"My hair awaits you along the
length of the tower..."

E Z R A   S C H A B A S

C A R L   M O R E Y

Opera

Canadian Opera Company

Viva

The First Fifty Years

D U N D U R N   P R E S S

T O R O N T O   •   O X F O R D

Editor: Barry Jowett
Design: John Lee
Design Assistant: Jennifer Scott
Printer: Transcontinental

Canadian Cataloguing in Publication Data

Schabas, Ezra, 1924-
    Opera viva: the Canadian Opera Company: the first fifty years

Includes bibliographical references and index.

ISBN 1-55002-346-2

I. Canadian Opera Company — History. I. Morey, Carl, 1934-   . II. Title.

ML28.T6C224 2000   782.1'09713'541   C00-931769-4

THE CANADA COUNCIL | LE CONSEIL DES ARTS
FOR THE ARTS | DU CANADA
SINCE 1957 | DEPUIS 1957

Canada

ONTARIO ARTS
COUNCIL

CONSEIL DES ARTS
DE L'ONTARIO

We acknowledge the support of the *Canada Council for the Arts* and the *Ontario Arts Council* for our publishing program. We also acknowledge the financial support of the *Government of Canada* through the *Book Publishing Industry Development Program*, *The Association for the Export of Canadian Books*, and the *Government of Ontario* through the *Ontario Book Publishers Tax Credit* program.

Care has been taken to trace the ownership of copyright material used in this book. The authors and the publisher welcome any information enabling them to rectify any references or credit in subsequent editions.

J. Kirk Howard, President

page ii: *Pelléas et Mélisande (2000)*.

Jean-François Lapointe as Pelléas and

Elzbieta Szmytka as Mélisande.

photo: Gary Beechey

Printed and bound in Canada.⊕
Printed on recycled paper.

www.dundurn.com

page iii: *Oedipus Rex (1997)*.

Michael Schade as Oedipus.

photo: Michael Cooper

Dundurn Press
8 Market Street
Suite 200
Toronto, Ontario, Canada
M5E 1M6

Dundurn Press
73 Lime Walk
Headington, Oxford,
England
OX3 7AD

Dundurn Press
2250 Military Road
Tonawanda NY
U.S.A. 14150

To the Memory of
Joan Parkhill Baillie
(1923–1997)

Don Carlos (1977).

Paul Plishka as Philippe II.

photo: Robert C. Ragsdale FRPS

Table of Contents

Fidelio (1970).

Act I. The prison.

photo: Robert C. Ragsdale FRPS

Both Carl Morey and I have thought about writing a history of the Canadian Opera Company (COC) since the mid-1990s. We both love opera and believe that the COC has done much to develop it in Canada. With the company approaching its fiftieth anniversary, it seemed an appropriate — perhaps urgent — time to record this Canadian success story — and to do it while there are still some of us who have been around since the company was founded.

Our work is not hagiography. It is a critical study of the COC, good and bad. There were times when it was in the doldrums, and other times when it seemed uncertain where it was going. And there were wonderful times, many of which we have tried to recapture in words and pictures for you, the reader.

I have written about the company's first twenty-five years, and Carl Morey about the second twenty-five years, leading up to the present. We could have written much more than we did. Where we lack exhaustive detail, the appendices fill in. They include: complete lists of COC productions, with their casts and production staffs; dates and locations of performances; and other information on COC activities.

We know or have known personally a good many of the COC's singers, conductors, directors, designers, administrators, and board members through the years. We have drawn heavily on them, through our recollections — especially of those no longer with us — and through interviews. Between us we have attended many of the COC productions and, on occasion, have written about them in journals. Some are still fresh in our minds, others nearly forgotten. The photos in this history will help you to remember them, too.

We are grateful to the COC for its interest in and support of this project, and especially for giving us the unrestricted use of its splendid Joan Baillie Archives. These archives were created almost thirty years ago by the late Joan Parkhill Baillie, and she managed them — always as a volunteer — until 1994, shortly before her death. We also

2

thank the present archivist, Birthe Joergensen, for her continued help and support. Without her patience and co-operation this book would not have been possible.

We have reviewed printed programs, press clippings, scrapbooks, photos, correspondence, minutes of board and committee meetings, and countless other COC documents and memorabilia in the archives. We have also drawn on *Opera Canada*, the magazine edited for so many years by still another professional volunteer, Ruby Mercer, as well as other Canadian periodicals. There is a short bibliography in the appendices.

We should point out that at no time did the present COC leadership question us on what we were saying about the company or in any way attempt to influence the outcome of our work. We hope that the many COC buffs who have followed the company's work over the years will agree more than disagree with our views.

A word about style. We have used original titles of operas, with this exception: non-English titles are given in English when an opera is done in an English translation, unless it is more well-known to English audiences in its original title.

We wish to thank Richard Bradshaw, general director of the COC, and Cathryn Gregor, its administrative director, for their unwavering support. We also thank the entire COC staff, which, in one way or another, has given us assistance whenever it was needed. In particular we want to mention Diana Justus, Susan Harrington, Jeremy Elbourne, Helmut Reichenbächer, Paul Caston, Wayne Vogan, and Ariel Fielding, all of whom had some direct association with this project. We gratefully acknowledge a research grant from the Social Sciences and Humanities Research Council of Canada, which was of indispensable support in developing this book.

Among those outside the COC who must be acknowledged here, foremost is our research assistant, Meran Currie-Roberts, who meticulously assembled the detailed performance and cast lists. Others who have helped along the way have been Michele Melady at CBC television archives, Miriam Newhouse at Actors' Equity, Russell Anthony of the Ballet/Opera House Corporation, Ann Schabas, and Stuart Hamilton.

Finally, we would like to thank our publisher, the Dundurn Group, Barry Jowett, who edited the manuscript with great care, and especially John Lee, who designed the book.

E.S.

Each of the following generously spoke at length, or corresponded, with one of or sometimes both the authors. The information and insights that they provided were essential to the writing of this book, and we gratefully acknowledge their contributions.

E.S., C.M.

Rodney J. Anderson
Joan Baillie
Robert Baillie
Margo H. Bindhardt
Philip Boswell
William Bowen
Richard Bradshaw
Elaine Calder
George Crum and Patricia Snell
Brian Dickie
Judith Forst
Sandra Gavinchuk
Margaret Genovese
Nicholas Goldschmidt

Michael Gough
Cathryn Gregor
Bruce Heyland
Joanne Ivey
Franz Kraemer
Murray Laufer and Marie Day
John Leberg
Trudi LeCaine
Gwen Little
William Lord
Lotfi Mansouri
Christopher Marsden
Ermanno Mauro
Bruce McMullan

Suzanne Mess
Mary Morrison
Cornelis Opthof
Rhyl Peel
Bob Rae
Harold Redekopp
Jan Rubes
Iain Scott
Douglas Sloan
Muriel Smith
Walter Stothers
Janet Stubbs
J.D. Woods
Jeannette and Elias Zarou

PRESIDENTS

Opera Festival Association of Toronto

R.H. Lorimer Massie	November 1950–June 1952
J.D. Woods	June 1952–June 1955
Richard S. Van Valkenburg	June 1955–April 1958
Frank F. McEachren	April 1958–May 1959
Floyd Chalmers	May 1959–January 1961

Canadian Opera Association

Frank F. McEachren	January 1961–February 1963
W. Preston Gilbride	February 1963–February 1965
Russell T. Payton	February 1965–February 1967
W.A. Curtis	February 1967–February 1969
Rodney J. Anderson	February 1969–January 1971
Robert L.T. Baillie	January1971–April 1973
E. Montague Larkin	April 1973–December 1974
Douglas A. Sloan	January 1975–December 1976

Canadian Opera Company

Rodney J. Anderson	January 1977–February 1978
Lionel C. Mohr	February 1978–January 1979
James M. Robertson	January 1979–March 1980
Walter G.D. Stothers	March 1980–October 1982

J.E. Mahoney	October 1982–October 1984
H.N.R. Jackman	October 1984–October 1986
Alastair Gillespie	October 1986–October 1988
A.J.R. Williams	October 1988–November 1990
Margo Bindhardt	November 1990–November 1992
Giles Meikle	November 1992–November 1994
John Cook	November 1994–November 1996
Georgia Prassas	November 1996–November 1998
Arthur R. A. Scace	November 1998–November 2000

THREE DAYS BEFORE CHRISTMAS 1825, in the town of York, as Toronto was called until 1834, a performance of the English opera *Mountaineers, or Love and Madness* was given in the Assembly Room of Franks' Hotel. This popular piece by Samuel Arnold had first been produced in London in 1793 and now served as the introduction to the pleasures of opera in the small and muddy administrative capital of the province of Upper Canada. The source of the production and the origins of the players are obscure, but a newspaper notice does say that the scenery and decorations had been brought over from a Rochester theatre, across Lake Ontario. The company played for two weeks. The entertainment was obviously well received since further performances in the next two years broadened the repertoire to include such popular hits as Henry Bishop's *The Miller and His Men*, Stephen Storace's *No Song, No Supper*, and John Braham's *The Devil's Brigade*. Braham had also been a famous singer — he created the role of Huon in Weber's *Oberon*, among other triumphs — and he became the first indisputable star to visit Toronto when he gave recitals in 1841.

By 1828 a theatrical entrepreneur from Buffalo proposed establishing a permanent theatre in York as part of a circuit that spread out from New York State. Something like a regular playhouse had to wait until 1833 when a Methodist chapel that had been abandoned by its congregation for larger quarters was converted into the grandly named Theatre Royal. Finally, in 1848, on the site of the Theatre Royal, the splendid Royal Lyceum was erected where the Toronto-Dominion Centre now stands and Toronto finally had a real theatre.

The 1840s saw the development of the operatic concert or the operatic soirée, often in costume, as a means for small ensembles to tour with truncated versions of operas, and as a source of entertainment when opera was a genuinely popular entertainment. The population of the eastern United States offered many towns in relatively close proximity to support such touring, and Lake Ontario — and after mid-century the railways — made

Der fliegende Holländer (1974).

Act 1. Phil Stark as The Steersman.

for easy access to the growing Canadian communities that stretched from Windsor in the west to Quebec City in the east. It was not long until Toronto, like so many other towns, became familiar with such pieces as Donizetti's *L'elisir d'amore, Lucia di Lammermoor,* and *La fille du régiment.* Auber's *Fra diavolo,* Rossini's *Il barbiere di Siviglia,* and Bellini's *Norma* and *La Sonnambula.* Performances were almost always given in English in keeping with the popular nature of the entertainment. In 1850 the celebrated soprano Rosa Devries appeared with a "French Opera Troupe" in programs that included music from such celebrated operas as Rossini's *Otello* and *Semiramide,* Meyerbeer's brand new *Le Prophète,* and Verdi's equally new *Jérusalem.*

In July 1853, Devries was also the star of *Norma,* the first fully staged opera performed in Toronto, complete with chorus and orchestra. The conductor was the young and brilliant Luigi Arditi, who would go on to an important international career and whose name lingered as the composer of a celebrated waltz song, *Il bacio.* The company returned the next year with *Lucia di Lammermoor, Lucrezia Borgia,* and *La fille du régiment.*

Touring companies now became regular visitors and brought to the city all of the standard repertoire, especially Italian works, including Verdi's *La Traviata* and *Il Trovatore* when they were still recent. The only German work to enjoy much success was Weber's *Der Freischütz* until the rage for Wagner at the end of the century.

The travelling troupe of George Holman played for a week at the Royal Lyceum in 1864 and returned the following year. Then in 1867 Holman leased the theatre and installed his company as the resident company. Suddenly, Toronto had an opera company. Whatever the group might have lacked by modern standards, it achieved great success, and Sallie Holman, one of George's daughters, became the toast of the town. Nevertheless, despite the introduction of a number of operas by Offenbach, Holman did little to expand the repertoire, and his audience appeared to lose interest. He gave up the Royal Lyceum after the close of the season in the spring of 1873 and moved to London, Ontario. The Holman company continued to tour and to pay short visits to Toronto for the next fifteen years, but after the deaths of both Sallie and her father George in 1888, the story of the troupe came to an end.

For the remainder of the nineteenth century, indeed until the outbreak of the First World War in 1914, enterprising companies continued to tour with all of the major operatic repertoire, companies that often included outstanding soloists and major conductors. The repertoire tended to be what has since become fixed as the "standard" repertoire, but there were also works that have now lost their popularity, such as Verdi's *Ernani*, Thomas' *Mignon*, Rossini's *Guillaume Tell*, Balfe's *Bohemian Girl*, Boito's *Mefistofele*, Massenet's *Thaïs*, Mascagni's *L'Amico Fritz*, and Montemezzi's *L'Amore dei tre Re*. Something of a novelty even in 1899 was John Philip Sousa's *The Bride Elect*, of which the *Globe* reviewer remarked that "Mr. Sousa is evidently far more successful as a composer of military marches than of comic opera music." (17/10/99)

The full company of the Metropolitan Opera Company of New York visited for three performances in 1899 with such artists as Marcella Sembrich, Edouard de Reszke, Pol Plançon, Emma Calvé, and Rosa Olitzka. They returned again in 1901 with *Lohengrin*, *Roméo et Juliette*, and *Carmen*. The orchestra had already appeared in 1892, 1893, and 1896 under the great Wagnerian conductor Anton Seidl, who brought to the city authentic Wagner performances by a conductor who had worked closely with the composer. Towards the end of the century, Wagner, in fact, was probably the city's favourite composer. Excerpts from his music dramas were heard regularly at orchestra concerts, often with great vocalists, and after 1887, when *Der fliegende Holländer* was performed, Toronto got to know *Lohengrin*, *Tannhäuser*, *Die Walküre*, and *Parsifal*. The Metropolitan Opera orchestra was back again in 1903 with Lillian Nordica and Edouard de Reszke.

The San Carlo Opera Company, a New York-based touring group, was characterized by Hector Charlesworth, the city's reigning music and art critic, as being "made up of Italian routinières" when they first appeared in Toronto in 1910. He was accurate in his assessment of a company that did not much change over its lifetime, but it continued to visit the city regularly during the next forty years and made up in enterprise what it lacked in finesse. At the least, it provided fully if inadequately produced performances of a wide repertoire, and the longevity of the organization attests to the fact that it satisfied a need, in Toronto and across the continent.

10

Dido and Aeneas

at Hart House Theatre, 1929.

Among the famous singers who appeared on the opera stage in Toronto were the great Canadian soprano Emma Albani as Lucia and Violetta, Maggie Teyte as Mimi in *La Bohème* and Marguerite in *Faust*, Feodor Chaliapin as Basilio in *Il barbiere di Siviglia*, Bidú Sayão as Massenet's Manon, Lily Pons as Lucia. The most famous singer in the second half of the nineteenth century, Adelina Patti, had first sung in Toronto in 1853 at the age of 10, and returned in 1887 in a costumed opera concert that featured her in the second act of Flotow's *Martha*. She was back again in 1892 with scenes from *Semiramide*, and again with *Martha* in 1894. Her conductor on each occasion was the same Arditi who had conducted the city's first complete operas some forty years before. At one of her last concerts in the city in 1903, Patti reminisced with the audience about her first appearance in Toronto fifty years before.

Unusual were the appearances of famous composers, but Mascagni conducted several concerts in 1902, including a performance of his *Cavalleria rusticana*. Not to be outdone by his countryman's success in North America, Leoncavallo followed in 1906 and conducted a concert performance of his already popular *I Pagliacci*.

Attempts to establish a local company had never advanced very far, and the economic and social disarray after the end of the war in 1918 did not present favourable conditions. Nevertheless, the Toronto Conservatory ambitiously set out to build an opera company in 1928. The fledgling company presented Humperdinck's *Hansel and Gretel* and Gilbert and Sullivan's *The Sorcerer* for a week in April at the Regent Theatre. The venture was successfully repeated the following April at Hart House Theatre with Purcell's *Dido and Aeneas* and a staged version of Bach's *Peasant Cantata*, in repertoire with Von Suppé's *Boccaccio*. Ernest MacMillan conducted the Purcell and Bach works, Thomas Crawford conducted *Boccaccio*, and sets and costumes were designed by the well-known painter, Arthur Lismer, a member of the celebrated Group of Seven. But the great stock market crash of 1929 and the subsequent depression put an end to further operatic development at the Conservatory until the 1940s.

Hugh the Drover at the Royal York Hotel, 1929.

The year of the great crash, 1929, saw the opening of the new CPR hotel in Toronto, the Royal York, a huge building that includes a large concert hall with curtained stage among its amenities. The musical festivities to mark the opening included performances of *Hugh the Drover*, a recent (1924) opera by the English composer Ralph Vaughan-Williams. Ernest MacMillan conducted, the set was designed by Arthur Lismer, and Allan Jones, who would later star in Hollywood films, was Hugh.

During the 1930s there were sporadic presentations sponsored by businessman Harrison Gilmour and his soprano wife Doris, and by a competing impresario, Braheen Urbane. In the 1940s James Rosselino managed a small company that sprang from his opera workshop at Central Technical School, and while it provided much-needed experience for young singers, it remained a small organization.

By mid-century Torontonians had had a century of regular operatic experience. They had seen most of what is still today the standard repertoire and, at least in concert, had heard all the great singers from Jenny Lind to Nellie Melba, from Enrico Caruso to Lauritz Melchior. Now with the growing population and the economic expansion that bloomed after the end of war in 1945, the stage was set at last for the establishment of a permanent company.

C.M.

Chapter 1

THE BEGINNINGS

August 1945. The war was over, and Canadian soldiers were on their way home after fighting hard and well. Canada was basking in national pride. Thanks to the war, its economic depression had disappeared, and signs of prosperity were everywhere. Subsidized university education was being provided for "demobs" by an appreciative government — a kinder reward than in 1918–19 when Canada offered little to its war-weary veterans.

The national radio network, the Canadian Broadcasting Corporation (CBC), had acquitted itself well at home and abroad during the war, as had the National Film Board (NFB). Yet cultivated Canadians noted sourly that Canada still had only a handful of good museums, art galleries, libraries, and symphony orchestras. Most live music was performed by church and community choirs, such as Toronto's Mendelssohn Choir. The music schools were mainly concerned with preparing diligent but reluctant children for graded examinations. Competitive music festivals that pitted child against child, band against band, and choir against choir, all purporting to improve the love of music

14

amongst the young, were at the height of their popularity. Canada had few musical institutions of merit, and the most promising musicians went abroad to study music and pursue their careers, few ever to return.

And then, in 1946, things began to happen. In Toronto the instigator on the operatic front, as twenty years earlier, was the Toronto Conservatory (it became "Royal" the next year), who launched Toronto's — and Canada's — first real opera school. The founding father was a German-speaking Czech pianist, composer, and critic, Arnold Walter. He was born in 1902 in Hannsdorf, a Moravian village in Austria-Hungary, the son of a high school principal. Both Mahler and Janáček were from the same region. Young Arnold showed much musical talent and was also an excellent all-round student. At 23, he earned his doctorate in law, summa cum laude, from Prague's Charles University, but this commendable achievement did not deter him from continuing his music studies. Law degree in hand, he went to Berlin to study musicology and piano.

Walter soon found that life as a musician wasn't easy in the Weimar Republic. He was a composer, and although his works attracted some attention they were only a minor source of income. It was as a pianist that he first

Arnold Walter

earned his living, playing background music for silent films. He also wrote, clearly and succinctly, about music and musical events, and this led to appointments as music editor for *Die Weltbuehne* and music critic for *Vorwarts*. Berlin was the musical capital of Europe in pre-Hitler years, with four opera houses, several symphony orchestras, much chamber music, and adventurous musical theatre. Contemporary and avant garde music thrived as nowhere else. Richard Strauss, Schoenberg, Schnabel, Furtwängler, Weill, Hindemith — they were all there. It was a musical feast for a young music critic, who dashed happily from one performance to another as part of his day's work.

And then came 1933. On the night of the infamous Reichstag fire, Walter was at his office dictating a review of a new production of Strauss's *Ariadne auf Naxos* when, as he related it, "the telephone rang and a voice said 'Don't go home tonight, the Reichstag is in flames, things are fishy.'" It was a timely warning; according to Walter, the editors of *Die Weltbuehne* were put in a concentration camp and his colleagues from *Vorwarts* were lined up against a wall with their hands up.

Walter fled Germany immediately, thanks to his Czech passport, and spent the next two years in Majorca. There, he taught at an international school and lived in Valldemosa, where Chopin had stayed almost a century earlier. In 1935 the Spanish Civil War broke out and Walter, considered suspect by both the left and right, went into hiding. With the help of the US consul he made his way to France on a British destroyer and, once his travel papers were sorted out, went on to England, where he joined his wife Maria, who had left Majorca earlier.

In London, Walter joined the staff at the Cecil Sharp House, a centre for British folk music studies. His work there was interesting but not lucrative. Europe's future looked bleak. He knew all too well that Nazi Germany was preparing for war. And then — it was 1936 — he had a stroke of luck. Toronto's Upper Canada College, a boy's school for Canada's wealthy families, was seeking a music master. Its headmaster, Terry MacDermott, was looking for a cultured European to "civilize" the boys. Walter heard about the job and was interviewed by Canadian High Commissioner Vincent Massey and his first secretary, Lester B. Pearson. (Thirty years later, Pearson told Walter that he remembered every word of the interview.)

16

Ettore Mazzoleni

photo: Henry Pratt

Walter got the job, but there were a few surprises in store for him. He had thought the college equivalent to a university; instead, it was a secondary school. Also, he knew nothing of the works of Gilbert and Sullivan which, he soon found out, he was expected to lead the students in annually. And, to make things worse, he found that very few students were interested in classical music. The boys, cruelly, called him the "Prussian," a description that stuck, even in his later years. This blond, rather short and stocky man with a German accent was, in fact, the furthest thing from a Prussian, both by birth and in outlook.

Six years was all he could take of Upper Canada College. In 1944, he and his musician colleague Ettore Mazzoleni, who taught English at the College, joined the Toronto Conservatory's staff. In the following year, Mazzoleni was appointed principal and Walter head of the newly formed Senior School, where advanced gifted students could enroll in a strenuous course of study similar to that given at New York's Juilliard School of Music. This in itself was a major step forward, but there was more to come. Walter, with the support of Edward Johnson, the Canadian manager of the Metropolitan Opera and head of the Conservatory's board, asked the University of Toronto, to whom the Conservatory reported, to allow the formation of an opera school to train opera singers, conductors, and repetiteurs. The university gave its permission but no money to help the school function. Whatever, it was a new beginning for opera in Toronto.

Arnold Walter needed two people to start the school: a pianist-conductor and a stage director.

photo: Henry Pratt

...olas Goldschmidt

The first appointment was Nicholas Goldschmidt, a Moravian like himself. Goldschmidt was an experienced singer, pianist, vocal coach, and conductor, who, in his early years, had worked in opera houses in Czechoslovakia. After emigrating to the United States in 1937, he had taught at the San Francisco Conservatory, Stanford University, and Columbia University, and in New Orleans and Lenox, Massachusetts.

By 1946, Goldschmidt, tall, thin, and energetic, was looking for a new challenge. Walter, in his quest, phoned Henry Levinger, assistant editor of the *Musical Courier* in New York, and asked him to suggest qualified people for the post. Goldschmidt, as luck would have it, was in Levinger's office when the call came through. Levinger promptly replied that he had just the man for the job sitting across the desk from him, and Goldschmidt, who didn't need much persuading, was soon on his way to Toronto. In later years Goldschmidt reminisced: "Was it destiny? Was it coincidence? Whatever it may have been, a new life had started for me on that day and Canada was to become my new home — and with it my professional and private life became a source of great happiness."

Yes, like Walter, the thirty-eight-year-old Goldschmidt was the right man in the right place at the right time. His enthusiasm was his calling card. When students had trouble with a role he encouraged them, and when they did well he praised them. He had extra-musical talents too: he mixed well with Toronto's society and eventually married Shelagh Fraser, a member of one of Toronto's leading families. She has been, throughout his life, his most staunch supporter.

Next Walter engaged Felix Brentano, a student of Max Reinhardt's and a prominent Broadway director. Together, Goldschmidt and Brentano set to work. The opera school held its classes and rehearsals in the forty-seven-year-old conservatory building located at one of Toronto's main intersections, College Street and University Avenue. (The Ontario Hydro Building is now on the site.) There were enough studios for lessons and practice, but only one room large enough to have group classes and stagings. This space was euphemistically called the Recital Hall, since student recitals were given there, but, in reality, it was a shared space — seats were removable — among several conservatory groups. There was no theatre, no place to store props and scenery, no real office for the staff. Yet the school made do.

The first opera students had little knowledge of opera but they wanted passionately to learn. Eager and intent, almost everything they did was a "first" for them. After only eight weeks of classes, Goldschmidt and Brentano, under Walter's watchful eye, produced an operatic excerpt show at Hart House Theatre — scenes from *La Bohème*, *Otello*, *Faust*, *La Traviata*, *Fidelio*, and *Der Rosenkavalier*. The theatre had some 450 seats, a small stage, and no orchestra pit. The singers performed in costume to a two-piano accompaniment. There were some props and assorted pieces of scenery. As was typical for years to come, the press and the public were amazed by the school's quality. Opera this good by young Canadians had heretofore seemed impossible. Few had doubted their singing ability, but acting was another story. At first the students were inhibited and disinclined to let themselves go, but they soon changed into good incipient singing-actors. A few prescient souls actually said that, thanks to the school, Canadian singers no longer had to go abroad to study the "foreign" art of opera.

In March 1947 the school gave Smetana's *The Bartered Bride* on two successive nights at the Eaton Auditorium. This handsome hall, completed in 1930, seated about 1,200. The school did the work in English, as it did nearly all of its productions in those first years. These 1947 performances were part of the Conservatory's diamond jubilee celebrations. They drew raves from the press. However, the audience was troubled by the orchestra, which played on the floor in front of the stage — as at Hart House Theatre, there was no pit. Undeterred, the school staged two performances of *Hansel and Gretel* there before Christmas. Gluck's *Orpheus and Euridice* was given two months later, followed by a lean but sprightly English version of Pergolesi's *La serva padrona* at the Toronto Art Gallery in April 1948.

La serva padrona was directed by Herman Geiger-Torel, a newcomer from South America, who was on a three-month teaching contract at the school. Shortly after his arrival, he was introduced to a small group of press and opera supporters at Shelagh Fraser's house. The rotund, cheerful, cigar smoking Geiger-Torel knew little English and aroused much hilarity as he fractured it before the assembly. The *Toronto Telegram* columnist Margaret Aitken commented on his courage and "refreshing abandonment. He describes a hoity toity opera singer: 'She has too much exclusivity'. When pleased he chortles 'Hurrah, hip! hip!'" (12/1/48) In comparing South American singers to Canadian singers he complained that the latter have "ambeetions" in their acting. What he meant was "inhibitions," but the word eluded him. Such malapropisms dogged Torel's speech for many years, although his written English was precise and perceptive.

Herman Geiger-Torel

In May, Brentano and Goldschmidt did Strauss's *Rosalinda (The Bat)* at the Royal Alexandra. It was the school's first venture in a large professional theatre, and the production came off well, helped in no small way by the theatre's professional accoutrements. Although dusty and a bit down at heel — it had been built in 1907 — the theatre had charm and atmosphere, a good stage, and a barely adequate orchestra pit.

By the late spring of 1948 it was clear that Brentano wasn't working out. He just didn't know enough about traditional opera. Goldschmidt recalls how Brentano unwisely wanted to cut the recitative before "Che Faro" in Gluck's *Orpheus and Euridice*. Goldschmidt protested, and Walter, as expected, sided with him. And Brentano

photo: Eaton's Portrait Studio

seemed to lack commitment to Toronto. Unlike Goldschmidt, he had not given up his New York ties, and continued to commute between New York and Toronto. After a year and a half it was time to let him go. Geiger-Torel was promptly hired as stage director in Brentano's place.

It was Nicholas Goldschmidt who had initially recommended Herman Geiger-Torel to Arnold Walter. The two had worked together in Czechoslovakia in the 1930s, where they had developed mutual respect and affection. Hermann Berthold Gustav Geiger was born in Frankfurt-am-Main in 1907. He came from a cultured German-Jewish family: his father was a lawyer, his mother, Rosy Geiger-Kullmann, a prominent composer. His Frankfurt forebears dated back to 1600. They were intellectuals, philosophers, rabbis, and cantors. His great-grandfather Abraham was one of the founders of liberal Judaism in Germany. Hermann studied piano and then violin but, recognizing that he was not especially brilliant at either, took up conducting. Successful to a degree, he was next drawn to staging opera. Fortunately, Lothar Wallerstein, the chief stage director at the Frankfurt Opera, took him on as an apprentice and, at the same time, urged him to continue his studies at the Frankfurt Conservatory in order to gain a broad historical and linguistic background in all aspects of opera. In 1930, Geiger joined Wallerstein at the Salzburg Festival to assist in preparing *Der Rosenkavalier*. In the cast were Lotte Lehmann, who played the Feldmarschallin, and Richard Mayr, the Baron Ochs. Geiger also worked under conductor Clemens Krauss of the Vienna State Opera and the legendary set designer Alfred Roller.

Geiger soon won appointments to Czech and German opera houses. Eventually, overwork led to pneumonia and pleurisy, and he was confined to hospital for nine months. Then came Adolf Hitler. The Nazis unhesitatingly cancelled Geiger's 1933–34 contract with the Mainz Opera. Clearly he had no future in Germany, so he gladly accepted a post as a staff director at the Teatro Colon in Buenos Aires. There, he directed leading singers, including Claudia Muzio, who sang in *La Traviata* and Catalani's *Loreley*. Alas, he crossed swords with Muzio over a staging she did not like, and Geiger refused to back down. The management, as expected, sided with her. The experience taught him to be wary of star singers. Opera houses of sixty years ago cherished their stars because they sang well — most of the time — and because they sold tickets. Directors were expendable.

Geiger returned to Europe in 1934 and worked for the next three years at the Troppau (Opava) Opera in Czechoslovakia. This was where he met the assistant conductor and chorus master Nicholas Goldschmidt. After a brief and dangerous visit to his family in Germany he went on to Paris, where he dropped the final "n" in "Hermann" and changed his last name to Geiger-Torel (informally he would, in future, be called simply Torel). The French, he said, had trouble pronouncing the G in Geiger and were getting tired of refugee Germans. Torel, a manufactured name, was, he thought, international in sound, and would work everywhere.

In 1938, Torel went back to the Colon. There, in the next two years, he directed some of the best singers of the day — Muzio, Lily Pons, Tito Schipa, Herbert Janssen, Max Lorenz, and Risë Stevens. The conductors he worked with were equally illustrious, including, among others, Erich Kleiber and Tullio Serafin. Between 1940 and 1943 he freelanced in Buenos Aires, and then, after working in a leather company for a year, he was appointed chief stage director at the National Theatre in Montevideo. Here his mandate was to build a Uruguayan national opera company. Although he couldn't know it at the time, it was excellent training for what was to come in Toronto.

A high-profile job followed, that of chief stage director of the Municipal Theatre in Rio de Janeiro, where he directed such outstanding artists as Mario del Monaco, Astrid Varnay, Ferruccio Tagliavini, Martial Singher, Bidú Sayão, Leonard Warren, Beniamino Gigli, and Zinka Milanov. Great as these singers were, Torel felt that he did not have enough rehearsal time with them to craft his productions. It was "instant" opera, the kind discriminating audiences spot readily, no matter how great the singing. In one three-month period Torel staged twelve operas, some mounted in just two or three days. After two years of this, he was ready to leave, and jumped at the opportunity to move to Toronto as Brentano's replacement. He never looked back.

Torel turned out to be an outstanding and dedicated teacher. He anticipated student needs and treated students as young professionals. Yet, warmhearted as he was, he would sometimes shout at students when they did wrong. In Canada's polite Anglo-Saxon world one simply didn't shout. However, after the initial shock, the students became accustomed to his outbursts, suspecting that he often staged them to get his point across. And, when all was said and done, he ended up smiling and laughing with them.

Torel knew the works he directed in depth and showed consistently good taste in realizing a composer's intentions. He was a practical director who only did works within the school's and, later, the company's grasp. He was not inherently adventurous, and was particularly cautious when it came to trying works he failed to understand or for which he lacked sympathy. His encyclopedic knowledge of the standard repertoire enabled him to refer confidently to minute details without referring to the score. Although first and foremost a director, he could see opera from the vantage point of the conductor, the singer, the designer, and the producer. He had played in orchestras, acted, and worked on sets, and he spoke six languages. George Crum, one of his musical assistants and later musical director of the National Ballet, said that, no matter what the problem in the opera house, one turned to Torel to solve it. The Conservatory Opera School and the Canadian Opera Company would reflect Torel's leadership, his points of view, his successes, and his failures, for the next twenty-eight years.

The Marriage of Figaro was the first opera he directed after settling in Toronto. Sung in English, it was performed for two nights in December 1948 at the Eaton Auditorium. The following spring he did *La Bohème* in the same venue. Audiences were enthusiastic, and so was the press. The school thrived. Was Toronto on the verge of having a professional opera company? The three Central Europeans — Walter, Goldschmidt, and Torel — dreamers and doers that they were, would soon see to it.

In the meantime, there was help from another quarter: the CBC. The 1940s and 50s have justifiably been called the "golden age" of CBC radio. Canada's national network had visionary and practical executives heading its French and English networks, and they were eager to exercise the CBC's mandate to produce quality shows featuring Canadian artists. Furthermore, they had the funds to do it. On June 11, 1948, Harry J. Boyle, program director of the CBC's Trans-Canada network, wrote to Walter that the Corporation, acknowledging the "pioneer work done in the training of singers by the Royal Conservatory of Music" and "realizing the limitations imposed on the futures of these singers by the fact that there was no permanent opera company in Canada," would form the CBC Opera Company. The opera school staff would provide the CBC with the required expertise, and advanced singers from the school would be called upon as needed. Boyle proposed collaborating with the school to present four operas on radio over the next ten months. The CBC's music staff, led by conductor Geoffrey Waddington and producer Terence Gibbs, would work together with Goldschmidt and George Crum. Crum, in his early twenties, was a fine pianist and a technically skilled conductor, and the CBC was quick to note this. An unspoken rivalry developed between Goldschmidt and Crum, but Goldschmidt usually held the reins. Torel soon joined the CBC team to help in selecting works and in casting.

The CBC did two productions in late 1948, *La Bohème* and *Orpheus and Euridice*. James (Jimmy) Shields sang Rodolfo in Bohème. He had started his career as an "Irish tenor," had sung with several name bands, and later became a popular radio singer on leading shows in both the USA and Canada. He was truly a "natural," and this CBC appearance launched him on a short but important career as a lyric tenor in Italian repertoire.

Another vocal find was Mary Morrison, a young soprano from Winnipeg. She was Mimi in *Bohème* and Euridice in *Orpheus*, and would later sing other leading roles at the school, on radio, and with the professional opera company. Edmund Hockridge, already a leading Canadian baritone, was a fine Marcello, and the following year he sang in CBC productions of *Don Giovanni* and the North American radio premiere of Benjamin Britten's *Peter Grimes*. It was Canada's loss when, in 1950, he left for England, where he sang in musical comedies in the West End and on the BBC for the next four decades. Czech-born bass Jan Rubes was the most dependable and durable of CBC opera singers in those beginning years. He would later be a mainstay of the Canadian Opera Company. Rubes had appeared in Prague and other Czech cities before coming to Toronto in 1948. His warm and engaging voice, and especially his splendid acting, attracted the favourable attention of critics. His trademark was versatility, and he could in turn be comical or villainous on stage. Of no little importance was that he generously helped his younger and less experienced colleagues in acting, stagecraft, and even dress.

Four days after he arrived in Toronto, Rubes met Goldschmidt. The persuasive Goldschmidt convinced him to join the opera school in order to sing in school productions. Even though he didn't need the training, this would, he promised, lead Rubes to paying roles in CBC operas. Accordingly, he first sang in the school's *Gianni Schicchi* and then in several CBC productions, including *Don Giovanni*, *La Traviata*, and *Fidelio*.

In sum, the CBC Opera Company gave singers invaluable experience and paid them well to boot. Singers such as Rubes and Shields would not have stayed in Canada without CBC fees, nor would many of the other young promising singers. The CBC was their main source of income for at least the first decade and a half after the war.

Late in 1949, the CBC did two public concert performances of *Carmen* at Massey Hall with the Toronto Symphony Orchestra (TSO). The cast included Margaret Kerr (Carmen), Mary Morrison (Micaela), Pierre Boutet (Don José), and Gilles Lamontagne (Escamillo). The audience loved it. The waters had been tested. There was unquestionably a growing public for live professional opera. It was time for the next big step.

Chapter 2

A COMPANY IS BORN

Late in 1949, Walter, Goldschmidt, and Torel boldly announced that, in February 1950, the Royal Conservatory Opera Company would mount an eight-day festival of three operas at the Royal Alexandra Theatre. The singers would include both professionals and students. Performing at the Royal Alec, as it was affectionately called, would be more costly than at Eaton Auditorium or Hart House Theatre, since the rent and union pay scales for singers, orchestras, and stage hands were higher. But it would be worth it, for the theatre was the closest thing Toronto had to an opera house. Its biggest drawback was the small orchestra pit. Good as it was to have one, it could only hold thirty players at best, and that only after removing three rows of orchestra seats. Frequently,

The Royal Alexandra Theatre as it was in 1950.

tympani, percussion, and double basses had to be placed in box seats on the side of the theatre, making them visible to the audience.

The university had grudgingly allowed the Conservatory to fund the festival. Principal Ettore Mazzoleni, with university president Sydney Smith growling in the background, warned Walter not to lose money. Smith's concern, it should be noted, was gratuitous, since the Conservatory was self-supporting and paid all of its bills without university help.

Walter, knowing that losses were almost inevitable, groaned but went ahead anyway. In a letter (22/11/49) to Toronto arts patron Fred MacKelcan, from whom he was trying to extract a donation for the festival, Walter explained with nervy optimism that he would stick to all his cost estimates: for rent, orchestra (he would not permit overtime), soloists, chorus, ballet fees, music rental, and royalties. Costumes, he said, would be paid for from a special fund. Other expense items he could not budget for but would control carefully

Planning the festival.

Clockwise, left to right: Edward Johnson, Nicholas Goldschmidt, Ettore Mazzoleni, Arnold Walter, Herman Geiger-Torel (back to camera).

photo: National Film Board

photo: Alex Gray

included scenery and props, stage hands, and publicity. Walter was a neophyte when it came to budgeting opera, yet such temerity was needed to do something new and daring in conservative Toronto.

Everything went ahead as Walter hoped. The first Toronto Opera Festival ran from February 3 to 11, 1950, with four performances of *La Bohème*, three of *Rigoletto*, and three of *Don Giovanni*. Many of the roles were done by the singers who had sung them in CBC productions, thus cutting coaching and rehearsal time. The opera orchestra, although hardly the equal of the TSO or CBC orchestra, was still a cut above the student orchestra used in earlier Conservatory productions. And the two busiest men in town were Goldschmidt and Torel, who conducted and directed all three operas.

The press, thoroughly won over, supported the festival with abundant publicity. The women's committee, which had been formed in 1947, sold thousands of tickets in all kinds of ways and added glamour to opera opening nights by wearing their best designer gowns — the men mostly wore white tie. Photos of the patrons at the theatre adorned the women's and social pages — important newspaper reading matter in the 1950s.

To everyone's surprise, the company played to near capacity audiences in the 1,500-

28

seat Royal Alec, and box-office income came to over $32,000. In a word, the festival was a revelation: Toronto had not seen or heard anything by local operatic forces to equal it. These were not helter-skelter performances with nondescript staging, so typical of touring groups such as the San Carlo, but thoroughly rehearsed operas, with all of the trappings.

The Globe and Mail, "recognizing the ... Festival as an event of importance in Toronto's musical history," brought in "distinguished critic" Thomas Archer of the Montreal Gazette, "to comment on this municipal achievement." (4/2/50) *Rigoletto* launched the festival. In his first review Archer hailed the company as national because, collectively, the principals came from six of Canada's ten provinces, and "doubtless the other four were represented in the chorus or the orchestra." About the Rigoletto, he particularly praised the leads, Gilles Lamontagne in the title role, and Jan Rubes as Sparafucile, "a conspirator to end all conspirators."

Jack Karr, The *Toronto Star*'s drama critic, also applauded the singing in Rigoletto and, in the same vein as Archer, wrote how proud he was that this was a Canadian production. (4/2/50) He also liked Goldschmidt's conducting and the ensemble singing. He called the sets "simple," "impressionistic," and "colourful without being gaudy."

Don Giovanni opened the next night to a sell-out audience. It was sung in English in Edward Dent's quite dull translation. Archer observed that it was done as comic opera, "a master stroke," rather than as quasi tragic grand opera, as the Metropolitan Opera did it! (Mozart and his librettist, Lorenzo Da Ponte, did call it a *dramma giocoso*.) (6/2/50) The audience laughed throughout because, as Archer wrote, it understood the dialogue, and the well-trained cast took advantage of every comical situation. Edmund Hockridge was the Don, Andrew MacMillan the Leporello. MacMillan, a brilliant actor with a rather modest voice, would also

Don Giovanni (1950).

Act 2. Left to right: Andrew MacMillan (Leporello), Edmund Hockridge (Don Giovanni). The statue of the Commendatore threatens Don Giovanni.

photo: Panda

serve as an assistant director to Torel for the next decade. Marguerite Gignac was the attractive Zerlina.

There was no letdown in quality in the third production, *La Bohème*. Pearl McCarthy of *The Globe and Mail* called it "astonishingly good," and singled out Torel's expert direction and the cast's joie de vivre. (8/2/50) The sets drew much praise from Rose MacDonald of the *Toronto Telegram*. (8/2/50) To show how times were changing, staid Toronto broke down and uninhibitedly demanded several curtain calls at the conclusion of each performance. And so, with good press and large audiences, the festival's eight days flew by, and the Conservatory's heads and board were ecstatic. When income and expenses were tallied up, the festival had actually made a small profit!

The school and "company" moved ahead. Later in the year Torel introduced "Opera Backstage," an operatic caricature-burlesque that, as its brochure pointed out, "poked fun at all the exaggerated stage mannerisms, wooden acting and unlikely turns that make opera look ridiculous beside modern theatre." Torel used eight or nine of his best singers to do the show, with George Crum at the piano. The group toured Canada from coast to coast, perhaps the first Canadian operatic group to do so. It was a trial balloon for the company tours that would come at the end of the decade.

Opera Backstage capitalized on typical operatic themes such as love, death, murder, curses, and vengeance, illustrating them in excerpts from the standard repertoire. Torel, whose wit and sense of humour were second to none, would, before each excerpt, point out to the audience how well or badly the opera dealt with the theme in question. In effect, he was doing what he did in actual rehearsals. Within five minutes of a show's beginning, he had the audience eating out of his hand.

By 1951, the opera school had attracted sufficient attention to prompt the NFB to produce a forty-

Opera Backstage in rehearsal.
Left to right: Ernest Adams, Joanne Ivey, Patricia Snell, Jan Rubes, Mary Morrison, Andrew MacMillan, George Crum (conductor).

minute documentary, "Opera School." It was shown in art theatres, usually as an extra to the feature film. It was a fictional step-by-step story of a young soprano student, played by Marguerite Gignac, from her entrance audition to her performance of Susanna in The *Marriage of Figaro* at the Royal Alexandra three years later. The film audited her classes with teachers and coaches, and her sessions with Arnold Walter who played his usual wise self, with Goldschmidt, the concerned musical director, and with Torel who gave instructions through a haze of smoke emitted from his ever-present cigar.

The three wise men, basking in the triumph of the 1950 festival, suspected that the university would turn thumbs down on a second festival. They even wondered whether its grudging support was best for opera in Toronto. For one thing, cutting financial corners to balance the Conservatory's books meant excessive artistic restraints. More money was needed to do things right, and perhaps it could be found elsewhere. All things considered, it appeared best to take the next step and form an independent company that would continue to collaborate with the Conservatory, where most of the singers would come from, and from which Goldschmidt and Torel would still draw salaries.

The enthusiastic Goldschmidt, with the support and encouragement of his wife and her friends on the women's committee, led the way in finding a small group of wealthy businessmen and professionals interested in supporting an opera company. Torel's operatic knowledge, colourful personality, and charm complemented Goldschmidt's organizing ability and made supporters confident that opera was in good and safe hands. Torel was always smiling as he explained matters in his inimitably rich and heavily accented English. As these talks for a second festival got under way, Walter stayed in the background. He was not completely in favour of setting the company loose from the school as yet but, in the rush of events, he soon changed his mind.

By October 1950, eight months after the first festival, the Conservatory board, as expected, raised serious doubts about having another festival without more support from the university. Goldschmidt and Torel promptly submitted their plan for an independent company. They had already solicited start-up pledges of funds from two Toronto businessmen, J.D. Woods ($5,000) and James Duncan ($1,000). Neither Woods nor Duncan were passionate opera lovers — both wanted their pledges to be anonymous — but they were civic minded and saw the need for a local, even a national, opera company. Their identities were revealed years later.

Goldschmidt and Torel next convinced Mazzoleni and Walter, if convincing was necessary, that a healthy relationship between the company and the school was essential to the success of both organizations. In an October memorandum, Torel explained to Mazzoleni how it would be done: the staff would be shared, preference would be given to school students and recent graduates when casting, and a large percentage of school students would be in the company's productions. (10/10/50)

Word came down from the university in November forbidding the Conservatory to be financially responsible for a commercial festival at the Royal Alexandra, no matter how much it would help opera school students or opera in Canada. The university saw producing opera as something outside its purview — this at a time when American universities such as Indiana were going all out to develop their opera schools. In fact, the university did not actually accept the opera school into its hallowed halls until 1968, when it approved a two-year diploma for opera students in the Faculty of Music.

But this was 1950. The university further decreed that if an independent opera company were formed, and if the company raised a minimum of $18,000, and if a general manager were appointed (not Torel, for fear that he would neglect his work at the school), it would permit the new company to use the Conservatory's facilities, students, and staff. In early November, the Conservatory ordered the new company to be in place within forty-eight hours, although it is not clear why such haste was necessary.

Opera supporters, mainly women, met on a few hours notice at the Goldschmidt home on Woodlawn Avenue in midtown Toronto to frame a response. (Evidently, a number of those present gave up their tickets to a Rudolf Serkin recital that evening in order to attend.) Mrs. Lorimer Massie and Mrs. Robert Dale-Harris (daughter of actor Leslie Howard) took on the immediate task of raising $12,000 on top of the Woods and Duncan pledges. According to Goldschmidt, Lorimer Massie was told by those present that he was to be the opera company's first president. Massie had no choice but to agree, even though he knew little about opera. Men of action that they were, Goldschmidt and Torel next enlisted Toronto lawyer John Godfrey (later Senator) to prepare the papers of incorporation.

The next day Goldschmidt and Torel marched into Mazzoleni's office and proudly showed the astonished Mazzoleni the company's provincial charter and the pledges of money it already had. Mazzoleni, acting on President Smith's behalf, was satisfied. The company's destiny was now clearly in the hands of Goldschmidt and Torel. As for Arnold Walter, it had been his dream to have a first-rate professional company working closely with his opera school, and this had now come to pass.

Goldschmidt and Torel had thought of almost everything — except to give the new company a name. And so, on the spur of the moment, they called it the Opera Festival Association of Toronto. It was a puzzling name for an opera company, but it lasted legally, if not publicly, until 1960. Edward Johnson, who had just retired as general manager of the Metropolitan Opera, agreed to be its honourary chairman, and Ernest Rawley, the manager of the Royal Alexandra, its general manager. Johnson's appointment was in name only; he played no role in the company. Rawley knew little about opera but did know how to cost shows and read balance sheets, skills the new company needed. Torel was called simply stage director, but he was really the company's general director, even though the Conservatory had decreed otherwise. He did the budgets with Rawley, decided on the operas and casting with Goldschmidt, and reported to the board through Mazzoleni. Goldschmidt was musical director and injected his own brand of operatic wisdom into the company. The twelve-man board — there were no women members — included Mazzoleni, Walter, and Rawley.

The board first met at the National Club on November 13, 1950, the day the charter was granted. After two more meetings that month a news release was issued, summarizing the company's creation and announcing the 1951 season: *The Marriage of Figaro* (in English), *Madama Butterfly*, and *Faust*. In the next few months, the board met frequently at J.D. Woods' house. The gatherings were as much social as business. To its great credit, the board, in short order, raised guarantees totalling over $30,000. The guarantees were not outright donations per se, but to be used only if needed. Among the guarantors were Edward Johnson, Vincent Massey, W.S. Low (the music publisher), Lady Eaton, Lady Kemp, E.P. Taylor, Sir Ellsworth Flavelle, Floyd Chalmers, and G.T. Heintzman (the piano manufacturer). On January 13, 1951, *The Toronto Star*'s Atkinson

Charitable Foundation gave the new company $5,000, a singularly large donation for those times, and this set an example for other foundations.

It was a dream come true. First the creation of an opera school, and then an opera company evolving from the school. The process was unusual. Yet, in retrospect, it was for the best. Toronto's staid citizenry might well have balked at forming an opera company straight away, given their resistance to the new and the different, and their view of opera as an alien art. Then, too, it would never have happened without Goldschmidt and Torel. They were so inspired and committed that the city's opera lovers found their plans irresistible. Their manner of speech, their eccentric behaviour, and their refusal to take no for an answer won over a legion of supporters.

Both men had their shortcomings. Torel shouted too much and lost his temper at rehearsals — although many believed that it was only an act. Goldschmidt was not an especially accurate pianist, and he conducted with a rather circular and imprecise beat. During performances he was prone to getting lost and even, occasionally, forgetting to conduct when caught up in the throes of the music. From one time to the next, he might change his mind about how a passage should be done, and this without warning, to the utter consternation of cast and orchestra. Yet all knew that this man loved what he was doing, that his fundamental musicianship was very sound, and that he had no fear of taking on difficult assignments.

In fact, the backers of the festival often relished seeing Goldschmidt and Torel squabble, screaming away at one another at rehearsals, and then making up thirty seconds later. Their company was a happy and spirited family and, unlike some fledgling opera companies, had few disputes among singers, staff, and board, and there were no prima donnas.

The 1951 festival was scheduled for February. The 1950 festival was used as a guide: one more performance was planned, and a small profit was courageously budgeted. Fees to singers, and to Goldschmidt, Torel, and Rawley, were minimal. Goldschmidt took only the conducting fees required by the Musicians' Union, Torel took a stipend of $5,500, and Rawley $1,000. Goldschmidt conducted all the performances for *Figaro* and *Butterfly* and shared the podium with George Crum for *Faust* — quite an endurance feat.

The young Suzanne Mess did the costumes for *Butterfly*, her first engagement with

34

The Marriage of Figaro (1951).
Act 2. Left to right: Patricia Snell
(Countess), Jean Edwards
(Susanna), Mary Alice Rogers
(Cherubino). Cherubino
serenades the Countess.

the company. She has since dressed at least five other *Butterflys* and, to this day, continues to work for many of the country's stage companies. Mess's ability to recycle costumes was a great asset in the opera company's early years when budgetary constraints were the order of the day. Torel was her mentor and severest critic, and she loved him for it.

The 1951 performances were as good and the press as glowing as in 1950, although the critics complained about the length of *Figaro*. Performances usually began at 8:30 p.m. *Figaro* was moved up to 8:15 and still concluded just ten minutes short of midnight. Andrew MacMillan as Figaro was the hit of the show, Marguerite Gignac was an engaging Susanna, and Ernest Adams a forceful Count. Patricia Snell, a high lyric soprano, was

Act 2. Jan Rubes as
Méphistophélès.

miscast as the Countess, a role she shared with Louise Roy. Eric McLean, writing for the
Montreal Star, seemed to be the only critic who knew this masterpiece well enough to dis-
cern that the young cast met its vocal and dramatic challenges. (17/2/51) He went on to
chastise his own city for its indifference to opera and asked why it didn't have a company comparable to Toronto's.

Leo Smith, a professor of music at Toronto, reviewed *Madama Butterfly* for *The Globe
and Mail* and thought June Kowalchuk, the Cio-Cio-San, not up to the role vocally.
(10/2/51) He complained especially about her vibrato, as he did Joan Hall's as Suzuki.
Smith took note of baritone James Milligan, who was singing a minor role. "[He] brought
vehemence and frenzy into his singing and he looked what he represented — the Asiatic
Priest." Torel admired Milligan's singing but thought him a poor actor. Milligan had a
short but brilliant international career, before his untimely death in 1961.

Faust was the company's most extravagant production to date, and decidedly the most
difficult to stage. The press singled out Jan Rubes for his fine singing and acting as
Méphistophélès. Choreographer Gweneth Lloyd, one of the founders of the Winnipeg
Ballet, prepared the ballet, and the chorus sang well. The press criticized Hans Berends'

Faust (1951).

Pierre Boutet (Faust),

Jan Rubes (Méphistophélès).

inventive sets for getting in the way of the action. (Berends was to be the company's principal designer for the next five years.) However, most of the adverse criticism was focussed on the production's dramatic aspects. It was clear that the young company had trouble handling the opera's changing character over the five acts.

Joanne Ivey, who played Marthe, remembered a major disruption at one of the *Faust* performances. Marguerite (Mary Morrison) was in her bedroom when Faust (Pierre Boutet) tried to reach her by ladder. He rested the ladder on the set's makeshift building with such force that the ladder toppled over, bringing most of the set with it. It was a nightmarish accident, but not that unusual in the world of opera. The show did go on.

With good houses and a net profit of over $2,000, the company's mood was upbeat. Convinced by now that Toronto really had an opera company, Torel brought a five-year plan to the opera board on June 9, 1951. His plan recommended — prematurely — that the company move its facilities out of the Conservatory in order to change the public's perception that it was a student group. It proposed seasons of three operas similar to the ones just completed and, for the fall of 1957, the start of light opera seasons of four works. This plan also recommended playing festival productions at other large Ontario centres. (Such post-festival run-outs to Hamilton, Kitchener, and London did actually begin in 1954.) Torel also wanted to tour some smaller productions — operas with piano accompaniment, and minimum props and costumes. (This had to wait until 1958, although *Così fan tutte*, under Conservatory auspices, did tour in this form in 1953 and 1956.)

Meanwhile, word got round that Toronto was becoming a good opera city, and so the Toronto Rotary Club, on the lookout for fund-raising schemes, sponsored the Metropolitan Opera to play at the city's hockey arena, Maple Leaf Gardens, in May 1952. Since other large groups, such as the TSO, had appeared there in the past, the Rotarians argued that the Gardens could be adapted for opera, albeit with voices and orchestra amplified. The Met, accustomed to playing on tour in roughly similar venues in the USA, looked over the Gardens and agreed that it would do.

The Met's plans presented Torel with an unexpected problem in setting the 1952 festival. He had planned to cash in on the 1950 success of *Rigoletto* by repeating it in 1952, but upon hearing that the Met would be doing it in May 1952, three months after the February festival, he hastily produced Massenet's *Manon* instead.

And so the third season got underway. To start it off, the company showed a decided spirit of adventure in mounting a new production of *The Bartered Bride*. It pleased every-one, as it had five years before. Jan Rubes was outstanding as Kezal — he seemed to have been born for the role. Thomas Martin, a staff conductor at both the Metropolitan and New York City opera companies who was accustomed to working with young and often inexperienced singers, conducted *Manon*, with Marguerite Gignac and Patricia Snell sharing the title role and the American tenor, John Alexander, singing Des Grieux. The rest of the cast were festival company regulars who learned much from Martin. *Manon's* set functioned well: Torel moved his forces sensibly about the stage, and the leads acted out the melodramatic text with some distinction.

Lois Marshall as the Queen of the Night in *The Magic Flute* attracted attention as she moved relentlessly through the Queen's two acrobatic arias. She shared the role with Patricia Snell. The opera marked the first appearance of bass-baritone Don Garrard, who played one of the high priests. He was another young singer who would go on to an inter-national career.

Each opera was done four times. *Manon* was an artistic success, but it brought in a deficit. The new set, Martin's fee, and the poor box office — 60 percent of capacity — were the causes. *The Flute* played to 94 percent capacity, and *The Bartered Bride*, some-what disappointingly, to 84 percent. The festival lost over $8,000, which the guarantors had to cover — a new experience for them. The board now knew that the business of opera was perilous, that fine productions did not necessarily mean good box-office, that production costs could get out of control, and that, generally, one must be ready for the worst as well as the best.

Manon's failure might have been expected. It is a difficult opera to mount, and does not win audiences easily outside of France. Nevertheless, Torel wondered whether Toronto's taste was forever limited to Mozart, Verdi, and Puccini. He saw that it would be more of a struggle than first anticipated to develop a sophisticated operatic public. It bothered him, too, that the board was upset about losing what was really very little

38

money. Had he taken unnecessary risks? Was he jeopardizing the company's future by doing works that he wanted to do rather than works that would please the public, assuming that one could gauge what the public wanted?

May came and Toronto enjoyed a second feast of operas and great singers. The Met's *Aïda* with Zinka Milanov, *La Bohème* with Jan Peerce and Eleanor Steber, *Carmen* with Ramon Vinay, Robert Merrill, and Herta Glaz, and *Rigoletto* with Leonard Warren made up a memorable week despite the setting, so redolent of hockey, hot dogs, and cola. The Met was pleased and continued to perform annually at the Gardens through 1960. And, in the long run, the Met's productions had a favourable effect on the festival's box office.

In the fall of 1952, at Edward Johnson's recommendation, the opera school — and, by extension, the company — engaged Ernesto Barbini as coach and conductor. Barbini, formerly with the Metropolitan Opera where he had coached Italian opera, wanted to conduct, and Toronto provided him this opportunity. Born and trained in Italy, he would be a decided asset to the company for the next two decades. Toronto singers clamoured to study Italian opera with him, even though they had to come to terms with his volatility, for Barbini could be gentle and kind or explosive and cruel, depending on his mood and the responses to his instruction. His English was poor, despite his haveing been in the USA since the late 1930s and had served in the American army during the war. Singers and orchestra were often left in the dark even after he explained what he wanted.

Ernesto Barbini

Barbini made his debut on the opening night of the 1953 festival, conducting *Madama Butterfly*. It was a regal evening with Governor General Vincent Massey in attendance. Barbini was on top of the work from the outset. He knew the score well and conducted it with rare attention to every note and nuance. In return, the orchestra, singers, and chorus performed with sensitivity and style. Irene Salemka, a twenty-two-year-old soprano from Manitoba, came close to mesmerizing the audience as

Cio-Cio-San. These two Toronto newcomers brought the opera festival to new levels of artistry.

The festival approached similar heights with its second production, Mozart's *Così fan tutte*. It is an extremely difficult work to put across because of its improbable — some would say impossible — plot. However, the music is heavenly, surely some of the finest Mozart ever wrote. The opera is in great measure dependent on ensembles, from duets to sextets, and leaves its six characters with challenges only superior casts can meet. The young company met them. Mary Morrison sang the vocally difficult role of Fiordiligi splendidly, and the young Sylvia Grant was a delightful and flighty Dorabella. The two cynical lovers were played by Edward Johnson (not the Met's Edward Johnson) as Ferrando and Don Garrard, showing his great promise, as Guglielmo. Jan Rubes as Don Alfonso had his usual good time, and the Despina role was shared by the diminutive Jacqueline Smith and Patricia Snell. Goldschmidt, who had previously conducted the work on CBC radio, had a fine grasp of it, and Torel, as was often his way, overdid its slapstick.

The Conservatory concert bureau arranged an Ontario tour of *Così* with two-piano accompaniment for later in the spring. It was as much a hit on the road as at the Royal Alexandra. In Peterborough it played two nights in a row. A delighted Robertson Davies, then editor of the Peterborough Examiner and probably the most informed and erudite opera critic in the province, said all of the things about the opera that Toronto critics, in good part, had failed to notice — how technically difficult it is, how the voices must match, how the singers "must have a musicianly regard for one another; balance and ensemble are everything in *Così*."

Returning to the company's Toronto festival, its third production was Gian-Carlo Menotti's *The Consul*. Torel had cast aside his worries about attendance and made what

Madama Butterfly (1953). Act 2. Sharpless (Gilles Lamontagne, right) advises a reluctant Cio-Cio San (Irene Salemka) to marry Yamadori.

some felt was an audacious choice. *The Consul* had been premiered in New York at the Ethel Barrymore Theatre in 1950, had subsequently won a Pulitzer Prize and a New York Drama Critics' Circle Award, and would eventually be translated into twelve languages and performed in twenty countries. Menotti was not only its composer and librettist, but had directed its premiere. The opera is a timely and relevant tragedy addressing the problems of people in a police state trying to get a visa to an unnamed country. A mid-century verissimo opera, *The Consul* makes for powerful drama, even though much of the music is rather mundane.

The Consul was an ideal piece to produce at the Royal Alexandra. Torel, who saw it as a director's dream, had a special empathy for the work because of his own experiences in Germany. It was a new kind of opera for Toronto and needed promotion and an exemplary cast to put it across. One thing seemed certain: since there were still only a few experienced and talented singing actors in the city, the company would have to import a soprano to play the leading part of Magda Sorel. Torel, therefore, went to New York with the avowed purpose of engaging Patricia Neway, who had created the role in the original production. While he was negotiating with Neway he auditioned a handsome expatriate Canadian soprano in her early thirties, Theresa Gray. She had studied extensively but as yet had not made much of an impression on the operatic and musical comedy stage. Torel was mightily impressed with her singing. It helped that she was Canadian, that she asked a lower fee than Neway, and that she would be available for extensive rehearsals. So he engaged her.

The Consul was a ground-breaking triumph for the Opera Festival Company. Gray was magnificent, as was the entire cast. In brief, the plot deals with Magda's efforts to save her husband, who has been arrested by the secret police. Her child dies, and she prepares to commit suicide as the curtain comes down. Gray's singing of the "Paper Aria" where she rebels against the consul's red tape, the dream sequence, and her final appearance at the consular office were especially memorable. The work is tonal, well-orchestrated, and, as in nearly all Menotti, kind to the voice. *The Consul* shows the composer's love for humanity. It is Menotti at his best.

The pathos and sorrow of this contemporary tragedy moved Toronto audiences enormously. It opened to a small house but, by its fourth performance — thanks to reviews and word of mouth — it almost sold out. Goldschmidt, Torel, and the board were so excited by its success that they decided to repeat it the following year. Alas, they would find that Toronto's public was not to be relied upon. It opened the 1954 festival with good attendance, but the next three performances played to half empty houses. The CBC had aired the work's worldwide television premiere with the opera company's cast a month before the festival, and this may have hurt ticket sales. Perhaps, too, Toronto's limited theatre and opera-going public simply couldn't take it a second time. Perhaps it was too much musical theatre, too much outside opera's mainstream for *Bohème* and *Butterfly* fans. Yet, in New York in 1950, it had run for eight months!

The Consul (1953).

Nellie Smith (Mother),

Theresa Gray (Magda Sorel),

Andrew MacMillan (Secret

Police Agent).

photo: Alex Gray

Chapter 3

FINDING ITS WAY

By 1954 the Opera Festival Company was firmly established, and its productions and casts compared favourably to first-rank smaller companies in North America and Europe. That year the festival made a profit of $1,000, perhaps more, since the bookkeeping was vague on this point. After the festival, Ettore Mazzoleni was appointed general director, and the company became known again as The Royal Conservatory Opera Company. Apparently there was no longer concern about coupling the company with the school, since the company's professional status was now secure. The surprising success of the first Stratford Shakespearean Festival in the summer of 1953 and the inspiring second May season of the Metropolitan Opera at Maple Leaf Gardens also helped to convince the company that there were audiences for quality entertainment. Met manager Rudolf Bing, not one for enthusiasm and overstatement, told The Globe and Mail that Toronto was the best opera city on the Met's annual continental tours. (22/2/54) *Carmen*, with the stunning Risë Stevens, played to over eleven thousand people, evidently a record at the time for indoor performances. It might still be.

Herman Geiger-Torel

43

44

School for Fathers (1954).
Act 2. Evelyn Gould (Lucinda),
Andrew MacMillan (Lunardo),
Joanne Ivey (Magherita).

School for Fathers (1954).
Act 1. Jon Vickers (Filipeto),
Sylvia Grant (Maria).

photo: Alex Gray

photo: Alex Gray

photo: Alex Gray

Rigoletto (1954).
Jon Vickers as the Duke.

Optimism was in the air. Canada was changing, and the performing arts were growing in importance. For many years Toronto's sole professional performing organization had been the TSO. Now local groups — the New Play Society, the Crest Theatre, the National Ballet, and the Opera Festival Association — were striving for places in the city's artistic life. Opera devotees were beginning to ask why the company didn't have a real opera house instead of merely a theatre. The opera board remained cautiously non-committal, since an opera house suggested major expansion and the need for large sums of money. The board was a notoriously poor fundraiser, compared to boards of American opera companies, and believed projects such as an opera house to be quite impossible. Fortunately, the Conservatory continued to support the company with services in kind — rehearsal space, salaries for Goldschmidt and Torel, music, and storage facilities. Mazzoleni, as cautious as the board, leaned heavily on Torel, who, with Goldschmidt's input, continued to select, cast, and budget operas. However, Torel still felt like an outsider and was intimidated by the board.

The company, nonetheless, moved ahead. In addition to the revival of *The Consul*, the 1954 festival performed Wolf-Ferrari's delightful but relatively unknown farce I quatro rusteghi, in English and re-titled *School for Fathers*. Suzanne Mess recalled that it had the distinction of being the first festival opera that was literally designed from scratch, with no hand-me-down costumes or scenery. Performed three times, it drew a reasonably good 76 percent house, as did *Rigoletto*. *Bohème*, at 87 percent, was the only box-office hit. The board, surprised that *Rigoletto* hadn't done better and discouraged by the Wolf-Ferrari reception, stressed that it wanted only traditional operas at its next festival.

In comparing the 1954 season with 1953's, there were sixteen performances of four operas instead of thirteen of three, attendance dropped a mere 1 percent, and income increased some $9,500; but when expenses were added up, there was a loss of around $10,000. Again the company had to ask the guarantors to bail it out. Instead of applauding the developing company, board members moaned loudly about the financial losses.

Nevertheless, artistic triumphs were, as in 1953, the order of the day. Barbini had evidently studied *School for Fathers* with the composer and he conducted it masterfully, as he did *Rigoletto*, again with Gilles Lamontagne as the tortured jester. The young Canadian

46

tenor, Jon Vickers, who had already gained an impressive reputation as an oratorio singer, sang the role of Filipeto in the Wolf-Ferrari piece, and the Duke in *Rigoletto*. Vickers, from Saskatchewan, had been urged by Mary Morrison to come to Toronto in the late 1940s. His voice was still relatively light, but its robust quality and cutting edge were more than evident to perceptive listeners. Vickers was a stiff actor who needed loosening up, but he learned fast. He would go on to become the leading heldentenor of his time.

Robert Goulet, a natural actor with a warm baritone voice, appeared in small roles in *School for Fathers*, *Bohème*, and *Rigoletto*. Only 21 at the time, this opera school student from Edmonton also sang in the chorus and was an assistant stage manager. (It was his only appearance with the company.)

After the festival there were runouts of *The Consul*, *Rigoletto*, and *Bohème*, to Hamilton, Kitchener, and London, but not further afield. When would the company become national? The board talked about a Western tour in 1955 and about sending Richard Van Valkenburg, its new president, to seek out engagements. Then it changed its mind. Van Valkenburg, the able director of Eaton's Art Gallery, was hardly qualified to book an opera tour despite his willingness to do so.

The company appeared to be going backwards when it mounted three, not four, operas in 1955. And all were standard works: *The Marriage of Figaro*, *La Traviata*, and *Die Fledermaus*. There were, as always, high spots. Marcella Reale, a young American soprano, was a superb Violetta in *Traviata*, and, with Jon Vickers as Alfredo and James Milligan as Germont, the opera was a vocal treat. Figaro benefitted from the Thomas Martin translation, with Jan Rubes as Figaro skillfully leading a strong cast. The broadly humorous *Fledermaus* revealed Torel's talent for staging Central European comedies. Even the rather tiresome jail scene went by quickly, thanks to the antics of the non-singing actor, Sammy Sales, who played the drunken Frosch. Joanne Ivey, looking every inch the bored and worldly Prince Orlofsky, drew much applause for her comments about contemporary Toronto in her second act monologue. Vancouver soprano Milla Andrew, singing for the first time at the festival, showed great promise as Rosalinda. She, also, would have a substantial international career.

La Traviata (1955).

Act 2. Germont (James Milligan) asks Violetta (Marcella Reale) to give up Alfredo.

photo: Alex Gray

The Marriage of Figaro (1955).
Act 3. Roma Butler (Susanna),
Mary Morrison (Countess).

Die Fledermaus (1955).
Act 3. In foreground: Karl
Norman (Alfred), Jean Ramsay
(Rosalinda), Andrew MacMillan
(Frank), Ernest Adams
(Eisenstein), Sammy Sales
(Frosch). In background: Lesia
Zubrack (Adele), Joyce Hill
(Fifi), in the jail.

48

This year the festival's income was up, as was attendance, all the more impressive since *Traviata* — unbelievably — was the poorest earner. The board was learning the hazards of trying to forecast ticket sales. But the festival lost money, due to the costs of mounting two new productions (*Traviata* and *Fledermaus*) and the fees for imports and dancers.

There were some signs of growth the next year: again only three operas, but eighteen instead of sixteen performances. *Carmen, Butterfly,* and *Don Giovanni* hardly added up to an adventurous season, but the *Carmen* production was new and came off very well. After hearing Risë Stevens and Blanche Thebom sing it for the Met at Maple Leaf Gardens, John Kraglund, music critic of *The Globe and Mail*, wondered how Toronto audiences would respond to the festival's *Carmen*. (25/6/55) Was he surprised!

Torel had engaged American mezzo-soprano Regina Resnik to do Carmen, and this helped Resnik launch a successful second career. Resnik had begun her career as a lyric-dramatic soprano and had sung major roles at the Met, Bayreuth, and other leading opera houses. She had just changed to a mezzo-soprano — in good measure the reason why the festival could afford her — and this was to be one of her first roles in her new tessitura.

Carmen (1956).

Regina Resnik (Carmen), Jon Vickers (Don José).

Resnik had a strong and vibrant voice, and was an intelligent musician and actor. A *Star* critic said that "she was pure alley-cat, and yet she gave the character a rough nobility based on the gypsy girl's own standard of morals and honour." (25/2/56) Her Carmen was, in a word, superb. She also influenced the Toronto cast with her professionalism, especially Jon Vickers, who sang Don José. His singing and acting in the "Flower Song" and in the final tragic scene were memorable. Resnik, aware of his great promise, encouraged him to move on to bigger and better things in the operatic world. (That summer they both sang in Britten's *The Rape of Lucretia* at Stratford — Resnik as Lucretia and Vickers as the Male Chorus. The next year Vickers was singing major roles at Covent Garden and in New York.)

As can sometimes happen in the best of opera companies, off-stage problems with *Carmen* arose. For rather murky reasons, Joanne Ivey, a fine actor but a modest singer and also Mazzoleni's wife, was double cast as Carmen and assigned three performances. She was under extraordinary strain from the outset to prove that nepotism had not gained her the coveted role. Some wondered why Ivey wasn't just a cover (one who stands by ready to step in if the principal becomes ill). Since there was always a day or two between performances, Resnik might easily have been persuaded to do all seven performances.

The problems began with an embarrassing exchange between Mazzoleni and Torel prior to the festival and the hapless Ivey was caught in the middle. To make things worse, Ivey was insufficiently coached in the role, she had little rehearsal time on stage, and didn't even get to try on all of her costumes before her opening night. Resnik had been testy even before she got to Toronto, having seen some newspaper clippings that made it appear that the press was paying more attention to Ivey than to her. Then she exploded at the beginning of a rehearsal because of another feature story on Ivey in the local press. Inevitably, Ivey gave poor performances. However, there was one lighter moment: on her opening night, her shawl got caught on a soldier's tunic at the start of the "Habañera," and the embarrassed chorus member had no alternative but to follow her closely about the stage as she gyrated to the music.

Robert Savoie, as Escamillo, and Marguerite Lavergne, as Micaela, were two of three French-Canadians singing at the festival that year. The third was the great lyric tenor,

Léopold Simoneau, who did Don Ottavio in *Don Giovanni*. Such was the impact of his Toronto performances that one bewitched *Montreal Star* journalist wished that Leporello or the Don had been written for tenor so that Simoneau could have sung one of those roles. (3/3/56) Simoneau, Lavergne, and Savoie, impressed with the festival, praised it beyond the call of duty in *The Toronto Star* and complained that Montreal's operatic efforts did not compare favourably with Toronto's. (22/2/56)

A new venture, aimed at grooming future audiences, was tried that year. High school students were invited to attend a dress rehearsal of the *Don*. They liked what they saw and heard, no doubt helped by the pleasant and informative introductions to different sections of the work by Boyd Neel, then dean of the Conservatory.

Madama Butterfly failed to attract audiences; perhaps Toronto had had too many *Butterfly*'s. Marcella Reale had been an enchanting Violetta the year before, but her Cio-Cio-San lacked intensity and dramatic power.

It was a season with one outstanding production and two good ones, the lowest box-office income in the company's history (72 percent), and the poorest attendance (75 percent). The company seemed to be on a down slope. Luckily, the Kitchener, Hamilton, and London performances were successful, both artistically and financially, as was the company's first ever appearance in Ottawa. In the final tally the company lost $30,000 for the year, a substantial sum for the times.

That season — so full of triumphs, disappointments, and internal problems — there was a major shakeup in the association. First came an overdue change in the company's leadership. Torel, having been offered the post of resident stage director at the Metropolitan Opera, went to the festival board to see whether it wished to entice him to stay in Toronto. Impressed, association president Van Valkenburg promptly raised his salary. A few weeks later he was appointed artistic director and his relationship with the Conservatory, where he would continue to teach, was clarified. He would, for the first time, be responsible directly to the board. Torel was now really in the driver's seat. In May, to wind up the reorganization, Mazzoleni resigned from the company, stating that his work as principal of the Conservatory left him little time to do his festival job.

The future of the company also brightened with the election of Floyd Chalmers to the board in the spring of 1956. President of the Maclean-Hunter publishing company and a driving force on the Conservatory's board for twenty years, he agreed to chair the opera board after the New Year. In May Torel confirmed the February 1957 operas and, as he had proposed five years earlier, announced that the company would give a season of light operas in October 1957, and do the 1958 festival in October, not February. The main reason for the change in dates was to gain a better orchestra. With only a limited pool of good orchestral players available, the new scheme would enable TSO players to join the opera orchestra prior to the beginning of the TSO season.

On January 3, 1957, the Opera Festival Association of Toronto announced its new board. It included the mayor of Toronto, the chairman of Metro, the president of the University of Toronto, and top business leaders from across the country who would enhance the company's national image and open the door for more funds. The association, tired of vacillating about its name, announced in November 1957 that "Canadian Opera Company (of Toronto)" would be used in the future. (The "of Toronto" was gradually dropped.) In 1960 the Opera Festival Association became the Canadian Opera Association. It was not until 1977 that "Canadian Opera Company" — finally — was adopted as its legal name.

As the 1957 opera season approached, support was growing for government funding for the arts, and the opera company would benefit from the movement. The federal government's Royal Commission on National Development in the Arts, Letters, and Sciences had published its Massey Report in 1951. The Report advocated federal aid to the arts and the establishment of a Canada Council to administer the grants. Arts groups were still waiting for action. The opera association, in a gesture it hoped would hurry the government along, dispatched a brief to the federal government, asking for an annual grant of $100,000. As anticipated, the government replied that there would not be any grants until the Canada Council was formed. However, with government aid to the arts becoming topical, the Municipality of Metropolitan Toronto, not be confused with the City of Toronto, gave its first grant of $10,000 to the association in 1957, the beginning

52

The Abduction from the
Seraglio (1957).

Léopold Simoneau as Belmonte.

The Abduction from the
Seraglio (1957).

Edita Symonek as Constanza.

of annual grants for years to come. That year, Metro, as the municipality was known, also gave grants of $15,000 each to the TSO and the National Ballet.

The 1957 festival should have been a joy, but Toronto audiences responded less than overwhelmingly to the three operas: *The Abduction from the Seraglio*, *Tosca*, and *Hansel and Gretel*. *The Abduction*, sung in English, had Edita Symonek as Constanza, Léopold Simoneau as Belmonte, and his wife, the lyric soprano Pierrette Alarie, as Blonda. Scene stealer Jan Rubes played Osmin. Torel was courageous indeed to have chosen such a little-known opera. The production was first class, although some complained that they couldn't understand the words, perhaps due to so many leads whose maternal tongue wasn't English.

Of the three *Tosca* principals, two were Americans: the soprano Ilona Kombrink as Tosca — she sang, acted, and looked the role splendidly — and the tenor Richard Cassilly as Cavaradossi; he had an imposing stage presence and ringing voice. Ilona Kombrink had married a Toronto musician and lived in Toronto. Cassilly and Kombrink would do other roles for the COC in the coming years. After attending Kombrink's second performance, *The Globe and Mail's* Kraglund, not one for superlatives, called her characterization "a great one." (27/2/57) This might also have been said about the production as a whole. The young bass-baritone, Victor Braun, made his first appearance with the COC in a minor role. Still a student, he was at the threshold of an impressive career that is continuing over four decades later. As for Hansel and Gretel, the rather frightening production drew large crowds, including many children.

Despite the season's overall excellence and generally good press the Mozart drew only 65 percent houses and *Tosca*, 77 percent. The Humperdinck work was the best attended at 85 per cent. Toronto's taste and artistic likes and dislikes continued to be a mystery.

Nicholas Goldschmidt took a leave of absence from the company after the February festival — as it turned out, never to return. He had been music director at the University of British Columbia summer school since 1950, and his work in opera there had attracted much attention. In 1955 he had organized the Vancouver International Festival and was subsequently appointed its artistic and managing director. Goldschmidt loved to start new ventures and thrived on the excitement and unpredictability that went with them.

His enthusiasm was as contagious in the British Columbia city as it had been in Toronto. The first Vancouver Festival would be held in the summer of 1958, with *Don Giovanni* and the Verdi *Requiem* the highlights. The big event of the 1959 festival would be the opening of the Queen Elizabeth Theatre, with Her Majesty present. Goldschmidt left Vancouver in 1962, and from 1964 to 1968 was chief of the performing arts division of the Centennial Commission. He has since organized and launched several other festivals in Canada.

An Act of Parliament in March 1957 finally constituted the Canada Council. (Succession duties from the estates of two recently deceased Canadians, Sir James Dunn and Isaac Walton Killam, provided the funds to establish it. Otherwise, as the more cynically inclined suggested, it might have continued to be but a pious wish.) The council's creation was a most significant event in Canada's cultural history. The Arts Council of Great Britain, an arm's-length body that had been formed after the war, was used, in part, as a model. The Canada Council's guidelines, "to foster and promote the study and enjoyment of, and production of works in, the arts," were sufficiently broad for it to respond to the arts community on a number of fronts, and it has done so ever since. Professional performing arts organizations needed money, and the twenty-one-member council addressed this immediately. The council also recognized how much young Canadian artists meant to the future of the country and took steps to help them with grants for training in Canada and abroad. Federal funding of artistic organizations and artists mattered a great deal in a country heretofore known primarily for its forests, mines, and fish.

In June 1957 Torel, moving quickly, met with Albert Trueman, director of the council, to discuss grants for a touring company and for commissioning operas by Canadian composers. Touring would be relatively easy to get under way, but finding composers interested in writing operas would be more difficult. (A decade would pass before the company finally did two commissioned works.) In November, Floyd Chalmers — he and Torel made a powerful pair — asked Trueman for $10,000 for touring. In his request, which was granted without delay, Chalmers pointed out that, in just ten years, the association and its predecessor, the Royal Conservatory, had produced 129 performances of

54

thirty operas, including some in Ontario cities other than Toronto, and that, in all, it had played to some 200,000 persons. It was an impressive record, even though much of Canada was still unaware of the company's existence.

The Canadian Opera Women's Committee (COWC) was lauded, deservedly, at the association's Annual General Meeting in the spring of 1957. Ten years had passed since nine prominent Toronto women interested in the Senior School and the Opera School had met for the first time in Arnold Walter's spartan office on the second floor of the Conservatory. Mrs. Floyd Chalmers (in those days only unmarried women used their Christian name) had chaired that first meeting. It's purpose was to form an "Opera and Concerts Committee" to promote the Conservatory's public performances, but it soon focussed its efforts on opera, and some years later renamed itself the COWC. Over the years it sold tickets, raised money, supplied props, and raised money for scholarships for students at the opera school. It also prepared sandwiches for casts, and put on opening night parties and other social events to enhance opera's image with the public.

Carousel (1957).

Joanne Ivey (Mrs. Mullin),

Don Garrard (Billy Bigelow).

For the 1957 festival the COWC sold more than half of the tickets and more than $5,000 worth of program ads, bringing in a net profit for the programs alone of over $3,000. The committee, with no letup, went on to work just as hard to sell the September operetta season, but with less success. Dressed to the nines, they came out in force for the three opening nights. The men were mostly in formal dress. Press cameras clicked away, re-enforcing the perception that opera — or operetta in this case — was an entertainment for the upper classes.

The operetta season should have gone better, with *Die Fledermaus*, Lehár's *The Merry Widow*, and Rodgers and Hammerstein's *Carousel*. Certainly the audiences enjoyed them. Yet the box office was discouraging, with *Carousel* the poorest seller. Company singers played the leading roles well, but the conducting was routine. Marie Day, on her first COC designing assignment, created an exciting set for *Carousel*, yet it didn't stop one *Star* critic from saying that it inhibited the actors. (22/10/57) There were concerns, initially, that Torel would fail to understand *Carousel*, and that it would need a Broadway director. Such was not the case. He caught the spirit of the work — it is based on Ferenc Molnar's *Liliom* — and the cast responded accordingly. All in all the season should have marked the beginning of annual operetta seasons at the Royal Alexandra, but it didn't.

The company's out-of-town appearances were just as discouraging. *Fledermaus* and *The Merry Widow* played in London and Ottawa, and *Fledermaus* in Montreal. Despite an $8,000 grant from the Canada Council, a Women's Committee grant of $15,000, and $9,000 from a special fund, the company lost $20,000. The only bright spot of the season was a greatly improved orchestra.

As Torel had proposed two years earlier, the next festival was to be held in the fall of 1958. Mrs. Fletcher Sharpe told the board's executive in January that the COWC, which she represented, was doubtful about Torel's wish to do Richard Strauss's *Ariadne auf Naxos*, a work not known to most Torontonians. The committee, with its considerable clout, got its way — *Ariadne* was put aside, never to be done by the COC in Torel's lifetime. He did, however, do a magnificent student production of the work at the opera school in the late 1960s.

Torel's compromise was *La Bohème*, under the baton of Walter Susskind, conductor of

photo: Alex Gray

La Bohème (1958).

Act 4. Plans are made to save Mimi. Left to right: Norman Mittelman (Marcello), Patricia Snell (Musetta), Jan Rubes (Colline), Andrew MacMillan (Schaunard), John McCollum (Rodolfo), Teresa Stratas (Mimi).

the TSO. It was Susskind's first time with the company. Although he was the best con-ductor the COC had engaged to date, his association with the COC was fraught with problems. To start with, he was nine days late for the beginning of the *Bohème* rehearsals. And there continued to be other scheduling difficulties involving rehearsal times and per-formance times. Susskind conducted seven COC productions over six seasons before finally leaving the company in 1963.

Mimi was the twenty-year old Teresa Stratas. She was a prize-winning Conservatory graduate who, in the next year, would be the co-winner of the Metropolitan Opera Auditions. She convinced Susskind and Torel that, despite her lack of experience, she was up to the role. Both men recognized her great talent and let her do it. Stratas, with her gorgeous dark spinto voice, also proved to be a gifted actor. She was a restrained Mimi at first, but her grasp of the role and her confidence improved with each performance. Marie Day did the sets and costumes, and Robert Gill of Hart House Theatre directed. He made his characters more believable than usual in this well-worn masterpiece, but the group scene in Act 2 was a hodgepodge of activity that disturbed rather than entertained.

The other two new productions in the COC's repertoire that season, Offenbach's *Tales of Hoffmann* and Verdi's *Un ballo in maschera*, were both well done, the former thanks to Elemer Nagy's direction and sets, and the latter because of memorable performances by Ilona Kombrink as Amelia and Guiseppe Campora as Riccardo, and because of Ernesto Barbini's fine conducting. The touring company's *Barber of Seville* rounded off the season.

The COC board, in an appreciative mood after its successful and quite adventurous 1958 season, recognized Torel's dedication, achievements, and prudence by appointing him general director at a salary of $1,000 per month. That fall the trio of Kombrink, Campora, and Barbini were a success again in another Verdi masterpiece, *La forza del destino*. The company, rather bravely, did a charming version in English of Prokofiev's *The Love for Three Oranges*. Susskind conducted, and actor/playwright Mavor Moore staged it. (Jean Gascon of Le Théatre du Nouveau Monde had initially agreed to direct it but had backed out on July 8 because he found the work incompatible with his direct-ing style.)

photo: Alex Gray

The Tales of Hoffmann (1958).
Donald Bartle
(Andrès/Cochenille), Jim
Hawthorne (Hoffmann).

photo: Alex Gray

Un ballo in maschera (1958).
Act 3, scene 1. Left to right:
Andrew MacMillan (Sam), Jan
Rubes (Tom), Harold Mossfield
(Renato).

La forza del destino (1959).
Act 1, scene 2. Ilona Kombrink as
Leonora. Designed by Laufer/Day.

photo: Alex Gray

58

The Love for Three Oranges (1959).
Don Garrard (The King of Nowhere), Alan Crofoot (Truffaldino).

photo: Alex Gray

This was Moore's first experience with opera direction — which, he admitted, was altogether different from directing plays. As he put it in *The Toronto Star,* "the composer has fixed in advance all those things which, in a dialogue play, only emerge as the end result: the length of time it takes to cross the stage to build up an emotion, to execute 'business,' to pause. A precise composer even indicates by his musical relation exactly how a tune is to be delivered — a trick far beyond the most explicit of playwrights." (14/10/59) Musical symbols, he said, "provide a cast-iron icing for which a stage director must then bake a cake."

The inventive designs and costumes for *The Love for Three Oranges* were done by Murray Laufer and Marie Day. (Both of them would work frequently with Torel over the

photo: Alex Gray

Otello (1960).

Act 1. Left to right: Aldo
Bertocci (Otello), Phil Stark
(Cassio), Wallace Williamson
(Roderigo).

Otello (1960).

Act 3. Louis Quilico as Iago.

photo: Alex Gray

next fifteen years.) This show, for children from ages 8 to 80, was beautifully sung and acted. It was a new kind of artistic triumph for the company, but, in great part, the public and press failed to appreciate it.

The tenth COC season (1960) was not up to the two previous seasons. Louis Quilico's Iago in *Otello* was the only forceful interpretation in an otherwise spotty production. Ilona Kombrink, who was having vocal problems that eventually brought her potentially great career to a halt, had to withdraw as Desdemona on opening night, although she did do the remaining six performances. An almost routine *Marriage of Figaro* was saved by Jan Rubes' Figaro and Peter Ebert's innovative staging, but nothing could save the poor production of Johann Strauss's *A Night in Venice*. That year, there were five more perfor-

60

mances than in 1959; attendance was poor and the deficit considerable. The COC, with some justification, blamed their difficulties on the grand opening of the O'Keefe Centre, which coincided with the opera season. Torel was determined to move the COC to the new hall.

The Marriage of Figaro (1960).
Act 2. Left to right: Patricia Rideout (Marcellina), Heinz Rehfuss (Count Almaviva), Phil Stark (Don Basilio), Andrew MacMillan (Dr. Bartolo), Jan Rubes (Figaro), Irene Salemka (Susanna), Mary Morrison (The Countess).

photo: Alex Gray

Chapter 4

A MAJOR NORTH AMERICAN COMPANY

One of the Canada Council's first grants was to the COC to help it form a touring company. The council — and the COC — believed that bringing live opera to remote places would help cultivate Canada's taste for opera. Also, the country would become more conscious of Canadian operatic talent, younger singers would gain invaluable experience, and the company would work for longer seasons.

Touring a Canadian opera group was almost an imperative at the end of the 1950s. The role of the performing arts in Canada's "search for identity" was becoming increasingly significant, thanks to the CBC, the Stratford Festival, the National Ballet, the Royal Winnipeg Ballet, the Canadian Players, and other such groups. They were all doing their share in helping the country grow up artistically. Now it was opera's turn.

Several matters clearly needed addressing before the COC could undertake a national tour: an opera with popular appeal and a relatively small cast had to be selected; flexible sets that would look well on both small and large stages and that were easy to transport had to be designed; and costumes that were light, yet sturdy, had to be made.

Finding sponsors and appropriate venues was the next step. Finally, the sequence of engagements had to be worked out to minimize travel times — so as not to tire unduly the cast and to keep costs down.

The first tour was planned for November and December 1958. It would last four weeks, with performances in Ontario and the Maritime provinces, including Newfoundland. The Royal Conservatory had toured an English version of *Così fan tutte* in Southern Ontario in 1953 and again in 1956, and these tours, with all of their trials and tribulations, would provide the model.

Surprisingly, finding sponsors was not as difficult as anticipated. A minor war was going on between Canadian concert-giving clubs in smaller centres and New York booking agencies, especially Columbia Concerts and its affiliate, Community Concerts. Many of the clubs were dependent on Community, which guaranteed an annual series of four or five concerts to suit a club's budget. The budget depended on the number of subscriptions the club sold, and so artists were not discussed until after the subscription sales were completed and the club knew how much money it had to spend. Then Community helped the club select and book artists within the club's price range. For these services, Community earned a percentage of the subscriptions called the differential. No single tickets were sold since this could endanger subscription sales. Community almost always promoted artists under contract with Columbia. Columbia then earned commissions from the artists, very few of whom were Canadian. Community argued that most Canadian artists were weak; but, as any one in the concert world knew, this was becoming less and less true.

Community actually thought this scheme benevolent. However, some Canadian clubs suspected that they were being taken, and a significant number of them defiantly began engaging Canadian artists directly. In some cases, and with a touch of reverse chauvinism, *only* Canadians were hired. Such changes in booking practices inevitably weakened the Columbia-Community hold and helped the COC find sponsors.

For this first tour, the COC booked six performances in Ontario and thirteen in Eastern Canada. The company would travel by bus for shorter trips (under three hundred miles), by rail and boat for longer trips, and by air home from Halifax at the end.

The COC would have to play in converted movie houses, high school auditoriums, and even gymnasiums; endure poor pianos and usually non-existent dressing rooms; and make do generally with conditions as they were, not as they should be.

Keeping these limitations in mind, Torel chose a comic opera, Rossini's *Barber of Seville*, for the first two tours. It had instant appeal, it would be sung in English, and much would be made of the opera's slapstick humour, which Torel typically enjoyed staging, perhaps too much so. Looking to the future, he envisaged the tour as a warm-up for the 1959 festival's production of this Rossini masterpiece and hoped to develop the best Toronto cast from the touring company.

And so some fourteen singers, a pianist-conductor, and a technician bravely set out. The company had the stamina to perform almost daily, sometimes after a strenuous day of travel. The leads were double cast, and they often did minor roles on "rest" days. They learned to cope with sore throats — the singer's nemesis — upset stomachs, and other maladies. Accommodation and meals, not Canada's strong suit in the 1950s, left much to

The Barber of Seville (1959).

John McCollum (Count Almaviva),

Alexander Gray (Figaro).

photo: Alex Gray

be desired, especially since the company could not afford up-market hotels and restaurants. Drafty halls and Canada's notorious winter weather didn't help either. The buses were usually overcrowded — piled high with people, costumes, scenery, and luggage. Members of the company frequently complained of "bus fever." On the plus side, there was a pervasive pioneering spirit that helped members put aside their personal problems, moderate their egos, and get on with the show. It was the beginning of a genuine *Canadian* company.

It helped that Canadian communities were eager for live opera. CBC radio and television operatic productions generated audiences, as did the Metropolitan Opera broadcasts. Long-playing albums, introduced in the late 1940s, featured complete operas, highlights, and great singers. Serious opera buffs in every corner of the country were collecting them. Opera was getting into their blood.

One glaring difference between the touring company and the Toronto company was that the former used a piano, the latter an orchestra. The COC simply could not afford to send an orchestra on tour. Tour sponsors and audiences were understandably disappointed, but this did keep the price down. (It would be ten years before the COC could travel with a small orchestra.) However, in a few large centres such as Halifax, Calgary, and Vancouver, where a sufficiently large pool of good musicians was available, an adequate orchestra was occasionally put together and used with COC productions. As expected, the performances were on the rough side because the singers had too few rehearsals and the players had too little operatic playing experience. In Halifax, COC pianist George Brough had to conduct the orchestra when the resident conductor declined to do so at the last minute. Brough, who had never conducted before, did admirably under the circumstances.

And so the piano was used for nearly all touring engagements in the COC's early tours. Of course, finding a good piano could in some communities be daunting. There were, in fact, communities where a grand piano was nowhere to be found. In many places the COC used instruments that hadn't been tuned for years and had broken strings, chipped keys, and other typical piano ailments.

That first year the scenery added up to four pieces — two folding screens, one collapsible prop piano, and one collapsible piano bench — plus hand props and, naturally, costumes. Ernest Adams doubled as company manager and singer — he shared the roles of Fiorello and the Policeman and played the Notary in every performance. The show, designed by Brian Jackson of the Stratford Festival, was later expanded for the Royal Alexandra performances. Jackson had already successfully designed the 1958 COC production of *Un ballo in maschera*.

Of the six Ontario performances, two were sponsored by universities (Queen's and Assumption, later renamed Windsor), one by London's Grand Theatre, two by concert clubs (in Whitby and St. Thomas), and one by the Lions Club of Wingham. The largest Ontario audience (1,900) was at Windsor's Capitol Theatre, yet the performance there received one of the tour's few half-hearted reviews. The *Windsor Star* complained, among other things, that there was no orchestra. In Halifax, all proceeds were donated to the recent Springhill mining disaster where seventy-four miners had lost their lives in a cave-in in the deepest mine in North America.

Wolfville had an especially appreciative audience of 1,500, mainly staff and students from Acadia University. At Mount Allison University in Sackville, music school students who attended confessed that they had never before been to an opera!

The COC covered nearly five thousand miles on this first tour. Torel — he had not travelled with the company — reported to the Canada Council that nearly every sponsor wanted return engagements. Torel's report underlined the tour's positive aspects because he wanted the council to continue its grants, which it did. Ernest Adams prepared an informal report that touched on some of the negative aspects: poor playing conditions, illness, fatigue, and tension among the cast.

For the next eighteen years, the COC continued to make annual tours of Canada and the United States, including Alaska. The 1959 tour gave twenty-two performances in Western Canada and covered nearly twice as many miles as the first tour. Torel, who was not above hyperbole when it helped sell tickets, said in a Canadian Press dispatch in the *Kirkland Lake News* that the COC's *Barber* was "interpretively superior" to the Metropolitan Opera's production at Maple Leaf Gardens and that it was "better rehearsed, fresher and had no stars." (17/10/59)

66

*The Merry Wives of Windsor
(1960).*
Touring company. Patricia Snell
(Alice Ford), Jan Rubes
(Falstaff), Elsie Sawchuck (Meg
Page).

photo: Alex Gray

Otto Nicolai's *The Merry Wives of Windsor* played in the East in early 1960 and in the West later in the year. Vancouver's Overture Concerts, directed by George Zukerman, booked the COC for seventeen of the forty Western performances. Overture, patterned after Community Concerts but not affiliated with any artist agency, would take the COC to small and remote centres as far north as the Arctic in the coming years.

Toronto had a chance to enjoy *The Merry Wives* when it played at Etobicoke Collegiate on March 14, 1960. *The Globe and Mail* generously praised the performance the next day, making special note, deservedly, of Mario Bernardi's conducting and pianistic skills. Then, in 1961 the COC did a hilarious version of Offenbach's parody on the Orpheus and Euridice legend, *Orpheus in the Underworld*. George Brough played and conducted a new English version written by Robert Fulford and James Knight. It was brilliantly cast, and featured some splendid singing actors. Phil Stark was one of the stand-outs as Orpheus. In a later tour of the work, Stark was described by the Columbus, Ohio *Citizen-Journal* "as one who sings like a poet, clowns like Zero Mostel, and plays the violin like a concert artist." (10/12/71) Another standout was Alan Crofoot, as Bacchus. He stopped the show when he sang his solo in the final act, bringing many, including the cast, to tears. Crofoot was described by the same critic as "suitably rotund, wistfully appealing, and endowed with the lyric tenor of an angel, if you'll excuse the theological mixture." *Orpheus* was one of the touring company's huge triumphs, both in its first tour in 1961, and in the revival in 1970–71. The 1961 tour gave thirty performances in the Atlantic provinces, and forty-four in the West. Overture arranged three performances with a Vancouver orchestra, two in Vancouver and one in Seattle, where it received rave reviews.

With three comedies under its belt, the company took on a more serious bent and toured *La Bohème* in 1962, both east and west. In Halifax the house was a sellout three days after the box office opened, and in St. John's, Newfoundland both performances were to full houses. Back in Toronto it played at a local high school before embarking on its Western tour and even pleased the local pundits who bemoaned the lack of an orchestra but still liked the production.

It was back to comedy in 1963 with *Così fan tutte*, followed by *Die Fledermaus* in 1964

top left: **Orpheus in the Underworld (1961).**
Touring company. Dodi Protero (Eurydice), Phil Stark (Orpheus).

top right: **Orpheus in the Underworld (1970 revival).**
Touring company. Alan Crofoot (Bacchus), Dodi Protero (Eurydice).

bottom left: **Così fan tutte (1963).**
Touring company. Left to right: Constance Fisher (Fiordiligi), Kathryn Newman (Despina), Cecilia Ward (Dorabella).

bottom right: **Così fan tutte (1963).**
Touring company. Left to right: Phil Stark (Ferrando), Jan Rubes (Don Alfonso), Alexander Gray (Guglielmo).

photo: Alex Gray

photo: Robert C. Ragsdale, FRPS

photo: Alex Gray

photo: Alex Gray

and 1965. The 1965 eastern tour included an appearance at Prince Edward Island's centennial celebrations. The western tour that year covered over twelve thousand miles for fifty-four performances. Opera was welcomed everywhere and return engagements were the order of the day. In 1966, the COC, mindful of linguistic imperatives, offered *Carmen* in both English and French, the latter for its Quebec performances. There were seventy-six performances of it in all, in the Maritimes, Quebec, Ontario, and the eastern United States.

In 1965, the Metropolitan Opera had launched a touring company of younger, less experienced singers much like the COC's. Risë Stevens, and her co-director Michael Manuel, programmed Rossini's *La Cenerentola*, Carlisle Floyd's *Susanna*, *Carmen*, and *Butterfly* for its first tour of some seventy cities in thirty-four weeks. The company played for a week at O'Keefe and in six other Canadian cities in addition to its USA tour. Their bookings showed confidence in Canada's growing enthusiasm for opera, and ultimately helped attendance at COC performances.

This cross-border touring worked both ways. More and more in the early 1960s, the COC's touring company looked south for engagements. Its fees, thanks to Canada Council subsidies, were low enough to compete with established American touring companies, and, quality-wise, it may have surpassed them. The realities of North American geography made it useful for the COC to find engagements in border states — Washington, Oregon, and Montana in the West, and Michigan, Ohio, and New York in the East — to round off tours. USA performances were good for the company's morale and tended to remind Americans that Canada was no operatic wasteland. Press reviews, even in large centres, were most

Don Pasquale (1968).
Touring company. Sheila Piercey
(Norina), Cornelis Opthof (Dr.
Malatesta).

laudatory. The American market would grow in the next few years, as the COC's reputation spread.

In the spring of 1967, even though the COC was very much absorbed with the centennial productions of its first two commissioned operas, *Louis Riel* and *The Luck of Ginger Coffey*, it found time to make its longest tour yet to the West with eighty-two performances of Donizetti's *Don Pasquale*. The company travelled to such distant places as Uranium City, Fort Smith, and Whitehorse in the Northwest Territories and the Yukon, and to Fairbanks, Anchorage, and Juneau in Alaska. Outside temperatures were often in the minus 50 degree range. Ruby Mercer, editor of *Opera Canada*, accompanied the group.

And then, finally, in 1968, a sixteen-piece orchestra joined the singers for the eastern tour, and became a fixture in subsequent tours. Small as the orchestra was, it was a vast improvement and gave the touring company a new lease on life. But it also created additional logistical problems with orchestra pits, travel, accommodation, and, naturally, performance fees. William Littler of *The Toronto Star* travelled to the far north with the company for a week in the fall of 1968. He admired the pluck of the cast, as they moved day after day from town to town, sometimes under very adverse conditions. It was their "sheer, hardened professionalism and that elixir of love known as audience rapport, that made it worthwhile for them and their public." (28/12/68) On a more sober note, this *Barber* tour lost money, due to cancellations and heavy travel costs — a plane had to be chartered for one engagement and the Juneau performance had to be cancelled because of bad weather.

Touring would continue for the ever-industrious COC until 1991. It gave an almost unbelievable 117 western performances of *Orpheus* in the winter of 1970–71, and then another ninety performances in the East later in the winter of 1971–72.

The company had many harrowing experiences on the tours, especially on the earlier ones. On one memorable evening in Saskatchewan, a piano leg actually collapsed during a performance. The pianist, James Craig, completed the act playing the instrument, such as it was, on a slanting keyboard! To make matters worse — this had nothing to do with pianos — a pot-bellied wood-burning stove half exploded and filled the theatre with smoke. At the other end of the country, in Nova Scotia, a piano's pedals ceased to function during the show, leaving the pianist to do what he could without them.

On another tour, Victor Braun and Cornelis Opthof, two strapping six-foot-plus baritones, were strolling down a street in Kenora, Ontario one late afternoon when a policeman stopped them. Because they were dressed casually, the policeman didn't believe their story — that they were in Kenora to sing in an opera. They were charged with vagrancy and trundled off to the police station. Thankfully, they were released in time for the performance, but it was obvious that the policeman knew little, and cared even less, about opera in his city. And to highlight how little theatre owners knew about opera's requirements, Jan Rubes remembered when the proprietor of a movie house in Fort William, Ontario (now part of Thunder Bay) refused to remove the projection screen! The tales go on and on, and retelling them has provided many laughs through the years.

To return to Toronto and back to 1961, the COC took a major step forward when it decided to move to the new O'Keefe (later Hummingbird) Centre, a 3,155-seat hall in downtown Toronto. The 1960 season at the Royal Alexandra had been discouraging, with only 59 percent attendance. The COC could look a half-mile to the east with envy to see O'Keefe selling out *Camelot* and a one-woman show with Marlene Dietrich.

E.P. Taylor, a prominent brewer and philanthropist, had originally planned to build a huge civic centre fashioned after New York's Rockefeller Center. It was to have a hotel, several restaurants, underground parking, and a complex of auditoriums, large and small. However, these plans were eventually scaled down to one large auditorium. Mayor Nathan Phillips granted Taylor Scott Lane, which crossed the auditorium's site, for $1. This done, Taylor then provided the $12 million necessary to build the Centre.

O'Keefe's planners had examined a number of large halls in North America and Europe before finalizing their plans. In the end, all this preliminary work yielded was a multi-purpose theatre that the cynical still call a "no-purpose" theatre. That said, the O'Keefe exterior is impressive. It is situated on a main Toronto thoroughfare (Front Street) and has a handsome facade with a marquee jutting out audaciously to the street and a driveway curving into the front entrance. There are several spacious lobbies. The main one is enhanced by a mural covering one complete wall, which Taylor commissioned from artist York Wilson; it is titled "The Seven Lively Arts." Unfortunately, the auditorium itself lacks intimacy, and singers and actors need amplification because of the hall's poor acoustics. The stage has a commendable sixty-foot proscenium and reasonable depth, but there is no way for actors to go from one side of the stage to the other without going down one flight, crossing over, and going up another. The original rigging tower was inadequate, and there were not enough light bridges and towers. These items could be improved, and eventually were, but not the orchestra pit, which still holds a maximum of seventy-six musicians, not really large enough for Wagner and Richard Strauss operas. To its credit, O'Keefe has a good rehearsal hall but, at least in its earlier years, this space was used mostly for storage, since storage facilities were meagre. Even so, a good deal of the scenery, costumes, and props had to be stored in other buildings until just prior to performances.

The O'Keefe Centre in 1961.

photo: O'Keefe Centre

A multi-purpose theatre is not an opera house, and O'Keefe had simply not been planned as one, even though its planners had consulted informed people in opera. It was and is mainly a venue for touring musicals, revues, jazz, vaudeville, and plays. On a different tack, little effort was made at first to accommodate made-in-Canada productions of opera, ballet, and theatre.

The Centre opened its doors in 1960 with a pre-Broadway run of the Lerner and Loewe musical, *Camelot*, with Richard Burton, Julie Andrews, and Canadian Robert Goulet. This show successfully launched a subscription series of popular road shows that suited the new hall. Torontonians and tourists liked the attractions, as well as the Centre itself, with its festive feeling, restaurant, art shows, and boutiques. (Its only drawback, hospitality-wise, was that it had to wait until 1965 for a liquor licence.) O'Keefe was the city's first new theatre in thirty years and a harbinger of other large buildings in Toronto's downtown.

Hugh Walker, the O'Keefe general manager, was interested in opera, and had even consulted Rudolf Bing when O'Keefe was being planned. He hoped this might convince the Metropolitan Opera, and its local sponsor, the Toronto Rotary Club, to play at the new hall in the spring of 1961, and so it did. The Met had already done nine annual week-long money-making seasons for Rotary at Maple Leaf Gardens, but the O'Keefe week, by comparison, did not go well. It was the end of the company's annual tour, and several leads in *Martha*, *Aïda*, and *La Traviata* were ill. The hall's acoustics were disconcerting for both the cast and the audience, and attendance was so-so. Rotary found the theatre's costs higher than anticipated, and the recently devalued Canadian dollar — down some five percent — further increased its payments to the Met. When Rotary announced that the Met would not play in Toronto in 1962, Torel expressed his disappointment in *The Globe and Mail*, for he believed that its singers served as an inspiration to the young singers in the COC. (5/1/62) Certainly the Met had made Toronto more opera conscious. Its main company would not return to Toronto until 1984.

The Met's experience with O'Keefe notwithstanding, the COC was still looking forward to playing at the Centre, never imagining that it would remain there for the rest of the century. For its first season in the fall of 1961, the COC scheduled five operas instead of three (two made up a double-bill), and cut its performances from twenty-one to seventeen. To kick-start the box office, COC president Floyd Chalmers persuaded a skeptical Hugh Walker, who thought little of the COC, to include COC performances in the Centre's subscription series. Walker agreed, but on condition that it would be for three years only.

Cavalleria rusticana (1961).
In foreground, Victor Braun (Alfio), Jon Crain (Turiddu).

Torel's choices for the COC's first season at O'Keefe were *Tosca*, *Carmen* (in English), *The Bartered Bride* (in English), and the double-bill of *Cavalleria rusticana* and *Pagliacci*. *Cavalleria*, staged by the experienced English director Joan Cross and done in traditional style in a workmanlike set by William Lord, left the audience unmoved. *Pagliacci*, on the other hand, was given an exciting, imaginative, and contemporary staging by young Leon Major. Set by designer Les Lawrence in the ruins of an Italian amphitheatre, the lamentable tale of love, jealousy, and betrayal was tautly executed and gripping to the end.

photo: Alex Gray

Inevitably, the large stage — so hard to fill in certain operas — and the troublesome acoustics caused problems for COC productions. The difficulties with the stage were gradually overcome by trial and error, but to cope with the acoustics, well-hidden amplification, taboo in respectable operatic circles, had to be used. The warmth and intimacy of Royal Alexandra productions was lost forever, but COC box-office receipts more than doubled, and there was even a surplus, at least in the first year.

photo: Alex Gray

above: **I Pagliacci (1961),** Act 2. Canio (Eddy Ruhl) has stabbed Nedda and Silvio.

right: **The Bartered Bride (1961).** Choreography by Don Gillies.

below: **Carmen (1961).** Jean Sanders (Carmen), Richard Cassilly (Don José).

photo: Alex Gray

In 1962, the COC took advantage of the orchestra pit — although it still wasn't large enough — to produce *Die Walküre*. Torel, to his discredit, made substantial cuts, saying that Toronto audiences would find the complete work boring. His real reason, one suspects, was to save costs of overtime for the orchestra and stage crew. In the same season Teresa Stratas, now a regular at the Metropolitan Opera,

Die Walküre (1961).
Paul Schoeffler as Wotan, and the Valkyries.

far left: **Madama Butterfly**
(1962).
Teresa Stratas as Cio-Cio-San.

left: **Rigoletto** *(1962).*
Act 3.

returned home to do *Madama Butterfly*, and Louis Quilico was a stunning *Rigoletto*, a role he would do in major opera houses throughout the world for the next thirty years. *Hansel and Gretel* was spruced up by director Leon Major and the creative sets of William Lord to round off the season.

In its third year at O'Keefe the company gave two masterpieces it could never have done at the Royal Alexandra, *Aïda* and *Der Rosenkavalier*. The Strauss work did badly, as much due to the poor amplification as to the mediocre singing by two of the leads. The bright spots were Helen Vanni's Octavian and Howell Glynne's Baron Ochs. It was an altogether different story with *Aïda*. It was well cast and brilliantly staged by Dino Yanopoulos, and the Laufer/Day sets and costumes were excellent. The two designers

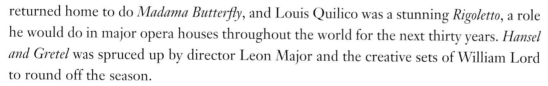

right: **Rigoletto** *(1973).*
Louis Quilico (Rigoletto), Maria Pellegrini (Gilda).

Der Rosenkavalier (1963).
Act 1. Marguerite Willauer (The
Feldmarschallin), Helen Vanni
(Octavian). The lovers in the
Feldmarschallin's boudoir.

photo: Alex Gray

Aïda (1963).
Cecilia Ward as Amneris in the
Triumphal Scene.

photo: Alex Gray

photo: Alex Gray

learned a great deal from the experienced and knowledge-able Yanopoulos. Torel wisely engaged Justino Diaz, a twenty-three-year-old Puerto Rican bass-baritone, to play Ramfis, a role he shared with Don Garrard. He also sang the Commendatore in *Don Giovanni*. Diaz, a Boris Goldovsky protegé, had won the Metropolitan Auditions and would go on to a major career at the Met and other leading opera houses in the years to come. (He would return to Toronto in 1970 to play the title role in *Don Giovanni*.) Heather Thomson did her first leading role of many with the COC as Mimi in *La Bohème*.

Don Giovanni (1963).

Act I.

This was the year that Walker, true to his word, took the COC off the O'Keefe 1964 subscription series despite Torel's protestations. Thus, the company was left to mount its fourth O'Keefe season independently. Torel, worried that it would lose most of O'Keefe's subscribers, moved cautiously and planned a repeat of *Aïda* and four other familiar operas to ensure good ticket sales: *Carmen*, *La Traviata*, *Fledermaus*, and *Madama Butterfly*. The *Carmen* cast included the lusty Mignon Dunn as Carmen, the now world-famous Jon

La Bohème (1963).

Act 4. Heather Thomson (Mimi), John Arab (Rodolfo).

photo: Alex Gray

right: Carmen (1964).
Act 1. Mignon Dunn
as Carmen.

below: Carmen (1964).
Act 4. Jon Vickers as Don José
gives himself up after slaying
Carmen.

photo: Alex Gray

photo: Alex Gray

Vickers as Don José, and Victor Braun, a leading baritone at the Frankfurt Opera, as Escamillo.

The *Aïda* repeat had two *contretemps*. In the second performance, Jon Vickers had to step in with only an hour's notice to sing Radamès, substituting for the accident-prone Richard Cassilly. Vickers knew the role well but not Torel's staging, yet he did the performance creditably. He wore Siegmund's costume from *Die Walküre* — there was nothing else close to being appropriate. The second incident also involved Cassilly, who, with Torel's permission, had gone to New York between performances to attend a dress rehearsal at the Met. He was about to embark for the trip back to Toronto when one of the plane's motors caught fire, leaving him to cool his heels at the airport until the next available flight.

To cope with the delay, O'Keefe provided complimentary sandwiches and non-alcoholic drinks to the capacity audience. Cast members joined the patrons in the lounges and chatted with them to help control tempers. As the number of those demanding refunds began to grow, Torel mounted the stage and, witty storyteller that he was, told anecdotes for a full hour, until Cassilly finally arrived with a police escort and the show went on. It ended at 1:30 a.m. There had been only a minuscule $2,000 in refunds.

Incidentally, Rudolf Bing, who was coming to Toronto to hear the still relatively unknown thirty-year-old Marilyn Horne as Amneris, was booked on the same aborted flight, but chose to return to his New York apartment. As with Justino Diaz, bringing Horne to the COC was a triumph for Torel, and he spoke of her appearance with relish for the next decade.

Prior to the season, John Kraglund of *The Globe and Mail* had asked why the company could not do at least *some* unfamiliar operas. He believed that the conservative choices would set the company back fifteen years artistically and he naughtily quoted an anonymous opera lover: "with such an adventurous program as they have lined up I'm

photo: Alex Gray

Aïda (1964),

Act 4. Radamés (Richard Cassilly), Aïda (Elizabeth Fretwell), and Amneris (Marilyn Horne) at the tomb.

surprised they haven't invited Nelson Eddy." (4/4/64) Yet, at the end of the season Kraglund had to say that "opera lovers were repaid with a season that must be considered excellent." (5/10/64) Torel sounded off with pride that the accolades could be attributed to Canadian talent: the permanent company of Canadian singers and the high proportion of Canadian stars (five out of eleven) among the "imported" artists.

Worries about having been cut from O'Keefe's subscription series proved groundless. Attendance had risen to 81 percent, ample proof that opera had caught on with the public in a city that was growing by leaps and bounds. The COC's independent series had attracted 6,113 genuine opera subscribers; most O'Keefe subscribers didn't care for opera and were glad to be rid of it. The subscription drive's success was in great part due to Danny Newman, the Chicago Lyric Opera's publicist, who advised the COC on selling techniques. The American Theatre Communication Group, with the assistance of the Ford Foundation, paid his fee. Newman, a performing arts evangelist, believed that the subscriber to an opera company or similar arts performing group makes a long-term commitment that leads to sophistication — being able to accept the new, the old, and the experimental — and ultimately results in loyalty and lasting devotion. His theme song was "I hate the single ticket buyer. I love the subscriber." He used extravagant brochures to encourage people to reap subscriber benefits, the principal one being saving money. Prior to his Toronto assignment, he had led a drive for Winnipeg's Manitoba Theatre Centre that brought a 70 percent increase in subscribers. Newman, assisted by Canada Council grants, would go on to help other large Canadian groups.

The COC's flourishing 1964 season — it was able to cut its $50,000 deficit in half — led Torel to be a bit more daring the next year. Accordingly, he presented *Rigoletto*, *Bohème*, *The Barber of Seville*, a lavish production of Puccini's *Turandot*, and a double-bill of Stravinsky's *Mavra* and Strauss's *Salome*. Margaret Tynes was a tantalizing Salome. Also well-cast was tenor Phil Stark, whose grating voice and superior acting skills made him an admirable Herod. Future COC *Salome*s had Stark as Herod, and his skill in the role brought him performances of it in major opera houses in North America and Europe.

In the next year, 1966, Torel did Verdi's *Macbeth* with Louis Quilico in the title role and Margaret Tynes as Lady Macbeth. In a mishap after the curtain at the end of Act 1,

photo: Alex Gray

photo: Alex Gray

far left: **Salome (1965).**
Jochanaan (Royce Reaves)
spurns Salome's (Margaret
Tynes) advances.

left: **Mavra (1965).**
Left to right: Geneviève
Perrault (a Neighbour), Sheila
Piercey (Parasha), Thomas
Clerke (Vassili), Patricia Rideout
(Mother of Parasha).

photo: Alex Gray

photo: Alex Gray

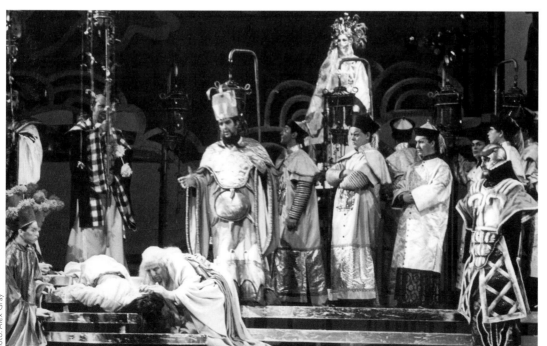

photo: Alex Gray

centre left: **Salome (1968 revival).**
Phil Stark as Herod.

above: **Turandot (1965).**
Act 3. Guiseppe Campora
(Calaf), Jeannine Crader
(Turandot). The lovers
are united.

left: **Turandot (1965),**
Act 3, scene 1. Liu stabs herself
to avoid revealing the Prince's
name.

82

Tynes fell from a six-foot height and broke her heel. A stagehand had forgotten to use a flashlight to help her descent. In great pain, she finished the performance using a cane and did all of the subsequent performances as scheduled. And then, in this same year, the COC did its first Canadian opera, Healey Willan's *Deirdre*. A Canada Council production grant of $30,000 and further assistance from the Ontario Arts Council (OAC), which had been created in late 1962 to be a funding agency for Ontario artists and groups, made this production possible. Playwright John Coulter was the librettist. The CBC had commissioned the work in 1943 and produced its first radio performance in 1946. In 1965 the Royal Conservatory's Opera School had done a revised version at the new MacMillan Theatre of the Edward Johnson Building on the University of Toronto campus. Ettore

Macbeth (1966).

Ermanno Mauro (Malcolm),

Margaret Tynes (Lady Macbeth),

Luigi Infantino (Macduff).

photo: Alex Gray

photo: Alex Gray

photo: Alex Gray

above: **Faust** *(1966).*

left: **Faust** *(1966).*

Heather Thomson as Marguerite.

photo: Alex Gray

La Traviata (1966).
Act 2. Alfredo (Luigi Infantino)
denounces Violetta (Maria
Chiara).

Mazzoleni, who had conducted the two earlier productions, also conducted the COC's.

Jeannette Zarou, who had shared the title role with Lilian Sukis in the school perfor-mances, played it again with the COC. *Deirdre* is a moving Celtic tale about the joys and sorrows of a girl who brings destruction to all who love her. The work owes much to Wagner but lacks his originality and theatrical instinct. Coulter had actually set up sev-eral highly dramatic sequences, but Willan had failed to capitalize on them musically. Such lost opportunities left the audience looking for action that never happened. Balance — or lack of it — was another problem: the music's rich texture and heavy orchestration often drowned out the singers.

The press reviews were mixed. *The Globe and Mail*'s John Kraglund applauded *Deirdre*, and the paper's drama critic, Herbert Whittaker, damned it. (26/9/66) *The Toronto Star*'s youthful reviewer William Littler didn't like it but tried his best to be respectful and make it appear at least a *succés d'estime*. (26/9/66) Some questioned why the COC did a work based on a Gaelic legend for its first Canadian opera, to which Coulter replied in the *Toronto Telegram*, "The art of a Canadian remains with but little differentiation the art of the country of his forebears, and the old world heritage of myth and legend remains his

84

photo: Ken Bell

John Coulter, Herman Geiger-Torel, Ettore Mazzoleni, and Healey
Willan discuss Deirdre in March 1965.

Deirdre (1966). Act 1, scene 2. Jeannette Zarou as Deirdre.

Deirdre (1966). Act 3. Patricia Rideout (Levercham), Jeannette
Zarou (Deirdre), Bernard Turgeon (Conochar). The death of
Deirdre.

heritage.... Music and poetry and painting must speak as yet in
old world voices." (24/9/66)

The next year was Canada's Centennial. The COC played
a significant role in this remarkable year. The Centennial
Commission had provided the funds for the COC to commission two new operas, one by Raymond Pannell and one by
Harry Somers, both of which the COC produced. (It also produced *Madama Butterfly, Il Trovatore, Tales of Hoffmann,* and
The Barber of Seville for insurance.) When the COC board

photo: Alex Gray

asked Torel if it was wise to do *two* new operas in the same season, Torel, with a sense of occasion, insisted that it *was* appropriate in Canada's birthday year. Pannell's *The Luck of Ginger Coffey*, with libretto by Ron Hambleton, is based on a Brian Moore novel. Somers' *Louis Riel*, with libretto by Mavor Moore, is an account of the life of a defiant and mystical Metis, and was derived in part from a John Coulter play.

Ginger Coffey, which opened the Centennial season at O'Keefe, was disappointing, being in great part a rather ineffective play with music that owes much to Menotti, Weill, and Bernstein. It is the story of an Irish immigrant who has difficulty coming to terms with Canada, and himself. Its interest depends on the words sung, but many of these were lost in the vast O'Keefe Centre. The work also lacks operatic drive, for want of a better word, despite excellent characterizations of the title role by Harry Theyard and of his wife by Mignon Dunn.

Torel had been close to *Ginger Coffey* from the beginning and had made a number of suggestions during its composition to a supremely confident Pannell, some of which were adopted reluctantly, others ignored. Pannell also made some last minute changes in the libretto without Hambleton's permission. No matter, Torel directed it as imaginatively as

top left: Il Trovatore (1967).
Act 2, the cloisters.

*above: The Barber of Seville
(1967).*
Jan Rubes (Don Basilio),
Alexander Gray (Figaro).

top: *The Luck of Ginger Coffey (1967).*

Act 1, scene 1. Designed by Schäfer/Hartman.

bottom: *The Luck of Ginger Coffey (1967).*

Act 3, scene 2. Harry Theyard as Ginger Coffey. The jail scene.

he could. One of the more impressive aspects of the show was designer Lawrence Schäfer's ingenious arrangement of three sets that could be moved quickly on and off stage to help execute the opera's thirteen scenes. As would be the case in *Louis Riel*, large photographic blowups and filmed projections — relatively new stage techniques — helped keep the audience abreast of the action.

Unlike *Ginger Coffey*, *Louis Riel* was an all out success, with its historical content, coincident drama, and unique mix of musical, visual, and dramatic effects. Moore wrote the libretto using both French and English, as befits the tale. French-Canadian writer Jacques Languirand collaborated with Moore on the French parts. No doubt Moore's past association with *Riel* — he had played the lead in the 1947 stage version — helped. Designers Laufer and Day checked settings, clothes, and even blankets worn by Metis, to make certain that their work was authentic. Leon Major was a happy choice as director, as was Victor Feldbrill as conductor. Feldbrill skillfully worked out the many diverse elements in an extremely complex score. Composer, conductor, director, and designers all worked closely together to create one of the COC's finest achievements.

Riel is first and foremost a drama; the music serves to intensify the action. It relates the life of the quixotic Metis, beginning with his involvement with the provisional government in Fort Garry in 1869, followed by the Prairie rebellions, his years of exile in Montana, the

Louis Riel composer Harry Somers (left) and librettist Mavor Moore.

photo of Harry Somers by Herbert J. Holtom

Frog Lake uprising in 1885, and, finally, his capture, trial, and execution in Regina. Somers called it a music drama with four different stylistic approaches: folk material that keeps recurring, however disguised, through the work; the orchestra, which "creates a platform of orchestral sound on top of which the singing is entirely apart"; some straight diatonic writing; and then the juxtaposition of all of them. Moore treats Riel as the idealist-dreamer who puts himself at the mercy of ruthless realists who eventually betray him.

Baritone Bernard Turgeon was cast as Riel, a role for which he seemed to have been born, and he played out its centrality superbly from beginning to end. Some people close to the production felt at times that Turgeon was so involved in the role that he was confusing his own identity with Riel's. He sang well, but it was left to Roxolana Roslak, who played Riel's wife Marguerite, to perform the musical highlight of the opera: an unaccompanied lullaby, "Kuyas," that she sang to her child to open Act 3. Based on an Indian tune, it sets the tone and mood for the impending tragedy.

The highlight of the Centennial year in Canada was the Montreal Exposition. The COC did both *Riel* and Peter Ebert's brilliantly staged production of Offenbach's *Tales of*

Louis Riel (1967).
Bernard Turgeon as Louis Riel.

Louis Riel (1967).
Act 3, scene 1. Riel (Bernard
Turgeon) with his wife
(Roxolana Roslak) and child.

Louis Riel (1968).
Act 2, scene 4. A public outcry
against Riel.

left: *Tales of Hoffmann (1967).*

below: *Tales of Hoffmann (1967).*
Alan Crofoot (Andrès/Cochenille), André Turp (Hoffmann).

Hoffmann at the Exposition, thanks to a generous grant from the Exposition Commission. "Expo" had booked six of the world's leading opera companies to perform in Montreal that year: the Royal Swedish, the Hamburg State, the Bolshoi, the Vienna State, the English Opera Group, and La Scala. Yet, beside the international competition, the COC did itself proud with its two productions.

Riel played three times again in Toronto in the 1968 opera season, but to smaller audiences than anticipated in spite of its success the year before. It was done on CBC television in 1969 and then put away until 1975 when the COC gave four performances of it at O'Keefe, one at the National Arts Centre, and one at the Kennedy Center in Washington D.C., as part of the USA's bicentennial celebrations.

Another initiative in the Centennial year was Prologue to the Performing Arts. Founded by a group of Toronto volunteers, Prologue sought to introduce children in the intermediate grades

photo: Alex Gray

photo: Robert C. Ragsdale, FRPS

The Glove (1975).

Prologue to the Performing

Arts. Left to right: Avo Kittask,

Michael Burgess, Andrea Martin

(lioness), Riki Turofsky, Martin

Short (lion).

to the arts through "in school" presentations by professional dance, theatre, and opera companies. Accordingly, under Prologue auspices the COC did thirty-seven performances of *La Serva Padrona*. Then, over the next ten years, also for Prologue, it gave similar capsulized versions of Menotti's *The Old Maid and the Thief* (68 performances), Wolf-Ferrari's *The Secret of Susanna* (129), Dominick Argento's *The Boor* (158), *The Barber of Seville* (13) and Donizetti's *Rita* (133), and two commissioned works: *The Spirit of Fundy* by Norman Symonds (55) and *The Glove*, with music by Tibor Polgar and text by George Jonas (100). Discussions with the students followed all performances, which, incidentally, were done with piano accompaniment.

Fundy was a great hit. Symonds had enlisted a group of school children to help him compose the piece, and credited them with some of its most outlandish — and successful — ideas. The music has traces of seventeenth-century operatic music and twentieth-century "silent movie" music. It may not be an opera in the conventional sense, but it has its appeal.

The even more successful *Glove* is based on a Schiller poem with descriptive and engaging music by Tibor Polgar. It is a comedy with three principal characters: a loud and conceited circus ringmaster, a selfish and vain princess, and a knight; two other roles, a male and a female lion, are played by actors. An ingenious set was designed by Lawrence Schäfer with "jungle gym" scaffolding that enabled director Alan Lund to have his cast effectively act, sing, and dance. The tale is simple: the princess tests her knight's love by dropping her glove in a lion's cage and asking him to retrieve it. This he does but then throws it in her face and departs.

Tosca (1968).

Marina Krilovici (Tosca),

Ermanno Mauro (Cavaradossi).

In the year following the centennial celebrations, the COC did a revival of *Bohème* and a new production of *Tosca*, with the sonorous Italian-Canadian tenor Ermanno Mauro singing Cavaradossi. Mauro, a graduate of the Conservatory opera school, had already made his mark as Malcolm in *Macbeth* (1966), and Manrico in *Il Trovatore* (1967), when he had stepped out of the chorus to substitute for Francisco Lazaro. Now he was joining the select group of young Canadian COC singers who had gone on to illustrious international careers. The other two principals were equally exciting: Louis Quilico as a terrifying Scarpia and Marina Krilovici, the Romanian dramatic soprano, as Tosca.

Leon Major directed and, according to Mauro, perhaps too much so. In his defence, Major wrote in *Opera Canada* that he was trying to overcome the attitude of some singers "whose only justification is the force of custom, the tradition of singing all B-flats down centre at the footlights, the tradition of finishing an aria and then relaxing to wait for the

Tosca (1968).

Louis Quilico as Scarpia.

Elektra (1969).

Astrid Varnay (Elektra), Eileen

Schauler (Chrysothemis).

photo: Ludvik Dittrich

next musical entrance." (v. 8, n. 2, p. 8) Like an increasing number of directors who looked critically yet constructively at the future of opera, Major expected the same serious approach to acting from singers that he got from actors.

That year, there was some excitement at the opening night, when Canada's new and popular Prime Minister Pierre Trudeau attended the premiere of yet another *Aïda*. He heard a good cast in what was becoming a slightly worn production. And it was the first performance of an eight-season partnership between the COC and the TSO. The TSO was a great improvement over the COC pick-up orchestra of previous years, but it would take time before it became a really competent opera orchestra. At first, some of its members resented playing opera, forgetting that many of the great orchestras of the world, including the Vienna Philharmonic, played for opera as part of their job and for most of the year.

Torel produced the long-awaited *Elektra* of Richard Strauss in 1969. Unfortunately, his choice for the title role, Astrid Varnay, was no longer up to it vocally, and Toronto's press berated Torel for choosing her. It should have been clear to him, many said, that she had already reached the end of her distinguished career. Another opera that year, *Turandot*, lost more money than expected because the sets, updated from the 1965 production, went over budget.

A year earlier the COC Planning Committee had urged Torel to travel abroad to hear star singers and, equally important, to hear younger singers on their way up who might be engaged at lower fees. His response to the committee — and it was a poor response — was that he didn't have time to travel. He used the same excuse for not attending opera conferences and other professional meetings. There was no question that his work, which was often criticized for being stereotyped and old fashioned, suffered from his lack of knowledge about what was going on in the international operatic world.

Following the 1969 season at O'Keefe, two of the season's operas, *Rigoletto*, with Louis Quilico, and, according to some an Americanized *Fledermaus*, were given at the newly opened and magnificent — there is no other word for it — National Arts Centre

Opera Theatre (now Southam Hall) in Ottawa. The company was overjoyed to be playing in such a fine house. It was the first of a decade of annual COC visits to the capital. The COC's successes in Ottawa helped to motivate the Centre to put on its own summer season of opera, "Festival Canada," in 1971.

photo: courtesy NAC Archives

The National Arts Centre
Opera (now Southam Hall).

Die Fledermaus (1969).
Howell Glynne as the jailer. He
died shortly afterwards.

photo: Ludvik Dittrich

Chapter 5

ART AND MONEY

By 1970 the COC could point with pride to its annual O'Keefe season, its tours, and its Prologue productions. And it had spawned several subsidiary organizations that were active and thriving. The Canadian Opera Women's Committee was busy raising money, and its Junior Opera Women's Committee was directing a variety of audience-building projects and introducing puppet shows of children's operas, such as Britten's *The Little Sweep*, into the public schools.

The COC was also proud of another offshoot, the Canadian Opera Guild (COG). Founded in 1959, the COG was sponsoring pre-performance opera lectures, producing a newsletter, and helping to establish affiliated guilds throughout Canada. Still ahead was a Toronto conference of guilds in 1974 at which forty-two opera companies would be represented. At the conference the COG would play a key role in creating Opera Guilds International and would ultimately focus much of its energy on developing this new group.

One of the COG's first projects in 1960 had been to publish the quarterly *Opera*

96

Canada. Its founder, Ruby Mercer, was a knowledgeable volunteer, with an American career in singing and broadcasting behind her. She was also *Opera Canada*'s editor and principal donor. By 1966, the COC had formally taken it over and had helped it grow into an impressive periodical that kept track of operatic events throughout the country and of Canadian singers abroad. It also included feature articles on opera and news of foreign opera companies and their productions.

And finally, there was the COC's Canadian Children's Opera Chorus, formed in 1968 by Lloyd Bradshaw, a prominent local choral conductor, and Ruby Mercer. It rapidly developed into an outstanding group of its kind. How many other opera companies anywhere were as active in so many different ways as the COC?

The company began 1970 with an extensive tour of the USA, booked by Columbia Artists with whom the COC was, by now, on excellent terms. In the fall came the O'Keefe season, with its artistic and box-office triumph, Beethoven's *Fidelio*, to commemorate the two hundredth anniversary of the composer's birth. Anja Silja, a leading European soprano and Wieland Wagner's mistress in the years before his death in 1966, was a striking Leonore.

Fidelio (1970).

Act 2. Anja Silva (Leonore),

Glade Peterson (Florestan).

Leonore and Florestan

are reunited.

photo: Robert C. Ragsdale, FRPS

Torel had sent Murray Laufer to Europe to meet Carlos Alexander, who had been engaged to direct *Fidelio*, and to see sets of the opera, since Laufer didn't know the work. It was one of those rare cases when the COC paid sufficient attention to a production's designs — *Aïda* and *Riel* were two others — and was prepared to spend money to assure their authenticity and see them completed before, as often happened, money ran out. While in Europe, Laufer met and heard Silja sing Leonore in Stuttgart; when she saw his set in Toronto she was full of praise. Fussy about directors, the soprano also praised Alexander's work.

The Toronto press lauded *Fidelio* but scolded Torel for scheduling it for only four performances! *Don Giovanni* had eight — with a fine cast, including Justino Diaz of the Met as the Don and Jan Rubes as Leporello — and *Carmen* and *La Traviata* seven each. So it went with the local press, who seemed intent on putting down the COC at every opportunity. The critics carped away at Torel's O'Keefe seasons with an unusual number of negative reviews. Torel suffered from them, as did a number of the singers. Jon Vickers, for one, threatened never to perform in Toronto again. Even when the critics praised a singer, a director, or a designer, the praise was given grudgingly. Torel firmly believed that poor reviews hurt ticket sales. Yet, oftentimes, works that got good reviews didn't sell, while those with bad reviews did.

The critics — and some of the public — also thought that Torel was an old-fashioned director, with antiquated ideas as to how things should go. His pre-planned stagings, some felt, were so predictable as to be boring. On occasion his casting seemed far off the mark, and his continual mounting of operatic warhorses bothered opera buffs, who were crying out increasingly loudly for new works.

Adverse criticism of Torel and the COC was festering in other circles too. The Ontario Arts Council was hinting that it would give the COC additional funds if the COC would put fifteen or more of its singers on permanent contract, but Torel thought it impractical, preferring to use such spare money for other purposes. His unsympathetic response to a good intention did not endear him to the OAC. COC President Rodney Anderson, did, however, send a wish list to the OAC on July 20, 1970: a longer O'Keefe season; more extensive tours; reduced ticket prices for students at student matinees; cheaper seats generally (the gap between high- and low-priced O'Keefe tickets was growing); more modern and daring operas; a chamber opera season; and increased use of multi-media devices. Torel later added to it a COC-owned rehearsal hall and a larger administrative staff.

The OAC took note of these items, but first it generously granted the company an additional $70,440 to reduce its accumulated deficit by half. In July, the Canada Council, no doubt influenced by the OAC, gave an additional $17,000, also to reduce the deficit.

photo: Robert C. Ragsdale, FRPS

Don Giovanni (1970).

Riki Turofsky (Zerlina), Justino Diaz (Don Giovanni).

Yet, despite their generosity, both groups continued to be critical of the COC's management, its repertoire, and its deficits. Torel blamed the deficits on inflation and unforeseen expenses. As for repertoire: on the one hand the COC board warned him to avoid box-office risks; on the other hand, the arts councils urged him to take risks with adventurous and new works, saying the box office would take care of itself. They were concerned about the COC's future and wanted Torel to come up with a long-range artistic plan even though they were unable to promise grant amounts more than one year in advance. How to plan under these circumstances? Torel was caught between a rock and a hard place.

Looking for a solution, the OAC, through its music officer Robert Sunter, concluded that an assessment of the COC by an outside authority might help in its deliberations. The Canada Council agreed. Accordingly, the Earl of Harewood, a first cousin of Her Majesty Queen Elizabeth II, was invited to come to Canada to assess the COC, and, more generally, opera in Canada. Lord Harewood was more than qualified for the task: he had been on the staff of Covent Garden and artistic director of the Edinburgh Festival, and now was general administrator of the English National Opera (formerly the Sadler's Wells).

The OAC wrote to Harewood: "opera lacks any sort of permanent base in Ontario... there is no internal dynamic demand for a change in opera in Canada, and it thus plods on a perpetual treadmill." It was an opinionated and downright negative introduction to Canadian Opera and would not help Harewood to give an unbiased and constructive assessment. After all, there had been practically no home-grown opera in Canada prior to the Second World War, and now there were opera companies in nearly all of the country's major cities. As for the COC, it was, by any measure, the fifth or sixth largest and most influential opera company on the continent. Surely, opera in Canada was not in as dismal a state as the OAC suggested.

Lord Harewood started his visit in the fall of 1971. First he attended the COC season. He thought the company's *Macbeth* "wholly disappointing," *The Merry Widow* "stylish," and *Lucia di Lammermoor* enjoyable but routine (he disliked Ernesto Barbini's conducting). Maria Pellegrini as Cio-Cio-San in *Butterfly* was "one of the best protagonists in the world today." *Die Walküre* "came off pretty well," and he praised Maureen Forrester as Fricka. On the whole, the judgments were fair, but patronizing. Harewood concluded that the COC needed "one or two better conductors ... and at least one other director of the stature of Leon Major," who had directed *The Merry Widow.*

Harewood had a point when it came to conductors. Torel hired conductors with whom he worked easily and liked personally even though some were not first class or, as was the case with Barbini, were losing their effectiveness. Loyalty was important to Torel. Barbini had been with the company since 1953. Torel would simply not dismiss him.

The touring company also came under fire. Harewood questioned whether its reduced versions, small orchestra, and limited sets did actually whet the public's appetite for opera. Needless to say, this struck a nerve, since audience response was nearly always good to excellent, and, from a practical point of view, the tours kept singers working for four to six months beyond the O'Keefe season. Harewood, instead, thought that the COC should tour its O'Keefe productions. He said little or nothing about costs, distances, and appropriate and available opera houses. Certainly there were no comparable logistical problems in England.

As expected, Harewood wanted the COC to do more contemporary opera, but he tempered his comments somewhat because the COC had already commissioned a new opera, *Héloise and Abélard,* by the Canadian composer Charles Wilson, to celebrate its twenty-fifth anniversary season. He criticized Torel's plan to put on Wagner's *Siegfried* and *Die Götterdämmerung* in two consecutive seasons, instead of giving the complete Ring cycle in one season. More generally, Harewood felt that Torel and the COC board were unimaginative regarding the COC's future. With some operas at O'Keefe playing to over 90 percent attendance, Harewood thought the COC far too conservative in merely projecting an increase to five weeks, two years hence.

Harewood suggested, rather, that the COC give two seasons a year, both to run in tandem with the National Ballet's two seasons, and with both groups using the same orchestra. He even raised the possibility of the two companies taking over the management of O'Keefe on a year-round basis. As an alternative to an extended O'Keefe season,

photo: Robert C. Ragsdale, FRPS

photo: Robert C. Ragsdale, FRPS

photo: Robert C. Ragsdale, FRPS

The Merry Widow (1971).
John Reardon (Danilo),
Lynn Cantlon (Anna
Glawari).

photo: Robert C. Ragsdale, FRPS

top left: **Macbeth (1971).**
Elinor Ross (Lady Macbeth), Louis Quilico (Macbeth).

top right: **Lucia di Lammermoor (1971).**
Don Garrard (Raimondo), Cristina Deutekom (Lucia).

above: **Madama Butterfly (1971).**
Michael Trimble (Pinkerton), Maria Pellegrini (Cio-Cio-San).

he suggested that the COC consider a spring season of small scale operas — Mozart, Rossini — at the Royal Alexandra. Whatever, he wanted the COC to do a lot more in Toronto than it was doing.

Lord Harewood next addressed audience building, opera for the young, and an opera-ballet house. Then he proposed that the company consider moving its operations to the NAC and travelling to Toronto annually for its O'Keefe season. It was really an impulsive recommendation inspired by his admiration for the NAC's fine opera house. Harewood also suggested a national booking agency to assist the COC and other touring companies, not knowing that the Canada Council was already putting a touring office in place.

The Merry Widow (1971).
Left to right: Alan Crofoot, Alexander Gray, Don McManus, Jan Rubes, John Reardon, Peter Milne, Allen Coates.

photo: Robert C. Ragsdale, FRPS

photo: Alex Gray

photo: Alex Gray

background: **Die Walküre**
(1971).

Maureen Forrester (Fricka),
Norman Bailey (Wotan).
Photo Robert Ragsdale, FRPS

top: **Siegfried (1972).**
Phil Stark (Mime), Karl-Josef
Hering (Siegfried).

bottom: **Siegfried (1972).**
Walter Cassel (The Wanderer),
Alexander Gray (Alberich).

photo: Alex Gray

Siegfried (1972).

Phil Stark (Mime), Walter

Cassel (The Wanderer).

As anticipated, when the Harewood Report appeared in July 1972 it attracted considerable attention. Most of Harewood's recommendations were shot down as impractical. Torel responded angrily to the report in an interview with a *Toronto Star* reporter on July 20, 1972. Harewood was acting as a critic, not as a professional, he said. Further, he was no musician and, therefore, not qualified to judge COC conductors; Torel, a musician to be sure, thought that the COC conductors *were* good. End of discussion.

The COC planning committee was more prudent in its response. Yes, it said, the COC would like to do more innovative operas, but on condition that the councils fund them. Yes, all things being equal, it would like conductors of higher calibre, but, it noted, the councils wanted the COC to use Canadian conductors, and how many good Canadian opera conductors were there? Yes, there were advantages in taking over

O'Keefe, but it was fundamentally unrealistic. Yes, the COC had explored, and would continue to explore, a combined season with the National Ballet.

Not surprisingly, talk of a new opera-ballet house had been percolating before Harewood's visit. Clearly, a new house would have considerable bearing on the O'Keefe Centre. Going back to 1968, increasing realty taxes and operating costs had prompted E.P. Taylor's Canadian Breweries and Argus Corporation to donate O'Keefe to the Metropolitan Toronto government. No matter, although O'Keefe was now publicly owned, it still paid realty taxes, two thirds of which went back, paradoxically, to the Metro government. The Centre had been having and continued to have operating losses with many of its road shows, even though it charged substantial rental fees for independently sponsored attractions. It certainly could not afford to lose the opera and the ballet.

Even before the Harewood Report, Hugh Walker had written to Torel urging him to give up any idea of a new opera house. (22/3/71) In a conciliatory mood, he suggested that the COC start its O'Keefe season earlier in the fall if it wanted a longer season, have a spring season also at O'Keefe, and, with O'Keefe, build an extension onto the hall to meet the COC's storage needs. However, he said nothing about reducing the rent, improving the acoustics, or cutting down the size of the hall to reduce and, hence, improve the seating. On this last point he claimed that all opera houses have some poor seats but that O'Keefe's best one thousand seats were as good as the best one thousand seats in any opera house in the world. Walker also added a warning: since Metro owned O'Keefe, it might look with disfavour on funding a new COC hall.

After the Harewood Report revived discussion of a new opera house, Walker made the mistake of telling John Fraser of *The Globe and Mail* how much O'Keefe had done for the COC since its debut there in 1961. (17/3/73) "We took the Opera Company, you know, when it wasn't much of anything." This was tantamount to waving a red flag in front of a bull, the bull being Herman Geiger-Torel. He wrote a stinging letter to Walker on April 6 reminding him of the fine productions the COC had done at the Royal Alexandra and accusing him of bad-mouthing the COC as an amateurish company before it played at O'Keefe. Walker then appeared before the COC board to plead his case that the company remain at O'Keefe. This especially aroused the ire of Douglas Sloan who, along with a few other board members and Lord Harewood, believed that O'Keefe was impossible and that the company's future depended on building a new opera house. Gradually, talk of a new opera house waned, and the COC settled back to business as usual.

In the summer of 1972, members of the COC had given a week of excerpts in costume at The Forum at Ontario Place — a park-like recreation centre on the shores of Lake Ontario. Both the TSO and the National Ballet had given successful programs at this indoor-out-door amphitheatre. There was no stage, and this necessitated a kind of theatre-in-the-round presentation. The one hundred singers and orchestra had to be amplified, and this, at first, caused many problems. Admission price was nominal in order to encourage attendance by the general public. The excerpts were chosen from operas scheduled for the upcoming O'Keefe season, and the soloists were mainly from the touring and Prologue companies.

The COC's fall 1972 season included the long-await-ed *Siegfried* and *Eugene Onegin* (in English), with the prominent American director Bliss Hebert staging *Onegin*. The *Onegin* performances had their ups and downs, although there were moving characterizations from Victor Braun as Onegin and the splendid Canadian soprano Heather Thomson as Tatyana.

Siegfried, always difficult to produce, needed more coherence and continuity. Part of the blame was Torel's; he cut forty-five minutes to save overtime costs. Then too, the audience had trouble comprehending the action;

above: Eugene Onegin (1972).

Act 1. Heather Thomson as Tatyana. The Letter Aria.

below: Eugene Onegin (1972).

Act 3. The final meeting between Tatyana (Heather Thomson) and Eugene Onegin (Victor Braun).

as Harewood was warned, the four operas of the Ring cycle — *Siegfried* is the third — should ideally be heard in sequence. There were good performances by Karl-Josef Hering (Siegfried), the experienced Walter Cassel (The Wanderer), and most of the other members of the cast. Ironically, the two new productions sold badly. A magnificent *Aïda* with Maria Pellegrini and the season's two other productions, *Tosca* and *La Bohème*, fared better.

For a week in the spring of 1973, the COC put on its touring production of *Così fan tutte* at the handsomely restored Royal Alexandra. It could have been the beginning of annual seasons of smaller scale operas, but it wasn't. *Così* had been a huge success on tour — over eighty performances earlier in the year in the United States and Western Canada. Sadly, however, only 1,150 of the Alec's 16,000 season subscribers chose to include it in their series, and there was but a modest call for single tickets. Torel, reporting to the board, attributed the poor attendance to the mixed press reviews: "the moment the tour

Aïda (1972).
Act 2, scene 2. Claude Corbeil as the King of Egypt, Ann Howard as Amneris, Maria Pellegrini (foreground) as Aïda, and Don Garrard (upper right) as Ramfis.

Aïda.
Maria Pellegrini (Aïda), Ann Howard (Amneris).

photo: Alex Gray

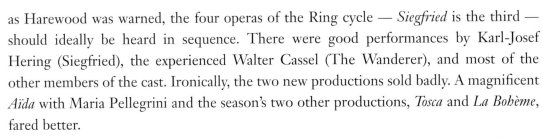

photo: Alex Gray

photo: Alex Gray

Così fan tutte at the Royal

Alexandra Theatre (1973).

Touring company.

Carrol Anne Curry (Dorabella),

Peter Barcza (Guglielmo).

photo: Robert C. Ragsdale, FRPS

hit our native city, our singers suddenly become poor, the music direction so sloppy and unstylish [sic], and the stage direction so overdone and slapsticky [sic] that our distinguished critics find enough food to tear us to pieces, then to devour us and keep our audiences away from the theatre." Undeterred, the COC did another ninety-one performances of *Così* in Eastern Canada, beginning in November. But it did not play at the Alec again for some years.

In September, again at The Forum, the company gave four Sunday evening programs built around specific composers — Puccini, Verdi, Rossini, and Lehár and Strauss. Unfortunately it was one of those years with an early fall, and opera lovers — and artists — shivered their way through each performance. Such programs might have eventually built audiences, yet they were dropped after 1973 because of lack of funds.

No matter, the 1973 fall season at O'Keefe was impressive and balanced. It featured new productions of *Rigoletto*, *Die Götterdämmerung*, and Guelph composer Charles Wilson's *Héloise and Abélard*, and revivals of *Fidelio*, *The Merry Widow*, and *The Barber of Seville*. *Héloise* was based on a radio play written for the BBC two decades earlier by Wilson's librettist, Eugene Benson. Benson rewrote it to suit Wilson's music, and the result was an effective music-drama that simply needed more passion. One wonders how Wilson and Benson, given this tragic love story, could have missed the point. As Arnold Edinborough put it in the *Financial Post*, "Instead of a gutsy tale of lust, love and longing, we got instead a closet-tragedy enmeshed in theological argument." (20/10/73) Most of the words went unheard, thanks to O'Keefe's faulty amplification.

However, two leading critics from abroad, Harold C. Schonberg of *The New York Times* and Alan Blyth of *The Times* of London, were more positive than the Canadian critics. Schonberg generously

top: Héloise and Abélard (1973). Don McManus as the wrathful Canon Fulbert and chorus.

right: Héloise and Abélard (1973). Heather Thomson (Héloise), Allan Monk (Abélard).

far right: Héloise and Abélard (1973). Abélard (Allan Monk) on trial.
photos:
Robert C. Ragsdale, FRPS

praised *Héloise*'s middle-of-the-road musical stance, "modernism without being *avant garde*, dissonance without being forbidding, electronics without scaring anybody away." However, he concluded by stating that the score had "no real character, no real distinguishing characteristics." (19/10/73) He believed that Wilson was at his best when writing for chorus. Wilson had explained in the fall issue of *Opera Canada* that the chorus, prominent and imaginatively treated throughout the work, depicts the authoritarian church and, as nuns, monks, or clergy, is a "brooding menacing backdrop to the love story." On one occasion it was even involved in a tavern brawl.

Schonberg also praised Murray Laufer's "cathedral-like set" and Victor Feldbrill's "superb conducting." He had heard the work at the National Arts Centre, where it had played with *Rigoletto*, and said it was "one of the best halls in the hemisphere."

Alan Blyth, who heard the work at O'Keefe, was quoted in the winter issue of *Opera Canada*. He was even more enthusiastic than Schonberg. He thought *Héloise* "properly constructed and paced for the stage ... a polished score ... pages of great beauty ... and enough of the real stuff of dramatic conflict ... to suggest that this is among the best new operas of the past decade, certainly surpassing anything heard in Britain, Tippett and Britten excluded."

A truncated version of *Die Götterdämmerung*, the final opera of The Ring, seemed, as with *Siegfried*, beyond the comprehension of some of the local press — and a good many of the audience — even though all admitted that the singing was first class, especially Ingrid Bjoner's Brünnhilde and William Wildermann's Hagen. A season high spot was Patricia Kern's coy and captivatiing Rosina in *The Barber*. In all, there were thirty-six performances in the 1973 season, five more than the preceding year, and the box-office receipts, thanks to an increase in prices, went from $568,918 in 1972 to $722,448; this was more than double that of the Expo year, although inflation had much to do with it.

Rigoletto (1973).

Act 3. Judith Forst (Maddalena),
Ruggero Bondino (The Duke).

photo: Robert C. Ragsdale, FRPS

photo: Robert C. Ragsdale, FRPS

photo: Robert C. Ragsdale, FRPS

*top: Die Götterdämmerung
(1973).*
Left to right: Janos Tessenyi
(Gunther), William Wildermann
(Hagen), Jean Cox (Siegfried).

Die Götterdämmerung (1973).
Left to right: Barbara Collier
(Gutrune), Jean Cox (Siegfried),
Ingrid Bjoner (Brünnhilde).

As the O'Keefe season grew longer, so did Torel's responsibilities. In January 1974 the COC announced that the ever-popular and amiable Jan Rubes had been appointed director of touring and program development. With close to one thousand appearances in the company behind him, Rubes now would be responsible for planning tour programs and those special projects that were not part of the O'Keefe season. No one knew more about touring, audiences, and community out-reach than Rubes.

His first new scheme, "OPERAtion ONTARIO," was an ingenious departure from one-night-stand touring, and expanded the company's scope. Rubes explained to *The Toronto Star* that he believed that "sneaking into town at 5 p.m. and leaving in the morning, without engaging in a dialogue with the community" was not the best way to do things. (3/2/75) He decided to change this pattern by scheduling a variety of programs in one community over a two- or three-day period, and with the community's active participation.

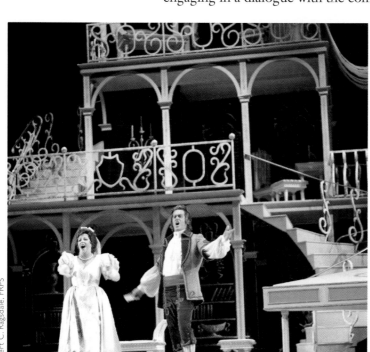

photo: Robert C. Ragsdale, FRPS

The Barber of Seville (1973).
Patricia Kern (Rosina), Cornelis
Opthof (Figaro).

And so, in early January 1975, the COC singers and orchestra moved to Niagara-on-the-Lake, the home of the Shaw Festival, where they rehearsed and did previews of *La Bohème*. There, the company prepared "Across the Land," a verbal history of the touring company, interspersed with significant operatic excerpts sung by COC members. Rubes hosted the show. The company also readied for performance "S.T.A.B.," a vocal revue of soprano, tenor, alto, and bass voices for schools, and "The Sounds of Music," an introduction to music for youngsters.

The workshops included: "The Opera Singer" (from the first lesson to the first engagement), with participants usually from local choruses; "The Musician" — instrumental workshops with participants from local orchestras or ensemble groups; and "Backstage" — a demonstration of the technical structure of an opera performance. The COC did these shows for a month in nine Southern Ontario cities and again in Eastern Canada in November 1975.

The highly original concerts and workshops — the singers still talk about them in glowing terms a generation later — were welcomed everywhere, as was *Bohème*. On one memorable occasion, the company did a concert at the Collins Bay Penitentiary in Kingston, where it won over the inmates in short order. There was another residency at Niagara-on-the-Lake in March 1976 when the company prepared *La Traviata* in Italian,

photo: Robert C. Ragsdale, FRPS

La Bohème, OPERAtion
ONTARIO 1975–76.

Left to right: James Anderson
(Schaunard), Barney Ingram
(Parpignol), Giulio Kukurugya
(Colline), Guillermo Silva-Marin
(Marcello), Ann Cooper (Mimi),
Glyn Evans (Rodolfo).

but set in 1911 instead of the mid-nineteenth century. A special provincial grant of $10,000, matched by the federal secretary of state's department, enabled Rubes to purchase new lighting equipment that could be easily set up and dismantled. (Evidently Rubes had modelled this equipment after the kind used by travelling rock and roll groups.) The tours in both the USA and Canada gradually wound down in 1976 and 1977. Rubes left the COC staff in 1976.

To return to July 1973, well before Rubes was appointed, the COC's Finance and Operating Committee recommended to the board that the general director "be instructed to make no plans for a tour in the 74/75 season." As we have seen, the tours went ahead, notwithstanding. There was more grumbling concerning Torel's effectiveness.

114

Back in 1968, Douglas Sloan had outlined an artistic structure that included not only the general director but a more or less permanent conductor, stage director, chorus leader, set and costume designer, workshop manager, and tour manager. This plan had still not been considered seriously six years later. Torel simply chose not to have permanent artistic personnel. And he selected each season's operas without formal input from staff, although he did listen to their suggestions as he did those from the board and the women's committee. Naturally, Torel's selections had to suit the company's finances, and the lack of adventurous operas was as much due to a conservative board worried about its mounting deficit as to Toronto's alleged preference for the operatic warhorses. Building an audience for innovative and contemporary opera is an uphill struggle that needs patience, money, and, of course, skillful producing.

The critical COC board pressed Torel to book more international stars to beef up ticket sales and was irritated when Torel was disinclined to do so. As always, he maintained that most stars would not rehearse enough with the company. True or not, Torel was really more interested in developing young Canadian singers and, as the record shows, he did just that. He never forgot his mission. It was also a hard fact that few board members took an active interest in the company, and fewer still raised funds for it. To sum up, the company's artistic policy in great part was driven by money, or the lack of it, not art.

Change was needed, and the board, exempting itself from blame for the company's shortcomings, pointed its finger at the general director. It questioned more and more openly Torel's artistic leadership, his repeated failure to stay in budget, and his limited view of the company's future. Did he know enough about operatic developments in the rest of the world? Were his errors in casting due to his dependence on what others told him about singers, rather than hearing them first-hand before booking them? One of Torel's classic errors along these lines was booking Marguerite Willauer, who turned out to be a barely adequate Marschallin in the 1963 *Der Rosenkavalier*. The opera director Dino Yanopoulos had recommended her. Torel had not known that Yanopoulos had a very personal interest in the soprano!

And then there were the inevitable questions. Was he getting too old? Had he been on the job too long? Some prominent board members felt that he should retire. Torel, hearing this, countered by accusing the board of being uninformed and ungrateful, and suggested that it knew nothing about opera, and that the company needed him. Matters were at an impasse.

Even if Torel wanted to retire, he couldn't afford to. His salary was small, far smaller than it should have been, and he had practically no retirement fund. Be that as it may, it was more to the point that, although Torel was in his late sixties, he was still in good health — or so he thought — and full of energy. He had always been a one-man show at the COC, not only as its general director but also as its de facto business administrator, even though others had always carried that title. It was no exaggeration that, for Torel, giving up the company was akin to giving up his life.

To defy his critics, he set a 1974 season that was the most diversified, daring, and substantive since the company's founding. It included, along with *Faust* and *Carmen*, no fewer than five new productions: a double-bill of Bartok's *Bluebeard's Castle* and Ravel's *L'heure espagnole*, which opened the season, *Der fliegende Holländer*, *La Traviata*, and the original version of Mussorgsky's *Boris Godunov*, this instead of the more popular Rimsky-Korsakov adaptation. And indeed, all of the operas were done well. *Bluebeard's Castle* had a stunning Laufer/Day Gothic-inspired set. However, the singing of Claude Corbeil and Lyn Vernon was, unfortunately, lost in great part because of the large orchestra and unpredictable O'Keefe amplification. John Leberg, who would play an important role in the company in the coming years, directed. *L'heure espagnole*, like the Bartok work, was sung in English, and its comedy got across to the audience thanks to a gifted Gwenlynn Little and broad characterizations by John Arab as Gonsalve and Alan Crofoot as the clockmaker, among others. The excellent *Boris* production, borrowed from the Cincinnati Opera, had Don Garrard as a reflective yet passionate Boris. It was one of Torel's great triumphs.

About 104,000 attended the season, the first time the COC's audience had reached six figures. Eighty-seven percent of all available seats were sold. The box-office take

photo: Robert C. Ragsdale, FRPS

photo: Robert C. Ragsdale, FRPS

photo: Robert C. Ragsdale, FRPS

top left: **Bluebeard's Castle (1974).**

Claude Corbeil (Duke Bluebeard), Lyn Vernon (Judith).

left: **Bluebeard's Castle (1974).**

Lyn Vernon (Judith), Claude Corbeil (Duke Bluebeard).

above: **L'heure espagnole (1974).**

Gwenlynn Little as Concepcion.

right: **Boris Godunov (1974).**
Henry Barney Ingram as The
Simpleton.

top: **Boris Godunov (1974).**
Don Garrard (Boris), William
Wildermann (Pimen).

bottom: **Boris Godunov (1974).**
Don Garrard (Boris), Kathleen
Ruddell (Feodor).
photos: Robert C. Ragsdale, FRPS

118

increased to $895,000, $170,000 more than in 1973. The company hadn't looked this good for several years, and Torel, flushed with success, paid Toronto its highest compliment by saying mischievously to the *Hamilton Spectator* that its operatic public had finally come of age. (26/10/74)

Yet, despite the good houses, at the end of the fall season there was a deficit of approximately $60,000. Going over budget had become an old story at the COC, but few expected the deficit to mount to over $100,000 by spring because of miscalculated sales tax, costly trucking of scenery, expensive costumes ($45,000 over budget for *Boris* alone), excessive stagehand costs, and expensive publicity and advertising. The accumulated deficit was now out of hand and led the board to place stringent controls on 1975 costs and to budget for an 80 percent box office, even though 1974's had been higher.

The board, in a decision-making mood, next addressed Torel's retirement. The powerful chairman of the Finance and Operating Committee Douglas Sloan — he would soon be COC president — prepared a retirement package. Torel would retire at the end of 1975, and then receive $12,000 annually, indexed to the cost of living, for the rest of his life. He would also receive an additional $3,000 annually for staging an opera for the COC. If there wasn't an opera that he wanted to direct, he would still receive this sum. Finally, he would be appointed a life member of the opera board.

At first, Torel wondered whether to refuse to retire, but he caved in on January 9, 1975. In a COC news release he said, "I have served the COC for some

Der fliegende Holländer (1974).

Don Garrard as Daland.

photo: Robert C. Ragsdale, FRPS

25 years. After such a long time I have come to realize — and I freely admit that it has not been easy to arrive at such a conclusion — that a change in the leadership of the COC may be desirable at a time when I am still in full possession of my physical and mental stamina...." He looked forward to spending more time with his wife and hoped that his life would "eventually develop into a spiritually and artistically rewarding activity of manifold tasks."

Still, opera insiders knew that he was simply being polite, that he wanted to stay on but the board wouldn't let him. Rather sadly, he took a dim view of his future as a freelance director and said to his friend William Lord, who had been COC company manager and designer, "Here I am at my age a journeyman director, to have to travel to make a living." In any event, a search committee of six, chaired by Rodney Anderson, was set to find a new COC general director.

As for the coming season, Torel and Bruce Chalmers, the COC business administrator, submitted a revised budget that the wary finance committee put through a wringer as soon as it hit the table. (An unforgiving Sloan said years later that Torel's budgets were prepared on the back of an envelope. He would not have said this if he had seen Torel's files and the countless draft budgets he drew up annually.)

Torel, in accordance with his retirement package, also submitted his plans for the 1976 O'Keefe season, when he would no longer be COC general director. Everything was going along smoothly until he heard that some board members had attended a meeting in Eastern Canada in March about the future of opera, without informing or inviting him. Upset, he complained bitterly to Sloan, saying that he should have been there. How right he was.

The COC told the public at its annual meeting in May that it had an accumulated deficit of $308,000, but neither would the season be curtailed nor would the quality of the casts and productions be lowered. It did manage to cut the company's operating costs slightly by reducing the annual number of *Opera Canada* issues from six to four. A subsequent committee report on *Opera Canada* provided the ammunition for the COC to withdraw all of its financial support, using the pretext that it was now a general opera magazine, and not a COC house organ *per se*. In early 1976, Ruby Mercer took it over per-

120

sonally and asked the Canada Council and other agencies to fund it.

Alas, the company's worries were only beginning. In early August 1975, the O'Keefe stagehands, members of the International Alliance of Theatrical Stage Employees, went on strike. They wanted a 20 percent increase to their hourly rate to match the rate at the Royal Alexandra and CBC. Obviously, the union had carefully chosen the time to strike, with the opera season less than a month away. Hugh Walker, on the brink of retirement, came to a tentative agreement with the union, but the O'Keefe chairman refused to ratify it. The COC, faced with the possibility of having to cancel its entire season, decided to move to the International Centre, a converted plane factory near Toronto's airport where the ill-fated Avro Arrow had been built almost twenty years earlier.

With O'Keefe about to lose the COC, it agreed, according to Sloan, to let Torel assist in the negotiations, since he was on good terms with the stagehands. An agreement was reached, and the season, thankfully, went on as originally planned. Walker, rather bitterly, said to *The Globe and Mail* that the O'Keefe stagehands would now be the highest paid stagehands in North America. (14/8/75)

Salome (1975).

Grace Bumbry as Salome.

During the strike, the COC Search Committee reported that, after considering 128 possible candidates and interviewing nine, it was recommending the appointment of Lotfi Mansouri of the Geneva Opera as the new general director. Torel, who had been consulted by the committee, endorsed the recommendation. Mansouri would take over on July 1, 1976 and then work with Torel for a three-month transitional period. Mansouri's salary would be $50,000, with annual increments of $5,000 over the length of his five-year contract. Torel's salary was $33,000. The COC board, as Sloan revealed in a *Star* interview, obviously thought Mansouri a much bigger fish than Torel. (22/12/75)

photo: Robert C. Ragsdale, FRPS

The 1975 season was not as varied as in 1974 but was certainly first-class. It was a Puccini year, to mark the fiftieth anniversary of the composer's death, but some press mischievously reminded their readers that the COC was a year late — Puccini died in 1924. In addition to *Salome* and *Riel*, there were no fewer than five new productions, *Die Fledermaus*, a double-bill of *I Pagliacci* and *Il Tabarro*, *Madama Butterfly*, and *Manon Lescaut*. *Lescaut* had been Puccini's first great success. When it had premiered in Turin in 1893, legend has it that Puccini took fifty curtain calls!

Among the season's stars were Grace Bumbry — who was then at the height of her career at the Met — as Salome, Victor Braun as Jochanaan, Maria Pellegrini as Cio-Cio-San, and the brilliant Canadian mezzo-soprano Judith Forst as Suzuki. Irving Guttman, a prominent Canadian opera director who had been a Torel student and assistant in the early days of the opera school, directed *Butterfly*. There was also a revival of *Riel*, which

below left: **Louis Riel (1975).** Act 2, scene 5. Left to right: Paul Trepanier (George Cartier), Jean-Pierre Hurteau (Bishop Taché), Donald Rutherford (Sir John A. Macdonald), Avo Kittask (Colonel Wolseley).

photo: Robert C. Ragsdale, FRPS

photo: Robert C. Ragsdale, FRPS

photo: Robert C. Ragsdale, FRPS

above: **Il Tabarro (1975).**
Louis Quilico (Michele), Lucine Amara (Giorgietta), Luciano Rampaso (Luigi).

left: **I Pagliacci (1975).**
Carrol Anne Curry (Nedda), Luciano Rampaso (Canio).

122

so many had been waiting for, and finally, *Fledermaus*, a *tour de force* with three fine Canadian leads: Lois McDonall as Rosalinda, Cornelis Opthof as Eisenstein, and Gwenlynn Little as Adele. All three were in the midst of busy international careers. In fact, the entire cast was Canadian, a reminder of the progress made in the twenty-five years since the company was formed. *Riel* and *Fledermaus* later played at the National Arts Centre. Riel was also taken to the Kennedy Center in Washington DC.

The double-bill of *I Pagliacci* and *Il Tabarro* added up to quite a bit of homicide. (Were these choices influenced by the growing violence of television shows and films?) Director Leon Major moved *Pagliacci* into the post-war era, which, as William Littler of the *Star* pointed out in his whimsical review, made "both operas virtually contemporary tales of illicit love and violent death among the impoverished working classes — soap operas without the detergent, if you will." (6/9/75)

Manon Lescaut (1975).

Act 2. Heather Thomson
(Manon), Peter Milne
(Geronte).

Manon Lescaut was the artistic triumph of the season. Heather Thomson and Ermanno Mauro were perfectly cast as the two leads, and Alexander Gray, a COC veteran, was a convincing Lescaut. James De Blasis, general manager of the Cincinnati Opera Company, directed, and Ernesto Barbini effectively made his way through the score. His tempi were usually up to speed, so as not to beg the criticism that a member of the *corps de ballet* had made a year or two earlier when he conducted: "O damn it," she had said, "you can only stay in the air so long."

Inexplicably, *Manon Lescaut* did not sell, nor did the double-bill, nor did *Riel*. There were twelve sell-outs: all four of the *Salome*s, four of the seven *Butterfly*s, and four of the seven *Fledermaus*es. The season's box office averaged 85 percent. The attendance was eight thousand fewer than in 1974, yet the COC took in $80,000 more. But it wasn't good enough. Subscriptions were down. Box-office expectations had risen in order to meet the increased costs

photo: Robert C. Ragsdale, FRPS

for stagehands. Business sponsorship was also disappointing. In December, Sloan said that the COC had a season deficit of between $150,000 and $220,000. Bruce Chalmers quietly left the company — there were omissions in his 1976 budget among other things — and was replaced by Gary Adamson, a former CBC project consultant and holder of an MBA degree. On January 15, 1976, Robert Lord, board finance chairman, said the deficit was much less, $117,000. The board, as one could see, still did not have a firm grip on it finances. The talk was that the accumulated deficit was around half a million dollars and this was the way it rested with the public. (The actual amount was $478,000.)

Whatever the deficit, the board had decided two months earlier to cut *Falstaff* and a revival of *Boris Godunov* from the 1976 season, leaving only four operas scheduled. By not mounting the two most expensive operas, it predicted a surplus of some $74,000 on the season, instead of a deficit that would, it believed, be "of the order of $250,000." Torel, guest directing in Winnipeg, wasn't present when the board made its decision. However,

photo: Robert C. Ragsdale, FRPS

Manon Lescaut (1975).

Act 4. Manon (Heather Thomson) dies in Des Grieux's (Ermanno Mauro) arms on the plains of New Orleans.

he wired the board, stating that the cut "may be the only easy way out" but it would be "a giant step backwards. Ten years of growth and artistic achievements could be wiped out if you are unable to make a major attempt to solve the problem on the revenue side. May I beg you to consider this from every point of view before making your decision."

His entreaties were to no avail. The executive committee, in its wisdom, then asked Torel to cancel the affected singers, hardly realizing what a terrible task that would be for a man in his sixty-ninth year and in his final season as COC general director. If nothing else, Torel coveted his reputation among artists as a man of his word, as a man of integrity.

Dutiful as always, he reported to the board on June 9, 1976 that nearly all of the now redundant singers had agreed to terms: some had accepted 50 percent of their projected fee, others had modified their contract and agreed to sing minor roles, and others had said that it would depend on whether they could get other engagements for the period. Torel then pared down the cost of costumes, sets, and rent, and the time needed for stagehands, orchestra, and lighting rehearsals. He told the board, "I will have to be there with a stop watch acting like a police watch-dog to save us any overtime which we cannot afford." He promised to produce the four operas within budget as best he could.

The board was resolved to wipe out its accumulated deficit in one fell swoop in order that Lotfi Mansouri begin his tenure, as William Littler put it, "with a bang, even if that meant Geiger-Torel would go out with a whimper." (25/9/76) The board organized a "Canadian Opera Rescue Fund" with a target of $803,000. Many were skeptical that it could be reached, for the COC was the poorest fundraiser of the seventeen major North American opera companies.

A disheartened Torel told the board at its June 9 meeting, "If you, Metro Toronto, and the Arts Councils had given the assistance which, for instance, the late Mr. Pompidou, Prime Minister of France, gave the general director of the Paris Opera ... I would have given you the *best* Opera Company in the world. Well, there is hope that in the coming years enough irrigation can be created to transform the Canadian operatic desert into a land of operatic fertility."

Maybe it wouldn't have been the best opera company in the world, but it would have been a much better one. Torel's German upbringing and his respect for authority had deterred him from speaking his mind in the past. The board told him what he could spend and he obeyed. Not many opera directors would have been as compliant, especially since the COC's financial troubles, as Sloan had said publicly to the *Star*, began with its disinterested board. (22/12/75) Its members, unlike their counterparts in the TSO, weren't required to buy season subscriptions, and, as Sloan said, "you'd be surprised at the number of board members who don't even do that."

The cancellation of the two operas seriously affected the TSO. The COC board had irresponsibly made its decision without consulting the TSO about a shortened season. Sloan, in a December 18 letter to TSO president Terence Wardrop, said that "neither myself nor Mr. Lord realized that we had a written commitment with the TSO for the 1976 season." It was an impertinent observation, since there was of course a written agreement that the COC had broken with impunity.

The TSO, generous to a fault, let the COC off the hook without penalty, did the reduced season, and paid its players in full. However, this ended an eight-year collaboration. The COC would begin its 1977 season later in the fall, thus conflicting with the TSO season, which would begin its season earlier. The COC would once more have to develop its own orchestra. An OAC-sponsored plan was submitted for a second major Toronto orchestra that would serve the COC, the National Ballet, and the CBC, but nothing came of it.

Torel's final season proved how thrifty he could be. Costs were less than budgeted, and the box office, at 88 percent, was better than anticipated. A grand opera season opened with the Offenbach operetta, *The Grand Duchess of Gerolstein..* Originally a Sante Fe Opera production, it was sung in French, and, bizarre as it may seem, the spoken sections were in English. Ann Howard — she had sung Amneris in the 1972 *Aïda* — was sparkling in the title role.

Die Walküre suffered appreciably from scaled-down sets and lighting. Murray Laufer, its principal designer, felt that his work had been so emasculated that he had his name removed from the credits. True, Laufer and his gifted wife Marie Day had often been considered extravagant in the past, but in this case Laufer was right. Leif Roar, the

The Grand Duchess of
Gerolstein (1976).
Ann Howard as the Grand
Duchess.

The Grand Duchess of
Gerolstein (1976).
Ann Howard (Grand
Duchess), James Atherton
(Fritz).

photo: Robert C. Ragsdale, FRPS

photo: Robert C. Ragsdale, FRPS

Danish baritone, was a strong Wotan, and an equally good Scarpia in *Tosca*. *Walküre* received the usual
mixed reviews. *La Bohème*, done by the COC for the
eighth time since 1950, had a sympathetic Mimi in
Jeannette Zarou. It was her last appearance with the
COC. And *Tosca*, the best production of this limited
season, was not only thanks to Roar but also to a
truly striking Marisa Galvany in the title role.

It was an artistically average season, but the balance sheet convinced the board that it had done the
right thing. Gary Adamson reported on November
18 that the accumulated deficit had been reduced by
$362,000 and now stood at $116,000, thanks to the

profitable season and a remarkable fundraising campaign led by Arthur Crockett of the Bank of Nova Scotia.

Tosca (1976). Act 2. Marisa Galvany (Tosca), Leif Roar (Scarpia).

128

Torel had agreed to speak on *Die Walküre* to the Toronto Wagner Society at the University of Toronto on October 6. As he mounted the steep steps of the Claude T. Bissell Building on St. George Street he had a heart attack and died thirty minutes later. Just a few days earlier he had spoken at an opera dinner. With humour that bordered on the ironic, he had reviewed the history of the COC from its beginnings to the present season — a season he was not proud of though he didn't say this. Now the cheerful, rotund, avuncular Torel — realist, romantic, compromiser, builder of opera in Canada — was gone.

Herman Geiger-Torel with his wife a few days before his sudden death.

photo: Robert C. Ragsdale, FRPS

A large on-stage celebration of Torel's years with the company had been planned for October 16, following the final opera of the season. Instead, a moving memorial tribute was held on October 12 at the MacMillan Theatre, where Torel had directed so many student productions. The Orford Quartet, members of the university Faculty of Music, and the Toronto Symphony performed. There were eulogies by Ezra Schabas, chair of the university's opera department, Walter Homburger, managing director of the TSO, and Robert Baillie, a past president of the COC — his wife Joan had voluntarily begun organizing the COC archives a few years earlier. And then Ermanno Mauro, one of a legion of Canadian singers who had learned so much from Torel, sang the "Ingemisco" from the Verdi *Requiem*. Lori Geiger-Torel, ill with cancer, was there, as were nearly a thousand other admirers who packed the hall, including Lotfi Mansouri, fresh from directing triumphs in Ottawa, Vancouver, and Vienna. The Mansouri years were about to begin.

Chapter 6

THE INTERNATIONAL STAGE
– Lotfi Mansouri

Lotfi Mansouri was born into a privileged Iranian family in 1929. He went to the United States and in 1953 graduated with a degree in psychology from the University of California at Los Angeles. But he quickly got caught up by theatre and opera, and also discovered that he had a passable tenor voice. He studied singing and began to direct small opera productions for local colleges in the Los Angeles area. His voice studies took him to Santa Barbara where he worked briefly with Lotte Lehmann and, fortuitously, with the Austrian stage director, Herbert Graf. When Graf became director of the Zurich Opera in 1960, he offered Mansouri a post as resident stage director. When Graf moved in 1965 to the larger and more prestigious Geneva Opera, Mansouri again followed. By this time he was guest directing at major Italian opera houses and in the United States. In 1963 he worked at San Francisco on six productions as a director with the company with which he had been a super when it visited Los Angeles and the company of which he would one day be the general director. It was during these years in Zurich and Geneva and in many theatres of Italy and Germany, as well as in San Francisco, that Mansouri

developed a wide network of friends and associates among artists on whom he would later draw to the benefit of the COC. When Herbert Graf died in 1973 and was succeeded by Jean-Claude Riber, Mansouri was ready to move on to a company of his own. When he came to the COC in 1976 he brought contacts throughout the international world of opera and extensive experience in a wide repertoire.

He also brought enthusiasm. Like Torel, Mansouri was a larger-than-life figure, capable of projecting a personality that seemed to epitomize the glamour and excitement of the theatre. Mansouri immediately became identified with opera in Toronto and his smiling face, a proclamation of confidence and success, was familiar in the media and in the advertising material of the company. He even had a signature licence plate for his automobile that read "OPERA."

Even before he had formally taken office, Mansouri was clear about his goals. At a meeting of the Planning Committee in January 1976, he indicated that he wanted a longer season, audience development, more adventurous repertoire and productions, and forward planning both financially and artistically. He wanted a "divorce" from the opera department at the University of Toronto and a resolution of the question of a company orchestra and the relationship with the Toronto Symphony Orchestra. A new theatre had to be considered, to which end he had already looked at the decrepit theatre that after later renovations would become the Elgin.

At the Planning Committee meeting in April 1976, Mansouri introduced the idea of Sunday matinees. It was agreed that they would be popular, but one comment unwittingly signalled the privileged point of view that is so often used to criticize opera as being elitist: the matinees would be in October and by then most people would have closed up their summer places.

Despite his wide experience in the theatre, Mansouri had never had to deal with the detailed business aspects of opera production. At Geneva, the budget was generously subsidized by government to an extent familiar in Europe but unknown in North America, and as a guest director in the United States he had never had to worry about anything but the artistic aspects of his productions within budgets determined by his host companies. The move to Toronto suddenly turned him into a businessman as well as a director; he

Lotfi Mansouri

132

photo: Gary Beechey

John Leberg

would be directly responsible for the administration of the budget and, moreover, be responsible for raising the funds needed to run the company, and maintaining contact with government agencies — the Canada Council, Ontario Arts Council, and the Metropolitan Toronto Arts Council.

He immediately set about learning about administration, fundraising, budgets, contracts, and the array of social and business obligations that fall to the manager of any cultural organization in North America. He attended seminars, used his contacts in American opera houses to find people who could advise him, and he looked for administrators who could handle the specialized jobs that he recognized needed to be filled. He quickly built a team around him that remained throughout his tenure with the company. From the Torel era, John Leberg provided continuity and a knowledge of the inner workings of the organization and assumed the new title of Director of Operations. Leberg had joined the company as assistant stage manager to Torel in 1967 and had intimate understanding of all aspects of the operation of the COC, both business and artistic. He had been committed to Torel and soon came to have a similar personal admiration for Mansouri that translated into a partnership that was essential for the growth of the company. Leberg did not care for the social aspects of running an opera company but he was high-energy, an astute manager, and completely devoted to the COC. His ideas and his skills did much to influence the company throughout Mansouri's tenure.

From outside the COC, Mansouri brought Margaret Genovese (whom he had met during a management seminar that he attended in California) to develop marketing and Dory Vanderhoof to raise money. An important figure who was not part of the administration was board member Walter Stothers, who was a member of the audit and the operating committees, and who would be president in 1980–82. He pressed hard questions about the finances, and he demanded, and even more importantly showed, how to get the detailed financial information that became standard during the Mansouri years. He was instrumental in developing the analyses and reports that Genovese became so good at and which were so important to future planning.

Philip Boswell was the junior appointment when he joined the artistic staff as assistant to John Leberg but he was to have the longest association with the company and arguably the greatest influence, after the general directors, for many years to come. Boswell was interviewed — on Hallowe'en, 1977 — for a job as director of touring, but he had done some work of that kind for the San Francisco Opera (he had also worked at Spoleto and for the Boston Opera) and, prophetically, was of the personal view that touring was too expensive and that the days were over when companies of any size would spend much time on the road. But he did accept a job working within the company and officially joined in January 1978 with his first task to schedule the complicated spring season at the Royal Alexandra Theatre. In 1981 Mansouri wanted someone to attend more carefully to seeking out singers and negotiating contracts, and Boswell took over the job as artistic administrator. All of these new appointments were people who were young, but they brought enthusiasm, dedication, and the specialized experience that was new to the company and that would change the COC. Not always for the better, in some views.

The promotional material took on an aspect of hucksterism that seemed inappropriate to the refined and socially effete world of opera, and fundraising at both the public and private levels was aggressive. The first company sponsors had been found while Torel was still director, but the new attitude to sponsorships and donations far exceeded anything that the COC had even considered possible. A considered policy underlay the expansion of financial support. Genovese and Vanderhoof worked within a framework that sought to establish a strong relationship between the company and the community, which also meant co-operation with the public relations director, Michael Howell, and his successor Karen Lynch. This in turn meant that all aspects of fundraising, marketing, and all artistic decisions were considered in conjunction with one another and how each segment would contribute to the overall projection of the company.

Artistic decisions were now made by Mansouri in conjunction with Leberg and Boswell, with strong input from Genovese, whose practical contribution was careful and highly detailed reports that forecast public and financial possibilities. The four were always in close communication and represented a spectrum from hard-headed and conservative practicality to a sense of challenging adventurousness. Vanderhoof developed

134

methods and a scope of fundraising that exceeded anything previously known by the COC and probably by any other cultural organization in Canada up to that time. Mansouri exuded the confidence and retained the ultimate authority that propelled the company, but he expected the same kind of leadership and commitment from all members of the team in respect to their own departments.

The new and highly charged emphasis on raising money brought the company into conflict with the Canadian Opera Guild. Raising money for the company was not a priority for the guild, whereas Genovese and Vanderhoof were trying to develop a donor program that had some benefits for the individual donor but that was directed principally towards the main company. The COC wanted to separate out the people who would give substantial amounts of money to help the company, not for community interest outside Toronto. In keeping with the new character of the COC administration, the company tended to view the guild as a somewhat old-fashioned remnant of the Torel years when what was now needed was something more orderly and more professionally run. The Toronto branch of the guild — but not the regional branches — was discontinued in 1979 and replaced with the Friends of the Canadian Opera Company. At the same time, the President's Council was established to engage those whose philanthropy placed them in the category of major donors. The success of the council was assured by the first chairman, Margo Bindhardt, who joined her intimate knowledge of the company to her broad connections and associations in the city's social and business circles.

And raising money was a priority. The financial disaster toward the end of the Torel era had been averted, as described earlier, with a one-time "save the opera" appeal and the accumulated deficit almost disappeared. But the 1978–79 season produced a new accumulated deficit of $451,000 from the Toronto activities, touring, and a new season in the spring. It was important that the company raise money based on its obvious strengths and development while underplaying the new financial difficulties.

With the administrative structure modernized, Mansouri turned to the Board of Directors, which had become cumbersome and unfocussed in its activities. In 1980 the structure of the board was simplified and a set of standing committees was created, thus defining the areas of board responsibilities and assigning to individual members a clear area of action to which they could be committed.

The fall 1977 season was the first produced entirely under Mansouri's auspices and it served notice of what would follow in the next eleven seasons: something different (*Don Carlos* in the French version), something popular (*The Magic Flute*), something light (*The Daughter of the Regiment*), and something demanding and probably modern (*Wozzeck*). *Don Carlos* opened the season with a brilliant cast drawn from international ranks that included Canadians: Ermanno Mauro as Carlo, Clarice Carson as Elisabeth, Victor Braun as Rodriguez, and Don Garrard as the Grand Inquisitor; artists from abroad, in this case the United States, were Tatiana Troyanos as Eboli, and Paul Plishka as Philippe II. It also marked the debut of set designs by Wolfram Skalicki, who would design nineteen productions for the company, sometimes with costumes designed by his wife, Amrei Skalicki. For *The Magic Flute*, the Irish conductor Kenneth Montgomery made his first appearance with the company and would return to conduct ten productions over the next seven years.

photo: Robert C. Ragsdale, FRPS

Don Carlos (1977).

The auto da fe scene. Clarice Carson (Elizabeth de Valois), Paul Plishka (Philippe II), Victor Braun (Rodriguez), Don Carlos (Ermanno Mauro).

The Daughter of the Regiment had the unusual talents of the great comedienne, Anna Russell as the Duchesse de Crackentorp, and the equally great contralto Maureen Forrester in the comic role of the Marquise de Berkenfeld. Russell had made a career spoofing opera and now she had the opportunity to bring her hilarity onto the operatic stage. Forrester's reputation was based on the serious song literature of such composers as Schumann, Brahms, and Mahler. Her few operatic performances, notably in works by Gluck and Wagner, gave no hint of the great good humour she brought to her portrayal

Die Zauberflöte (1977).

Leo Goeke (Tamino) and Robert Lloyd (Sarastro) on the steps, Patricia Wells (Pamina) kneeling.

Daughter of the Regiment (1977).

Maureen Forrester (Marquise de Berkenfield), Anna Russell (Duchess of Crackentorp), Norma Burrowes (Marie).

of the Marquise. Boris Brott, who had considerable success as a symphonic conductor, made an inauspicious debut and did not return to the company.

Impressive as *Don Carlos* was, it was *Wozzeck* that crowned Mansouri's first season. Even half a century after its Berlin premiere in 1925, the opera was still a challenge and by no means a standard work anywhere, especially outside Germany. This was its first performance in Canada. Not only was the production a triumph, it was realized with performances mainly by native singers and producers. Mansouri himself directed the production with sets by Murray Laufer and costumes by Marie Day. The conductor was Raffi Armenian, director of the Kitchener-Waterloo Orchestra, and Lyn Vernon and Allan Monk took the leading roles. The cast was rounded out with Ara Berberian (Doctor), William Neill (Drum Major), Martin Chambers (Andres), and Janet Stubbs (Margret). The American tenor, William Neill, would return to the COC and later establish himself as an important teacher, first in Toronto and then in Montreal. Janet

Stubbs had been working her way up through the chorus to small roles at O'Keefe and as Rosina in *The Barber of Seville* on tour, and would take on increasingly important roles over the next decade.

During Mansouri's term as director, a general principle for repertoire and casting evolved. Money would be directed toward a particular star who would bring lustre to the company and whose choice of role would likely determine the repertoire. At the other extreme, an operetta would be chosen for its popular appeal at the box office and be cast as singers were available. In between, and in the end the most notable, were the "esoteric" works that were not widely performed and that were chosen precisely for their artistic novelty, works for which singers had to be found who would devote time to roles that they seldom sang or were learning for the first time.

Wozzeck (1977).

Allan Monk as Wozzeck with

Lyn Vernon as Marie.

The casting of the 1977 season also introduced, albeit discreetly, the new director's view that he was head of an international company, not a provincial or even a national one. Torel had certainly had important guests from abroad, but the presence of Plishka and Troyanos, who were major singers at the Metropolitan Opera, served notice that foreign stars were more welcome than in the past. If the previous administration had taken the attitude that its first responsibility was to Canadian singers, producers, and designers, the new administration was primarily concerned with mounting productions that would match those in theatres abroad — or more precisely, in the United States — and with both singers and designers who would be chosen for their appropriateness to a role and for their star quality, rather than for their nationality. It is a difficult argument to dispute, and one that tends to be put aside when things go well, only to be revived when an imported singer seems no better than an available Canadian. In some views, Mansouri was thought to have turned away from Canadian singers in favour of foreign artists. He did indeed engage singers from abroad, not all of whom were by any means stars, but his record overall is favourable to Canadians, and the prominence of Canadian singers in major roles in his first season is noteworthy. Furthermore, most of the minor roles were cast with Canadian singers, although almost all the Canadians had previously appeared with the COC. Among those in small roles who were appearing for the first time were Martin Chambers (Andres in *Wozzeck*), who would sing many notable character roles; and Gino Quilico (a Corporal in *Daughter of the Regiment*), son of the great baritone Louis Quilico who would himself become one of the principal baritones of his generation. Jeanette Aster was also engaged for the first time as a stage manager; she would go on to a career as a director and eventually head Ottawa's Opera Lyra.

The retrenchment in 1976 from thirty-six to twenty-four performances was maintained in 1977, as it would be again in 1978, with twenty-five performances. The number of subscriptions held in 1977 at 10,253 and increased the next year to 12,025, the highest they had ever been. Overall, attendance was 85 percent in 1977 and 88 percent in 1978 in a theatre that held 3,100 people. Among opera companies in North America, during the 1978–79 season only five opera companies exceeded the COC in total attendance — the Metropolitan, New York City Opera, San Francisco, Houston, and Chicago Lyric.

As soon as the 1977 Toronto season ended, the fall tour immediately went into production. Mansouri directed *The Barber of Seville* and John Leberg took on *La Traviata*. Timothy Vernon, later director of Pacific Opera in Victoria, was the conductor of both productions. In November and December, the touring company visited all the Atlantic provinces, including Newfoundland and Prince Edward Island, and in January and February of the new year they travelled in the United States from Michigan to Florida.

One of Mansouri's most urgent ambitions was the expansion of the season and the move from an isolated period in the fall to the so-called *stagione* system where productions were spread over many months rather than clustered in one period. It was out of the question for the TSO to play for an expanded opera season during its concert season because rehearsals and performances with the COC would take up too much time. There was, moreover, a financial question. When the COC engaged the TSO, it hired the entire orchestra regardless of what or how many players were needed for individual productions. Although it would be cheaper to hire casual players who would be paid by engagement, this could result in a vastly inferior orchestra in the pit, and while the audience might think it goes to hear the singers, no performance, and certainly no company, can survive a weak orchestra. Even before Mansouri's arrival there had been discussions about terminating the arrangement with the TSO and embarking on a plan for an opera orchestra. At the meeting of the Planning Committee in April 1975, the question of an extended season was discussed. It was realized that a move away from the short season in the fall would mean the end of the affiliation with the TSO, but there was also a question of the chorus.

The University of Toronto Opera Division began its session late in the fall term specifically so that its members would be available to the COC chorus. The students did not comprise the entire chorus, but they were a substantial and dependable part of it, and just as an extended season would affect the company's relationship with the TSO, so would it affect its ability to draw on the opera students for the chorus. The problem of establishing a chorus independent of the school posed fewer problems, however, than the creation of a new orchestra. Early in 1976 John Leberg had reported to the Planning Committee on the possibility of an independent orchestra and Mansouri took up the subject as soon as he joined the company. There was concern that there would not be enough good freelance players available in the city, especially as the National Ballet took some of the players from its orchestra on tour, thereby reducing the pool of potential players for the opera; and there were rumblings at the musicians' union that another orchestra would draw funding away from the TSO. As it turned out, none of the fears were realized. The TSO continued to expand its own season; funding for the COC was for the company, not for its orchestra, and did not affect other orchestra subsidies; and there was an abundance of good players, frequently young musicians who could not find the very few jobs that came up in the established Canadian orchestras. If the new orchestra was technically a pick-up group at first, it soon coalesced into a regularly contracted ensemble. In a similar way, there were enough singers in Toronto who were good enough and interested enough to provide a substantial professional chorus. The disciplined chorus and the high

140   standard of orchestral playing would become distinguishing features of the COC.

With the orchestra question resolved for the 1977 season, the other major limitation that Mansouri had to face was access to the O'Keefe Centre. As long as the opera played only for a few weeks in the fall, its was, in Mansouri's view, merely an "exotic bird" that flew in and out of the city but made no lasting impression. But to break out of that fall confinement, the COC had to have access to the O'Keefe stage in the winter and spring as well as in the fall. The Centre was a municipal theatre but its policy was that of a road-house in which the COC and National Ballet of Canada were tenants in competition with such hits as *Evita*, Harry Belafonte, and Liberace. Even an increase in the length of the fall season was seen by the O'Keefe management as an incursion into its own subscription series and it was unwilling to give up more time to opera and ballet. The grants from Metropolitan Toronto to the COC were tied to the rent that the COC paid to O'Keefe, although in fact Metro's grant was always less than what the company paid in rent. In a way, Metro was shifting money from one of its pockets to another and making a profit to boot — for example, in the 1979 season the grant from Toronto was $56,953 but the theatre rent was $278,691 — but its continuing support on this basis was crucial to expanding the season; without an increased grant from Metro related to the increased rent that the COC would pay O'Keefe, there would be no hope of expanding the opera season. It would take another two years before a new balance of grant and rent was established.

It was at this time that Floyd Chalmers approached Mansouri with a project for a new opera to follow up on his sponsorship of *Louis Riel* ten years before. Chalmers wrote to Mansouri in November 1977 to ask for the return of a book he had loaned to Mansouri on Sioux music. Chalmers remarked that he was getting his Sitting Bull books together "in order to make another attempt at developing a plan for an opera." The plan advanced to the point where Mavor Moore, librettist for *Louis Riel*, completed the text and the Calgary composer Gregory Levin completed a first version of the score. But there it stalled. In April 1984 there was a meeting with Moore, Levin, Mansouri, Leberg, Floyd Chalmers, and Joan Chalmers. Moore afterwards wrote angrily to Mansouri complaining that the libretto had not been read, tapes of Levin's music had not been listened to, and that Mansouri lacked any committed interest in the piece. Despite the animosity of his letter, Moore wrote again to Mansouri the following September about the possibility of giving *Ghost Dance*, as the opera was to be called, at Expo 86 in Vancouver in co-operation with the COC and the Minnesota Opera, but nothing came of the idea. The opera had two workshop performances in Toronto produced by Comus Music Theatre in the fall of 1986, but after that it was not heard again.

In anticipation of the extension to a year-round series of performances, a spring season was instituted in April 1978 at the Royal Alexandra Theatre where the COC had begun its professional life. The entrepreneurial Ed Mirvish, whose fortune — based on a huge discount department store — belied a man of culture and generosity, now owned the theatre. When he bought the fifty-five-year-old Royal Alexandra in 1962, he literally saved it from demolition and soon re-established it as one of the country's major theatres. The COC's *Così fan tutte* had earlier been included in a Mirvish season. Despite the lack of box-office success of that earlier partnership, Mirvish supported the new COC initiative by including the spring opera season in the highly successful subscription series that he operated in his theatre. The COC was spared the enormous financial risks involved in its new enterprise and had a large guarantee in the subscriber audience.

The Royal Alexandra season included *The Marriage of Figaro*, *La Traviata*, and *The Barber of Seville*, with casts that were made up almost entirely of young Canadian singers. *Figaro* was given a special distinction by the fact that it was directed by the great sopra-

below left: La Traviata (1978) at the Royal Alexandra. Maria Pellegrini (Violetta) and Martin Chambers (Alfredo).

below: The Marriage of Figaro (1978) at the Royal Alexandra. Raymond Hickman (Count Almaviva), Joel Katz (Antonio), Janet Stubbs (Cherubino), Pamela Myers (Countess Almaviva), Barbara Shuttleworth (Susanna).

photo: Robert C. Ragsdale, FRPS

photo: Robert C. Ragsdale, FRPS

142

no, Graziella Sciutti, who was now turning to stage direction after a brilliant career as a singer, especially of Mozart. A spring season was repeated in April 1979 with *Carmen* and

La Cenerentola and with outstanding singers, among whom were Judith Forst (who had spent several seasons at the Metropolitan), Janet Stubbs, Diane Loeb, and Gino Quilico. The continuation of the company's extensive tours, to which the spring season was now added, meant the engagement of a large number of singers and maintained the presence of the COC across the continent. In 1977–78, the first full season entirely under Mansouri's direction, there were twenty-five performances in Toronto in the fall and thirty-two in the spring; twenty-two performances of *La Traviata* and *The Barber of Seville* in Eastern Canada and seventeen in Ontario; and thirty performances in the United States. There were also fifty performances of a capsule *Barber* for Toronto schools under the Prologue to the Performing Arts program, making a total of 176 performances in all

La Cenerentola (1978) at the Royal Alexandra.

Janet Stubbs as Cinderella, with Caralyn Tomlin (Clorinda) and Susan Gudgeon (Tisbe).

categories in Canada and the United States. The long tours in the 1960s had often run to an impressive number of performances, but never had the total included so many fully produced main-stage performances in Toronto.

The enthusiastic promotion of the company and its search for new subscribers met a storm of criticism in the spring of 1978. The popular American actor, Tony Randall, was engaged to make a promotional recording that was distributed in June to radio stations, and in the form of a small LP, to the public at large through mailings and as a magazine insert. Journalists and critics complained that the admittedly engaging Randall had overstepped the bounds of good taste in his breezy and flippant comments on *Rigoletto, Der Rosenkavalier,* and *Don Giovanni,* comments that they found sexist and vulgar. William

Littler in *The Toronto Star* summed up the negative view when he asked "whether any organization which undertakes the custodianship of art has the right to demean and misrepresent the true nature of that art for the sake of selling tickets." But Littler had to report that the campaign seemed to be working if the marked increase in subscription sales was any indication.

The 1978 season at the O'Keefe Centre went ahead in the fall as usual, with the same successful variety that had marked the previous season. *Rigoletto* with Louis Quilico in the title role was the first of several COC productions in which father and son, Louis and Gino, would appear together. The title role of *Don Giovanni* was shared by Michael Devlin and Justino Diaz. These two operas were the familiar items, with *Der Rosenkavalier* as the well-known yet seldom given piece. Kenneth Montgomery returned to conduct the Strauss opera, Heather Harper was a radiant Marschallin, and Judith Forst and Lyn Vernon shared the role of Octavian with equal brilliance. The novelty was Tchaikovsky's *Joan of Arc* in its continental premiere and, indeed, in one of its few performances since the nineteenth century. Although it had immediate success in 1881 at its first performance in St. Petersburg, the opera soon fell from popularity and its few productions have been mainly as vehicles for a star mezzo-soprano in the title role. The COC was no exception when it had Lyn Vernon to sing Joan, a role that suited her dramatic stage presence and vocal intensity. Mario Bernardi returned to conduct after an absence from the company since 1970. Not least among the performers in *Joan of Arc* was the opera-loving secretary of state in the federal government, John Roberts, who as an extra was cast as a monk. He had been a Bishop in *Don Carlos* the previous season and remarked that only Lotfi Mansouri could have demoted him so quickly! The production was also seen at the National Arts Centre in Ottawa and broadcast on CBC television on the program "Live from the NAC," the first COC production to be televised.

top: *Rigoletto (1978).*
Louis Quilico in the title role,
with Gino Quilico as Marullo

bottom: *Der Rosenkavalier*
(1978).
Heather Harper as the
Marschallin, with Pierre Duval
(The Italian Singer) and Artur
Korn (Baron Ochs).

Joan of Arc (1978). Lyn Vernon as Joan.

The touring company that for many years had set out after the end of the O'Keefe season continued to operate, this time with a production of *The Marriage of Figaro*. The previous year the tour had been to Eastern Canada. This year, 1978–79, the company visited Ontario and the West as well as the United States, making thirty-six stops in Canada and forty-eight in the United States, to play to 81,661 people. It was to be the last tour to cover such distances and to be on the road for so long a period of time. Touring was becoming expensive and more and more difficult to justify, especially the trips to the USA. And Mansouri had other plans

The fall seasons had traditionally ended by mid-October to enable the O'Keefe Centre to open its own shows in the fall. Mansouri had negotiated with the Centre to extend the 1977 season to the end of the month and in 1978 the season had edged into

November by a few days. Finally, in 1979 Mansouri was able to negotiate a new arrangement with O'Keefe that allowed him to establish a season from fall to spring at that theatre, and as well to return to six main productions instead of the four that had been instituted in 1976 because of the financial crisis. The rental costs for the theatre suddenly rose to $544,432 but the grant from Metropolitan Toronto rose correspondingly to $531,000. The spring season at the Royal Alexandra was discontinued. Each of the six operas in 1979–80 had its own time period, beginning with *Simon Boccanegra* in September and ending with *Peter Grimes*, which closed in early May. Not least of the advantages of the new arrangement was a gain in the already high rehearsal standards that Torel had imposed since the beginning and which the company never lost. Now preparation was not so pressed for time as had been the case when all productions had to be rehearsed and performed within a matter of weeks.

The first nine-month season was one of premieres for the COC when five of the six pieces were given for the first time by the company — *Boccanegra, Tristan und Isolde, L'elisir d'amore, Werther*, and *Peter Grimes*. It was a bold choice of works; the only opera from the "standard" repertoire was *Madama Butterfly. Simon Boccanegra* again brought together Louis Quilico as Simon and Gino Quilico in the important role of Paulo. *Tristan* was notable for the vast out-in-space designs of Annelies Corrodi, and for Spas Wenkoff and Johanna Meier in the title roles. He was the reigning Tristan of the moment. Meier was singing her first Isolde and would repeat it at Bayreuth in 1981. Maureen Forrester was Brangäne. Mansouri directed and his assistant for this production was the young Toronto director Robert Carsen, who would soon enjoy international success. In the spring of 1980 Leon Major returned to direct a delicate and moving production of Massenet's *Werther*, with Benito Maresca in the title role and Judith Forst as Charlotte. Kenneth Montgomery conducted a gripping *Peter Grimes* with William Neill as Peter, Heather Thomson as Ellen, and Thomas Stewart as Balstrode. The accumulated deficit, however, had grown to $685,328, and would continue to mount.

With the season now extended from fall to spring, the 1980–81 season was something of a climax in repertoire and casting, a remarkable achievement by Mansouri and his team after only four years. *Otello* opened the season and was double cast with James

photo: Robert C. Ragsdale, FRPS

photo: Robert C. Ragsdale, FRPS

photo: Robert C. Ragsdale, FRPS

above: **Simon Boccanegra (1979).**

Louis Quilico (Simon) with Gino Quilico (Paolo).

above right: **Tristan und Isolde (1979).**

Spas Wenkoff and Johanna Meier.

right: **Peter Grimes (1980).**

Thomas Stewart (Balstrode) and William Neill (Peter Grimes).

McCracken and Richard Cassilly in the title role. Cassilly had appeared often with the company since its early days, but McCracken's only previous appearance in Toronto had been in 1956 during a visit by the Metropolitan Opera when he had sung the messenger in *Aïda* and the toy-seller in *La Bohème*. Allan Monk added Iago to his gallery of villains for the COC, and Mariana Niculescu sang Desdemona.

Lulu attracted international attention. Alban Berg had died with the opera incomplete and it had been performed in two acts with a truncated final scene to complete the action. Only after the death of Berg's widow and some legal wrangling was the scoring of the opera completed by Frederic Cerha. The full three-act opera was first performed in Paris

Otello (1980).

James McCracken as Otello, with Mariana Niculescu as Desdemona.

photo: Robert C. Ragsdale, FRPS

in February 1979, and in July of the same year at Santa Fe, New Mexico. The COC's production in November 1980 was only the third of the complete opera. Carole Farley and Claudia Cummings shared the title role, Evelyn Lear was the sadly tragic Countess Geschwitz, and Victor Braun was Dr. Schön. The conductor was Kenneth Montgomery, who had conducted *Tristan* and *Peter Grimes* the previous season and who was quickly establishing himself as the company's principal conductor, especially for its most demanding scores.

One of the most striking women on the operatic stage, Elisabeth Söderström, made her only appearance with the company as a luminous Merry Widow to the Count Danilo of Alan Titus. The comic roles were in the skillful hands of actor/dancer Gerald Isaac as Njegus and actress Barbara Hamilton as Prasowia.

The stellar season was capped with Joan Sutherland and Tatiana Troyanos in *Norma*. If any event marked the character of the company as Mansouri was developing it, it was the appearance of Sutherland now and in future seasons. She was the reigning *diva* of the day and she brought a new lustre to the COC stage. For all the distinguished singers who had appeared with the company, to have singers of the renown and stature of Sutherland, Troyanos, Söderström, and McCracken in one season was unprecedented.

The season was rounded out with Mozart's *Die Entführung aus dem Serail*, conducted by Bernardi, *Madama Butterfly*, and *Der fliegende Holländer*, with Marita Napier, Albert Remedios, and Leif Roar.

The proposed transmission of *Norma* in a live telecast in the spring of 1981 almost foundered on a series of misunderstandings and problems in contract negotiations. When matters were settled, a labour dispute at the CBC caused the cancellation of what would have been the first live telecast of the COC from O'Keefe Centre. Fortunately, the dispute did not prevent the taping of the production, and it was broadcast later in May.

The two spring seasons at the Royal Alexandra in 1978 and 1979 with the emphasis on young Canadians were virtually a projection of one of Mansouri's most fervent ambitions, the establishment of an ensemble of young singers. In Switzerland he had worked closely with Herbert Graf who had established opera studios in Zurich and in Geneva that

photo: Robert C. Ragsdale, FRPS

photo: Robert C. Ragsdale, FRPS

photo: Robert C. Ragsdale, FRPS

top left: **Lulu** *(1980).*
Lulu (Carole Farley) leans over the body of Dr. Schön (Victor Braun), watched by the Countess Geschwitz (Evelyn Lear) and Alwa (William Pell), with the Schoolboy (Ferguson MacKenzie) in the shadows.

left: **Claudia Cummings as Lulu** *(1980).*

bottom left: **The Merry Widow** *(1981).*
Anna Glawari, the Merry Widow (Elisabeth Söderström), arrives at the Act 1 ball.

below: **Norma** *(1981).*
Joan Sutherland (Norma, seated) and Tatiana Troyanos (Adalgisa).

photo: Robert C. Ragsdale, FRPS

were closely associated with the operas in those cities but which provided specialized teaching and training for young professionals. From his first visits to Toronto, Mansouri spoke about the need for such a program at the COC, a program that was not in competition with the University of Toronto's Opera Division but that would act as a bridge to professional life for a select group of talented singers. As early as February 1976 (Mansouri took office in July 1976) there was mention at the Planning Committee of a "resident company" and by April the committee agreed that there would be a spring season in 1978 built around a Resident Artists program.

It was not until October 23, 1979 that a formal proposal was presented to the Executive Committee that set out the need for a permanent body of singers and how such a group could be established. There was a strong element of self-interest in the proposal, beginning with the first sentence: "The Canadian Opera company needs to have increased and continual visibility in both Metropolitan Toronto and in the province of Ontario in order to insure long-term audience and development support." The proposal also makes the point that rising production costs make future touring less and less likely, an activity which, in any case, has provided work but not a level of training that young singers should have.

It was also seen as essential that the COC retain an outreach program if levels of government funding were to be maintained. The solution was to create a Resident Ensemble Program. "Nine young Canadian singers, the best talent available from across Canada, would be contracted by the Canadian Opera company to participate in a year's program that would provide professional performing opportunities, as well as serving the community through a variety of outreach marketing/audience development projects." The members of the Ensemble would have supporting roles in the O'Keefe season, appear in other smaller productions, and visit schools and communities for workshops and performances. The proposal was accepted and the Ensemble formally came into being in May 1980. Stuart Hamilton, well-known as accompanist and coach and the founder of Opera in Concert in Toronto, was appointed musical director. The first group comprised eleven singers, and Derek Bate as conductor.

To institute a full program, considerable funding would be needed and here the sup-

Members of the first
Ensemble, 1980/81. Back, left
to right: Michael Shust,
Caralyn Tomlin, Roxolana
Roslak, Barry Stillwell, Shawna
Farrell, Mark Pedrotti, Stuart
Hamilton, Theodore Baerg,
Guillermo Silva-Marin,
Deborah Milsom. In front:
Eleanor James, Janet Stubbs.

port of the Canada Council, Imperial Oil, and a training grant from the federal
Manpower Program were essential. The initial sponsor was Imperial Oil Company, and
Margo Bindhardt was first chair of the Advisory Board. In its first season, 1980–81, the
Ensemble consisted of eleven singers, among whom were some who already had substantial professional experience, such as Theodore Baerg, Mark Pedrotti, Roxolana
Roslak, and Janet Stubbs. All but two of the members appeared in small parts on the main
stage and in larger parts on tour. Beginning in 1983–84, there would be two categories of
regular members and apprentices, the latter those singers who were not yet sufficiently
experienced or advanced to enter the full program. It seems to have been recognized at
once from the cross-country auditions that there were singers with potential but without

adequate background for the Ensemble and in the summer of 1981 a draft proposal was drawn up for a Resident Training Program with the Royal Conservatory in Toronto. Nothing came of this proposal and the COC retained the two-tier division of membership.

The COC lived up to its promise of providing outstanding coaches and experience with major directors and conductors, but the Ensemble was not quite everything that it seemed. It was never a permanent core to the company in the way that it was sometimes described. The intention was always that young singers would spend a year or two in the group and then move on to independent professional life. Moreover, in many if not most cases, that professional life would not include the COC. The company seemed to allow few of the Ensemble members to grow within the COC; they were fine for small parts, but they would have to go elsewhere to gain major experience. Small roles and small productions, as well as special performances for patrons or in schools, were the limits of many Ensemble members' experience.

At worst, the Ensemble was seen to be a device for the COC to attract funding, and to be exploitative of young singers, to the extent that there were sometime problems with Canadian Actors' Equity, the union to which singers belonged. Equity's position was that Ensemble members were professional singers, however embryonic their careers might be, and they had to be engaged within the broad terms of the general agreement between Equity and the COC. Even taking into account the training aspect of the Ensemble, Equity often found that members were overworked and sometimes were treated as a convenient group that could be slotted into any kind of subsidiary activity. The wide-ranging "outreach" engagements were particularly troubling insofar as they seemed to advance the company at the expense of the singers. However, where the outreach involved patrons, it meant that people got to know young Canadian singers and this in turn consolidated their interest in the COC, to the ultimate advantage of everyone. And where "outreach" meant school programs, there could always be an anticipated, even if undefined, educational value for those young listeners who might discover opera for the first time.

In defence of the COC, Mansouri always took the attitude that the Ensemble was a stepping-stone to a career, not necessarily a career in Canadian opera or with the COC. People were brought in to work with the Ensemble whose contacts and recommendations could lead to engagements elsewhere, and behind the scenes Mansouri himself vigorously promoted members with other directors. The view that the COC was a growing international company precluded using young singers of limited experience and no reputation in major roles, no matter how good they were. It is an argument that often resurfaces. There have been singers who rose to prominence quickly once they left the COC and on whom the COC might have been expected to take a chance. Equally, there are singers who have been given growing opportunities within the COC. Finally the choice of singers comes down to the preference of the general director in conjunction with his immediate artistic associates in any company, and it is not easy to marshal arguments either for or against nationalism in making those decisions. On balance, if the COC benefitted from the Ensemble, there is no doubt but that the young singers also benefitted, often taking their first major steps toward a career.

The Ensemble also had a function in the growth of opera companies in Canada. In the first paragraph of the 1979 proposal the point was made that the COC "must continue to serve in the Canadian cultural community as a leader in the training of young Canadian talent." The Ensemble did in fact become a resource for the increasing development of new and already established companies in the 1980s. No other organization in Canada had the resources of the COC or the possibility of financing such an operation, not even in Montreal where the success of individual productions was weakened by the erratic history of companies in that city (although l'Opéra de Montréal, established in 1980, soon followed suit with its Atelier lyrique in 1984). If this could be interpreted as Toronto-centric arrogance, the fact is that in the 1980s the COC was the flagship of the fleet. In Torel's era there had hardly been a fleet and the first objective had been to establish one major, permanent company, but now companies were developing across the country and increasingly they not only needed singers, they could provide stages for younger Canadians, many of whom had been with the Ensemble.

The idea of engaging the touring groups to participate in schools in the towns that were visited, an idea developed first by Jan Rubes, was now renewed. In its first three sea-

photo: Gary Beechey

top: *Little Red Riding Hood (1981/82).*

A scene from a school performance as part of Toronto's
Prologue to the Performing Arts.

bottom: Harbourfront Centre — inside the tent.

sons, 1980–83, the Ensemble appeared "in residence" in fifty-one Ontario communities outside Toronto. In its first ten years, this number increased to an astonishing 127 towns, many of them on two or more occasions, plus visits to twenty-seven communities elsewhere in Canada, from Gander in Newfoundland to Kitimat in British Columbia. These visits, which could last as long as three days in any one town, varied in presentation from a full production through highlights concerts to children's programs and workshops in schools. In Toronto, it was now the Ensemble that participated in the school system's Prologue to the Performing Arts.

For some years the COC had participated in a successful civic venture, the Metropolitan Toronto International Caravan, which featured pavilions around the city reflective of the many nationalities and cultural organizations represented in the city's population. The COC lost $6,000 on its 1979 pavilion and withdrew from Caravan, thus opening the way for the first venture that drew directly on the new Ensemble, a series of weekend performances in July and August 1980, at the Harbourfront Festival on Toronto's lakeshore. Abridged thirty-minute versions of *Hansel and Gretel, La Bohème,* and Kurt Weill's *Little Mahagonny* were given along with an operatic review, *I Love You! I Hate You! Drop Dead!* Performances were given cabaret-style with tables ranged around a large tent. The Harbourfront productions continued until 1985 and provided patrons with the opportunity to hear future stars in capsule versions of roles — Ben Heppner as Hoffmann, Theodore Baerg as Figaro, Joanne Kolomyjec as Micaela, Gaétan Laperrière as Germont, Kimberley Barber as Prince Orlofsky, Odette Beaupré as Carmen, John Fanning as Escamillo.

The first winter season for the Ensemble was a busy one. A special school program of *Madama Butterfly* was given in twenty-seven Toronto schools and twenty-four elsewhere in Ontario, an activity that with some variation was to become standard for the next decade. In February 1981 a concert presentation was given of Purcell's *Dido and Aeneas* with excerpts from his *The Fairy Queen*. Karl Richter, the great German specialist in baroque music, was to have conducted, but he died just eleven days before the performance and Kenneth Montgomery stepped in. Benjamin Britten's opera for children, *The Little Sweep*, was performed at Harbourfront in the same month. Six singers from the Ensemble appeared at the annual ball at the Metropolitan Opera House in New York on April 4, 1981, in a special revue composed for them by David Warrack, *One Step at a Time*. And through January and February, the Ensemble was on tour through twelve Ontario cities and towns with Rossini's *Cinderella* and an entertainment arranged by Mavor Moore, *The Magic of Mozart*. In addition to the performance activity in that first season, Ensemble members had musical and dramatic coaching, sometimes with people who were working with the main company, sometimes with people brought in especially for them.

An ambitious project was undertaken in the 1981–82 and 1982–83 seasons with a special du Maurier Series. A few performances of the principal O'Keefe productions were given with members of the Ensemble in the major roles, but the costs and complications of such a program limited it to these two seasons.

Ensemble members were limited in their main-stage appearances, but they were the principal performers in some notable smaller productions. In June 1984, the COC produced what was billed as the North American Premiere of the early seventeenth-century stage work, *La rappresentazione di Anima et di Corpo* by Emilio de' Cavalieri. Mansouri had been assistant to Herbert Graf when Graf directed this rarely seen piece at the Salzburg Cathedral, and the COC used the costumes from that production. Performances were in St. Michael's Cathedral, the cast of thirteen was almost entirely present or former members of the Ensemble, and the choruses were sung by the boys of St. Michael's Choir School. In February and March, 1985, a charming *Così fan tutte* was given at the Bluma Appel Theatre, with Joanne Kolomyjec, Odette Beaupré, Peter Blanchet, and John

photo: Gary Beechey

La Rappresentazione di Anima e di Corpo (1984). Interior of St. Michael's Cathedral with members of the COC Ensemble and the boys of St. Michael's Choir School.

Fanning/Gaétan Laperrière as the lovers, conducted by Derek Bate. The theatre is a playhouse with about nine hundred seats. Acoustically it proved to be rather dry, and the orchestra pit was small. This was the only COC production there. A year later, in 1986, the Ensemble gave *The Beggar's Opera* to inaugurate the Joey and Toby Tanenbaum Opera Centre and the Texaco Opera Theatre, followed by a Brecht/Weill evening as part of the Brecht Festival. In 1988 there was a splendid production, also at the Centre, of Britten's *Turn of the Screw*, conducted by Martin Isepp.

The Ensemble was now in effect the touring arm of the COC and the productions that had been assembled especially for touring for so many years were abandoned. The extensive and wide-ranging tours were also curtailed, being confined mainly to Ontario. It was not until 1987 that the tour extended once more to the Atlantic provinces. Because

photo: Robert C. Ragsdale, FRPS

Così fan tutte (1985) at the Bluma Appel Theatre.
Left to right: Joanne Kolomyjec (Fiordiligi), Gaétan Laperrière (Guglielmo), Brian McIntosh (Don Alfonso), Peter Blanchet (Ferrando), and Odette Beaupré (Dorabella).

the members of the Ensemble were not sufficient to fill all the roles, other young singers were sometimes engaged. In 1981, for example, Ben Heppner, then at the University of Toronto, sang King Kaspar in *Amahl and the Night Visitors*.

With the season expanded and the Ensemble established, Mansouri's attention turned to real estate. The COC had had a series of administrative homes in rented premises around the city, and rehearsals had been equally peripatetic, sometimes in the comparative luxury of the MacMillan Theatre at the University of Toronto, but frequently in church halls. With the development of the Harbourfront complex on the city's central waterfront, the company moved its offices there and also was able to use an old ice-house as a scene shop. The ice-house had the advantage of unobstructed space, and was later turned into an art gallery and the du Maurier Theatre Centre, but Mansouri real-

photo: Michael Cooper

The Turn of the Screw (1988).
The ghosts, Peter Quint and Miss Jessel.

ized that the COC's tenure at Harbourfront would not be permanent. If the company could not have its own theatre (a story to be taken up later), it could have its own production and administrative premises and to this end a suitable building was sought. The choice finally came down to a set of buildings on Front Street at Berkeley. In the 1980s this was a forgotten corner of Toronto despite its proximity to downtown, which lay further to the west. There was little commercial or residential development in the area at a time when the city elsewhere was bustling. The building at 227 Front Street East had been built as a woolen mill and had been designed by one of the city's most famous architects, E.J. Lennox. In 1888 Consumers' Gas Company constructed an enormous building next to the mill as a purifying plant. In 1938, Dalton's, a manufacturer and importer of baking and other food goods, bought the mill, and in 1967 acquired the adjacent property as well. In 1984 the COC bought the group of Dalton buildings and embarked on extensive renovations.

The buildings would not have been acquired without the help of three private supporters of the COC. Paul Hellyer, an MP, cabinet minister, and sometime amateur singer, guaranteed the down-payment. Hal Jackman provided money but especially his influence and contacts. And Joey Tanenbaum provided a million dollars. With additional grants from federal and provincial governments, the old mills building was converted to offices and prop storage, and the vast space of the old gas building (it was twelve metres high and had a floor-space about twenty-four by forty-two metres) became a combination theatre and rehearsal space. A hydraulic stage in two sections could turn the cavernous room into a studio theatre, and the floor area was great enough to prepare a production as it would appear on the O'Keefe stage and have space left over. A third commercial building was also obtained, and the completed unit, with offices, studios and rehearsal rooms, provided all the administrative and rehearsal needs in one building.

The Joey and Toby Tanenbaum Opera Centre, as the entire unit was called, opened on November 5, 1985, and in February 1986, the Ensemble's performances of *The Beggar's Opera* inaugurated the Texaco Opera Theatre, as the studio theatre was named. With a corporate change in 1989, the theatre was re-named the Imperial Oil Opera Theatre.

With the Opera Centre established, Mansouri and Leberg attended to another need of any major opera company, a scene shop. The construction of costumes, props, and sets requires special workshops, but none is more difficult to accommodate than the need for large spaces in which to prepare the sets that fill a stage. A building was being used for this purpose on Melita Avenue, an out-of-the-way street next to a railway line in the middle of the city. A draft proposal for renovations to the building was made at the end of 1985, and a year later, on November 24, 1986, the property was bought by the company. With the addition of the Melita Avenue building to the Joey and Toby Tanenbaum Opera

left: The Joey and Toby Tanenbaum Opera Centre. The large building houses the theatre/rehearsal space, with the buildings behind for studios and administration.

below left: Interior of the Joey and Toby Tanenbaum Opera Centre set up for rehearsal. The area can be reconfigured into various arrangements for concert and opera performances.

below: The Melita Avenue scene shop.

photo: Gary Beechey

photo: Gary Beechey

Centre, the COC suddenly had extensive real estate of its own that housed its complete production and administrative needs and provided production and rehearsal space second to none. All that was missing was an opera house.

The idea of the company having its own theatre had remained alive since the early 1970s in the Torel era. During 1972–73 the Planning Committee, urged on by the Harewood report, discussed possibilities, one of which was to take over management of the O'Keefe Centre, an idea quickly rejected on the grounds that such a move would decrease the chance of building a new theatre later on. There was also discussion about the old Odeon Carlton cinema on Carlton Street just east of Yonge. The theatre had opened in 1948, had a seating capacity of 2,300 and was built with at least the vague idea that it could be used for live productions. In 1950 the touring San Carlo Opera Company performed there, taking advantage of the modest but adequate stage and the orchestra pit. When the cinema closed, the public parts of the theatre seemed to offer an opportunity for the COC to acquire a home of its own. Unfortunately, the stage area and pit were not nearly large enough for the regular use of a major opera company, and the placement of the building and adjoining streets made any substantial enlargement impossible. After various attempts to save it as a historic building, the Odeon Carlton was torn down in 1973.

A more realistic possibility was for the company to join in the development of the new Metro Centre announced by the city in 1972 to cover a large area west of University Avenue and south of King Street. There was already a New Massey Hall Committee to build a new concert hall to replace the venerable but faded Massey Hall. In 1973 representatives of the concert hall committee and the COC Planning Committee had an informal discussion at which there was general agreement that it would be ideal if the new hall and the opera house were in the same large area under development. At the meetings in April and May, 1974, the Planning Committee decided to proceed with plans for a new theatre, to apply for a grant to make a study of all aspects of the new house, and to acquire land at Metro Centre adjacent to the new concert hall. The new concert hall eventually turned out to be Roy Thomson Hall, which opened in 1982, but the opera house was not to be its neighbour. The COC did, however, join in the activities during the opening week of the hall with a concert performance of Strauss's *Capriccio*.

By 1976 other possibilities were being examined by the COC. The city and the federal government had announced plans to rejuvenate lands on Lake Ontario east of Spadina Avenue and there was some discussion about including an opera house in the new development. One of the more bizarre suggestions was to construct a theatre of about 1,500 seats in the old warehouse of a supermarket chain on the edge of the new Harbourfront. Slightly more realistic was the potential offered by the renovation of two old theatres on Yonge Street that were restored as the Elgin and Winter Garden theatres, and although the Elgin was eventually used by the COC, its stage area and pit were much too small for the grander of grand operas and there was little room in which to enlarge them.

In the fall of 1976 Douglas Sloan, president of the COC, made it clear that he opposed the COC's taking on the sole responsibility for the theatre; he favoured an arrangement by which a separate group would undertake the project as was then being done for the new concert hall. Roy Thomson Hall, as the concert hall became, remains in the hands of a board, and the Toronto Symphony Orchestra, whose home the hall is, is the chief rent-paying tenant, an arrangement that has drawbacks for the orchestra that the opera did not originally wish to embrace. Indeed, the opera and the ballet virtually had that arrangement with O'Keefe Centre.

The idea of sharing a new theatre with the National Ballet of Canada had come up as early as November 1972. By 1977 the COC and the NBC had agreed informally to their co-operation in a new theatre and they engaged the consulting firm of Woods, Gordon to examine various proposals that had arisen.

In February 1978, the first of a long series of studies appeared: *Feasibility Study of a New or Remodelled Opera/Ballet Building in Toronto*. In June of the same year there was a formal motion by the Executive Committee of the opera to meet with the National Ballet for the express purpose of forming an opera/ballet theatre corporation along the lines suggested by Sloan. Nevertheless, it was not until the fall of 1982 that a small committee was formed, to be called the Opera/Ballet Group until formal incorporation took place. The group was acting on a resolution accepted jointly by the boards of the COC and the

NBC whereby both companies authorized the formation of a new corporation whose main function would be to obtain financing to construct and operate a theatre primarily for the use of opera and ballet. Three major sites had already been isolated — Bay and Wellesley, Harbourfront, and North York — and Arcop Associates was engaged to report on these and other possibilities by February 1983. This was to be the second of at least thirteen feasibility and planning reports that would be written between 1978 and 1988. The Opera/Ballet Group was formally incorporated in November 1983 as The Opera/Ballet Hall Corporation.

In March 1983, Mel Lastman, the mayor of North York and future mayor of an amalgamated Toronto, launched a proposal and a drive for public support to have the theatre located in his city. At the time, North York was a separate municipality on the northern border of the City of Toronto and Lastman had ambitious plans for its development. The care-fully considered campaign included a lavish folder and supporting documents but the proposal was not accepted by the Opera/Ballet Hall Corporation. Lastman did get his theatre and concert hall complex but it was not to be the opera house, although the idea that it should be briefly surfaced again in 1999.

Scenery stored outside the O'Keefe Centre between performances. The theatre does not have the space to store multiple sets during repertoire performances of operas.

photo: Michael Cooper

The mayor of Toronto, John Sewell, also had an opinion. In the summer of 1983 he was saying publicly that the old Imperial Theatre should be turned into the new ballet/opera house and he wrote twice to the board with this suggestion. The Imperial was beautifully renovated as the Pantages Theatre by the commercial group Livent, but like all these old theatres, it could not have been sufficiently enlarged in the stage and pit areas to accommodate the repertory needs of an opera company. The idea had already been examined and rejected in the Arcop report. To complicate matters still further, the city was examining the renovation and use of the O'Keefe Centre and engaged a group of consultants to prepare the report, *The Future of O'Keefe Centre in Relation to Opera and Ballet*, which appeared in June 1984.

For several years representatives of the ballet and the opera had been quietly working behind the scenes to obtain the support of the provincial government that finally led to the confirmation to the board in January 1985 by Premier William Davis of the donation of a large block of land owned by the government at the corner of Bay and Wellesley streets. In the summer, meetings took place with Bernard Ostry of the Ontario Ministry of Culture and Marcel Masse, federal minister of communications. It was agreed that a target figure of forty million dollars was realistic for private fundraising. The expectation was that the new theatre would open in 1988. But there were clouds on the horizon. William Davis and the Conservatives lost the election in June 1985 and the new Liberal Premier of Ontario, David Peterson, was quoted in *The Toronto Star* for March 5, 1986, as saying that he could not support the new theatre because he was supporting a domed sports stadium. In a letter dated April 1, 1986, Lily Munro, the Ontario Minister of Citizenship and Culture refers to "many pressing demands for capital funding" and despite Premier Davis's announcement the year before regarding the donation of the land, she says that "the question of the site at Bay and Wellesley is being reviewed with the Ministry of Government Services." She did say that she would "continue to seek all possible consideration of this project." In fact, the property never was signed over to the corporation.

In November the name was changed to the Ballet/Opera House Corporation, Hal Jackman succeeded Ephraim Diamond as Chairman, and the projected opening was advanced to 1991. It was also in 1987 that Mansouri drew in Janet Stubbs who would quietly have important positions for the next few years. She was thinking of ending her singing career and Mansouri asked her to represent him on the ballet/opera house committee. She continued with the last of her musical engagements but did move to administration and worked closely on the design process and selection of the architect for the new theatre. In addition to her musical background, Stubbs was a fully qualified lawyer who had been called to the bar before she decided to be a singer.

The corporation pressed on and by June 1987 a process was set up to choose an architect. Even this did not go smoothly. For one thing, the funds of the Ballet/Opera House Corporation were exhausted, but they were shored up in December 1987 with a $950,000 grant from the Ontario government and a further $1,200,000 from the federal government in April 1988. There was also growing concern about the escalating costs, and particularly about the effect the new house would have on the operating budgets of the two companies once they moved into their new home with substantially fewer seats than the O'Keefe. The Toronto Society of Architects protested to Mansouri that an anonymous open competition should be established with adjudication by a jury of experts; and in an article in *The Globe and Mail*, (20/6/87) architecture writer Adele Freedman accused the Corporation of keeping the selection "as close and cozy as possible."

Moshe Safdie, who had leapt to international fame with his apartment-house design for Expo 67 in Montreal, was chosen as architect in March 1988. The following July, Lily Munro announced that the Government of Ontario would contribute the site at Bay and Wellesley as well as $65 million, conditional on support from the federal government. The huge site, on government land adjacent to the provincial parliament buildings, was also to include residential developments, and the sale of parcels of land by the government would provide the funds for the grant. A squabble broke out at City Hall where some politicians were fiercely opposed to the provincial gift of the land because of a complicated transfer of building densities, something that the politicians claimed was the exclusive prerogative of the city. But by then Lotfi Mansouri had resigned.

Throughout the 1980s Mansouri had continued to press ahead with the building of the company while the opera house became more and more a chimera. The 1981 season opened with *Un ballo in maschera* and *Les contes d'Hoffmann*, the latter in the fantastic designs of Gunther Schneider-Siemssen. Mariana Niculescu returned as Violetta in *La Traviata*. A radiant *Jenufa* was conducted by Mario Bernardi with Patricia Wells, Elizabeth Connell, William Neill and William Pell.

Louis Quilico added another of his famous roles to his COC list when he sang Falstaff to open the 1982 season. *Die Zauberflöte* was seen in the lush and entertaining designs of the famous illustrator of children's books, Maurice Sendak, and directed by Frank Corsaro. A frothy *La belle Hélène* lightened a wintry January in 1983, but was balanced against a sensational *Elektra* with Olivia Stapp and Maureen Forrester that was received

above left: **Un ballo in maschera (1981).**
Martina Arroyo as Amelia.

above: **Les contes d'Hoffmann (1981).**
Spalanzani (André Lortie) shows off the
doll Olympia (Carol Gutknecht) as
Hoffmann (Neil Shicoff) watches.

far left: **La Traviata (1982).**
Mariana Niculescu as Violetta with John
Brecknock as Alfredo.

left: **Jenufa (1982).**
Elizabeth Connell as Kostelnicka and
Patricia Wells (kneeling) as Jenufa.

Jenufa (1982). Eleanor James (Grandmother Buryjovka), Patricia Wells (Jenufa), William Neill (Laca).

Falstaff (1982). Louis Quilico as Falstaff.

with roars of approval. A parade of western wagons and horses on Yonge Street heralded the company's first *La fanciulla del West*. Despite the hoopla, the production was of a high order and starred Johanna Meier as Minnie. Authenticity was assured when Meier got to use her skills as a rider to arrive on horseback in the final scene. Monteverdi's early seventeenth-century masterpiece, *L'incoronazione di Poppea*, that closed the season, could well have been lost in the expanses of the O'Keefe Centre, but the production managed a balance between baroque authenticity and the demands of grand opera. With *Elektra* on January 21, 1983, the COC introduced the revolutionary idea that is its most distinctive contribution to the international opera world — Surtitles. The idea had occurred to

Die Zauberflöte (1982).
Papageno (Theodore Baerg)
eats while Tamino (Anson
Austin) plays the magic flute.

Mansouri and was taken up by John Leberg. Subtitled films had been around for years and the more recent telecasts of opera had used the same cinema technique on the television screen. Why not adapt the idea to the theatre and live performance? A much older tradition of singing an opera in the language of the audience had virtually disappeared, especially as jet aircraft enabled singers to wing around the world performing their roles in the one language in which they knew them and not re-learning them to suit individual audiences. Opera lovers everywhere had become used to hearing performances of which they understood not one word, but now Mansouri's constant search for ways to build audiences became the impetus to finding a remedy for this state of opera-going.

The specific concern was with Strauss's *Elektra* and Monteverdi's *L'incoronazione di Poppea*, both of them highly literary operas where a subtle understanding of the text was needed to understand fully the characterizations and development of the musical drama. Bruce McMullen, the company's technical director, and Leberg explored the possible technical means for projecting a running translation synchronized to the unfolding drama on stage. Sonya Friedman, who had provided the translation subtitles for the Metropolitan Opera telecasts, provided the capsulized texts. At first standard slides in three projectors were operated by a member of the musical staff. Between eight hundred and one thousand slides were required for one production and were projected onto a

photo: Robert C. Ragsdale, FRPS

La belle Hélène (1983).
A day at the beach.

right: *Elektra (1983).*
Klytemnestra (Maureen
Forrester) confronts Elektra
(Olivia Stapp).

far right: *La fanciulla del West*
(1983).
Johanna Meier as Minnie and
Giorgio Lamberti as Dick
Johnson.

photo: Robert C. Ragsdale, FRPS

photo: Robert C. Ragsdale, FRPS

L'incoronazione di Poppea
(1983).
The final scene with Carmen
Balthrop as Poppea and
Michael Myers as Nero.

photo: Robert C. Ragsdale, FRPS

screen about twenty metres by a metre and a half at the top of the proscenium above the stage. Soon a more sophisticated technique using a computer and a video projector was introduced that streamlined and simplified the basic principle. The COC licenced *Surtitles* as a trademark, but only the name: because the technique employed existing apparatus, the company could not retain rights to what was only an idea and benefit financially from them. Other companies simply used the idea with different names.

After Toronto, Artpark in upper New York State, near Niagara Falls, employed the *Elektra* surtitles, and in the fall the New York City Opera titled Massenet's *Cendrillon*. If there were a few purists who objected to the distraction of the constantly changing texts above the stage, surtitles quickly caught on with audiences who discovered the pleasure of actually being able to understand the details of the action on stage that was unfolding in a foreign language. The COC's idea so changed attitudes in the opera house that by the end of the century there were few major companies anywhere that did not title their performances.

The COC's first *Lohengrin* was a disappointment amidst high expectations. The set and the eccentric direction by Nando Schellen were more of a distraction than a fresh view of the work, and the title role was unequally shared by Siegfried Jerusalem and the over-extended Warren Ellsworth. The notable aspect was the debut in the pit of Swiss conductor Michel Tabachnik. *Turandot*, which shared the fall season with *Lohengrin*, was visually unimpressive but Martina Arroyo and Ermanno Mauro provided high-powered singing in the two principal roles.

The spring of 1984 brought the return of Joan Sutherland in the title role of *Anna Bolena* with Judith Forst as Giovanna Seymour, a brilliant pairing that provided brilliant and intense singing from both artists. Spring also brought the Canadian premiere of Benjamin Britten's last opera, *Death in Venice*. Based on Thomas Mann's celebrated novella about a writer's passionate attraction to the beautiful Polish boy, Tadzio, the opera depends to a great extent on the dramatic and vocal style of the tenor role of Aschenbach. Kenneth Riegel brought great skill and insight to his portrayal of the tragically inhibited but obsessed Aschenbach, and the enormous cast was distinguished throughout, notably Allan Monk in the varied baritone roles.

photo: Robert C. Ragsdale, FRPS

photo: Gary Beechey

photo: Gary Beechey

photo: Robert C. Ragsdale, FRPS

above: Lohengrin (1983).

Siegfried Jerusalem as Lohengrin and Nicola Fabricci as the dead Telramund.

below: Anna Bolena (1984).

Joan Sutherland in the title role with Judith Forst as Giovanna Seymour.

above: Turandot (1983).

Turandot (Martina Arroyo) poses the riddles to Calaf, the Unknown Prince (Ermanno Mauro).

below: Death in Venice (1984).

A scene at the Venetian lido, Kenneth Riegel as Aschenbach.

One of the greatest triumphs of Mansouri's regime was the production of *Die Meistersinger* in May 1985. Within the somewhat musty but still effective sets by Robert O'Hearn that were borrowed from the Metropolitan were magnificent performances by Mari Anne Häggander, William Johns, and John Reardon, crowned by the superb Hans Sachs of Siegfried Vogel, the whole under the authoritative baton of Gabor Otvös. There was an integrity to the production that resulted in performances that soared beyond the sum of its distinguished parts. Coupled with *Die Meistersinger* was the sharply contrasting *Rake's Progress* by Stravinsky, played in the famous sets that the British painter David Hockney had originally designed for the Glyndebourne opera and which subsequently were seen in other theatres.

Ambroise Thomas's *Hamlet* has seldom been performed since the nineteenth century except as a revival. It was the vehicle for Joan Sutherland's return in the fall of 1985 for her last new stage role as Ophelia, a role that includes one of the celebrated mad scenes of nineteenth-century opera. When she came back in the spring of 1987 it was for the title role in Cilea's *Adriana Lecouvreur*, like *Hamlet* an opera that is now not often seen except in revival for a great soprano.

The 1980s continued to offer varied and notable performances, among them a strong *Salome* with Stephanie Sundine; Poulenc's *Les dialogues des Carmélites* in the spring of 1986; *Macbeth* with Allan Monk and Sylvia Sass; and Mozart's relatively seldom-heard *Idomeneo* in a striking production designed by Les Levine, conducted by Leopold Hager, with a cast of Carol Vaness, Dolores Ziegler, Ruth Ann Swenson, and Siegfried Jerusalem in the title role.

Idomeneo (1987).

Idomeneo (Siegfried Jerusalem) unites Idmante (Delores Ziegler, left) and Ilia (Ruth Ann Swenson).

photo: Robert C. Ragsdale, FRPS

The company had undertaken its first large-scale concert with Renata Scotto and Carlo Bergonzi in the fall of 1978, in celebration of the two hundredth anniversary of the opening of the grandest of grand opera houses, La Scala in Milan. Another concert, also

photo: Robert C. Ragsdale, FRPS

photo: Robert C. Ragsdale, FRPS

photo: Robert C. Ragsdale, FRPS

photo: Gary Beechey

photo: Robert C. Ragsdale, FRPS

top left: **Die Meistersinger von Nürenberg** *(1985).*
Janet Stubbs (Magdalena), James Atherton (David), Mari Anne Häggander
(Eva), William Johns (Walther), and Siegfried Vogel (Hans Sachs).

top right: **Die Meistersinger von Nürenberg** *(1985).*
The final scene. Walther (William Johns) sings the Prize Song to win Eva
(Mari Anne Häggander).

left: **The Rake's Progress** *(1985).*
Tom Rakewell (John Stewart) tries the "fantastic baroque" bread machine
as Nick Shadow (Allan Monk) watches. Designs by David Hockney.

above: **Hamlet** *(1985).*
Joan Sutherland (Ophélie) with Gaétan Laperrière (standing, as Horatio)
and John Brocheler (Hamlet).

below: **Adriana Lecouvreur (1987).** Joan Sutherland as Adriana with Gary Relyea as the Prince de Bouillon.

right: **Salome (1986).** Stephanie Sundine as Salome, Phil Stark as Herod.

bottom: **Les dialogues des Carmélites (1986).** Carol Vaness (at right) as Mme. Lidoine and Janet Stubbs (third from right) as Mother Marie.

below right: **Macbeth (1986).** Allan Monk in the title role with Sylvia Sass as Lady Macbeth.

photo: Gary Beechey

photo: Robert C. Ragsdale, FRPS

photo: Gary Beechey

photo: Robert C. Ragsdale, FRPS

Lady Macbeth of Mtsensk

(1988).

Mary Jane Johnson as Katerina

Ismailova and Michael Myers

as Sergey.

Lady Macbeth of Mtsensk

(1988).

Ben Heppner as Zinovy

Ismailov and Cornelis

Opthof as Boris Ismailov.

photos: Robert C. Ragsdale, FRPS

at O'Keefe, featured Birgit Nilsson in October 1979. The great soprano had been absent from North America because of tax problems and this concert marked her return. The Toronto Symphony Orchestra had presented Luciano Pavarotti in a benefit concert at Maple Leaf Gardens in 1985 and the COC now took a leaf from the TSO book and announced a concert, also at the Gardens, by Placido Domingo for January 1986. Unfortunately, Domingo missed his plane that was to have brought him from Europe and the concert had to be cancelled. It was rescheduled for March 1, 1987, when 17,500 people attended. A dinner followed at the Tanenbaum Opera Centre to celebrate Mansouri's ten years with the company.

The 1987–88 season included another of the unconventional repertoire choices that proved a great success. Shostakovich's *Lady Macbeth of Mtsensk* had had extraordinary success after its premiere in Leningrad in 1934. Its earthy and violent drama and powerful musical style assured its performances throughout the world. But Stalin saw it in 1936 and the decadence and distorted realism of the work made it a pawn in the Soviet attack on the arts. The opera disappeared from sight. In the 1960s a much revised version appeared, called *Katerina Izmaylova*, but it was not until the 1970s that Shostakovich's original opera was again available. It was this authentic version that was so powerfully produced at the COC in January 1988.

On the Sunday morning of the last performance of *Lady Macbeth* Michael Myers, the Sergey of the production, awoke to discover he had lost his voice and could not sing that afternoon. The suddenly voiceless singer is the dread of opera companies everywhere. In some cases it might lead to cancellation but in its first fifty years the COC has never cancelled. William Lewis, who had been singing Danilo in *The Merry Widow*, was intercepted just as he was about to

photo: Robert C. Ragsdale, FRPS

photo: Michael Cooper

Ariadne auf Naxos (1988).
Left to right: Guillermo Silva-
Marin (Scaramuccio), Theodore
Baerg (Arlecchino), Tracy Dahl
(Zerbinetta), Christopher
Cameron (Truffaldino) and
Dennis Giesbrecht (Brighella).

Jan Rubes as Majordomo in
Ariadne auf Naxos (1988).

leave Toronto and pressed into service. Lewis saved the Sunday matinee performance by singing from the side while Myers acted the role.

In the spring, a visually rich *Ariadne auf Naxos* in 1988 was matched vocally by Judith Forst, Elizabeth Connell, and William Johns. Not least of the distinctions of the *Ariadne* production was the appearance as the Majordomo of Jan Rubes in his last role with the company of which he had been a founding member in 1950.

In March 1986 the music office of the Canada Council proposed a special grant to the COC to produce a piece as part of the "Year of Canadian Music." Mansouri was already thinking about ways to stimulate composers to think along operatic lines, but in this case there was not time to turn to an inexperienced composer or to commission a major new work. John Leberg was familiar with *Patria II*, a part of an extensive cycle of musical/theatrical works by R. Murray Schafer and was curious about the first part, which had not been performed. The decision was made to take advantage of the Canada Council's interest and to produce *Patria I: The Characteristics Man* at the Tanenbaum Opera Centre. Substantial grants were obtained from the Canada Council, the Ontario Arts Council,

Patria I (1987)

at the Texaco Opera Theatre,
the chorus in tiers above the
orchestra, Robert Aiken,
conductor. Some of the
television screens that figured
prominently are visible.

photo: David Cooper

and the Maclean-Hunter Foundation. Robert Aitken would conduct and the director was to be Christopher Newton, artistic director of the Shaw Festival at Niagara-on-the-Lake, Ontario.

Almost at once differences developed — mostly animosities among the composer, director, and designers — that led to probably the most strained production in the COC's history. The COC kept its problems out of the public eye, but Schafer published his dissatisfaction with the presentation of *Patria I* in the *Journal of Canadian Studies* (1988). He complained that early in the discussions he had not qualified his conditions for the production of his work with the result that he was effectively cut out of the production development, that his suggestions were ignored by the COC, and that in the end he disapproved of virtually every aspect of the venture. He attended none of the performances. For its part, the COC found the composer dictatorial and indifferent by turns, and Newton, who persevered to produce the final show, privately expressed his dismay at conditions that he found sometimes appalling, sometimes insulting. Nevertheless, the six performances of this new and difficult work in the three-hundred-seat Texaco Opera Theatre were sold out, but the critical reception was mixed. The headline for Robert Everett-Green's review summed it up in *The Globe and Mail* (23/11/87): "Undisciplined script detracts from *Patria's* superb music." In Everett-Green's view, Schafer's "accomplished music-writing" was "layered in with the scatter-gun vagaries of an inept script." The script was also Schafer's.

Patria I (1987)

photo: David Cooper

The *Patria I* exercise did focus the problem of the relationship of the company to new works. The cold statistic that could not be ignored was that the production cost an average of about $222 per seat when total budget was averaged by total attendance. By comparison, a million-dollar production played to an 80 percent house for six performances at O'Keefe would cost about sixty-five dollars. The COC's experience with the commissioning of new works had been limited to *Louis Riel* and *The Luck of Ginger Coffey* for the centennial celebrations in 1967, and *Héloise and Abélard* in 1973; and to more modest pieces for use in the schools, *The Spirit of Fundy* in 1972, and *The Glove* in 1975. New works would always be expensive and for the most part they would likely attract smaller audiences than could be justified by an O'Keefe production.

The solution was to make long-term plans for major new works, and to develop a program that would generate a number of smaller works in which composers could explore the special demands of the musical theatre. With the financial assistance of TransCanada Pipelines, a composer-in-residence program was set up in 1987 for young composers and librettists who would work with established professionals in the field to develop the particular skills required to write for the theatre. Three composers were chosen for the first year, and the result was the performance of three new works in May 1988 at the Texaco Opera Theatre: *Réalitillusion* by Michel-Georges Brégent; *Zoé* by Richard Désilets; and *Dream Play* by Timothy Sullivan.

Although not a part of the new composer-in-residence program, a newly commissioned opera for children was premiered in 1987. *Rose is a Rose* was written and composed by the popular folk and blues singer, Ann Mortifee. As it turned out, the text proved too complicated for young children, and the vocal writing did not take into account the techniques and ranges of the classically trained singers of the Ensemble, who performed it. If the decision to engage a pop artist in such a project was adventurous, the results proved less than were hoped for.

Broadcasting also expanded notably in the 1980s. COC productions had been seen irregularly on CBC television since the broadcast in 1978 of *Joan of Arc* from Ottawa. Subsequent CBC-TV transmissions — all of them produced by Norman Campbell and all from the O'Keefe Centre — were *Norma* (with Sutherland and Troyanos) (1981), *Anna Bolena* (with Sutherland and Forst) (1984), *The Rake's Progress* (1986), *Les dialogues des Carmélites* (1987), *La forza del destino* and *Don Giovanni* (1988), *Tosca, The Makropulos Case*, and *La Bohème* (1989).

Around 1981 discussions were held between the COC and the CBC about ways in which to add COC productions to radio programming. One of the chief problems had to do with the extra payments that must be made to performers when a performance is broadcast. The CBC had standing agreements with the unions that required them to pay performance fees that made the costs of the COC productions impossibly high. However, the COC could negotiate directly with its own orchestra and singers, and a system was worked out whereby the CBC provided broadcasting services but the COC would negotiate and own all broadcast rights. In the United States, the Texaco company was the sponsor of the Metropolitan Opera broadcasts and Texaco Canada agreed to a similar sponsorship for the COC, where six Toronto performances would be taped during performance in one season and broadcast the following fall before the Metropolitan transmissions began. The broadcasts began on the CBC network in Canada in 1983 and in 1984 and 1985 they were also heard in the United

photo: Robert C. Ragsdale, FRPS

Don Giovanni (1988).
Don Giovanni (Gino Quilico)
toasts the arrival of the masked
guests, received by Leporello
(Louis Quilico).

States on some two hundred stations of the National Public Radio Network.

Broadcasting on both television and radio and the activities of the Ensemble enhanced the reputation of the company in Toronto, across the country, and throughout North America. The evidence of success could be measured in the steady growth of the number of subscribers along with the expansion of the season. In 1979–80, the first season spread over the year, there were 11,323 subscribers and thirty-five performances. By 1989–90 the number of performances at O'Keefe Centre had grown to fifty-three and the number of subscribers to 19,190. In addition, there were the performances at the Tanenbaum Opera Centre. The only thing lacking was an opera house.

In the fall of 1988 Mansouri announced that he had accepted the post as director of the San Francisco Opera Company and that he would leave Toronto at the end of December. Speculation was rife over whether he would have stayed on if the new opera house had been built, but all Mansouri would say was that he had done everything he could in Toronto and that it was best for him and for the COC if he moved on. In any case, how could he have turned down an invitation to lead one of the three major opera companies in the USA after the Metropolitan and the one, moreover, that would bring his career full circle: he would be head of the company where, as a youthful super, he had been first bitten by the opera bug. He inherited from Torel a high standard of performance and a secure foundation on which to build. By the time he left, Mansouri had a company that owned its own scene-shop, administrative offices, rehearsal rooms, and studios, and a small opera theatre. He had understood the necessity to de-mystify opera and worked aggressively to draw in new audiences, to which end he developed the Harbourfront activities, the extended school performances, and a range of works from *The Merry Widow* to *Lulu*. The Ensemble program was firmly established with a remarkable series of successful singers among its ranks. The popular repertoire had been the core of the productions, but in addition there had been major works of the twentieth century that were less often seen. There had always been judicious balance between standard works and more adventurous choices, although the productions themselves were always fundamentally traditional. Mansouri himself had directed forty-four main-stage productions (including four revivals) as well as productions for tours and the summer festivals. He was always thoroughly professional and totally involved in anything that he did but it was the unusual works — mainly modern — that most fired his imagination and stimulated his best work. Freed from the routine of familiar repertoire, he discovered a range of expression that he delivered with moving impact in such operas as *Death in Venice* and *Jenufa*. Overall, Mansouri had wisely invested his inheritance from Torel to build a major enterprise.

Chapter 7

THE DICKIE ERA

The search committee, secure in the understanding that it was looking for a head for a company of international standards and one that must continue to grow, advertised widely both in Canada and abroad. The committee sought advice from members of the musical community both in Toronto and outside the city, and from staff members and singers with the company. One of the primary decisions that had to be made was whether the new head would be another stage director, as Torel and Mansouri had been, or a musician, or whether the company should now have at its head someone who was not personally involved in production but who would oversee the artistic and business aspects of the company as a general administrator. The model of the general administrator with overall responsibilities was accepted, and from about sixty-five candidates and nine interviews, the vote went to Brian Dickie.

Brian Dickie went from his university days at Trinity College, Dublin, directly to work for the celebrated Glyndebourne Opera Festival in 1962. He was also director of the Wexford Festival in Ireland during 1967–73, a festival noted for its productions of

unusual repertoire, and advisor to the Théâtre musical de Paris, 1973–81. But it was at Glyndebourne where he made his mark and rose through the administration to become the general administrator in 1981. There he was soon credited with strengthening the already distinguished musical standards of the festival and with bringing adventurous stagings to the theatre. After more than twenty-five years at Glyndebourne it seemed time to make a move, and the idea of a move to Toronto seemed to be the right one at the right time. As it turned out, the results were mixed for both the COC and for Dickie.

Brian Dickie took up the post of general director in January 1989. At once he observed that not a single major Canadian director had been engaged at the COC by Mansouri. Although all the heads of the COC since Torel have been criticized at one time or another for not sufficiently promoting Canadians, Dickie's personal view was that a country's performing arts organizations are in the end defined by contributions made by the residents of that country, but that the dramatic standards should be the highest whatever the origins of the director. He immediately set about finding directors in Canada and elsewhere who would bring original perspectives to the opera. His policy was to choose directors and allow them free rein in what they did, but the trick was to match the director with the work.

There were some striking successes: Robin Phillips, Robert Carsen, Richard Monette, Robert Lepage, and Brian Macdonald from Canada; Nicholas Muni and Nicholas Lehnhoff from abroad. A corollary to this was the need for sets and costumes to match the original ideas of the directors. Dickie especially disliked the habit of recycling parts of sets into new sets in order to save money, something that Skalicki had been especially good at for Mansouri. If Mansouri had brought to Toronto the designs of such impressive international figures as Schneider-Siemssen, Sendak, Bjornson, Maximowa, and Hockney, they had all been borrowed and arguably had little to do with the Canadian theatre scene. To change all this, of course, would cost money. Mansouri had in fact saved the company a great deal of money by directing so many operas himself. (His contract had left the decision to him how many productions he would direct, but with the stipulation that he would receive no additional remuneration for his directorial work with the company.) Now the company was faced with the full costs of a director for every pro-

Brian Dickie

photo: Michael Cooper

The Makropulos Case (1989).

Stephanie Sundine as Emilia Marty and Richard
Margison as Vitek.

photo: Robert C. Ragsdale, FRPS

Andrea Chénier (1989).

Aprile Millo as Maddalena and Ermanno
Mauro as Chénier.

duction, usually with new sets. If this resulted in some striking productions, it
also resulted in some striking costs. Mansouri knew how to do things on a
shoestring, but Dickie's view was conditioned first by artistic demands and
only second by costs. Almost immediately things began to go wrong. The
years in the genteel and privately financed world of Glyndebourne provided no
training for the rough marketplace of opera in Canada, where vast sums of
money had to be raised each year and where subsidies from governments provided a crucially important but relatively small part of the budget.

When Dickie took up office in January 1989, the season planned by
Mansouri was still in progress, distinguished particularly by Janacek's
Makropulos Affair, sung in Czech and coached by one of the greatest inter-
preters of the role of Emilia Marty, Elisabeth Söderström. Aprile Millo and
Ermanno Mauro starred in a traditional but stirring *Andrea Chénier*. The
Ensemble presented an imaginative version of Monteverdi's *Il ritorno d'Ulisse
in patria* at the Texaco Opera Theatre in the Tanenbaum Opera Centre. The
choice of the Monteverdi opera would open the way to a series of early operas

that served the needs of the Ensemble especially well — large casts, relatively modest instrumental requirements, dramatic demands, vocally rewarding.

Mansouri returned in the 1989–90 season to direct a moving new *Wozzeck* with aus-tere and imposing sets by Michael Levine, with Judith Forst and Allan Monk. *Der Rosenkavalier*, in the spring of 1990 brought honour to no one. It was acceptably sung by Josephine Barstow and Dolores Ziegler as the Marschallin and Octavian, with veteran conductor Julius Rudel, but they were weighed down by unfortunate sets and direction.

The program for young composers and librettists that Mansouri had initiated in 1987–88 extended into the first months of Dickie's management when again three one-act operas were given in May 1989: *An Expensive Embarrassment* by Denis Gougeon, *The Unbelieveable Glory of Mr. Sharp* by Andrew MacDonald, and *Dulcitius: Demise of Innocence* by Peter Paul Koprowski. In 1990–91 there was a single resident composer, John Oliver of

photo: Michael Cooper

Il ritorno d'Ulisse in patria (1989). Ensemble production at the Texaco Opera Theatre.

Vancouver, who was commissioned to write a full-length work. The COC in collabora-tion with the Banff Centre presented his opera *Guacamayo's Old Song and Dance* in the spring of 1991 at the newly renamed Imperial Oil Opera Theatre. The young Winnipeg composer Randolph Peters followed Oliver as composer-in-residence for 1991–93, dur-ing which time he composed *Nosferatu* with a text by Marilyn Gronsdal Powell based on a story by Thom Sokoloski. The opera was premiered in December 1993 to full houses at the du Maurier Theatre Centre, and considerable critical notice, a harbinger of a more celebrated commission that was to come to Peters with *The Golden Ass*.

The beginning of the fall season in 1991 marked the beginning of Dickie's effective control of the repertoire. *Eugene Onegin*, with Carol Vaness and Sergei Leiferkus, led off the season in a production directed by John Copley. The conductor was Richard Bradshaw, who had been brought from San Francisco in 1989 to be the chief conductor.

top left: **Wozzeck (1990).**
Allan Monk as Wozzeck and
Stuart Kale as the Captain.

top right: **Guacamayo's Old
Song and Dance at the
Imperial Oil Theatre (1991).**
Gary Rideout as Guacamayo
and Valerie Gonzalez as
Hunahpu.

bottom left: **Nosferatu at the
du Maurier Theatre Centre
(1993).**
Sally Dibblee (Camilla) and
Marcia Swanston (Nzbana).

bottom right: **Eugene Onegin
(1990).**
Sergei Leiferkus (Onegin) and
Carol Vaness (Tatyana).

photo: Robert C. Ragsdale, FRPS

photo: Michael Cooper

photo: Michael Cooper

photo: Robert C. Ragsdale, FRPS

photo: Michael Cooper

photo: Michael Cooper

Dickie also engaged the veteran British director, Anthony Besch, to freshen up *Die Fledermaus*. Besch was an older alumnus of Glyndebourne and had been briefly stage director of the opera school at the University of Toronto (1968–69), but he had never directed at the COC. The spring production included a striking new *Lulu*, starring Rebecca Caine, with Victor Braun as Dr. Schön. Caine, a Canadian, had made her reputation in the London production of *Phantom of the Opera*, and now made what was to many a surprising but brilliant transition to one of the most demanding roles in opera. The director was Nicholas Muni, who would bring further imaginative productions to the company.

In the spring of 1991 the company marked the two hundredth anniversary of the death of Mozart with three distinguished productions. Nicholas Lehnhoff was one of the

above left: *Lulu (1991).*
Rebecca Caine as Lulu, with
Victor Braun (Dr. Schön, standing) and Barry McCauley
(Alwa).

above right: ***Così fan tutte***
(1991).
Joanne Kolomyjec (Fiordiligi)
and Anthony Michaels-Moore
(Guglielmo) on the stairs, with
Richard Croft (Ferrando) and
Louise Winter (Dorabella).

left: ***La clemenza di Tito***
(1991).
Richard Margison as Tito, with
Susan Quittmeyer (Sextus) and
Donna Brown (Servilia).

photo: Robert C. Ragsdale, FRPS

most notable of operatic directors and more than fulfilled Dickie's desire to introduce important directors to the COC stage. His production of *Così fan tutte* shared the Mozart season with *Le nozze di Figaro* and *La clemenza di Tito*. Despite Lehnhoff's presence, in some ways it was *Tito*, Mozart's last opera, that stole attention, partly because of the young American director, Stephen Wadsworth, and the conductor, Leopold Hager, and partly because of the brilliant cast that included Jean Stilwell, Donna Brown, Susan Quittmeyer, Margaret Marshall, and Richard Margison as Tito.

The Elgin Theatre after its restoration.

photo: Courtesy of the Ontario Heritage Foundation, photographer: Hill Peppard

The Mozart operas were all given in the Elgin Theatre, which had reopened in December 1989 after lavish renovations. The theatre had been built in 1913 as an elegant Lowe's vaudeville house. It had declined to a seedy movie theatre when the Government of Ontario bought the property in 1981 and restored it to its original elegance with greatly improved stage and audience facilities. This was during the heady days of a burgeoning commercial theatre business in Toronto and it seemed both historically apposite and a sound business investment that the provincial government should undertake such a venture. The building, in fact, contained two theatres — a Winter Garden on the top floors, designed to look like an enormous forested bower, complete with real leaves; and a traditional theatre on the lower floors with boxes, a grand proscenium, lavish decoration, and much gilt and *faux* marble. The beautifully restored, 1,550-seat Elgin, as the large theatre was called, would figure prominently in Dickie's plans for the COC.

The 1991–92 season brought new directors from within the Canadian theatre community. The season opened with *Fidelio* with Helena Does in the title role, conducted by Bernardi, and directed by the well-known actor, director, and head of the Stratford Festival, Richard Monette. A new production of *La Traviata* starred Nancy Gustafson in the role of Violetta in a somewhat eccentric modernist production directed by Brian Macdonald. Macdonald had been a notable choreographer before he had equal success in directing musical theatre and opera. In January Bernard Uzon, director of the Opéra de Montréal, directed Gounod's *Roméo et Juliette*. Britten's *Albert Herring* was given a humorous and stylish production at the Elgin. As with *Lady Macbeth* a few years previously, events conspired around *La Bohème* in January and February to test the company's resourcefulness. Keith Olsen, who was singing Rodolfo, was not well and after three performances he had to abandon the role to the understudy J. Hunter Morris. Olsen felt better enough to resume the part in the fifth performance only to have to bow out after the first act, leaving Morris to complete the performance. Finally, Richard Margison stepped in and sang brilliantly for the remaining four performances. To complicate matters further, Gianna Rolandi, Musetta in the production, was indisposed at the second performance and was hastily replaced by Catherine Janus.

Memory of the winter misfortunes of *La Bohème* faded with the coming of spring. To close the season in May, Robert Carsen directed the premiere of Harry Somers' *Mario and the Magician*. *Mario* had been commissioned by Mansouri and Leberg in 1988. The first intention had been to give the new opera at the Texaco Opera Theatre, but that idea was changed in favour of a main-stage production at the Elgin. It fell to Dickie to see the work through to performance, and it was he who brought director Robert Carsen and designer Michael Levine into the creative team while the opera was being written. Librettist Rod Anderson (the same Rodney Anderson who had played such important roles on the board of the COC) fashioned an effectively theatrical drama out of Thomas Mann's 1928 novella about the rise of fascism in an Italian vacation town. To this, his seventh opera, Somers brought the full measure of his long experience in the theatre and as composer of some of the most important music composed in Canada.

Mann's story had been eerily predictive. By 1929 the Fascist movement under Mussolini was firmly in control of Italy, a control that played on nostalgia and intense xenophobic nationalism that at the time included strong anti-German sentiment. The brooding and repressive atmosphere of the story reaches a climax when the magician, Cipolla, who represents the manipulative fascists, grotesquely seduces the young waiter,

photo: Mark Spiteri

Albert Herring (1991). Sid (Gerald Finley) teases Albert (Craig Ashton).

*top: Mario and the Magician
(1992).*
Stefan (Theodore Baerg) strolls
among the Italians, while a portrait of Mussolini looks on.

*bottom: Mario and the Magician
(1992).*
Cipolla (David Rampy) begins the
humiliation of Mario (Benoit
Boutet).

Mario, in front of an audience. The young man, horrified at his shame, kills Cipolla. In directing the opera, Robert Carsen accepted the unavoidable fact that a modern audience knew too well the consequences of fascism and incorporated references that made specific what was only anticipated in Mann's novella. Michael Levine continued his brilliant work for the COC that had begun with *Idomeneo* and *Wozzeck* with a bleak set that was wonderfully adaptable in Carsen's hands. *Mario and the Magician* brought an ambitious season to a striking conclusion.

Important as he saw the visual realization of an opera, Dickie considered the music to be fundamental; raising the musical standards was a priority. The company had never had an official music director, although Mansouri had flirted with the possibility and in the early days Goldschmidt had been in effect just that. One of Dickie's first appointments was Richard Bradshaw, who had been charged with the specific responsibility of strength-ening the orchestra. Bradshaw was born in England, was trained there, and worked for a time at Glyndebourne where he and Dickie became friends. In 1977 Bradshaw went to the San Francisco Opera as resident conductor and remained there until Dickie invited him to Toronto in 1989.

Bradshaw had already been a guest at the COC for *The Merry Widow* and for *Tosca*. He liked the city, the company, and especially the promise of a new opera house. It had been a strategic decision by Mansouri not to put great emphasis on orchestra development, partly because of an inclination always towards the stage rather than to the pit, partly because the inadequate acoustics of the O'Keefe Centre would, in his view, obviate any improvements in the actual quality of the instrumentalists. Nevertheless, a master agreement with the musicians' union in 1985 had already established a regular orchestra; now Bradshaw's job would be to enhance the qual-ity of the ensemble and ensure its stability. There was no shortage of good players but to guarantee that they would

photo: Michael Cooper

photo: Michael Cooper

stay in Toronto and stay with the opera, they needed more than just a contract.

The plan was to develop concerts outside O'Keefe where the orchestra could hear themselves better than in the pit and where automatically there would be a demand for a higher level of performance that would in turn provide greater satisfaction for the musicians. Concerts, and recordings, would not only enhance the quality of the playing; such events would help fill in the gaps between the periods of opera performance. A regular series of concerts and concert performances of operas varied the fare offered by the COC and would eventually give players and audiences the experience of hearing them in the superb George Weston Recital Hall of the Ford Centre. In 1997 there was an ensemble of fifty-four players, not enough to play some of the bigger works but enough for much of the repertoire and more than enough to provide the consistent solid core to which extra players might be added as needed.

There were significant administrative changes. John Leberg resigned in the fall of 1988 and joined Mansouri in San Francisco. Dory Vanderhoof had substantial differences with Dickie and he left in February 1989. Margaret Genovese followed in April 1989. Philip Boswell stayed on for a time but left in the summer of 1992. Janet Stubbs had been appointed Director of Music Administration in the spring of 1989 but left in October 1991. Felicity Jackson, whom Dickie knew from Glyndebourne, was appointed in Boswell's place, but no new group was created with the collective association of the old Mansouri team that was now gone.

Subscriptions began to fall disastrously. They had reached a peak of 19,190 in the 1989–90 season for seven operas but then began to decline to 12,738 in 1993–94 and to 9,283 in 1994–95 for a season of six operas, the lowest number of subscribers since 1970. An analysis of the seasons from 1990–91 to 1994–95 charted a decline in annual attendance of almost fifty thousand patrons. Several factors probably contributed to the change. Economically, things had been very good up to about 1990, after which recession set in and governments made much of the necessity to eliminate deficit budgets, conditions that encouraged a pessimistic view in many quarters as people found taxes rising, wages frozen, and services declining. This was also the period in which the federal government introduced a new tax, the GST, that contributed to a noticeable increase in ticket prices.

Probably there had also been too many changes in performance and subscription poli-cies. Dickie wanted to expand the company to a point that would make the leap to the new theatre logical. Fifty-three performances of seven operas in 1989–90 increased to sixty-six performances of nine operas in the following season. An abrupt return to fifty perfor-mances of six operas in 1993–94 was too late to stem the subscriber loss and probably con-tributed further to subscriber confusion. Performances were given in two theatres — the O'Keefe and the Elgin — which added to the changing patterns of pricing and assignment of seating; in 1993–94, four of the six operas were given at the newly rebuilt Elgin theatre. A prime rule in nourishing subscription is to avoid making too many changes too quickly that will introduce confusion into subscribers' decisions to renew. Furthermore, in some indefinable way, the public seemed to be losing confidence in the COC.

There had been a particularly bad gamble on *Carmen* in the fall of 1993. When the opera had been given in 1989–90 there were ten performances that attracted attendance of slightly more that 97 percent capacity. Dickie decided to move the company away from total dependence on subscriptions and to emulate the big musicals that were then having spectacular success in the city. Accordingly, thirteen non-subscription performances of *Carmen* were given in the expectation that the remounting of the earlier production would meet with a repeat of its success. Unfortunately, the public did not flock to see a second time what it had seen a few years before; *Carmen* attracted slightly under 60 per-cent attendance.

The Elgin Theatre was a key in Dickie's strategy to bring the company into the new opera house. It was essential that production expand during the period preceding the move into the new house, something that was impossible within the confines of the arrangement with the O'Keefe Centre. There were limitations in the size of the stage and the orchestra pit, but the Elgin was adequate nonetheless for a substantial part of the opera repertoire, and Dickie would have some splendid successes there. But the Elgin, like the opera house, became a victim of the recession. It had been rebuilt to serve as a serious house for transfers of good work of whatever kind from smaller theatres, but it quickly became apparent that the costs of sustaining such a theatre were greater than anticipated. A quick-fix solution was to rent the Elgin for long-term attractions from the popular commercial theatre. In the long-run this was not a solution, but the policy had the effect of evicting the COC with its periodic short-term bookings. The Elgin proved to be a sub-plot in the unravelling theatre saga.

When Brian Dickie took over the company, the ballet/opera house was still in development stages, but the site had been secured at Bay and Wellesley Streets, provincial funding had been promised, and the design team continued to examine theatres in Europe and in the United States. An architectural model was unveiled in June 1989 for a spectacular building that was scheduled to open in 1994. It was to stretch almost the entire block from Bay Street to Yonge Street, and included, in addition to a five-tiered, two-thousand-seat horseshoe auditorium, two side stages and two rear stages beyond the main stage, separate rehearsal rooms for both ballet and opera, storage space, offices, and impressive foyers. It was designed by Moshe Safdie to be one of the most spectacular theatres in the world. In November 1989 the federal government made a grant of $4.5 million to complete the planning and design of the new theatre. The project had become

photo: Steve Rosenthal

The model for the proposed ballet/opera house in 1989.

enormous and very costly at $230 million, without even considering the operational costs of such a building. In part this was because the building was to provide not merely a theatre but offices, costume and prop-shops, and rehearsal space, things that the opera had but which the ballet badly needed. If the ballet's needs were legitimate, they nonetheless fuelled a competition of egos between the two companies. In retrospect it seems clear that the theatre was a building for the 1980s but that it was greatly over-extended in the economic chill of the 1990s. It had also bogged down in endless studies and planning that used up money and time, and produced ever more grandiose versions. Then unexpectedly, the provincial government changed again.

At the fall election in 1990, the Liberals were defeated and the New Democratic Party formed the government with Bob Rae as premier. Soon after he took office, Rae called a meeting of representatives of the Ballet/Opera House Corporation and made clear to them that there were grave financial problems that he had to face. The Art Gallery of Ontario was in serious difficulty and it was apparent that the new domed stadium was going to cost the province a great deal of money. There appeared to be opposition to the theatre project within his government, and Rae saw the ballet/opera house as being far too big and far too expensive both to build and to maintain — the overall budget was now about $300 million. But Rae was personally supportive of the project and he made clear that he did not want it to fail; he asked that the project be scaled back and that a reduced scheme be negotiated. By this time plans were far advanced, with construction virtually about to begin. Discussion was divided, but the prevailing opinion was to refuse to consider an extensive re-working of the plans at this point. The view was that a magnificent building had been designed, that much money and time had gone into it already, and that to alter the project now would be a betrayal. With no reduction in the building plan, Rae announced on November 9, 1990, that the government was cancelling its financial commitment, although the promise of the land would be retained while the Ballet/Opera House Corporation sought other ways to finance construction. In fact, the operations of the corporation were now effectively terminated.

Two years later, in November 1992, the government also withdrew its commitment to provide the land with the announcement that it would be used for "affordable housing." The property had never actually been signed over to the Ballet/Opera House Corporation, although there was often the impression that it had been. The financing from government sources had always been a house of cards, and with the withdrawal of the Ontario government, the funding from federal and city sources also collapsed. The National Ballet turned to developing its own rehearsal and support facilities similar to those already enjoyed by the opera at the Tanenbaum Centre, and despite various proposals for a smaller building — and even renewed discussion about the renovation of O'Keefe Centre by the city — the Ballet/Opera House Corporation distributed its few remaining assets to the COC and NBC in July 1993, and went out of business. The site at Wellesley and Bay would be developed privately as condominiums to be called, ironically, "Opera Place," with future tenants left to wonder at the inappropriateness of the name. For many, the residential development would be a monument to what would have been one of Toronto's most distinctive and impressive buildings, a structure of international significance.

In parallel to the saga of the ballet/opera house was the story of the much-vaunted SkyDome, in which the Ontario government was deeply involved and which affected the demise of the ballet/opera house project. The stadium's financial failures led to Premier Rae's desire to remove the province from its part in the finances of the building. In 1994, the stadium was sold for $151 million, by which time its debts had risen to $358 million. The Ontario government had contributed $30 million to the original cost. The government kept $125 million from the sale, leaving a bill of $263 million as the government's effective contribution to the SkyDome debacle, more than enough to build an opera house. (Peter Foster, "The Money Pit," *Toronto Life*, 33/9 (June 1999), p. 89) It is not surprising that the cost of the stadium to provincial coffers coloured the Premier's view of the ballet/opera house.

Through the optimism about the new theatre and then through the crushing disappointment of its cancellation, the company continued to develop. The Ensemble had been seen by Mansouri largely as a training unit with at best incidental connection to the mainstage productions. Dickie was not happy with the idea that the COC should be in the training business at all and thought of the "ensemble" as being the core part of the company that performed regularly and often in the main productions. At one point he explored the possibility of re-joining the training part of the Ensemble to the opera division at the University of Toronto in something like a return to the arrangement at the beginning of the histories of both the school and the company, but nothing came of that for complex reasons on both sides. At the very least, he wanted a smaller ensemble that was not necessarily a source for casting small roles in main productions. He did develop the idea that it was important for young singers to understudy principal roles, although even here he did not confine such engagements to members of what was now called the Ensemble Studio. To provide some opportunity for the artistic growth of young singers, a recital series was inaugurated in 1990–91 to present members in song repertoire, not from opera, but this lasted only a few seasons.

The production of Monteverdi's *Il ritorno d'Ulisse in patria* that had been given by the Ensemble in Toronto in February and March 1989 provided the point of departure for a new touring initiative by Dickie. He turned to Monteverdi's *L'incoronazione di Poppea* for touring in the fall of 1990. Like *Ulisse*, *Poppea* was a masterpiece by a great composer, rewarding for the singers, but relatively modest in its instrumental requirements. The production was of a high standard with fine singers mostly from the current or recent Ensemble program, conducted by Daniel Beckwith and directed by Stephen Wadsworth. It was given in Toronto and in six other cities in Ontario but its reception did not match its artistic standard. Dickie's view was that the earlier policy of touring only operas from the most popular repertoire was limiting to both the company and to the audiences in smaller centres, and that a community should have a performance as carefully prepared and with the same quality as a Toronto performance, something that was impossible if only the big popular operas were to be done in scaled-down versions suitable for travelling. But the fact was, those smaller centres had come to look forward to that repertoire, and the sudden shift to the esoteric, even if carefully prepared, qualities of *Poppea* was unexpected and audiences and sponsors withdrew. Publicity had billed the opera as "Steamy *Poppea*" with "parallels with modern politics, big business and sex scandals," but Urjo Kareda found the Toronto performances badly wanting in passion and urgency (*The*

Globe and Mail, 29/10/90) and although a few critics had good things to say about the tour, too many found the piece boring and frustrating.

In any case, touring was not nearly the viable enterprise it had been when the company first undertook tours in 1958. The touring productions had often had to manage in unsatisfactory theatres in small centres, and with the growth of major companies in most of the principal Canadian cities, and the easy transportation along good roads in modern automobiles, grand opera was within reach of most of the thinly spread Canadian population. The COC had done its job of fostering opera across the country. Now with escalating costs, it was time to abandon touring.

If touring had brought the COC literally into communities throughout most of Canada, the radio broadcasts that had begun on the CBC national network in 1983 brought the company to listeners across the country for six weeks each fall. These broadcasts depended on the sponsorship of Texaco Canada, but Texaco and Texaco Canada underwent financial and corporate changes (Texaco Canada was sold to Imperial Oil) that brought about the end of sponsorship of the broadcasts at the same time that the COC orchestra demanded a considerable increase in the broadcast fee. Attempts to find a new sponsor failed, mainly because potential sponsors wanted more exposure than the discreet acknowledgement that had satisfied Texaco Canada, and a greater advertising component on radio was against CBC policy. Although Dickie held to the personal view that the CBC as a public broadcaster had a responsibility to carry such programs as the COC productions, he worked with Harold Redekopp at the CBC to find a solution, but without success. The costs of meeting the orchestra demands made the broadcasts prohibitive for both the CBC and the COC, and the series was cancelled in 1993. Henceforth, only an occasional COC production would be heard in a series on the CBC that presented various companies from Canada and abroad.

The 1992–93 Toronto season led off with a controversial production of *Rigoletto*. George Tsypin designed a setting of large surfaces in primary colours that provided changeable playing spaces but that had nothing to do with the ornate renaissance palaces and murky streets that usually serve the opera. It was not enough that Rigoletto be deformed; Nicholas Muni put him into a kind of wheelchair that he propelled about the stage with his feet. Brent Ellis was the jester. He not only managed the chair, but realized perfectly Muni's concept of Rigoletto as confined by his physical condition, repressed by the moral contagion of the court, and dominated by his love for Gilda. Scenically, it was the most radical departure the COC had made in the presentation of a standard work of the repertoire.

The other great event of the 1992–93 season was the double-bill in January of Bartok's *Bluebeard's Castle* and Schoenberg's *Erwartung*. The director was the celebrated Robert Lepage from Quebec, whose theatrical works had won him international praise

photo: Michael Cooper

photo: Michael Cooper

above left: Rigoletto (1992). Brent Ellis as Rigoletto and Jorge Lopez-Yanez as the Duke of Mantua.

above right: Rigoletto (1992). The final scene, with Young Ok Shin (far left, as Gilda), Mark S. Doss (Sparafucile), and Jean Stilwell (Maddalena).

photo: Michael Cooper

left: Victor Braun as Bluebeard and Jane Gilbert as Judith in *Bluebeard's Castle (1993).*

but who had not previously worked in opera. The surrealism of both operas was exploited by Lepage and designer Michael Levine with a set that was held in a huge frame within which the dreamlike dramas were enacted with the precise yet mysterious images that Lepage is able to draw up from the subconscious. Victor Braun powerfully portrayed the anguished Bluebeard in the encounter with his new wife, the enigmatic and implacable Judith of Jane Gilbert. The role of the unamed Woman in *Erwartung* poses formidable demands on the soprano whose long monologue constitutes the entire action of the opera. Rebecca Blankenship achieved both a musical and a dramatic triumph in the role. The productions immediately became the talk of the city and attracted audiences for whom traditional opera had held little attraction. The double-bill became the COC's most celebrated production. In February 1993 the entire company took the productions to the Brooklyn Academy, and in August of the same year they performed at the Edinburgh Festival where the COC won the Scotsman Hamada Festival Prize for music and drama, and the 1993 International Critics' Award for music. The production, with local orchestras and some changes in conductor and singers, was seen in Australia at Melbourne in October 1994, and at the Hong Kong Festival in February 1996. It was re-mounted with the original performers in Toronto in 1995.

A significant element in the success of the double-bill was the outstanding playing of the orchestra under Bradshaw's direction. The Schoenberg score in particular presents enormous difficulties, but the orchestra performed with a suppleness and lustre of tone that contributed substantially to the effect of the production, even in the ungrateful acoustics of the O'Keefe Centre.

If the company had never looked better on the surface — notable performances, higher general artistic standards, the orchestra's growing into a major ensemble — internally there were serious problems brewing by 1993. The ballet/opera house had been lost and the Elgin soon would be. An economic depression was settling in and the value of the Canadian dollar was declining, which greatly increased the cost of hiring foreign artists. An integrated management team had not been established, and to many people Brian Dickie did not have the business acumen to run a large company, especially under stressful economic conditions. Dissatisfaction was spreading, especially as Dickie came to feel

Erwartung (1993).

Rebecca Blankenship as The

Woman with Noam Marcus

as The Lover.

that he had been brought to Toronto under false pretenses — that he had come to Toronto, as he put it, "to build a theatre and to build a company" — but now that the whole theatre project had fallen through he became frustrated with attempts to continue in the O'Keefe Centre, which he considered to be totally inadequate for opera. Moreover, he felt that he did not have the support of the board, some of whom did not share Dickie's conviction that a new theatre was absolutely necessary to the continued growth of the company.

It was equally true that Dickie alienated people in management and among supporters of the COC. He was often seen to be patronizing and arrogant, a kind of tactless British officer bringing enlightenment to the colonies. In his view, there was a built-in problem in the COC's policy of changing presidents every two years. He felt that it takes time for a director to forge a productive relationship with the president, something that is impossible if the position revolves through the membership of the board. In his own case, he was appointed when Alastair Gillespie was president, but when he took up the post the president was A.J.R. Williams, who in turn was followed by Margo Bindhardt. He personally felt the relationship with Williams was harmonious, but tensions quickly arose between him and Bindhardt and signalled the troubles to follow. In any case, his interests and his talents were in artistic matters, but the nature of the job demanded that he give most of his time to administrative matters at which he was not skilled and which did not interest him. The loss of many administrators meant that there was no institutional memory to provide continuity, and many appointees, whatever their experience, had often no experience of running an opera company or any other kind of performance organization. All of this exacerbated the feeling of many that Dickie, in his dissatisfaction, patronized them when they themselves needed strong leadership.

If it is not easy to pinpoint all the problems that were besetting the company, the financial problems were clear. In 1988–89 (seven operas, fifty-one performances), with a budget of $15.5 million, government grants had totalled $4.6 million and private fundraising provided $3.8 million. Total revenue was $20,000 over expenses and the accumulated deficit had been reduced to $160,000. Four years later, in 1992–93 (eight operas, sixty-eight performances) the budget was $15.7 million with total government grants increasing slightly to just over $4.6 million. Fundraising dropped somewhat to just over $3 million. However, attendance fell from 88.9 percent of capacity to 68.7 percent and production expenses had almost doubled, situations that combined to produce a year deficit of almost $1.5 million, and an accumulated deficit of $2.9 million.

By the summer of 1993 matters were coming to a head. The COC board member and future president, Georgia Prassas, wrote bluntly to Dickie about what she considered to be his "insolent behaviour." A good deal of behind-the-scenes controversy now took fire, culminating in an announcement in *The*

Erwartung (1993). Rebecca Blankenship (The Woman) lying on the floor, with a reflection in a pool of water at the front of the stage.

photo: Michael Cooper

Globe and Mail on October 4 that Dickie was leaving. This was supported with a statement from board chairman Margo Bindhardt, only to have the COC president Giles Meikle (he had succeeded Bindhardt as president) issue a contradictory statement. It was apparent that Dickie, who was out of town while all this was happening, was not the only one who could be accused of inefficiency, although in a sense, both Bindhardt and Meikle were correct: the matter had been effectively settled (Bindhardt) but the *Globe* report had been leaked and was not yet official (Meikle). After two weeks of silence, the COC finally released a statement on October 19 that Brian Dickie had resigned as general director of the company.

It was an unhappy ending to what had started out five years before as an optimistic beginning of a brave new era. The artistic stature of the COC had unquestionably been raised by Dickie, but the company itself was disorganized and demoralized, and it had become too apparent that there had been a serious mismatch between the man and the company. Ironically, it was Dickie's vision that had developed and confirmed the individual character of the COC, a quality that had always been at the core of the company but that began to mature with his direction. Unfortunately, it was not enough to resolve current difficulties. Although the troubles had been brewing for some time, the abrupt climax of events meant that no one was in charge. Board members were volunteer and were neither available nor qualified to attend to the day to day running of the operation, and there was no one within the management who had sufficient knowledge or experience to take over in an emergency. Something had to be done quickly. A search committee was convened at once, the first business being to examine various administrative models to determine whether there should be a new arrangement for the COC. In early December the committee recommended a dual leadership model divided on artistic and administrative lines.

Chapter 8

RICHARD BRADSHAW

Richard Bradshaw had been chief conductor since 1989 and had presided over some of the greatest musical successes of Brian Dickie's regime. Unlike Dickie, with whom he had shared a background and long friendship, Bradshaw liked Toronto and had no personal reason to leave. He was also more in tune with the exigencies of operatic life in North America, having spent much of his artistic life in San Francisco and Toronto. A tentative inquiry as to whether he might be interested in being the new general director had met with no enthusiasm from Bradshaw, but he was willing to consider a role that was less demanding from an administrative point of view. Given the necessity to act swiftly, he was the obvious and natural choice and was made artistic director and music director in January 1994.

Among the administrative staff of the COC there was an alarming lack of sense of direction. Some board members, notably Meikle and Prassas, undertook some working meetings with staff while the search committee sought someone to take over the business management. In June Elaine Calder was appointed general manager. The new

arrangement seemed practical and ideally would provide efficient administration, but it was to be short-lived.

Elaine Calder came to the COC from the Shaw Festival at Niagara-on-the-Lake where she was in her fifth season as administrative director. Among other jobs before that she had held similar positions with the Grand Theatre in London, Ontario and with Toronto Free Theatre. While she had extensive experience in the performing arts, this was her first association with a musical organization, although she personally had a passionate interest in opera. Her main tasks were to bring some order to the administration, to renew morale among the staff, and to concentrate the company on recovering subscriber confidence and on raising money from private and government sources. She hired a number of new people who, if they did not turn out to be the long-term team of the Mansouri years, did provide some stability; and some people stayed on, such as public affairs director Susan Harrington, to help rebuild administrative continuity. With the increasing agitation for a new theatre, Calder felt herself to be drawn in two administrative directions: one towards the development of the new house, the other towards the running of the company. Unsatisfied with her increasingly dual role, she abruptly resigned in November 1997. But by this time Calder had done much to reorganize the administration and Bradshaw, who had had no experience of that kind of thing, had been able to watch and learn. In January 1998 the COC announced a return to the previous single-management status with Bradshaw as general director.

The second in command was to be Cathryn Gregor, who had been musical administrator since the fall of 1991 and had worked previously in various management positions with Toronto musical organizations. She would oversee finance and administration and report to Bradshaw while those on the artistic side would report directly to him. The ebullient and aggressively optimistic Bradshaw and the measured and efficient Gregor proved an effective combination. Bradshaw approached former artistic administrator Philip Boswell to ask if he would act as a consultant to the company since he had so intimate an understanding of it from his days with Mansouri. Boswell declined to act as consultant, but Bradshaw caught Boswell at a fortuitous moment; with the new change in management, he was interested in resuming his old job, which he did.

206

below left: Le nozze di Figaro (1993).
Left to right: Peter Strummer (Dr. Bartolo), Marcia Swanston (Marcellina), John Kriter (Don Curzio), Dwayne Croft (Count Almaviva), Gerald Finley (Figaro), and Wendy Nielsen (Countess Almaviva).

below right: Die Zauberflöte (1993).
Left to right: Russell Braun (Papageno), Norine Burgess, Monica Whicher, and Tania Parrish as the Three Ladies, and Michael Schade (Tamino).

Calder and Bradshaw enjoyed a stroke of financial luck that greatly helped the budget. In the 1980s, the provincial Ministry of Culture and Communications had promoted an Investment in the Arts program, which was a dollar-matching program that had ended in 1989. There had been a five-year restriction on use of the funds, but when the money became available in 1994 and was applied against the year deficit, the 1993–94 loss was converted to a $379,000 surplus. Furthermore, an Expansion Fund that had been set up within the company in 1990 was drawn on to provide $850,000 against the accumulated deficit. Financial problems were by no means solved, but a good deal of pressure was taken off the new management for the moment. Unfortunately, by 1995–96, government grants would drop precipitously by almost 14 percent.

Artistically, what Dickie had set in motion continued to move ahead in the 1993–94 season. His departure left behind a remarkable *Le nozze di Figaro* at the Elgin directed by Robin Phillips, one of the most authoritative classical directors in the country, with the young and increasingly commanding Canadian baritone Gerald Finley in the role of Figaro. A production of *Die Zauberflöte* at the same time was thoroughly disliked by audiences and critics but did have the negative merit of introducing the closest thing the company has had to a scandalous production. The production was shared with Glimmerglass, a summer festival in New York State, and was directed by Martha Clarke,

photo: Michael Cooper

who had been a founder of the dance troupe Pilobolus, was chiefly a choreographer, and was determinedly *avant garde*. By contrast, a beautifully stark but moving *Katya Kabanová* was directed by Robert Carsen at the Elgin in January 1994, conducted by Bradshaw, with Stephanie Sundine and Felicity Palmer.

If *Katya* was sublime, *Le Comte Ory* came dangerously close to the ridiculous through a series of mishaps that produced what was probably the company's greatest production nightmare. The production had been mounted at Glimmerglass and was now to be re-done in Toronto. The original director, Keith Warner, was to re-stage the piece but just as rehearsals were to begin he became ill and sent his young assistant to begin. It soon became apparent that Warner was not going to appear. At an early rehearsal the tenor Jorge Lopez-Yanez fell from a portable stairway in the set and had to withdraw because of injuries. The tenor from Glimmerglass, Paul Kelly, was engaged but he could not do the entire run, so Charles Workman was also engaged for the last few performances. The relatively inexperienced assistant director was proving unsatisfactory and after two weeks of the four-week rehearsal period, the original assistant for the production, Pierre Péloquin, was engaged as director and he set about a rescue operation. The singer in the role of the Countess was already unhappy with the original concept of the production when a descending picture-frame that was part of the set landed on her neck. She withdrew and a new Countess had to be found a few days before the opening. The American soprano Susan Patterson knew the role in Italian and she gamely joined the production and quickly re-learned the part in the original French, the language of the COC production. Press reviews of the opening performance were mixed, but it was a miracle that there was an opening to review. Patterson, Kelly, and Péloquin, who collectively saved the show, did not appear again in a main production of the company.

The company's continual quest for new audiences and new ways to bring opera to wider attention brought it back to Harbourfront in the summer of 1995. With the sponsorship of Altamira Investments Services, three concerts were given in the outdoor

photo: Michael Cooper

Katya Kabanová (1994).

Jane Gilbert (Varvara), Felicity Palmer (Kabanicha) and Stephanie Sundine (Katya).

top left: **Le Comte Ory (1994).** Adèle (Susan Patterson), Isolier (Kimberly Barber) and Count Ory (Paul Austin Kelly).

photo:Robert C. Ragsdale FRPS

photo: Edward Kowal

photo: Michael Cooper

top right: An Altamira concert at night at Molson Place, Harbourfront on Lake Ontario.

above: Richard Margison sings at an Altamira concert in the first season, 1995, with Richard Bradshaw and the COC Orchestra at Molson Place.

Molson Place on the lake. If occasional airplanes and the noises of pleasure boats on the bay sometimes intruded on the music, they did nothing to dampen the enthusiasm of thousands who filled the amphitheatre and spilled into the space around for three free concerts in July that included among the soloists Richard Margison, Russell Braun (the son of Victor Braun), and Norine Burgess. A week-long summer camp was also inaugurated to introduce children in the city to the fun and wonder of what goes into the creation and production of an opera.

Bradshaw continued the composer-in-residence program with a commission for a new work from Gary Kulesha, a Toronto composer whose large and varied output had included incidental music but, so far, no opera. Carol Bolt had written a highly successful play, *Red Emma: Queen of the Anarchists*, based on the life of the American political activist Emma Goldman, who died in Toronto. In November and December 1995 at the du Maurier Theatre at Harbourfront, *Red Emma* had an imaginative premiere directed by David William, a former artistic director of the Stratford Festival.

There were especially fine roles for the two young singers who sang Emma, Anita Krause, and Sonya Gosse.

Bradshaw was now in artistic control and he continued the adventurous dramatic standards that Dickie had established. In the fall of 1994 a production of *Don Pasquale* humorously set in an American frontier town was a delight and served for the debut of Bramwell Tovey, conductor of the Winnipeg Symphony Orchestra.

Eugene Onegin, in the spring of 1995, suffered another of those emergency situations brought about by a suddenly indisposed singer. During the first act on opening night, Gwynne Geyer, who was singing Tatyana, lost her voice. She had been unwell, but no one was prepared for this situation. However, Sonya Gosse, who was the understudy, was in the audience and she sang the rest of the performance from the orchestra pit while Geyer acted the part. Gosse filled the role at the second performance and Ljuba Kazarnovskaya took over the remaining performances. Kazarnovskaya would appear again with the company in 1996 as Salome

photo: Michael Cooper

Red Emma at the du Maurier Theatre Centre (1995).

Left to right: Nathalie Paulin (Helen), Dan Chamandy (Fedya) and Anita Krause (Emma).

Gwynne Geyer was fully recovered when she returned in January 1995 for a moving performance in the title role of *Jenufa*. A new and unorthodox production of *Der fliegende Holländer*, directed by Christopher Alden, was given in January 1996, without intermission and in a single set that was essentially a large tipped box. The figure of the Dutchman, sung by Richard Paul Fink, was presented in stark white make-up and a prison uniform that explicitly called up reference to the Holocaust. Ben Heppner, who was by now the world's leading heroic tenor, made a striking appearance as Canio in *I Pagliacci*. *Rigoletto* was repeated in Tsypin's sets but directed by Frank Matthus with markedly less success than had been the case with Nicholas Muni in 1992. The old set by

above: **Don Pasquale (1994).**
Tracey Welborn as Ernesto has
a bath, assisted by COC chorus
members Ingrid Martin,
Stephanie Petropoulos, and
Marianne Bindig.

right: **Jenufa (1995).**
Gwynne Geyer (Jenufa), Judith
Forst (Kostelnicka), and Quade
Winter (Laca).

top: **Der fliegende Holländer (1996).**
Act 3, with the Dutchman's ghostly crew below.

above: **Der fliegende Holländer (1996).**
Eva-Marie Bundschuh as Senta, and Richard Paul Fink as the Dutchman.

photo: Michael Cooper

Skalicki for *Ariadne auf Naxos* was re-used for a new production by Tom Diamond that updated the theatrical context to make the commedia dell'arte figures into punk figures from popular culture. If the basic idea was engaging, the execution was often cheap laughs at the expense of the music.

The success of the composer-in-residence program continued in 1996 with the announcement that Alexina Louie had been commissioned to compose a new opera. Louie, who was originally from Vancouver but now living in Toronto, had been enjoying increasing acclaim for her colourful and distinctive instrumental music. The text for the new work, which would be called *The Scarlet Princess*, was to be by the American writer David Henry Hwang whose play, *M. Butterfly*, had won him a Tony Award on Broadway.

photo: Michael Cooper

I Pagliacci (1996).
Tonio (Sigmund Cowan) clasps the dying Canio (Ben Heppner) as Nedda (Helena Kaupová) lies murdered beside them.

The 1996–97 season offered an interesting balance of works from the seventeenth to the twentieth century. The season led off with *Salome* and *Elektra*, both on basically the same fundamental set, but the first directed by the celebrated filmmaker Atom Egoyan, the latter by James Robinson, both directors taking highly unconventional approaches to the operas. Egoyan set *Salome* in some kind of fascist spa and used television images and projections to striking, if not always intelligible, effect. Robinson stripped down both set and action and threw the emphasis on exaggerated and forceful characterization. At the du Maurier Theatre Centre at Harbourfront, the Ensemble did a modernist version of Cavalli's seventeenth-century *La Calisto*. In January, Robin Phillips returned to direct an elegant production of Berlioz's seldom performed *Béatrice et Bénédict*, as successful a realization of this theatrically problematic work as it is likely to have. Gordon Gietz and Jane Gilbert brought both vocal and visual charm to the performances. *Les dialogues des Carmélites* was revived in the old sets of Skalicki, but now directed by Diana Leblanc, an actress and director who had recently enjoyed brilliant success at Stratford. If less rewarding than Mansouri's realization of 1986, the production was distinguished by Nadine

Canadian Opera Company

THE FIRST FIFTY YEARS

212

above: Salome (1996).
Jane Gilbert (Herodias), David Rampy
(Herod), and Ljuba Kazarnovskaya
(Salome), with Slavko Hochevar in the
background as the Executioner.

right: Elektra (1996).
Susan Shafer as Klytemnestra and Susan
Marie Pierson as Elektra.

top right:: Béatrice et Bénédict (1997).

bottom right:: Béatrice et Bénédict (1997).
Jane Gilbert as Béatrice, Gordon Gietz
as Bénédict.

Denize as Mother Marie and Rita Gorr as the Old Prioress. Gorr was then at the end of a career that had begun almost fifty years before but she was still a compelling figure on stage. The season ended with a well-sung but conventional *Manon Lescaut* and an equally conventional *Luisa Miller*. But the latter brought the debut of Marina Mescheriakova who created a sensation in the title role.

Meanwhile, if the ballet/opera house project had died, the question of a suitable theatre for the opera remained very much alive. O'Keefe Centre had never been the problem for the National Ballet in the way it was for the COC, and with the NBC's acquisition of new premises for rehearsal and administration the matter of a new theatre lost much of its urgency. The thrust towards a new theatre was bedevilled by ever-renewing discussions about rebuilding the O'Keefe in some way. In 1994 there were extensive considerations about renovation schemes, one of which would cost about $75 million. In addition to the eternal question of where the money would come from, there were also concerns over governance of the theatre, the position of the COC and the NBC in the managing of a theatre neither of them owned, as well as questions about when such renovations might be made, a question that made season and repertoire planning extremely

left: **Les dialogues des Carmélites** *(1997).*
Rita Gorr as the Old Prioress.

right: **Luisa Miller** *(1997).*
Marina Mescheriakova as Luisa and Evgenij Dmitriev as Miller.

photo: Michael Cooper

photo: Michael Cooper

difficult. The subject arose yet again in February 2000 when the former O'Keefe Centre, newly renamed the Hummingbird Centre, announced plans to rebuild the interior to house a two-thousand-seat theatre and an improved stage. No discussion with the COC preceded the announcement.

By 1995 it was apparent that the interminable debate over the O'Keefe Centre would go nowhere and in August of that year Bradshaw made a passionate argument for the COC's going it alone, and immediately, in building a new theatre. It would not be physically grandiose but would have fine acoustics and stage facilities sufficiently large to mount at least three productions at a time in repertory. Early in 1996 a plan was developed that would not expand the main season for the present, but with a two-pronged strategy aimed at recovering subscriber confidence and financing and building a theatre.

In the fall of 1996, as the result of a large corporate donation for the refurbishing of O'Keefe Centre, the theatre changed its name officially to the Hummingbird Centre. There were some modifications to the lobby area, and a new stage curtain was hung. The principal benefit for the audience was the introduction of an elaborate and highly sophisticated "sound enhancement" system. For years, the COC had employed varying degrees of electronic amplification in attempts to compensate for the unsatisfactory acoustics of the Centre. The new system was still artificial, but it produced a far more balanced and acceptable quality of sound than had ever been possible before. The same system was used in other opera theatres — the Muziektheater in Amsterdam, the Brooklyn Academy, and, perhaps most surprising of all, the Staatsoper unter den Linden in Berlin. It was arguably the way of the future, but the COC was convinced that the power of opera lay in the direct sound of voices and instruments, and that the company would only fully realize its potential in a theatre with fine natural acoustics.

In 1995 the third change of the provincial government in ten years brought the Conservatives back into power under Premier Mike Harris, who was unyielding in his refusal to assist with the building of an opera house in any way. There were quiet negotiations with the province, but the only response was to bring together the company and the real estate arm of the government to explore a possible commercial deal. On July 9, 1997 the COC announced that it had completed arrangements to buy a block of land at

University Avenue and Queen Street from the provincial government for the market-value price of $16 million, which must be the first time any government has extracted from, rather than contributed to, a cultural organization on such a scale. Five architectural firms were invited to meet with the building committee, with the final decision going to A.J. Diamond, Donald Schmitt and Company to design the new opera house. There was a momentary flurry of opposition by a group who wanted the theatre to be designed by the Canadian-born architect, Frank Gehry, who had become the toast of the international architectural community with his Guggenheim Museum in Bilbao, Spain. But the group offered no support for the considerable additional financing that such a design would cost, and the COC stood by its decision to engage Diamond and Schmitt.

The company triumphed in its 1997–98 productions. *Turandot* led off in a spare production quite opposite to the extravagant scenic designs that are conventionally lavished on this opera. If Galina Kalinina was a smaller-voiced singer than has become associated with the title role, she brought a lyrical presence in both voice and acting that made a more believable princess who succumbed to the prince of Jon Villars. The second night of the season brought to the stage a production to rival Lepage's *Erwartung/Bluebeard* duo, the double-bill of Stravinsky's *Symphony of Psalms* and *Oedipus Rex*. Director François Girard had an impressive reputation as a filmmaker but this was his first encounter with opera. The *Symphony* was starkly presented with the chorus lined across the stage but sunk a little below the floor level. The association of the concept with AIDS was made specific by a series of figures who moved down through the theatre with books full of names of victims as names simultaneously appeared across the floor of the stage. The actor Colm Feore sat passively at the side of the stage but rose to become the narrator in *Oedipus Rex*, and the ancient plague that terrorizes the people of Thebes was joined to the present-day plague of AIDS. Michael Levine designed a great mound of shapeless forms surmounted by a gigantic throne-chair where Oedipus is first seen. The

Turandot (1997).

Turandot (Galina Kalinina) surrenders to the love of Calaf (Jon Villars).

photo: Michael Cooper

216

Actor Colm Feore, who was
witness to the *Symphony of
Psalms* and The Speaker in
Oedipus Rex (1997).

*The Emperor of Atlantis at the
Imperial Oil Theatre (1997).*
James Westman as Emperor
Overall.

mountain gradually took shape as a mass of human beings who seek deliverance. Girard's stark vision of the two disparate but here totally connected works of Stravinsky, and Levine's tragic design produced an overwhelming effect.

The singing matched the concept, especially the Jocasta of the magnificent Judith Forst and the gripping presence and singing of Michael Schade as Oedipus. As the imposing Creon, Victor Braun marked the fortieth anniversary of his debut with the company. In a long series of original and compelling productions, the Stravinsky double-bill rose to an achievement that was remarkable even by the COC's own standards. At the annual Dora Mavor Moore awards for theatrical productions in the city, it swept the board — for the production itself, and for Girard, Forst, Bradshaw, Levine, Alain Lortie (lighting), and Donna Feore (choreography), all of whom won individual awards related to the double-bill.

The double-bill in October was followed by another harrowing work in November, *The Emperor of Atlantis* by Viktor Ullmann. Ullmann had been one of the young composers in the Schoenberg circle in Vienna. He was pursuing a successful career when he was interned in a Nazi concentration camp in 1942 where he managed to complete his opera the following year. He was killed at Auschwitz in 1944. The one-act opera centres on a King who carries out limitless slaughter as part of warfare, and Death who is repulsed by the loss of meaning in life and death and who goes on strike.

Recordings were also expanding the influence of the company. CBC Records produced *Rarities by*

Rossini and Verdi, featuring the COC Orchestra and Chorus, in 1995, followed the next year with *Richard Margison Sings French and Italian Opera Arias*. A 1997 recording with Michael Schade and Russell Braun, titled *Soirée française*, won a Juno award in Canada and the Gabriel Fauré Award of the Academie du disque lyrique in France. Parallel to the recordings was an expansion of the concert activity of the COC. The stage of the George Weston Recital Hall was large enough to accommodate the orchestra and chorus, and concerts there became a regular COC event. The Rossini/Verdi recording was launched with a concert at the Recital Hall and in the next few years the orchestra was joined by such artists as Ben Heppner and Dmitry Hvorostovsky. There were choral works such as Verdi's *Requiem* and Berlioz's *L'enfance du Christ*, and concert versions of Tchaikovsky's *Iolanthe* and Verdi's *Giovanna d'Arco*. There were also public concerts at the Glenn Gould Studio organized by radio producer Neil Crory for the CBC that featured Joanne Kolomyjec, Judith Forst, Michael Schade, Russell Braun, Gerald Finley, Isabel Bayrakdarian, Benjamin Butterfield, and Brett Polegato.

The season continued with two productions that brought back to the company the combined talents of director Frank Corsaro and the celebrated artist and designer Maurice Sendak. A charming *Hänsel und Gretel* included the debut of Isabel Bayrakdarian in the role of the Sandman. But the notable work was the COC's fourth addition to its Janacek productions with *The Cunning Little Vixen*. This odd but moving tale of humans and animals had had its premiere in 1924, but it was only after the 1950s that it began to achieve limited but growing popularity. Rebecca Caine added the title role to her portrayal of unusual heroines for the COC.

The 1998–99 season got off to a solid start with a visually unusual but impressive *Norma* by James Robinson and Allan Moyer, the same team that had produced *Der fliegende Holländer* in the 1995–96 season. There was also a conventional but fine production of *Tosca* that was notable for the unconventionally girlish Tosca of the French soprano, Sylvie Valayre. The Ensemble continued its encounters with baroque opera with a production of Franceso Cavalli's 1649 Venetian opera, *Giasone*.

The Cunning Little Vixen (1998). The Vixen (Rebecca Caine, seated at right) with the Fox (Beth Clayton) surrounded by creatures of the forest. Set designed by Maurice Sendak.

photo: Michael Cooper

Norma (1998).

Marina Mescheriakova (Norma)
and Ruxandra Donose
(Adalgisa).

photo: Michael Cooper

Giasone (1998).

An Ensemble production at
the du Maurier Theatre Centre,
with Liesel Fedkenheuer
(Giasone), Tamara Hummel
(Isifile), Krisztina Szabó
(Medea), and Michael Colvin
(Aegeus).

photo: Michael Cooper

It was the second part of the season that held the surprises. Russell Braun returned for his now famous Figaro in *Il barbiere di Siviglia*, but the two singers engaged for Rosina and Almaviva did not come up to expectation, and although they each retained a couple of performances, the opening and the majority of performances to follow were given to two young singers plucked from the minor roles. Isabel Bayrakdarian was beginning to make an impressive career after having won the Metropolitan Opera auditions and she was scheduled for two performances of Rosina. Now she was propelled to lead position and proved to be in every way a charming and vocally brilliant Rosina. Her Almaviva had been scheduled to sing the minor role of the Officer, but Michael Colvin shot to principal tenor and immediately confirmed the confidence that the company placed in him.

Along with *Il barbiere* was a production of Handel's *Xerxes* in a production that had originated at the New York City Opera and which charmed its audiences far beyond what they could have anticipated. The director, Stephen Wadsworth, was no stranger to the COC, and with *Xerxes* he more than exceeded even what he had previously done with the company. In his own idiomatic translation into English, Wadsworth created a production

Il barbiere di Siviglia (1999).
Isabel Bayrakdarian (Rosina),
Donato Di Stefano (Dr.
Bartolo), Umberto Chiummo
(Don Basilio), Russell Braun
(Figaro), and Michael Colvin
(Almaviva).

Xerxes (1999).

Kimberly Barber (Xerxes),

Phyllis Pancella (Amastre),

David Daniels (Arsamene),

Kathleen Brett (Romilda), and

Jan Opalach (Ariodate).

photo: Michael Cooper

that blew away the affectations that so often weigh down Handel revivals. Kimberley Barber was a wonderful Xerxes, and Kathleen Brett, always an admirable singer, emerged as a singer to be reckoned with. The young American counter-tenor, David Daniels, sang ravishingly and brilliantly as Arsamene.

In the spring, Richard Margison sang one of his most celebrated roles, that of Manrico in *Il Trovatore*, in a bizarre modernist production by Nicholas Muni, designed by John Conklin. But even with Margison in the cast, the scene-stealer was the fiery Irina Mishura as Azucena. The spring was also the occasion for the first major COC commission since *Mario and the Magician*, Randolph Peters and Robertson Davies' *The Golden Ass*.

Probably no production in the COC's history attracted so much attention, not even

Il Trovatore (1999).

Irina Mishura as Azucena and

Richard Margison as Manrico.

photo: Michael Cooper

Louis Riel in 1967. Robertson Davies had a long career as one of the most distinguished writers in Canada, but from the 1970s his reputation grew to international proportions enjoyed by few other Canadians. He was also an avid opera fan and had long been a familiar figure at COC performances. He had already written a modest libretto for a children's opera composed by Derek Holman, *Dr. Canon's Cure*. Prophetically, he had written a novel in 1958, *A Mixture of Frailties*, that revolved around the composition of an opera to be called *The Golden Asse*. Richard Bradshaw had been urging Davies to write a full-length libretto for some years before the writer quietly decided to get on with it. When he did, he returned to his fictional opera based on a Roman story by Apuleius, and produced the text for *The Golden Ass*.

left:: Author and librettist of **The Golden Ass,** Robertson Davies.

photo: Gary Beechey

right: Richard Bradshaw with Randolph Peters, composer of **The Golden Ass.**

photo: Edward Kowal

Bradshaw scored another success in bringing Davies and Randolph Peters together in what proved a fruitful meeting, and the two men set off to write their opera. Davies finished the text, but he died on December 2, 1995, without having been able to revise and re-work his text as the opera took final form. Fortunately, the great English director, Colin Graham, was a friend of Davies and had been engaged to direct the premiere, and it fell to him to act as dramaturge in the final revisions of the piece for the stage. While Peters had the success of *Nosferatu* behind him for the COC, he did not have a widely popular reputation, not even in the rarefied world of serious composers, but a new opera with a libretto by Davies captured attention across Canada and even abroad.

The rich and handsome Lucius is sidetracked from his amorous pursuit of Fotis by his desire to master the magic arts of Pamphilea, Fotis's mistress. His attempts at magic only result in his being turned into an ass. Lucius the ass undergoes a series of trials and indignities until Fotis gives him the perfect rose that will restore his humanity. But she tells him "You must die to self" and Isis instructs him to forego pleasure, desire, and pride. With the wisdom of self-knowledge, Lucius enters the mystic order as a priest of Isis in a scene reminiscent of Tamino's enlightenment at the conclusion of *Die Zauberflöte.*

photo: Michael Cooper

photo: Michael Cooper

The Golden Ass (1999).
Rebecca Caine as Fotis and
Kevin Anderson as Lucius.

The Golden Ass (1999).
Pamphilea (Judith Forst) works
her magic.

The first performance took place on April 13, 1999. Some critics found the work wanting in its unusual story of love and magic, or in the decidedly conservative musical language of Randolph Peters. Audiences, however, had no doubts about it. In the company's budgeting, it was expected that the box-office success of *Il Trovatore* would carry the expensive but unknown *The Golden Ass*. Word spread quickly, however, and performances sold so well that it was the *Ass* that carried the Troubadour.

In the fall of 1999, the company entered its fiftieth season with optimism and determination. The success of previous seasons had climaxed in the new opera of Peters and

Davies, subscriptions were rising after several years of poor sales, production standards were high, the orchestra and chorus were outstanding. The opera house project, however, got caught in yet another snag.

Livent, the company that had run the theatre complex in North York, now called the Ford Centre, collapsed and the city was faced with ownership of a large theatre and a concert hall that it did not wish to finance. The suggestion was made that the COC should occupy the now problematic large Apotex Theatre, but the stage had been designed to hold only a single long-running show and was totally inadequate for the needs of an opera company. To rebuild the structure would have cost almost as much as a new theatre, and still have been makeshift. The proposed theatre at University and Queen was to be incorporated into a skyscraper in a partnership deal between the COC and the Cadillac Fairview company that was to have provided a financial basis for the opera house. Across the street, however, was the venerable seat of the Law Society of Upper Canada, Osgoode Hall, and in the spring of 1999 the barristers complained that the new tower would cast an unacceptable shadow over their distinguished building. Cadillac Fairview meanwhile had second thoughts about the practicality of adding another large building to the downtown core and resolved the Law Society's distress by withdrawing from its arrangement with the company. Toughened by decades of setbacks and delays, the COC gamely announced that it would continue alone with the free-standing theatre without benefit — or hindrance — of an attached office tower, and at a height that would not cast the Law Society in the shade. Funding for the new theatre still seemed a mystery, but the company bravely set up a model for it in the Hummingbird lobby at the beginning of the new season and confidently expected to spend its next fifty years in its own home.

The 1999–2000 season opened with two productions that could hardly have been different in concept but each of which, in its way, represented the strengths of the company at the half-century mark. The veteran *basso*, Paolo Montarsolo, directed *L'elisir d'amore* in a traditional style that probably had not much changed from Donizetti's days, and if to some it seemed unredeemably old-fashioned, it had unquestioned charm and style.

L'Elisir d'Amore (1999).

Michael Schade as Nemorino
and Henriette Bonde-Hansen
as Adina.

photo: Michael Cooper

Musically, it was elegantly sung by a cast headed by Michael Schade and the Danish soprano Henriette Bonde-Hansen. Against this was set a radically new production of *La Traviata* around which there was such a swirl of anticipation that all performances were sold out before the first night. The Russian director Dmitry Bertman and his designer Igor Nezhny set the opera in a dual world of nineteenth-century dreams and contemporary disco club culture. And Violetta died — or at least was lost to the world — in a hospital. If the production did not work in all its details, the boldness of the concept nevertheless brought new perspectives to the opera. Zvetelina Vassileva was a compelling Violetta, and in the orchestra Bradshaw eliminated the accretions of tradition to deliver

La Traviata (1999).
The final scene with Zvetelina
Vassileva as Violetta and
Vladimir Grishko as Alfredo.

photo: Michael Cooper

a musical rendering that was taut and true to Verdi's original intentions. The full houses responded enthusiastically both positively and negatively; virtually unknown at COC productions, some people loudly booed the production.

The production of *La Traviata* also was the occasion of the anniversary of one of the COC's most enduring and valued singers. In the role of Baron Duphol, Cornelis Opthof marked forty years and forty-three productions with the company.

Following the Hummingbird productions, the Ensemble distinguished itself with a searing production of Britten's *Rape of Lucretia*, directed by Diana Leblanc at the du Maurier Theatre. Ensemble productions had always been notable for the quality of the singing and the integrity of the performances, but the eight young singers in this case excelled, even by their own high standards. The COC co-operated with the opera division of the University of Toronto, which the week before *Lucretia* had mounted Britten's

photo: Michael Cooper

Krisztina Szabó as Lucretia
and Andrew Tees as
Tarquinius in *The Rape of
Lucretia at the du Maurier
Theatre Centre (1999)*.

Don Giovanni (2000).
Isabel Bayrakdarian as Zerlina
is wooed by Giovanni (Davide
Damiani).

Midsummer Night's Dream, to produce a small but impressive Britten festival, including the presence of Britten's biographer, Donald Mitchell, for a series of lectures as the Wilma and Clifford Smith Visitor at the university.

In November, the company announced that Randolph Peters would write a new opera with a libretto by novelist and poet Margaret Atwood on the subject of the nineteenth-century poet Pauline Johnson. And there would be a new children's opera composed by the young Newfoundland composer Dean Burry, who was director of an after-school opera program.

The season continued with *Don Giovanni* which, like *La Traviata* in September, was completely sold out before it opened; and a return of the radical production of *Der fliegende Holländer* from 1996, albeit with some revisions that eliminated the Holocaust reference and made the Dutchman a more generalized symbol of loneliness and alienation. Gidon Saks sang the title role. Frances Ginzer, who had not been heard with the company since 1981 when she sang Antonia in *Les contes d'Hoffmann*, returned as a dramatic soprano in the part of Senta.

The season concluded with the tried and true — *La Bohème* — and the novel — *Pelléas et Mélisande*. *La Bohème* had opened the first season of the Opera Festival fifty years before and it was fitting that it should round off the half-century mark. If *La Bohème* represented the traditionalist values of the company, *Pelléas et Mélisande* carried on the line of powerfully new and original productions. Although Debussy's only opera was almost a century old, it remains more admired than performed and this was the COC's first production of it, and only the second time the work had been seen in Toronto. The darkly threatening production directed by Nicholas Muni and designed by Dany Lyne realized the frustration of Golaud and the passion of Pelléas and Mélisande in the shadowy ambiguity that envelops this troubling and evocative drama. With Debussy's notoriously demanding masterpiece from the beginning of the twentieth century, the COC confidently entered the twenty-first.

Subscriptions were rising, morale was high, public interest was intense. The Canadian

photo: Michael Cooper

photo: Michael Cooper

Der fliegende Holländer (2000).
Frances Ginzer as Senta and Gidon
Saks as the Dutchman.

Opera Company entered the new millennium with optimism and confidence. Then, unexpectedly, the progress toward the opera house suffered yet another setback. When the company prepared to close the land deal with the provincial government on March 15, 2000, the government withdrew from the agreement and refused to sell the property at Queen Street and University Avenue, arguing that the federal government had failed to make a clear commitment to support the project.

Despite prodigious and often passionate response from the COC's supporters against government inaction, by the spring of 2000 the questions of the new house had bogged down in backstage bickering among federal, provincial, and municipal governments, each of them protesting enthusiasm for the theatre, none of them willing to offer unequivocal support. Secure in its artistic standards and assured by its audiences, the company was undaunted. Richard Bradshaw made clear the company's determination: "As long as land can be bought or given, the Board of the Canadian Opera Company intends to forge ahead. Whatever happens, we intend to build an opera house."

With determined optimism for the future, the COC at its centenary will predictably chronicle the triumphs in a new theatre that will magnify the success of its first half-century.

230   # Archival Sources and Bibliography

Archives:

The principal archival collection is the Joan Baillie Archives of the Canadian Opera Company. This includes the correspondence of the General Directors, complete minutes of the Board of Directors and its committees, reports and business papers regarding publicity, marketing, and touring, photographs of all the productions, miscellaneous scrapbooks, and various records and reports that relate to the artistic and business administration of the company. All financial information used in this book is drawn from these sources. As well, there are extensive records relating to the Ballet/Opera House Corporation.

In addition to materials in the COC archives, the Archival Fonds and Collections of the Music Division, National Library of Canada (Ottawa) contains the papers of Ernesto Barbini, Herman Geiger-Torel, Nicholas Goldschmidt and Arnold Walter.

Joan Baille (1923–1997),

founder of the COC

Archives and first archivist.

Bibliography

Baillie, Joan Parkhill. *Look at the Record.* Oakville, ON.: Mosaic Press, 1985.

Canadian Opera Company 1950–1971. n.a. Toronto: The Canadian Opera Company, n.d.

Canadian Opera Company 1950–1977. n.a. Toronto: The Canadian Opera Company, n.d.

Cooper, Dorith. "Opera in Montréal and Toronto: A Study of Performance Traditions and Repertoire 1783–1980." PhD dissertation, University of Toronto, 1983.

Encyclopedia of Music in Canada, 2nd ed. Helmut Kallmann and Gilles Potvin, eds., Robin Elliott and Mark Miller, assoc. eds. Toronto: University of Toronto Press, 1992.

Fairman, Richard. "What are We Really Hearing?" *Opera* 50/8 (August 1999): 888–893.

Foster, Peter. "The Money Pit." *Toronto Life* (June 1999): 82–96.

Harewood, the Earl of (Lascelles, George). *Opera in Canada, a Report.* Ontario Arts Council/Canada Council, 1972.

Knelman, Martin. "Exit, Stage Left." *Toronto Life* (April 1994): 41–46.

Mansouri, Lotfi, with Aviva Layton. *An Operatic Life.* Toronto: Mosaic Press/Stoddart Publishing, 1982.

Morey, Carl. "Nineteenth-century Opera in Toronto." In C. Morey, *An Opera Sampler: Miscellaneous Essays on Opera,* pp. 73–81. Toronto: Dundurn Press, 1998.

Morey, Carl. "Harry Somers: Opera as Politics." In C. Morey, *An Opera Sampler: Miscellaneous Essays on Opera,* pp.143–152. Toronto: Dundurn Press, 1998.

The New Grove Dictionary of Opera. Stanley Sadie, ed. London: MacMillan, 4 vols., 1992.

Opera Canada. Toronto: Opera Canada Publications, 1960– .

Peglar, Kenneth. *Opera and the University of Toronto, 1946–1971.* Toronto: University of Toronto, Faculty of Music, 1972.

Remembered Moments of the Canadian Opera Company 1950–1975. n.a., n.d. (1976?)

Russell, Hilary. *Double Take: The Story of the Elgin and Winter Garden Theatres.* Toronto: Dundurn Press, 1989.

Schabas, Ezra. *Toronto's New Orchestra.* Toronto: 1976

Schafer, R. Murray. *"Patria I: The Characteristics Man." Journal of Canadian Studies* 23/1 and 2 (Spring/Summer, 1988): 207–218.

Walker, Hugh. *The O'Keefe Centre: Thirty Years of Theatre History.* Toronto: Key Porter Books, 1991.

APPENDICES

Opera Diva

photo: Michael Cooper

Thomas Goerz as The Merchant. *The Golden Ass* (1999).

Productions by Composer

Operas on Tour

Seymour Barab
Little Red Riding Hood 1981–1982

Georges Bizet
Carmen 1966

Gaetano Donizetti
Don Pasquale 1967, 1968

Engelbert Humperdinck
Hänsel und Gretel 1980–1981

Franz Lehár
The Merry Widow 1983–1984

Claudio Monteverdi
L'incoronazione di Poppea 1990–1991

Mavor Moore
The Magic Mozart 1979–1980

Wolfgang Amadeus Mozart
*Così fan tutte 1963, 1972–1973,
1973–1974
Le nozze di Figaro 1978–1979,
1979–1980, 1989–1990*

Otto Nicolai
Die lustigen Weiber von Windsor 1960

Jacques Offenbach
*Les contes d'Hoffmann 1987–1988,
1988–1989
Orphée aux enfers 1961, 1970–1971,
1971–1972*

Giacomo Puccini
*La Bohème 1962, 1974–1975, 1975–1976,
1976–1977, 1984–1985
Hello .....Boheme (La Bohème) 1980–1981*

Gioacchino Rossini
*Il barbiere di Siviglia 1958, 1959, 1968,
1969–1970, 1976–1977, 1977–1978,
1981–1982
La Cenerentola 1979–1980, 1986–1987*

Johann Strauss, Jr.
Die Fledermaus 1964, 1965, 1982–1983

Giuseppe Verdi
*La Traviata 1975–1976, 1976–1977,
1977–1978, 1985–1986*

Mainstage Operas in Toronto

Bela Bartok
*Bluebeard's Castle 1974, 1992–1993,
1994–1995*

Ludwig van Beethoven
*Fidelio 1970, 1973, 1991–1992,
1997–1998*

Vincenzo Bellini
Norma 1980–1981, 1998–1999

Alban Berg
*Lulu 1980–1981, 1990–1991
Wozzeck 1977, 1989–1990*

Hector Berlioz
Béatrice et Bénédict 1996–1997

Leonard Bernstein
Candide 1984–1985

Georges Bizet
*Carmen 1956, 1961, 1964, 1970, 1974,
1979 (Spring), 1983–1984, 1989–1990,
1993–1994*

Benjamin Britten
*Albert Herring 1991–1992
Death in Venice 1983–1984
Peter Grimes 1979–1980
The Rape of Lucretia 1999–2000
The Turn of the Screw 1987–1988*

Emilio de' Cavalieri
*La rappresentazione di Anima e di Corpo
1983–1984*

Francesco Cavalli
*La Calisto 1996–1997
Giasone 1998 – 1999*

Francesco Cilea
Adriana Lecouvreur 1986–1987

Claude Debussy
Pelléas et Mélisande 1999–2000

Gaetano Donizetti
*Anna Bolena 1983–1984
Don Pasquale 1994–1995
L'elisir d'amore 1979–1980, 1999–2000
La fille du régiment 1977
Lucia di Lammermoor 1971, 1981–1982,
1986–1987, 1994–1995*

234

John Gay
The Beggar's Opera 1985–1986

W. S. Gilbert and Arthur S. Sullivan
The Mikado 1985–1986

Umberto Giordano
Andrea Chénier 1988–1989

Charles Gounod
Faust 1951, 1966, 1970, 1974, 1984–1985
Roméo et Juliette 1991–1992

George Freiderich Handel
Xerxes 1998 – 1999

Engelbert Humperdinck
Hänsel und Gretel 1957, 1962, 1963,
1992–1993, 1997–1998

Leos Janácek
The Cunning Little Vixen 1997–1998
Jenufa 1981–1982, 1995–1996
Katya Kabanov 1993–1994
The Makropulos Case 1988–1989

Gary Kulesha
Red Emma 1995–1996

Franz Lehár
The Merry Widow 1957 (Fall), 1971,
1973, 1980–1981, 1983–1984,
1987–1988

Ruggiero Leoncavallo
I Pagliacci 1961, 1966, 1975, 1990–1991,
1995–1996

Pietro Mascagni
Cavalleria rusticana 1961, 1966

Jules Massenet
Manon 1952
Werther 1979–1980, 1992–1993

Gian–Carlo Menotti
The Consul 1953, 1954

Claudio Monteverdi
L'incoronazione di Poppea 1982–1983
Il ritorno d'Ulisse in patria 1988–1989

Wolfgang Amadeus Mozart
La clemenza di Tito 1990–1991
Così fan tutte 1953, 1973, 1984–1985,
1990–1991, 1992–1993

Don Giovanni 1950, 1956, 1963, 1970,
1978 (Fall), 1987–1988, 1992–1993,
1999–2000
Die Entführung aus dem Serail 1957,
1980–1981
Idomeneo 1986–1987
Le nozze di Figaro 1951, 1955, 1960, 1978
(Spring), 1990–1991, 1993–1994
Il rè pastore 1994–1995
Die Zauberflöte 1952, 1977, 1982–1983,
1988–1989, 1993–1994

Modest Mussorgsky
Boris Godunov 1974, 1986–1987

Jacques Offenbach
La belle Hélène 1982–1983
Les contes d'Hoffmann 1958, 1967,
1981–1982, 1987–1988
La grande duchesse de Gérolstein 1976

John Oliver
Guacamayo's Old Song and Dance
1990–1991

Raymond Pannell
The Luck of Ginger Coffey 1967

Randolph Peters
The Golden Ass 1998–1999
Nosferatu 1993–1994

Francis Poulenc
Dialogues des Carmélites 1985–1986,
1996–1997

Sergei Prokofieff
The Love for Three Oranges 1959

Giacomo Puccini
La Bohème 1950, 1954, 1958, 1963, 1965,
1968, 1972, 1976, 1983–1984, 1988–1989,
1991–1992, 1994–1995, 1999–2000
La fanciulla del West 1982–1983
Gianni Schicchi 1995–1996
Madama Butterfly 1951, 1953, 1956,
1962, 1964, 1967, 1971, 1975,
1979–1980, 1985–1986, 1990–1991,
1993–1994, 1997–1998
Manon Lescaut 1975, 1996–1997
La rondine 1989–1990
Suor Angelica 1990–1991
Il Tabarro 1975
Tosca 1957, 1961, 1968, 1972, 1976,
1984–1985, 1988–1989, 1992–1993,

1998–1999
Turandot 1965, 1969, 1983–1984, 1997 –
1998

Maurice Ravel
L'heure espagnole 1974

Rodgers and Hammerstein
Carousel 1957 (Fall)

Gioacchino Rossini
Il barbiere di Siviglia 1959, 1965, 1967,
1973, 1978 (Spring), 1984–1985,
1989–1990, 1991–1992, 1998–1999
La Cenerentola 1979 (Spring), 1995–1996
Le Comte Ory 1993–1994

R. Murray Schafer
Patria 1 1987–1988

Arnold Schoenberg
Erwartung 1992–1993, 1994–1995

Dmitri Shostakovich
Lady Macbeth of Mtsensk 1987–1988

Bedrich Smetana
The Bartered Bride 1952, 1961,
1992–1993

Harry Somers
Louis Riel 1967, 1968, 1975
Mario and the Magician 1991–1992

Johann Strauss, Jr.
Die Fledermaus 1955, 1957 (Fall), 1964,
1969, 1975, 1981–1982, 1986–1987,
1990–1991
A Night in Venice 1960

Richard Strauss
Ariadne auf Naxos 1987–1988, 1995–1996
Elektra 1969, 1982–1983, 1990–1991,
1996–1997
Der Rosenkavalier 1963, 1978 (Fall),
1989–1990
Salome 1965, 1968, 1975, 1985–1986,
1996–1997

Igor Stravinsky
Mavra 1965
Oedipus Rex with Symphony of Psalms 1997
– 1998
The Rake's Progress 1984–1985

Pyotr Ilyich Tchaikovsky
Eugene Onegin 1972, 1990–1991,
1994–1995
Joan of Arc 1978 (Fall)
The Queen of Spades 1988–1989

Ambroise Thomas
Hamlet 1985–1986

Viktor Ullmann
The Emperor of Atlantis 1997–1998

Giuseppe Verdi
Aïda 1963, 1964, 1968, 1972, 1985–1986
Un ballo in maschera 1958, 1981–1982,
1989–1990
Don Carlos 1977, 1988–1989
Falstaff 1982–1983, 1991–1992
La forza del destino 1959, 1969,
1987–1988
Luisa Miller 1996–1997
Macbeth 1966, 1971, 1986–1987
Otello 1960, 1980–1981, 1989–1990
Rigoletto 1950, 1954, 1962, 1965, 1969,
1973, 1978 (Fall), 1986–1987,
1992–1993, 1995–1996
La Traviata 1955, 1964, 1966, 1970,
1974, 1978 (Spring), 1981–1982,
1985–1986, 1991–1992, 1993–1994,
1999–2000
Il Trovatore 1967, 1984–1985, 1998–1999
Simon Boccanegra 1979–1980

Richard Wagner
Der fliegende Holländer 1974, 1980–1981,
1995–1996, 1999–2000
Götterdämmerung 1973
Lohengrin 1983–1984
Die Meistersinger von Nürenberg
1984–1985
Siegfried 1972
Tristan und Isolde 1979–1980, 1987–1988
Die Walküre 1962, 1971, 1976

Healey Willan
Deirdre 1966

Charles Wilson
Héloise and Abélard 1973

Ermanno Wolf–Ferrari
I quatro rusteghi 1954

Robert Wright and George Forrest
Kismet 1986–1987

Appendix II

Productions of the Canadian Opera Company
1950–2000

Unless otherwise indicated, Toronto productions took place in the Royal Alexandra Theatre until 1961, and after that date at the O'Keefe Centre (renamed the Hummingbird Centre in 1996). Toronto productions of the Canadian Opera Company Ensemble are included in the main list and are designated as COCE. Ensemble productions that were given outside Toronto are included under COC Tours. Titles of operas are always given in the original language with the exception of works in Russian and Czech, for which the most familiar English title is used. If an opera was performed in an English translation and not in the original language, this is noted in the entry.

1950

Rigoletto   **Giuseppe Verdi**
February 3, 8, 11, 1950
Conductor: Nicholas Goldschmidt
Director: Herman Geiger-Torel
Set Designer: George Englesmith
Costume Designer: Stewart Bagnani

Rigoletto	Gilles Lamontagne
Duke of Mantua	Roger Doucet
Gilda	June Kowalchuck
Maddalena	Margaret Kerr (Feb. 3, 11); Joan Hall (Feb. 8)
Count Ceprano	Ernest Adams
Marullo	Andrew MacMillan
Monterone	William B. Williams
Sparafucile	Jan Rubes
Borsa	Frank Crane
Countess Ceprano	Patricia Snell
Giovanna	Margaret Hitchcock
Page	Marguerite DesJardins
Usher	Glenn Gardiner

Don Giovanni   **Wolfgang Amadeus Mozart**
In English
February 4, 9, 11, 1950
Conductor: Nicholas Goldschmidt
Director: Herman Geiger-Torel
Set: George Englesmith
Costume Designer: Stewart Bagnani

Leporello	Andrew MacMillan
Donna Anna	Louise Roy
Don Giovanni	Edmund Hockridge
The Commendatore	Jan Rubes

Don Ottavio	Pierre Boutet
Donna Elvira	Elizabeth Benson Guy
Zerlina	Marguerite Gignac
Masetto	Glenn Gardiner
Innkeeper	Ernest Adams
Maid	Marguerite DesJardins

La Bohème   **Giacomo Puccini**
February 7, 8, 10, 1950
Conductor: Nicholas Goldschmidt
Director: Herman Geiger-Torel
Set: J.H.C. Heitinga
Costume Designer: Stewart Bagnani

Marcello	Ernest Adams
Rodolfo	James Shields
Colline	Jan Rubes
Schaunard	Andrew MacMillan
Benoit	Glenn Gardiner
Mimi	Mary Morrison
Parpignol	Pierre Daniel
Musetta	Beth Corrigan (Feb. 7, 8); Patricia Snell (Feb. 10)
Alcindoro	Earl Dick
Sergeant	Jack Asher
Sergeant	Sydney Melville

1951

Le nozze di Figaro   **Wolfgang Amadeus Mozart**
In English
February 8, 10, 14, 16, 1951
Conductor: Nicholas Goldschmidt
Director: Herman Geiger-Torel
Set: Eduardo Loeffler
Costume Designer: Stewart Bagnani

Figaro	Andrew MacMillan
Susanna	Marguerite Gignac, Jean Edwards
Count Almaviva	Ernest Adams
Countess Almaviva	Louise Roy (Feb. 8, 10, 14); Patricia Snell (Feb. 16)
Cherubino	Marjorie Hays (Feb. 8, 10, 14); Mary Alice Rogers (Feb. 16)
Marcellina	Virginia Lippert
Dr. Bartolo	John Asher
Don Basilio	Victor White
Don Curzio	Douglas Scott

Antonio	Glenn Gardiner
Barbarina	Beth Corrigan (Feb. 8, 14, 16); Barbara Franklin (Feb. 10)
First Peasant Girl	Fiona Skakun (Feb. 8, 14); Yolanda Di Paolo (Feb. 10, 16)
Second Peasant Girl	Joan Maxwell (Feb. 8, 14); Roma Butler (Feb. 10, 16)

Madama Butterfly   **Giacomo Puccini**
February 9, 12, 14, 17, 1951
Conductor: Nicholas Goldschmidt
Director: Herman Geiger-Torel
Set: Hans Berends
Costume Designer: Suzanne Mess

Cio-Cio-San	June Kowalchuck
Suzuki	Joan Hall
Pinkerton	James Shields
Sharpless	Gilles Lamontagne (Feb. 9, 12, 17); Norman Summers (Feb.14)
Goro	Earl Dick
The Bonze	James Milligan
Prince Yamadori	Reginald Heal (Feb. 9, 14); Glenn Gardiner (Feb. 12, 17)
Commissioner	Robert I. Foster
Kate Pinkerton	Elizabeth Murray (Feb. 9, 17); Joan Maxwell (Feb. 12, 14)
Dolore	Leslie Nash

Faust   **Charles Gounod**
February 13, 15, 17, 1951
Conductor: Nicholas Goldschmidt/George Crum
Director: Herman Geiger-Torel
Set: Hans Berends
Costume Designer: Elizabeth Willes-Chitty

Faust	Pierre Boutet
Méphistophélès	Jan Rubes
Valentin	Gilles Lamontagne (Feb. 13, 15); Ernest Adams (Feb. 17)
Wagner	Glenn Gardiner
Siébel	Marguerite DesJardins (Feb. 13, 17); Virginia Lippert (Feb. 15)
Marguerite	Mary Morrison
Marthe	Joanne Ivey

1952

The Bartered Bride   **Bedrich Smetana**
In English
February 21, 23, 26, 29, 1952
Conductor: Nicholas Goldschmidt/George Crum
Director: Herman Geiger-Torel
Set: Hans Berends
Costume Designer: Elizabeth Willes-Chitty

Marie	Elizabeth Benson Guy
Jenik	Reginald Heal
Kezal	Jan Rubes
Vasek	Victor White
Krushina	Glenn Gardiner
Ludmila	Louise Roy
Springer	Ernest Adams
Esmerelda	Sylvia Grant
Muff	George Barrs
Hata	Nora Conklin
Misha	James Milligan
Circus Manager	Ernest Adams

Die Zauberflöte   **Wolfgang Amadeus Mozart**
In English
February 22, 23, 27, March 1, 1952
Conductor: Nicholas Goldschmidt
Director: Herman Geiger-Torel
Set: Hans Berends
Costume Designer: Rodolfo Nicoletti

Pamina	Mary Morrison
Tamino	Robert Price
Papageno	Andrew MacMillan
Papagena	Jean Edwards; Barbara Franklin
Queen of the Night	Lois Marshall; Patricia Snell
First Spirit	Ruth Gillis
Second Spirit	Sylvia Grant
Third Spirit	Joanne Ivey
First Lady	Elizabeth Benson Guy
Second Lady	Margo McKinnon; Shirley Sproul
Third Lady	Joan Hall
Sarastro	Russell Skitch; Jan Rubes
Speaker	Don Garrard; Glenn Gardiner
Monostatos	Ernest Adams
First Armoured-Man	Joseph Cooper
Second Armoured-Man	Vaclovas Verikaitis

Manon   **Jules Massenet**
February 25, 27, 28, March 1, 1952
Conductor: Thomas Martin
Director: Herman Geiger-Torel
Set: Hans Berends
Costume Designer: Suzanne Mess/Elizabeth Willes-Chitty

Manon Lescaut	Marguerite Gignac; Patricia Snell
Chevalier Des Grieux	John Alexander
Lescaut	Gilles Lamontagne
De Brétigny	James Milligan; Andrew MacMillan
Count Des Grieux	John Nedra
Guillot De Morfontaine	Ernest Adams; Earl Dick
Poussette	Doreen Vogel
Javotte	Andrée Thériault

238

Rosette	Joanne Ivey
Innkeeper	Vaclovas Verikaitis
First Guardsman	Milton Jiricka
Second Guardsman	Ralph Roose
Maid	Claudette LeBlanc
A Monk	Carman Fleisher
Sergeant	Bernard Turgeon

1953

Madama Butterfly   Giacomo Puccini
February 11, 13, 16, 18, 1953
Conductor: Ernesto Barbini
Director: Herman Geiger-Torel
Set: Hans Berends
Costume Designer: Suzanne Mess

Cio-Cio-San	Irene Salemka
Suzuki	Joan Hall
Pinkerton	James Shields
Sharpless	René Bouchard
Goro	Ernest Adams
The Bonze	Jan Rubes (Feb. 11, 16); Charles Couture (Feb. 13, 18)
Prince Yamadori	Victor White (Feb. 11, 13, 18); Alexander Gray (Feb. 16)
Commissioner	Ralph Roose
Kate Pinkerton	Margo McKinnon
Dolore	James Shields, Jr.
Registrar	Clarence Fleiger

Così fan tutte   Wolfgang Amadeus Mozart
In English
February 12, 14 (matinée and evening), 18, 20, 1953
Conductor: Nicholas Goldschmidt
Director: Herman Geiger-Torel
Set: Hans Berends/Elizabeth Willes-Chitty
Costume Designer: Suzanne Mess

Fiordiligi	Louise Roy (Feb. 12, 14 (mat.), 18); Mary Morrison (Feb. 14 (eve), 20)
Dorabella	Sylvia Grant
Despina	Jacqueline Smith (Feb. 12, 14 (mat), 20); Patricia Snell (Feb. 14 (eve.), 18)
Ferrando	Edward Johnson
Guglielmo	Don Garrard
Don Alfonso	Jan Rubes (Feb. 12, 14 (eve.), 18); Andrew MacMillan (Feb. 14 (mat.), 20)

The Consul   Gian-Carlo Menotti
February 17, 19, 21 (matinée and evening), 1953
Conductor: Nicholas Goldschmidt
Director: Herman Geiger-Torel
Set: Hans Berends
Costume Designer: Suzanne Mess

John Sorel	Glenn Gardiner
Magda Sorel	Theresa Gray
Mother	Nellie Smith
Secret Police Agent	Don Garrard; Andrew MacMillan
The Secretary	Joanne Ivey
The Magician	Ernest Adams
Mr. Kofner	Jan Rubes
Vera Boronel	Catherine Akos
The Foreign Woman	Suzette Nadon; Louise Roy
Anna Gomez	Doreen Vogel
Assan	Ralph Roose
First Plainclothesman	Charles Couture
Second Plainclothesman	Clarence Fleiger

1954

The Consul   Gian-Carlo Menotti
February 20, 23, 27, March 2, 1954
Conductor: Nicholas Goldschmidt
Director: Herman Geiger-Torel
Set: Hans Berends
Costume Designer: Suzanne Mess

John Sorel	Glenn Gardiner
Magda Sorel	Theresa Gray
Mother	Nellie Smith
Secret Police Agent	Andrew MacMillan
The Secretary	Joanne Ivey
The Magician	Ernest Adams
Mr. Kofner	Jan Rubes
Vera Boronel	Catherine Akos
The Foreign Woman	Suzette Nadon; Milla Andrew
Anna Gomez	Andrée Thériault; Roma Butler
Assan	Bernard Turgeon
First Plainclothesman	William Copeland
Second Plainclothesman	Charles Couture

La Bohème   Giacomo Puccini
February 22, 24, 26, March 3, 6, 1954
Conductor: Ernesto Barbini
Director: Herman Geiger-Torel
Set: J.H.C. Heitinga
Costume Designer: Suzanne Mess

Marcello	Gilles Lamontagne (Feb. 22, 26, Mar. 3); James Milligan (Feb. 24, Mar. 6)
Rodolfo	James Shields
Colline	Jan Rubes
Schaunard	Andrew MacMillan
Benoit	Glenn Gardiner
Mimi	Irene Salemka
Parpignol	Walter Dinoff
Musetta	Jacqueline Smith (Feb. 22, 26, Mar. 3); Lavone Skaven (Feb. 24, Mar. 6)
Alcindoro	Ernest Adams
Sergeant	Charles Couture
Sergeant	Robert Goulet
Sergeant	Robert Doane

I quatro rusteghi   **Ermanno Wolf-Ferrari**
In English
February 27, March 3, 5, 1954
Conductor: Ernesto Barbini
Director: Herman Geiger-Torel
Set: Hans Berends
Costume Designer: Suzanne Mess

Lucinda	Evelyn Gould
Margherita	Joanne Ivey
Lunardo	Andrew MacMillan
Maurizio	Bernard Turgeon
Maria	Sylvia Grant
Servant	Patricia Rideout (Feb. 27, Mar. 5); Phyllis Mailing (Mar. 3)
Filipeto	Jon Vickers
Simone	Glenn Gardiner
Felicia	Mary Morrison
Cacian	James Milligan
Count Riccardo	Ernest Adams
Columbine	Lesia Zubrack
Harlequin	Alexander Gray
Night-Watchman	William Copeland
Young Man	Robert Goulet
Young Woman	Dolores Huck

Rigoletto   **Giuseppe Verdi**
March 1, 4, 6, February 25, 1954
Conductor: Nicholas Goldschmidt
Director: Herman Geiger-Torel
Set: George Englesmith
Costume Designer: Suzanne Mess

Rigoletto	Gilles Lamontagne
Duke of Mantua	Jon Vickers
Gilda	Patricia Snell
Maddalena	Joan Hall (Feb. 25, Mar. 6); Catherine Akos (Mar. 1, 4)
Count Ceprano	Charles Couture
Marullo	Alexander Gray
Monterone	James Milligan
Sparafucile	Jan Rubes
Borsa	Ernest Adams
Countess Ceprano	Jeannine Perron (Feb. 25, Mar. 6); Katherine McBain (Mar. 1, 4)
Giovanna	Irene Loosberg (Feb. 25, Mar. 6); Helen Spicer (Mar. 1, 4)
Page	Claudette LeBlanc (Feb. 25, Mar. 6); Dolores Huck (Mar. 1, 4)
Usher	Robert Goulet

1955

Die Fledermaus   **Johann Strauss, Jr.**
In English
February 25, 28, March 2, 5, 11, 12, 1955
Conductor: Nicholas Goldschmidt

Director: Herman Geiger-Torel
Set: Nicholai Soloviov/Rudi Dorn
Costume Designer: Suzanne Mess

Rosalinda	Milla Andrew (Feb. 25, 28, Mar. 5, 11); Jean Ramsay (Mar. 2, 12)
Eisenstein	Ernest Adams
Adele	Evelyn Gould (Feb. 25, 28, Mar. 2, 11); Lesia Zubrack (Mar. 5, 12)
Alfred	Karl Norman (Feb. 25, 28, Mar. 5, 12); Jon Vickers (Mar. 2, 11)
Frank	Andrew MacMillan
Prince Orlofsky	Joanne Ivey
Dr. Falke	Don Garrard
Frosch	Sammy Sales
Dr. Blind	Bernard Turgeon
Fifi	Lesia Zubrack (Feb. 25, 28, Mar. 2, 11); Joyce Hill (Mar. 5, 12)
Ivan	Robert Doane

Le nozze di Figaro   **Wolfgang Amadeus Mozart**
In English
February 26, March 4, 8, 10, 1955
Conductor: Nicholas Goldschmidt
Director: Herman Geiger-Torel
Set: Eduardo Loeffler/Hans Berends
Costume Designer: Suzanne Mess

Figaro	Jan Rubes
Susanna	Roma Butler
Count Almaviva	Andrew MacMillan
Countess Almaviva	Mary Morrison
Cherubino	Marjorie Hays
Marcellina	Milla Andrew (Feb. 26, Mar. 8); Irene Loosberg (Mar. 4, 10)
Dr. Bartolo	Don Garrard
Don Basilio	Karl Norman
Don Curzio	Ernest Adams
Antonio	Bernard Turgeon
Barbarina	Jean Edwards
First Peasant Girl	Katherine McBain (Feb. 26, Mar. 8); Angela Antonelli (Mar. 4, 10)
Second Peasant Girl	Helen Albert

La Traviata   **Giuseppe Verdi**
March 1, 3, 5, 7, 9, 12, 1955
Conductor: Ernesto Barbini
Director: Herman Geiger-Torel
Set: Hans Berends
Costume Designer: Suzanne Mess

Violetta	Marcella Reale (Mar. 1, 5, 7, 12); Patricia Snell (Mar. 3, 9)
Alfredo	Jon Vickers
Germont	James Milligan
Flora	Andrée Thériault (Mar. 1, 3, 12); Irene Loosberg (Mar. 5, 7, 9)
Annina	Phyllis Mailing (Mar. 1, 7, 12); Patricia

	Rideout (Mar. 3, 5, 9)
Gaston	Karl Norman (Mar. 1, 5, 9, 12); Ernest Adams (Mar. 3, 7)
Baron Douphol	Bernard Turgeon (Mar. 1, 3, 12); James Whicher (Mar. 5, 7, 9)
Marquis	Alexander Gray
Dr. Grenvil	Andrew MacMillan
Giuseppe	Walter Dinoff
Messenger	Severin Weingort

1956

Carmen   **Georges Bizet**
February 24, 27, 29, March 3, 6, 8, 10, 1956
Conductor: Ernesto Barbini
Director: Herman Geiger-Torel
Set: Robert Prévost
Costume Designer: Suzanne Mess

Moralès	Alexander Gray
Micaela	Marguerite Lavergne
Don José	Jon Vickers
Zuniga	Andrew MacMillan
Carmen	Regina Resnik (Feb. 24, Mar. 3, 6, 10); Joanne Ivey (Feb. 27, 29, Mar. 8)
Frasquita	Patricia Snell
Mercédès	Patricia Rideout
Escamillo	Robert Savoie
El Remendado	Bernard Turgeon
El Dancairo	Ernest Adams

Don Giovanni   **Wolfgang Amadeus Mozart**
In English
February 25, 29, March 2, 7, 9, 1956
Conductor: Nicholas Goldschmidt
Director: Herman Geiger-Torel
Set: Hans Berends
Costume Designer: Suzanne Mess

Leporello	Andrew MacMillan
Donna Anna	Sylvia Grant
Don Giovanni	Don Garrard
The Commendatore	Sidney Melville
Don Ottavio	Léopold Simoneau (Feb. 25, 29, Mar. 2); John McCollum (Mar. 7, 9)
Donna Elvira	Patricia Snell (Feb. 25, 29, Mar. 2); Milla Andrew (Mar. 7, 9)
Zerlina	Evelyn Gould
Masetto	Bernard Turgeon

Madama Butterfly   **Giacomo Puccini**
February 28, March 1, 3, 5, 7, 10, 1956
Conductor: Ernesto Barbini
Director: Herman Geiger-Torel
Set: Hans Berends
Costume Designer: Suzanne Mess

Cio-Cio-San	Marcella Reale
Suzuki	Joan Hall
Pinkerton	James Shields
Sharpless	Harry Mossfield
Goro	Ernest Adams
The Bonze	Vaclovas Verikaitis
Prince Yamadori	James Whicher
Commissioner	Wilson Patterson
Kate Pinkerton	Katherine McBain
Dolore	Grant Robert
Yakuside	Alan Crofoot
Mother	Rhoda Pendleton
Cousin	Angela Antonelli
Aunt	Dolores Del Grande

1957

Die Entführung aus dem Serail   **Wolfgang Amadeus Mozart**
In English
February 25, 27, March 2, 5, 1957
Conductor: Nicholas Goldschmidt
Director: Herman Geiger-Torel
Set: Hans Berends
Costume Designer: Suzanne Mess

Belmonte	Léopold Simoneau
Osmin	Jan Rubes
Pedrillo	Ernest Adams
Selim Pasha	Joseph Fürst
Konstanze	Edita Symonek
Blondchen	Pierette Alarie
A Mute	Donald Bartle
Chief of the Guard	Don McManus

Tosca   **Giacomo Puccini**
February 26, 28, March 4, 6, 8, 9, 1957
Conductor: Ernesto Barbini
Director: Herman Geiger-Torel
Set: Hans Berends
Costume Designer: Suzanne Mess

Cesare Angelotti	Don McManus
A Sacristan	Bernard Turgeon
Mario Cavaradossi	Richard Cassilly
Tosca	Ilona Kombrink
Baron Scarpia	Harold Mossfield
Spoletta	Alan Crofoot
Sciarrone	Victor Braun
Shepherd Boy	Manley Stark
Jailer	Willam Bourns (Feb. 26, Mar. 8, 9); Osyp Hoshuliak (Feb. 28, Mar. 4, 6)

Hänsel und Gretel   **Engelbert Humperdinck**
In English
March 1, 2, 6 (matinée and evening), 9 (matinée and evening), 1957
Conductor: Nicholas Goldschmidt/Mario Bernardi

Director: Herman Geiger-Torel
Set: Hans Berends
Costume Designer: Suzanne Mess

Gretel	Angela Antonelli
Hänsel	Marie Gauley
Mother	Constance Fisher (Mar. 1, 2); Irene Loosberg (Mar. 6, 9)
Father	Bernard Turgeon
The Sandman	Patricia Rideout
The Dew Man	Sheila Piercy
The Witch	Milla Andrew

1957 (Fall)

Carousel   **Rodgers and Hammerstein**
October 21, 22, 23 (matinée and evening), 24, 25, 26 (matinée and evening), 1957
Conductor: Mario Bernardi
Director: Herman Geiger-Torel
Set: Marie Day
Costume Designer: Suzanne Mess

Carrie Pipperidge	Lillian Bozinoff (Oct. 21, 23 (eve), 24, 26 (mat); Elizabeth Mawson (Oct. 22, 23 (mat), 25, 26 (eve))
Julie Jordan	Lesia Zubrack (Oct. 21, 23 (eve), 24, 26 (mat)); Marie Gauley (Oct. 22, 23 (eve), 25, 26 (eve))
Mrs. Mullin	Joanne Ivey
Billy Bigelow	Don Garrard
First Policeman	Donald Bartle
David Bascombe	Alexander Gray
Nettie Fowler	Sylvia Grant (Oct. 21, 23 (eve), 24, 26 (mat)); Phyllis Mailing (Oct. 22, 23 (mat), 25, 26 (eve))
Enoch Snow	Karl Norman
Jigger Craigin	Don McManus
Hannah	Mary Andrews
Arminy	Hazelanne Guloien (Oct. 21, 23 (eve), 25, 26 (eve)); Teresa Stratas (Oct. 22, 23 (mat), 25, 26 (eve))
Second Policeman	James Whicher
Captain	Victor Braun
Heavenly Friend	Andrew MacMillan
Starkeeper	Bernard Turgeon
Enoch Snow, Jr.	Brian Beaton
Principal	Alan Crofoot
Doctor Seldon	Bernard Turgeon

The Merry Widow   **Franz Lehár**
In English
October 28, 29, 30 (matinée and evening), 31, November 1, 2 (matinée and evening), 1957
Conductor: Ernesto Barbini
Director: Herman Geiger-Torel
Set: John Engel

Costume Designer: Suzanne Mess

St. Brioche	Alan Crofoot
Baron Zeta	Andrew MacMillan
Valencienne	Marie Gauley
Camille	Karl Norman
Cascada	Alexander Gray
Kromov	Don McManus
Olga	Joanne Ivey
Bogdanowitsch	Harold Mossfield
Sylvaine	Constance Fisher (Oct. 28, 30 (mat), Nov. 2); Patricia Snell (Oct. 29, 30 (eve), 31, Nov. 1)
Njegus	Bernard Turgeon
Anna Glawari	Sylvia Grant (Oct. 28, 29, 30 (mat), Nov. 1, 2 (eve)); Elizabeth Mawson (Oct. 30 (eve), 31, Nov. 2 (mat))
Count Danilo	Ernest Adams
Lolo	Lesia Zubrack (Oct. 28, 30 (eve), 31, Nov. 2 (mat)); Lillian Bozinoff (Oct. 29, 30 (mat), Nov. 1, 2 (eve))
Dodo	Joyce Hill
Waiter	Igor Gavon (Oct. 28, 30 (mat), 31, Nov. 2 (eve)); James Whicher (Oct. 29, 30 (eve), Nov. 1, 2 (mat))

Die Fledermaus   **Johann Strauss, Jr.**
In English
November 4, 5, 6 (matinée and evening), 7, 8, 9 (matinée and evening), 1957
Conductor: Ettore Mazzoleni
Director: Herman Geiger-Torel
Set: Nicholai Soloviov/Rudi Dorn
Costume Designer: Suzanne Mess

Rosalinda	Ilona Kombrink
Eisenstein	Andrew MacMillan
Adele	Patricia Snell (Nov. 4, 6 (eve), 8, Nov. 9 (mat)); Lesia Zubrack (Nov. 5, 6 (mat), 7, 9 (eve))
Alfred	Alan Crofoot (Nov. 4, 6 (eve), 7, 9 (mat)); Karl Norman (Nov. 5, 6 (mat), 8, 9 (eve))
Frank	Ernest Adams
Prince Orlofsky	Joanne Ivey
Dr. Falke	Harold Mossfield
Frosch	Sammy Sales
Dr. Blind	Bernard Turgeon
Fifi	Lillian Bozinoff
Ivan	James Whicher

1958

Un ballo in maschera   **Giuseppe Verdi**
Oct. 13, 15, 18, 22, 24, 1958
Conductor: Ernesto Barbini
Director: Herman Geiger-Torel
Set: Brian Jackson

242

Costume Designer: Brian Jackson

Samuele	Andrew MacMillan
Tommaso	Jan Rubes
Oscar	Sheila Piercey (Oct. 13, 15, 18); Luba Hanushak (Oct. 22, 24)
Riccardo	Giuseppe Campora
Amelia	Ilona Kombrink
Renato	Harold Mossfield
Judge	James Whicher
Ulrica	Irene Loosberg
Silvano	Alexander Gray (Oct. 13, 18, 24); Donald Young (Oct. 15, 22)
Servant	Walter Dinoff

Les contes d'Hoffmann Jacques Offenbach
In English
October 14, 17, 20, 22, 25, 1958
Conductor: Ettore Mazzoleni
Director: Elemer Nagy
Set: Elemer Nagy
Costume Designer: Suzanne Mess

Lindorf/Coppélius/Dappertutto/Dr. Miracle	Morley Meredith
Andrès/Cochenille/Pittichinaccio/Franz	Donald Bartle
Luther	James Whicher
Herman	Donald Young
Nathanael	Alan Crofoot
Hoffmann	Jim Hawthorne
Nicklausse/Muse	Margaret Schelin (Oct. 14, 17); Joanne Ivey (Oct. 20, 22, 25)
Spalanzani	Ernest Adams
Olympia/Stella/Giulietta/Antonia	Marguerite Gignac
Schlemil/Crespel	Jan Rubes
The Voice of Antonia's Mother	Patricia Rideout

La Bohème   Giacomo Puccini
October 16, 18, 21, 23, 25, 1958
Conductor: Walter Susskind
Director: Robert Gill
Set: Marie Day
Costume Designer: Marie Day

Marcello	Norman Mittleman
Rodolfo	John McCollum
Colline	Jan Rubes
Schaunard	Andrew MacMillan
Benoit	Ernest Adams
Mimi	Teresa Stratas
Parpignol	Walter Dinoff
Musetta	Patricia Snell
Alcindoro	Alan Crofoot
Sergeant	Victor Braun
Sergeant	James Whicher

1959

La forza del destino   Giuseppe Verdi
October 12, 14, 17, 20, 23, 1959
Conductor: Ernesto Barbini
Director: Elemer Nagy
Set: Elemer Nagy
Costume Designer: Suzanne Mess

Marchese Di Calatrava	Victor Braun
Leonora	Ilona Kombrink
Curra	Arlene Meadows
Don Alvaro	Giuseppe Campora
Alcalde	Donald Young (Oct. 12, 20); Cornelis Opthof (Oct. 14, 17, 23)
Don Carlo Di Vargas	James Milligan
Trabuco	Donald Bartle
Preziosilla	Mary McMurray
Fra Melitone	Gerhard Pechner
Padre Guardiano	Jan Rubes
Surgeon	Severin Weingort

The Love for Three Oranges   Sergei Prokofieff
In English
October 13, 16, 21, 22, 24, 1959
Conductor: Walter Susskind
Director: Mavor Moore
Set: Murray Laufer
Costume Designer: Marie Day

The King of Nowhere	Don Garrard
Pantaloon	James Whicher
Truffaldino	Alan Crofoot
Leandro	Victor Braun
Princess Clarissa	Mary McMurray
Smeraldina	Patricia Rideout
Celio	Paul Fredette
Fata Morgana	Sylvia Grant
The Prince	John Arab (Oct. 13, 22, 24); Roger Doucet (Oct. 16, 21)
The Cook	Ernest Adams
Linetta	Darlene Hirst
Ninetta	Barbara Strathdee
Nicoletta	Sheila Piercey

Il barbiere di Siviglia   Gioacchino Rossini
In English
October 15, 17, 19, 21, 24, 1959
Conductor: Ettore Mazzoleni
Director: Herman Geiger-Torel
Set: Brian Jackson
Costume Designer: Brian Jackson

Fiorello	Victor Braun
Count Almaviva	John McCollum
Figaro	Alexander Gray
Dr. Bartolo	Andrew MacMillan
Rosina	Patricia Snell

Don Basilio	Jan Rubes
Berta	Patricia Rideout
Sergeant	Donald Bartle
Notary	Victor Braun

1960

Otello **Giuseppe Verdi**
October 10, 12, 15, 18, 20, 22, 24, 1960
Conductor: Ernesto Barbini
Director: Herman Geiger-Torel
Set: Brian Jackson
Costume Designer: Brian Jackson

Montano	Cornelis Opthof (Oct. 10, 12, 18, 20); Donald Young (Oct. 15, 22, 24)
Cassio	Phil Stark
Iago	Louis Quilico
Roderigo	John Arab (Oct. 10, 12, 15, 18, 20, 22); Wallace Williamson (Oct. 24)
Otello	Norman Harper (Oct. 10, 20); Aldo Bertocci (Oct. 12, 15, 18, 22, 24)
Desdemona	Ilona Kombrink
Emilia	Elsie Sawchuck
A Herald	Severin Weingort
Lodovico	Osyp Hoshuliak

Le nozze di Figaro **Wolfgang Amadeus Mozart**
In English
October 13, 15, 19, 21, 27, 29, 1960
Conductor: Walter Susskind
Director: Peter Ebert
Set: Peter Rice
Costume Designer: Suzanne Mess

Figaro	Jan Rubes
Susanna	Irene Salemka
Count Almaviva	Heinz Rehfuss
Countess Almaviva	Mary Morrison
Cherubino	Darlene Hirst
Marcellina	Patricia Rideout
Dr. Bartolo	Andrew MacMillan
Don Basilio	Phil Stark
Don Curzio	Alan Crofoot
Antonio	Alexander Gray
Barbarina	Daphne Drake
Peasant Girl	Kathryn Newman
Peasant Girl	Peggy McMurray

A Night in Venice **Johann Strauss, Jr.**
In English
October 14, 17, 19, 22, 26, 28, 29, 1960
Conductor: Ettore Mazzoleni
Director: Mavor Moore
Set: Clare Jeffery
Costume Designer: Clare Jeffery

Pappacoda	Alan Crofoot (Oct. 14, 19, 22, 29); Ernest Adams (Oct. 17, 26, 28)
Mario	Robert Briggs
Del'Aqua	Andrew MacMillan
Lorenzo	Nuni Naneff
Bartoldi	Cornelis Opthof
Ciboletta	Dodi Protero (Oct. 14, 19, 26, 28); Barbara Strathdee (Oct. 17, 22, 29)
Caramello	Alexander Gray
Francesco	Maurice Brown
Duke of Palobino	John McCollum
Barbara Del'Aqua	Arlene Meadows (Oct. 14, 19, 26, 28); Joanne Ivey (Oct. 17, 22, 29)
Serafina	Daphne Drake
Agrippina	Slava Ziemelyte
Centurio	Donald Young
Nina	Sheila Piercey

1961

Carmen **Georges Bizet**
In English
September 30, October 3, 5, 7, 13, 1961
Conductor: Walter Susskind
Director: Joan Cross
Set: Joanne Hall/Robert Prévost
Costume Designer: Suzanne Mess

Moralès	Severin Weingort
Micaela	Micheline Tessier
Don José	Richard Cassilly (Sept. 30, Oct. 3, 5); Eddy Ruhl (Oct. 7, 13)
Zuniga	Jan Rubes
Carmen	Jean Sanders
Frasquita	Constance Fisher
Mercédès	Darlene Hirst (Sept. 30, Oct. 7, 13); Elsie Sawchuk (Oct. 3, 5)
Escamillo	Victor Braun
El Remendado	Alan Crofoot
El Dancairo	Phil Stark

Cavalleria rusticana **Pietro Mascagni**
October 2, 4, 10, 12, 14, 1961
Conductor: Ernesto Barbini
Director: Joan Cross
Set: William Lord
Costume Designer: William Lord

Santuzza	Mary Simmons (Oct. 2, 4, 12, 14); Lise Joanisse (Oct. 10)
Mamma Lucia	Patricia Rideout
Alfio	Victor Braun
Turiddu	Jon Crain
Lola	Darlene Hirst

I Pagliacci **Ruggiero Leoncavallo**
October 2, 4, 10, 12, 14, 1961

Conductor: Mario Bernardi
Director: Leon Major
Set: Les Lawrence
Costume Designer: Suzanne Mess

Tonio	Benjamin Rayson
Canio	Eddy Ruhl (Oct. 2, 4, 10); Richard Cassilly (Oct. 12, 14)
First Villager	Arthur Appy
Second Villager	Tito Dean
Nedda	Sylvia Grant
Beppe	Alan Crofoot
Silvio	Ronald Nelsen

The Bartered Bride   Bedrich Smetana
In English
October 4, 6, 11, 1961
Conductor: Ettore Mazzoleni
Director: Mavor Moore
Set: Murray Laufer
Costume Designer: Clare Jeffery/William Lord

Marie	Sheila Piercey
Jenik	John McCollum
Kezal	Jan Rubes
Vasek	Alan Crofoot
Krushina	Victor Braun
Ludmila	Arlene Meadows
Springer	Phil Stark
Esmeralda	Dodi Protero
Muff	Maurice Brown
Hata	Elsie Sawchuk
Tobias Misha	Vaclovas Verikaitis

Tosca   Giacomo Puccini
October 7, 9, 11, 14, 1961
Conductor: Ernesto Barbini
Director: Herman Geiger-Torel
Set: Hans Berends
Costume Designer: Suzanne Mess

Cesare Angelotti	Vaclovas Verikaitis
A Sacristan	Ernest Adams
Mario Cavaradossi	Richard Verreau
Floria Tosca	Ilona Kombrink
Baron Scarpia	Benjamin Rayson
Spoletta	Phil Stark
Sciarrone	Ronald Nelsen
Shepherd Boy	Eva Szilard
Jailer	Maurice Brown

1962

Madama Butterfly   Giacomo Puccini
October 13, 16, 18, 22, 24, 1962
Conductor: Ernesto Barbini

Director: Andrew MacMillan
Set: Les Lawrence
Costume Designer: Suzanne Mess

Cio-Cio-San	Teresa Stratas
Suzuki	Patricia Rideout
Pinkerton	William Lewis
Sharpless	Alexander Gray (Oct. 13, 16, 22); Victor Braun (Oct. 18, 24)
Goro	Alan Crofoot
The Bonze	Peter Van Ginkel
Prince Yamadori	William Copeland
Commissioner	Tito Dean
Kate Pinkerton	Jean MacPhail (Oct. 13, 18, 24); Mona Kelly (Oct. 16, 22)
Dolore	Tricia Adams

Rigoletto   Giuseppe Verdi
October 15, 17, 20, 24, 26, 1962
Conductor: Ernesto Barbini
Director: Leon Major
Set: Murray Laufer
Costume Designer: Suzanne Mess

Rigoletto	Louis Quilico
The Duke of Mantua	Enrico DiGiuseppe
Gilda	Gwenlynn Little
Maddalena	Mary McMurray
Count Ceprano	Maurice Brown (Oct. 15, 20, 24); William Copeland (Oct. 17, 26)
Marullo	Ronald Nelsen
Count Monterone	Victor Braun (Oct. 15, 20, 26); Alexander Gray (Oct. 17, 24)
Sparafucile	Jan Rubes (Oct. 15, 17, 20, 24); Peter Van Ginkel (Oct. 26)
Borsa	Thomas Clerke (Oct. 15, 20, 24); Wallace Williamson (Oct. 17, 26)
Countess Ceprano	Franki Pannell (Oct. 15, 20, 26); Diane Gibson (Oct.17, 24)
Giovanna	June Grant
Page	Diane Gibson (Oct. 15, 20, 26); Franki Pannell (Oct. 17, 24)
Usher	Tito Dean (Oct. 15, 20, 24); Maurice Brown (Oct. 17, 26)

Hänsel und Gretel   Engelbert Humperdinck
In English
October 17, 19, 20, 27, 1962
Conductor: Ettore Mazzoleni
Director: Leon Major
Set: William Lord
Costume Designer: William Lord

Gretel	Dodi Protero
Hänsel	Mary McMurray
Gertrude	Elsie Sawchuk
Peter	Cornelis Opthof
The Sandman	Patricia Rideout

The Dew Man   Heather Thomson
The Witch   Phil Stark

Die Walküre   **Richard Wagner**
October 23, 25, 27, 1962
Conductor: Walter Susskind
Director: Herman Geiger-Torel
Set: Louis Kerenyi
Costume Designer: Csilla Marki

Siegmund	Karl Liebl
Sieglinde	Mary Simmons
Hunding	Jan Rubes
Wotan	Paul Schoeffler
Brünnhilde	Gladys Kuchta
Fricka	Arlene Meadows
Gerhilde	Constance Fisher
Waltraute	Elizabeth Elliott
Schwerleite	Irene Loosberg
Ortlinde	Sylvia Grant
Helmwige	June Grant
Siegrune	Elsie Sawchuck
Rossweise	Marguerite DesJardins
Grimgerde	Mona Kelly

1963

Der Rosenkavalier   **Richard Strauss**
In English
September 21, 24, 26, October 2, 9, 1963
Conductor: Walter Susskind
Director: Herman Geiger-Torel
Set: Horst Dantz
Costume Designer: Horst Dantz

Octavian	Helen Vanni
Feldmarschallin	Marguerite Willauer
Major-Domo	Wallace Williamson
Baron Ochs	Howell Glynne
Attorney	Maurice Brown
A Milliner	Carrol Anne Curry (Sept. 21, 26, Oct. 9); Roxolana Roslak (Sept. 24, Oct. 2)
An Animal Tamer	Danny Tait (Sept. 21, 26, Oct. 9); Bernard Fitch (Sept. 24, Oct. 2)
Valzacchi	Phil Stark
Annina	Patricia Rideout
Noble Orphan	Eleanor Calbes
Noble Orphan	Kathryn Newman
Noble Orphan	Naomi Alexandroff
A Singer	Alan Crofoot
Leopold	Ron Hastings
Herr Von Faninal	Bernard Turgeon
Sophie	Marjorie Hays
Marianne	Elizabeth Elliott
Major-Domo of Faninal	Garnet Brooks
Innkeeper	Thomas Clerke
Police Commissioner	Peter Van Ginkel

Mahomet	Cathy Ball
Footman	Ernest Atkinson
Footman	Garnet Brooks
Footman	Tito Dean
Footman	David Geary
Waiter	Ernest Atkinson
Waiter	Tito Dean
Waiter	William Perry
Waiter	David Geary

Aïda   **Giuseppe Verdi**
September 23, 25, 28, October 1, 4, 10, 1963
Conductor: Ernesto Barbini
Director: Dino Yannopoulos
Set: Murray Laufer
Costume Designer: Marie Day

Ramphis	Don Garrard (Sept. 23, Oct. 10); Justino Diaz (Sept. 25, 28, Oct. 1, 4)
Radames	Richard Cassilly
Amneris	Cecilia Ward
Aïda	Ella Lee
The King of Egypt	Osyp Hoshuliak (Sept. 23, 25, Oct. 1); Maurice Brown (Sept. 28, Oct. 4, 10)
Messenger	Arthur Apy (Sept. 23, 28, Oct. 1); Wallace Williamson (Sept. 25, Oct. 4, 10)
Priestess	Maria Pellegrini (Sept. 23, 28, Oct. 1); Norma Lewicki (Sept. 25, Oct. 4, 10)
Amonasro	Victor Braun

La Bohème   **Giacomo Puccini**
September 25, 28, October 2, 5, 11, 1963
Conductor: Mario Bernardi
Director: Andrew MacMillan
Set: Marie Day
Costume Designer: Suzanne Mess

Marcello	Cornelis Opthof
Rodolfo	John Arab
Colline	Peter Van Ginkel
Schaunard	Bernard Turgeon
Benoit	Tito Dean
Mimi	Heather Thomson
Parpignol	Arthur Apy (Sept. 25, Oct. 2, 11); Ernest Atkinson (Sept. 28, Oct. 5)
Musetta	Constance Fisher
Alcindoro	Phil Stark
Custom-House Sergeant	Wallace Williamson
Custom-House Sergeant	Joseph Macko
Headwaiter	Ron Hastings

Don Giovanni   **Wolfgang Amadeus Mozart**
In English
September 27, 30, October 3, 5, 12, 1963
Conductor: Walter Susskind/Mario Bernardi
Director: Mavor Moore
Set: Rudi Dorn

246

Costume Designer: Suzanne Mess

Leporello	Jan Rubes
Donna Anna	Beverly Bower
Don Giovanni	Don Garrard
The Commendatore	Justino Diaz
Don Ottavio	Frank Porretta
Donna Elvira	Sylvia Grant
Zerlina	Sheila Piercey
Masetto	Alexander Gray

Hänsel und Gretel   Engelbert Humperdinck
In English
October 7, 8, 9, 12, 1963
Conductor: Ettore Mazzoleni
Director: Leon Major
Set: William Lord
Costume Designer: William Lord

Gretel	Dodi Protero
Hänsel	Edith Evans
Gertrude	Irene Loosberg
Peter	Cornelis Opthof
The Sandman	Kathryn Newman
The Dew Man	Carrol Anne Curry
The Witch	Arlene Meadows

1964

La Traviata   Giuseppe Verdi
September 12, 16, 19, 25, October 1, 1964
Conductor: Ernesto Barbini
Director: Irving Guttman
Set: Jean-Claude Rinfret
Costume Designer: Suzanne Mess

Violetta	Maria Di Gerlando
Alfredo	John Arab
Germont	Victor Braun
Flora	Helly Sapinski
Annina	Maria Pellegrini
Gastone	Wallace Williamson
Baron Douphol	William Copeland
Marquis	Tito Dean
Dr. Grenvil	Peter van Ginkel
Giuseppe	Nuni Naneff

Carmen   Georges Bizet
September 14, 18, 23, 1964
Conductor: George Crum
Director: Leon Major
Set: Robert Prévost/Joanne Hall
Costume Designer: Suzanne Mess

Moralès	Tito Dean
Micaela	Joan Patenaude

Don José	Jon Vickers
Zuniga	Peter van Ginkel
Carmen	Mignon Dunn
Frasquita	Muriel James
Mercédès	Geneviève Perreault
Escamillo	Victor Braun
El Remendado	Bernard Fitch
El Dancairo	Phil Stark

Die Fledermaus   Johann Strauss, Jr.
In English
September 15, 19, 24, 30, October 3, 1964
Conductor: Ettore Mazzoleni
Director: Andrew MacMillan
Set: John Wilson
Costume Designer: William Lord

Rosalinda	Heather Thomson
Gabriel Von Eisenstein	Cornelis Opthof
Adele	Sheila Piercey
Alfred	John Arab (Sept. 15, 24, Oct. 3); Garnet Brooks (Sept. 19, 30)
Frank	William Copeland
Prince Orlofsky	Jan Rubes
Dr. Falke	Alexander Gray
Frosch	Ron Hastings
Dr. Blind	Richard Braun
Fifi	Eleanor Calbes
Ivan	Robert Carley

Madama Butterfly   Giacomo Puccini
September 17, 26, 29, October 3, 1964
Conductor: James Craig
Director: Werner L. Graf
Set: Les Lawrence
Costume Designer: Suzanne Mess

Cio-Cio-San	Mietta Sighele
Suzuki	Fernande Chiocchio
Pinkerton	Garnet Brooks
Sharpless	Alexander Gray
Goro	Phil Stark
The Bonze	Peter van Ginkel
Prince Yamadori	Richard Braun
Commissioner	Tito Dean
Kate Pinkerton	Lilian Sukis
Dolore	Dina Mammon
Yakusidé	Nuni Naneff
Mother	Marcelle Zonta
Cousin	Jeannette Zarou
Aunt	Ruth Shakarian

Aïda   Giuseppe Verdi
September 22, 26, 28, October 2, 1964
Conductor: Ernesto Barbini
Director: Herman Geiger-Torel
Set: Murray Laufer

Costume Designer: Marie Day

Ramphis	Jan Rubes
Radames	Richard Cassilly (Sep. 22, 28, Oct. 2); Jon Vickers (Sep. 26)
Amneris	Marilyn Horne
Aïda	Elizabeth Fretwell
The King of Egypt	Osyp Hoshuliak
Messenger	Wallace Williamson
Priestess	Jeannette Zarou
Amonasro	Napoléon Bisson

1965

Turandot　　　　　**Giacomo Puccini**
September 17, 21, 27, October 2, 6, 9, 1965
Conductor: Ernesto Barbini
Director: Leon Major
Set: Murray Laufer
Costume Designer: Marie Day

A Mandarin	Donald Young
Liu	Jeannette Zarou (Sep. 17, 27, Oct. 2); Helly Sapinski (Sep. 21, Oct. 6, 9)
Calaf	Giuseppe Campora
Timur	Howell Glynne
Prince of Persia	Ermanno Mauro
Ping	Bernard Turgeon
Pang	Garnet Brooks
Pong	Thomas Clerke
The Emperor	Danny Tait
Princess Turandot	Jeannine Crader

Il barbiere di Siviglia　　　　**Gioacchino Rossini**
In English
September 18, 22, 25, October 1, 4, 1965
Conductor: Mario Bernardi
Director: Irving Guttman
Set: William Lord
Costume Designer: Suzanne Mess

Sergeant	Thomas Park
Fiorello	Richard Braun
Count Almaviva	John Arab
Figaro	Alexander Gray
Dr. Bartolo	Bernard Turgeon
Rosina	Barbara Strathdee
Don Basilio	Jan Rubes
Berta	Patricia Rideout
Notary	Heinar Piller
Ambrogio	Abbott Anderson

Rigoletto　　　　　**Giuseppe Verdi**
September 20, 24, 30, October 6, 9, 1965
Conductor: Ernesto Barbini
Director: Leon Major

Set: Murray Laufer
Costume Designer: Suzannr Mess

Rigoletto	Peter Glossop
The Duke of Mantua	Gianni Savelli
Gilda	Maria Pellegrini
Maddalena	Arlene Meadows (Sep. 20, 24, Oct. 9); Darlene Hirst (Sep. 30, Oct. 6)
Count Ceprano	Oskar Raulfs
Marullo	Donald Young
Count Monterone	Howell Glynne
Sparafucile	Jan Rubes
Borsa	Wallace Williamson
Countess Ceprano	Joanna Myhal (Sep. 20, 30, Oct. 6); Roxolana Roslak (Sep. 24, Oct. 9)
Giovanna	June Grant
Page	Nancy Gottschalk
Usher	Paul Frederics

La Bohème　　　　　**Giacomo Puccini**
September 23, 28, October 2, 8, 1965
Conductor: James Craig
Director: Andrew MacMillan
Set: Marie Day
Costume Designer: Warren Hartman

Marcello	Alexander Gray (Sep. 23, Oct. 8); Peter Glossop (Sep. 28, Oct. 2)
Rodolfo	Jean Bonhomme
Colline	Maurice Brown
Schaunard	Tito Dean
Benoit	Richard Braun
Mimi	Dorothy Coulter (Sep. 23, 28, Oct. 8); Lilian Sukis (Oct. 2)
Parpignol	Ermanno Mauro
Musetta	Dodi Protero (Sep. 23, Oct. 2, 8); Eleanor Calbes (Sep. 28)
Alcindoro	Phil Stark
Sergeant	Paul Frederics
Sergeant	Herman Rombouts

Salome　　　　　**Richard Strauss**
September 25, 29, October 5, 7, 1965
Conductor: Wolfgang Martin
Director: Herman Geiger-Torel
Set: Brian Jackson
Costume Designer: Suzanne Mess

Narraboth	Garnet Brooks
A Page	Darlene Hirst
First Soldier	Donald Young
Second Soldier	Maurice Brown
A Cappadocian	David Geary
Salome	Margaret Tynes
A Slave	Roxolana Roslak (Sep. 25, Oct. 5); Joanna Myhal (Sep. 29, Oct. 7)
Jokanaan	Royce Reaves
Herod	Phil Stark

Herodias	Arlene Meadows
First Jew	Thomas Park
Second Jew	Danny Tait
Third Jew	Ian Garratt
Fourth Jew	Wallace Williamson
Fifth Jew	Tito Dean
First Nazarene	Oskar Raulfs
Second Nazarene	Ermanno Mauro
Naaman	Abbott Anderson

Mavra　　　　　　**Igor Stravinsky**
In English
September 25, 29, October 5, 7, 1965
Conductor: Mario Bernardi
Director: Werner L. Graf
Set: Brian Jackson
Costume Designer: Suzanne Mess

Parasha	Sheila Piercey (Sep. 25, Oct. 5, 7); Dodi Protero (Sep. 29)
Vassili	Thomas Clerke
Mother of Parasha	Patricia Rideout
A Neighbour	Geneviève Perreault

1966

Faust　　　　　　**Charles Gounod**
September 15, 19, 23, October 1, 5, 8, 1966
Conductor: Pierre Hétu
Director: Leon Major
Set: Les Lawrence
Costume Designer: Suzanne Mess

Faust	Jean Bonhomme
Méphistophélès	Jan Rubes
Valentin	Cornelis Opthof
Wagner	Richard Braun
Siébel	Geneviève Perreault
Marguerite	Heather Thomson
Marthe	Elizabeth Mawson

Macbeth　　　　　　**Giuseppe Verdi**
September 16, 22, 26, 28 1966
Conductor: Ernesto Barbini
Director: Herman Geiger-Torel
Set: Marie Day
Costume Designer: Marie Day

Macbeth	Louis Quilico
Banquo	Osyp Hoshuliak
Lady Macbeth	Margaret Tynes
A Servant	Lloyd Dean
Macduff	Luigi Infantino
Malcolm	Ermanno Mauro
Lady-in-Waiting	Sheila Piercey
Murderer	Leonid Skirko

Murderer	Thomas Park
Fleance	Phillip Blackford
Warrior Apparition	Stan Kane
Bloody Child	Nancy Greenwood
Crowned Child	Nancy Gottschalk
Physician	Richard Braun
King Duncan	Herman Rombouts

Cavalleria rusticana　　　**Pietro Mascagni**
September 17, 21, 27, 30, October 6, 8, 1966
Conductor: Nello Segurini
Director: Irving Guttman
Set: William Lord
Costume Designer: William Lord

Santuzza	Helly Sapinski
Mamma Lucia	Patricia Rideout
Alfio	Bernard Turgeon
Turiddu	Francisco Lazaro (Sep. 17, 21, 27, 30); Gianni Savelli (Oct. 6, 8)
Lola	Geneviève Perreault
A Woman	Nicole Lorange

I Pagliacci　　　　**Ruggiero Leoncavallo**
September 17, 21, 27, 30, October 6, 8, 1966
Conductor: James Craig
Director: Leon Major
Set: Les Lawrence
Costume Designer: Warren Hartman

Tonio	Bernard Turgeon
Canio	Francisco Lazaro (Sep. 17, 21, 27, 30); Gianni Savelli (Oct. 6, 8)
First Villager	Giuseppe Macina
Second Villager	Stan Kane
Nedda	Maria Pellegrini
Beppe	Garnet Brooks (Sep. 17, 21, Oct. 8); Thomas Park (Sep. 27, 30, Oct. 6)
Silvio	Alexander Gray

La Traviata　　　　**Giuseppe Verdi**
September 20, 24, October 1, 3, 7, 1966
Conductor: Ernesto Barbini
Director: Irving Guttman
Set: Jean-Claude Rinfret
Costume Designer: Suzanne Mess

Violetta	Maria Chiara (Sep. 20, 24, Oct. 3, 7); Maria Di Gerlando (Oct. 1)
Alfredo	Luigi Infantino
Germont	Louis Quilico
Flora	Elizabeth Mawson
Annina	Kathryn Newman
Gastone	Wallace Williamson (Sep. 20, Oct. 1, 7); Garnet Brooks (Sep. 24, Oct. 3)
Baron Douphol	Howard Mawson
Marquis	Philip May

Dr. Grenvil	Maurice Brown
Giuseppe	Giuseppe Macina

Deirdre   **Healey Willan/John Coulter**
September 24, 29, October 4, 1966
Conductor: Ettore Mazzoleni
Director: Herman Geiger-Torel
Set: Lawrence Schäfer
Costume Designer: William Lord

Cathva	Howell Glynne
Conochar	Bernard Turgeon
Fergus	Oskar Raulfs
Levercham	Patricia Rideout
Deirdre	Jeannette Zarou
Naisi	Gianni Savelli
Ardan	Richard Braun
Ainnle	Thomas Park
A Fighter	Howard Mawson
A Spy	Maurice Brown
Levercham's Helper	Nancy Greenwood
Levercham's Helper	Nancy Gottschalk
Levercham's Helper	Maida Rogerson

1967

The Luck of Ginger Coffey   **Raymond Pannell/Ronald Hambleton**
September 15, 19, October 2, 1967
Conductor: Samuel Krachmalnick
Director: Herman Geiger-Torel
Set: Lawrence Schäfer
Costume Designer: Warren Hartman

Ginger Coffey	Harry Theyard
Voice in the Pit	Garnet Brooks
Voice in the Pit	Ernest Atkinson
Voice in the Pit	Franki Pannell
Voice in the Pit	Sheila Piercey
Priest	Maurice Brown
Achille Beauchemin	Alexander Gray
Veronica	Mignon Dunn
Paulie	Doreen Millman
Michel	Robert McLennan
Gerry Grosvenor	William Pickett
Hickey	Donald Rutherford
Fox	Ernest Atkinson
Kenny	Jacques Lareau
Oona	Dodi Protero
Clarence	Alan Crofoot
Old Billy	Peter Milne
MacGregor	Eugene Green
Madame Beaulieu	Geneviève Perreault
Annette	Elsie Sawchuk
Melody Ward	Franki Pannell
Bruno	Robert Jeffrey
Sammy	Richard Braun

Torchy	Daniel Saunders
Rose	Sheila Piercey
Rhodes	Garnet Brooks
First Cop	Donald Rutherford
Second Cop	Thomas Park
Jailer	David Geary
Voice in Tank	Oskar Raulfs
Voice in Tank	Lloyd Dean
Voice in Tank	Peter Milne
Judge	Maurice Brown

Il Trovatore   **Giuseppe Verdi**
September 16, 21, 27, October 3, 7, 9, 13, 1967
onductor: Ernesto Barbini
Director: Rexford Harrower
Set: Enzo Deho
Costume Designer: Casa d'Arte Fiore

Ferrando	Maurice Brown
Inez	Kathryn Newman (Sept. 16, 27, Oct. 7, 13); Marilyn Carley (Sept. 21, Oct. 3, 9)
Leonora	Jeannine Crader (Sept. 16, 21, 27, Oct. 7, 9); Helly Sapinski (Oct. 3, 13)
Count Di Luna	Victor Braun
Manrico	Francisco Lazaro, (Ermanno Mauro)
Azucena	Mignon Dunn (Sept. 16, 21, 27); Dorothy Cole (Oct. 3, 7, 9, 13)
An Old Gypsy	Lloyd Dean
A Messenger	Remo Marinucci
Ruiz	Ermanno Mauro

Il barbiere di Siviglia   **Gioacchino Rossini**
In English
September 18, 22, 30, October 5, 10, 14, 1967
Conductor: Ernesto Barbini
Director: Irving Guttman
Set: William Lord
Costume Designer: William Lord

Fiorello	Richard Braun
Count Almaviva	Perry Price
Figaro	Alexander Gray
Dr. Bartolo	Eugene Green
Rosina	Colette Boky (Sept. 18, Oct. 5, 10, 14); Sheila Piercey (Sept. 22, 30)
Don Basilio	Jan Rubes (Sept. 18, 22, 30); Joseph Rouleau (Oct. 5, 10, 14)
Berta	Patricia Rideout
Sergeant	Thomas Park

Les contes d'Hoffmann   **Jacques Offenbach**
September 20, 25, 29, October 5, 7, 12, 14, 1967
Conductor: Otto-Werner Mueller
Director: Peter Ebert
Set: Brian Jackson
Costume Designer: Suzanne Mess

Lindorf/Coppélius/Dappertutto/Dr.Miracle Andrès/Cochenille/Pittichinaccio/Franz	Norman Mittleman Alan Crofoot (Sept. 20, 25, 29, Oct. 5, 7); André Lortie (Oct. 12, 14)
Luther	Oskar Raulfs
Hermann	Lloyd Dean
Nathanael	Ernest Atkinson
Hoffmann	André Turp (Sept. 20, 25, 29, Oct. 5, 7, 14); David Astor (Oct. 12)
Nicklausse	Geneviève Perreault
Spalanzani	Phil Stark
Antonia/Giulietta	Roxolana Roslak; Heather Thomson
Olympia/Stella	Colette Boky (Sept. 20, Oct. 7, 12); Eleanor Calbes (Sept. 25, 29, Oct. 5, 14)
Schlémil/Crespel	Jan Rubes
Antonia's Mother	Nancy Greenwood

Louis Riel   **Harry Somers/Mavor Moore**
September 23, 28, October 11, 1967
Conductor: Victor Feldbrill
Director: Leon Major
Set: Murray Laufer
Costume Designer: Marie Day

William McDougall	Howell Glynne
A Soldier	George Reinke
Ambroise Lépine	André Lortie
Thomas Scott	Thomas Park
Joseph Delorme	Jacques Lareau
Janvier Ritchot	David Geary
Elzéar Goulet	Lloyd Dean
André Nault	Phil Stark
Baptiste Lépine	Ermanno Mauro
Elzéar Lagimodière	Donald Rutherford
Louis Riel	Bernard Turgeon
Dr. Schultz	Peter Milne
Charles Mair	Donald Saunders
O'Donaghue	John Arab
Bishop Taché	Joseph Rouleau
Sir John A. Macdonald	Cornelis Opthof
Sir George Cartier	Perry Price
Donald Smith	Ernest Atkinson
Julie Riel	Patricia Rideout
Sara Riel	Mary Morrison
Colonel Wolseley	Maurice Brown
Hudson's Bay Scout	Robert Jeffrey
Marguerite Riel	Roxolana Roslak
Gabriel Dumont	Garnet Brooks
James Isbister	Lloyd Dean
Poundmaker	Oskar Raulfs
General Middleton	Ernest Atkinson
Father André	André Lortie
Wandering Spirit	Herman Rombouts
Clerk of the Court	Donald Saunders
Judge	Maurice Brown
F. X. Lemieux	John Arab
B. B. Osler	David Geary
Dr. François Roy	Robert Jeffrey

Prison Guard	George Reinke

Madama Butterfly   **Giacomo Puccini**
September 26, 30, October 4, 6, 1967
Conductor: Ernesto Barbini
Director: Herman Geiger-Torel
Set: Les Lawrence
Costume Designer: Suzanne Mess

Cio-Cio-San	Nagisa Kai
Suzuki	Nancy Greenwood
Pinkerton	Harry Theyard
Sharpless	William Pickett
Goro	Phil Stark
The Bonze	Howell Glynne
Prince Yamadori	Richard Braun
Commissioner	Peter Milne
Kate Pinkerton	Lois Gyurica
Dolore	Caroline Hughes
Yakusidé	Herman Rombouts
Mother	Marilyn Carley
Cousin	Carmen Gagnon
Aunt	Renée Rosen

1968

Aïda   **Giuseppe Verdi**
September 13, 18, 28, October 1, 5, 7, 10, 1968
Conductor: Ernesto Barbini
Director: Herman Geiger-Torel
Set: Murray Laufer
Costume Designer: Marie Day

Ramphis	Joseph Rouleau
Radames	Carlos Barrena
Amneris	Gloria Lane
Aïda	Mirna Lacambra
The King of Egypt	Osyp Hoshuliak (Sep. 13, 18, Oct. 1, 7); Maurice Brown (Sep. 28, Oct. 5, 10)
Messenger	Peter Milne (Sep. 13, Oct. 1, 10); Donald Rutherford (Sep. 18, 28, Oct. 5, 7)
Priestess	Margaret Zeidman (Sep. 13, 28, Oct. 1, 7); Nancy Gottschalk (Sep. 18, Oct. 5, 10)
Amonasro	Louis Quilico (Sep. 13, 18, 28, Oct. 10); Bernard Turgeon (Oct. 1, 5, 7)

Louis Riel   **Harry Somers/Mavor Moore**
September 16, 20, 24, 1968
Conductor: Victor Feldbrill
Director: Leon Major
Set: Murray Laufer
Costume Designer: Marie Day

William McDougall	Howell Glynne
A Soldier	George Reinke
Ambroise Lépine	André Lortie
Thomas Scott	Thomas Park

Joseph Delorme	Jacques Lareau
Janvier Ritchot	David Geary
Elzéar Goulet	Lloyd Dean
André Nault	Phil Stark
Baptiste Lépine	Ralph Oostwoud
Elzéar Lagimodière	Donald Rutherford
Louis Riel	Bernard Turgeon
Dr. Schultz	Peter Milne
Charles Mair	Garnet Brooks
O'Donaghue	John Arab
Bishop Taché	Joseph Rouleau
Sir John A. Macdonald	William Pickett
Sir George Cartier	Paul Trépanier
Donald Smith	David Astor
Julie Riel	Patricia Rideout
Sara Riel	Gwenlynn Little
Colonel Wolseley	Maurice Brown
Hudson's Bay Scout	Danny Tait
Marguerite Riel	Roxolana Roslak
Gabriel Dumont	Garnet Brooks
James Isbister	Lloyd Dean
Poundmaker	Oskar Raulfs
General Middleton	David Astor
Father André	André Lortie
Wandering Spirit	Herman Rombouts
Clerk of the Court	Donald Rutherford
Judge	Maurice Brown
F. X. Lemieux	John Arab
B. B. Osler	David Geary
Dr. François Roy	Danny Tait
Prison Guard	George Reinke

Tosca **Giacomo Puccini**
September 21, 26, October 2, 4, 8, 12, 1968
Conductor: Ernesto Barbini
Director: Leon Major
Set: Lawrence Schäfer
Costume Designer: Suzanne Mess

Cesare Angelotti	Maurice Brown
A Sacristan	Jan Rubes
Mario Cavaradossi	Ermanno Mauro
Floria Tosca	Marina Krilovici
Baron Scarpia	Louis Quilico
Spoletta	André Lortie
Sciarrone	Oskar Raulfs
Shepherd Boy	Renée Rosen
Jailer	Herman Rombouts

La Bohème **Giacomo Puccini**
September 23, 28, October 3, 5, 9, 11, 1968
Conductor: James Craig
Director: Constance Fisher
Set: Marie Day
Costume Designer: Warren Hartman

Marcello	Alexander Gray
Rodolfo	Pierre Duval
Colline	Jan Rubes

Schaunard	Peter Milne (Sep. 23, 28, Oct. 5); Donald Rutherford (Oct. 3, 9, 11)
Benoit	Richard Braun
Mimi	Heather Thomson
Parpignol	Remo Marinucci
Musetta	Sheila Piercey (Sep. 23, 28, Oct. 5); Roxolana Roslak (Oct. 3, 9, 11)
Alcindoro	Phil Stark
Sergeant	Herman Rombouts
Sergeant	Giuseppe Macina

Salome **Richard Strauss**
September 25, 27, 30, October 3, 10, 12, 1968
Conductor: Samuel Krachmalnick
Director: Herman Geiger-Torel
Set: Brian Jackson
Costume Designer: Suzanne Mess

Narraboth	Garnet Brooks
Page	Geneviève Perreault
First Soldier	David Geary
Second Soldier	Jacques Lareau
A Cappadocian	Lloyd Dean
Salome	Maria Kouba
A Slave	Nancy Gottschalk (Sep. 25, 30. Oct. 3); Lorna Hearst (Sep. 27, Oct. 10, 12)
Jokanaan	William Pickett
Herod	Phil Stark
Herodias	Gloria Lane (Sep. 25, 27, Oct. 3, 12); Elsie Sawchuk (Sep. 30, Oct. 10)
First Jew	Thomas Park
Second Jew	Danny Tait
Third Jew	Ernest Atkinson
Fourth Jew	Ralph Oostwoud
Fifth Jew	Richard Braun
First Nazarene	Oskar Raulfs
Second Nazarene	Giuseppe Macina
Naaman	Vance Davis

1969

La forza del destino **Giuseppe Verdi**
September 12, 17, 22, 27, October 9, 11, 1969
Conductor: Ernesto Barbini
Director: Anthony Besch
Set: Murray Laufer
Costume Designer: Suzanne Mess

Marchese Di Calatrava	Howell Glynne
Leonora	Marina Krilovici
Curra	Elsie Sawchuk
Don Alvaro	Salvador Novoa
Alcalde	Steven Henrikson
Don Carlos	Benjamin Rayson
Trabuco	Robert Glover
Preziosilla	Mignon Dunn
Fra Melitone	Peter Milne

| Padre Guardiano | Don Garrard |
| Surgeon | Igor Saika-Voivod |

Die Fledermaus   **Johann Strauss, Jr.**
In English
September 15, 19, 27, 30, October 2, 8, 11, 1969
Conductor: Victor Feldbrill
Director: Leo Nedomansky
Set: John Wilson
Costume Designer: Warren Hartman

Rosalinda	Milla Andrew
Eisenstein	Cornelis Opthof
Adele	Gwenlynn Little
Alfred	Alan Crofoot (Sep. 15, 19); John Arab (Sep. 27, 30, Oct. 2, 8, 11)
Frank	Richard Braun
Prince Orlofsky	Jan Rubes
Dr. Falke	Donald Rutherford
Frosch	Howell Glynne
Dr. Blind	Steven Henrikson
Fifi	Riki Turofsky
Ivan	Herman Rombouts

Elektra   **Richard Strauss**
September 20, 24, October 3, 1969
Conductor: Heinrich Bender
Directo: Herman Geiger-Torel
Set: Lawrence Schäfer
Costume Designer: Marie Day

Serving Woman	Joan Maxwell
Serving Woman	Kathryn Newman
Serving Woman	Leah Wertman
Serving Woman	Dodi Protero
Serving Woman	Elsie Sawchuk
Overseer	Stephanie Gerson
Elektra	Astrid Varnay
Chrysothemis	Eileen Schauler
Klytemnestra	Mignon Dunn (Sept. 20, 24); Elsie Sawchuk (Oct. 3)
Confidante	Sonia Rohozynsky
Trainbearer	Lorna Hearst
Young Servant	Paul Trépanier
Old Servant	Steven Henrikson
Orestes	Richard Mundt
Guardian of Orestes	Herman Rombouts
Aegisthus	Phil Stark

Turandot   **Giacomo Puccini**
September 23, 26, October 4, 6, 1969
Conductor: Ernesto Barbini
Director: Leon Major
Set: Murray Laufer
Costume Designer: Marie Day

| A Mandarin | Peter Milne |
| Liù | Heather Thomson |

Calaf	Richard Cassilly
Timur	Jan Rubes
Prince of Persia	Remo Marinucci
Ping	Donald Rutherford
Pang	Phil Stark
Pong	Garnet Brooks
The Emperor of China	Robert Glover
Princess Turandot	Marion Lippert

Rigoletto   **Giuseppe Verdi**
September 25, 29, October 1, 4, 7, 10, 1969
Conductor: Mario Bernardi/Alfred Strombergs
Director: Leon Major
Set: Murray Laufer
Costume Designer: Suzanne Mess

Rigoletto	Louis Quilico
The Duke of Mantua	Pierre Duval
Gilda	Urszula Koszut
Maddalena	Joan Maxwell
Count Ceprano	Herman Rombouts
Marullo	Richard Braun
Count Monterone	Don Garrard
Sparafucile	Richard Mundt
Borsa	Paul Trépanier
Countess Ceprano	Lorna Hearst
Giovanna	Kathryn Newman
Page	Renée Rosen
Usher	Igor Saika-Voivod

1970

La Traviata   **Giuseppe Verdi**
September 19, 23, 26, October 2, 6, 12, 15, 1970
Conductor: Ernesto Barbini
Director: Sonja Frisell
Set: Jean-Claude Rinfret
Costume Designer: Warren Hartman

Violetta	Urszula Koszut
Alfredo	John Arab
Germont	Louis Quilico (Sep. 19, 23, 26, Oct. 2, 6, 12); Abe Polakoff (Oct. 15)
Flora	Sonia Rohozynsky
Annina	Kathryn Newman
Gastone	Roelof Oostwoud
Baron Douphol	Allen Coates
Marquis	Steven Henrikson
Dr. Grenvil	Herman Rombouts
Giuseppe	Remo Marinucci (Sep. 19, 26, Oct. 6, 15); Antonio Zanet (Sep. 23, Oct. 2, 12)

Carmen   **Georges Bizet**
September 22, 26, October 1, 5, 10, 14, 16, 1970
Conductor: Mario Bernardi/Alfred Strombergs
Director: David Peacock

Set: Joanne Hall/Robert Prévost
Costume Designer: Suzanne Mess

Moralès	Steven Henrikson
Micaela	Roxolana Roslak
Don Jose	Jean Bonhomme
Zuniga	Claude Corbeil
Carmen	Ruza Baldani
Frasquita	Sheila Piercey
Mercedes	Sonia Rohozynsky
Escamillo	Cornelis Opthof
Remendado	Alan Crofoot
Dancairo	Phil Stark

Faust   **Charles Gounod**
September 25, 29, October 3, 8, 17, 1970
Conductor: Ernesto Barbini
Director: Leon Major
Set: Les Lawrence
Costume Designer: Suzanne Mess

Faust	John Walker
Méphistophélès	Don Garrard
Valentin	Cornelis Opthof
Wagner	Steven Henrikson
Siébel	Renee Rosen
Marguerite	Jeannette Zarou
Marthe	Leah Wertman

Fidelio   **Ludwig van Beethoven**
October 3, 7, 9, 13, 1970
Conductor: Heinrich Bender
Director: Carlos Alexander
Set: Murray Laufer
Costume Designer: Marie Day

Jaquino	Phil Stark
Marzelline	Dodi Protero
Rocco	Don McManus
Leonore	Anja Silja
Don Pizarro	Chester Ludgin
First Prisoner	Ernest Atkinson
Second Prisoner	Herman Rombouts
Florestan	Glade Peterson
Don Fernando	Claude Corbeil

Don Giovanni   **Wolfgang Amadeus Mozart**
In English
September 18, 24, 28, 30, October 10, 17, 1970
Conductor: Victor Feldbrill/Alfred Strombergs
Director: Herman Geiger-Torel
Set: Lawrence Schäfer
Costume Designer: Suzanne Mess

Leporello	Jan Rubes
Donna Anna	Eileen Schauler
Don Giovanni	Justino Diaz

The Commendatore	Don McManus
Don Ottavio	Garnet Brooks
Donna Elvira	Heather Thomson
Zerlina	Gwenlynn Little (Sep. 18, 24, 30, Oct. 10, 17); Riki Turofsky (Sep. 28)
Masetto	Claude Corbeil

1971

Lucia di Lammermoor   **Gaetano Donizetti**
September 17, 22, 27, October 2, 5, 9, 14, 1971
Conductor: Ernesto Barbini
Director: Sonja Frisell
Set: Lawrence Schäfer
Costume Designer: Suzanne Mess

Normanno	Edward Matthiessen (Sep. 17, 27, Oct. 5, 14); David Meek (Sep. 22, Oct. 2, 9)
Lord Enrico Ashton	Louis Quilico (Sep. 17, 22, Oct. 2); Cornelis Opthof (Sep. 27, Oct. 5, 9, 14)
Raimondo	Don Garrard
Lucia	Cristina Deutekom
Alisa	Kathryn Newman
Edgardo	Ermanno Mauro
Lord Arturo Bucklaw	Garnet Brooks

The Merry Widow   **Franz Lehár**
In English
September 18, 23, 25, 29, Oct. 8, 11, 12, 16, 1971
Conductor: Victor Feldbrill
Director: Leon Major
Set: Murray Laufer
Costume Designer: Marie Day

St. Brioche	Alan Crofoot
Baron Zeta	Jan Rubes
Valencienne	Gwenlynn Little
Camille	John Arab
Cascada	Alexander Gray
Kromov	Don McManus
Olga	Sheila Piercey
Bogdanowitsch	Peter Milne
Sylvaine	Sonia Rohozynsky
Njegus	Allen Coates
Anna Glawari	Lynne Cantlon
Count Danilo	John Reardon
Lolo	Judith Lebane
Dodo	Kathleen Ruddell
Waiter	Herman Rombouts (Sep. 18, 25, Oct. 8, 12); Richard Braun (Sep. 23, 29, Oct. 11, 16)
Jou Jou	Clare Bewley

Madama Butterfly   **Giacomo Puccini**
September 21, 24, 30, Oct. 2, 4, 7, 14, 16, 1971
Conductor: Alfred Strombergs

254

Director: Carlos Alexander
Set: Les Lawrence
Costume Designer: Suzanne Mess

Cio-Cio-San	Maria Pellegrini
Suzuki	Patricia Rideout
Pinkerton	Michael Trimble
Sharpless	Cornelis Opthof (Sep. 21, 30, Oct. 7, 16); Alexander Gray (Sep. 24, Oct. 2, 4, 14)
Goro	Phil Stark
The Bonze	Avo Kittask
Yamadori	Antonio Zanet (Sep. 21, 30, Oct. 4, 14); Richard Braun (Sep. 24, Oct. 2, 7, 16)
Commisioner	Peter Barcza (Sep. 21, 30, Oct. 4, 14); Gary Relyea (Sep. 24, Oct. 2, 7, 16)
Kate Pinkerton	Kathleen Ruddell
Dolore	Lillian Brych
Registrar	Gerard Boyd
Yakusidé	Remo Marinucci
Mother	Florence Maltese
Cousin	Judith LeBane
Aunt	Anne Marie Clark

Macbeth   **Giuseppe Verdi**
September 28, October 6, 9, 15, 1971
Conductor: Ernesto Barbini
Director: Georg Philipp
Set: Marie Day
Costume Designer: Marie Day

Macbeth	Louis Quilico
Banquo	Don McManus
Lady Macbeth	Elinor Ross
A Servant	Lloyd Dean
Macduff	John Arab
Malcolm	Garnet Brooks
Lady-in-Waiting	Lynn Blaser (Sep. 28, Oct. 9); Ann Cooper (Oct. 6, 15)
Murderer	Avo Kittask
Fleance	Christopher Svensson (Sep. 28, Oct. 9); Michael Kennard (Oct. 6, 15)
Warrior Apparition	Peter Barcza (Sep. 28, Oct. 9); Gary Relyea (Oct. 6, 15)
Bloody Child	Nancy Greenwood
Crowned Child	Roxolana Roslak
Physician	Richard Braun (Sep. 28, Oct. 9); Herman Rombouts (Oct. 6, 15)

Die Walküre   **Richard Wagner**
September 25, October 1, 7, 13, 1971
Conductor: Heinrich Bender
Director: Herman Geiger-Torel
Set: Louis Kerenyi
Costume Designer: Csilla Marki

Siegmund	Richard Cassilly
Sieglinde	Helly Sapinski
Hunding	Don Garrard

Wotan	Norman Bailey
Brünnhilde	Klara Barlow
Fricka	Maureen Forrester
Gerhilde	Gwenlynn Little
Waltraute	Raisa Sadowa
Schwerleite	Patricia Rideout
Ortlinde	Dodi Protero
Helmwige	Roxolana Roslak
Siegrune	Elsie Sawchuk
Rossweise	Nancy Greenwood
Grimgerde	Renée Rosen

1972

Siegfried   **Richard Wagner**
September 15, 21, 27, 30, 1972
Conductor: Heinrich Bender
Director: Herman Geiger-Torel
Set: Murray Laufer
Costume Designer: Marie Day

Mime	Phil Stark
Siegfried	Karl-Josef Hering
Der Wanderer	Walter Cassel
Alberich	Alexander Gray
Fafner	Jan Rubes
Forest Bird	Ann Cooper
Erda	Nina Vanderlinden
Brünnhilde	Klara Barlow

Eugene Onegin   **Pyotr Ilyich Tchaikovsky**
In English
September 16, 22, 28, October 7, 10, 12, 1972
Conductor: James Craig
Director: Bliss Hebert
Set: Murray Laufer
Costume Designer: Suzanne Mess

Tatyana	Heather Thomson
Olga	Judith Forst
Madame Larina	Sonia Rohozynsky
Filipyevna	Patricia Rideout
Lensky	John Walker
Eugene Onegin	Victor Braun
A Captain	Donald Oddie
Triquet	Edward Matthiessen (Sep. 16, 22, Oct. 7, 12); David Meek (Sep. 28, Oct. 5, 10)
Zaretsky	Avo Kittask
Guillot	Herman Rombouts
Prince Gremin	Don Garrard

Aïda   **Giuseppe Verdi**
September 19, 23, 29, October 2, 5, 11, 14, 1972
Conductor: Ernesto Barbini
Director: Herman Geiger-Torel
Set: Murray Laufer

Costume Designer: Marie Day

Ramfis	Don Garrard
Radames	Pedro Lavirgen
Amneris	Ann Howard
Aïda	Maria Pellegrini
King of Egypt	Claude Corbeil
Messenger	Antonio Zanet (Sep. 19, 29, Oct. 5); Remo Marinucci (Sep. 23, Oct. 2, 11, 14)
Priestess	Judith Lebane (Sep. 19, 29, Oct. 5); Stephanie Bogle (Sep. 23, Oct. 2, 11, 14)
Amonasro	Cornelis Opthof

La Bohème　　　　**Giacomo Puccini**
September 20, 23, 25, October 3, 6, 12, 14, 1972
Conductor: Jean Deslauriers
Director: Carlos Alexander
Set: Marie Day
Costume Designer: Andrea Grainger/Warren Hartman

Marcello	Alexander Gray
Rodolfo	Ermanno Mauro
Colline	Claude Corbeil
Schaunard	Peter Milne (Sep. 20, 25, Oct. 3); Peter Barcza (Sep. 23, Oct. 6, 12, 14)
Benoit	Don McManus
Mimi	Urszula Koszut
Parpignol	Remo Marinucci
Musetta	Nicole Lorange (Sep. 20, 23, Oct. 3, 6, 14); Riki Turofsky (Sep. 25, Oct. 12)
Alcindoro	Alan Crofoot (Sep. 20, 23, Oct. 12, 14); Phil Stark (Sep. 25, Oct. 3, 6)
Customs Officer1	Allen Coates
Customs Officer2	Gary Relyea

Tosca　　　　**Giacomo Puccini**
September 26, 30, October 4, 7, 9, 13, 1972
Conductor: Ernesto Barbini
Director: Leon Major
Set: Lawrence Schäfer
Costume Designer: Suzanne Mess

Angelotti	Don McManus (Sep. 26, Oct. 7, 13); Herman Rombouts (Sep. 30, Oct. 4, 9)
Sacristan	Jan Rubes
Cavaradossi	Luciano Rampaso
Tosca	Clarice Carson
Scarpia	Louis Quilico
Spoletta	John Arab
Sciarrone	Gary Relyea (Sep. 26, Oct. 7, 13); Donald Oddie (Sep. 30, Oct. 4, 9)
Shepherd Boy	Renée Rosen
Jailer	Allen Coates

1973

Così fan tutte　　　　**Wolfgang Amadeus Mozart**
In English
Royal Alexandra
March 21, 22, 23, 24 (matinée and evening), 1973
Conductor: John Fenwick/Errol Gay
Director: Herman Geiger-Torel
Set: George Schlögl
Costume Designer: Andrea Grainger

Ferrando	Garnet Brooks (Mar. 21, 23, 24 (mat)); John Arab (Mar. 22, 24 (eve))
Guglielmo	Peter Barcza (Mar. 21, 23, 24 (mat)); Donald Oddie (Mar. 22, 24 (eve))
Don Alfonso	Peter Milne (Mar. 21, 23, 24 (mat)); Jan Rubes (Mar. 22, 24 (eve))
Fiordiligi	Barbara Collier (Mar. 21, 23, 24 (mat)); Helly Jedig (Mar. 22, 24 (eve))
Dorabella	Kathleen Ruddell (Mar. 21, 23, 24 (mat)); Nancy Greenwood (Mar. 22, 24 (eve))
Despina	Ann Cooper (Mar. 21, 23, 24 (mat)); Gwenlynn Little (Mar. 22, 24 (eve))
Servant	Phil Stark
Servant	Steven Thomas

Götterdämmerung　　　　**Richard Wagner**
September 7, 12, 15, 20, 1973
Conductor: Heinrich Bender
Director: Herman Geiger-Torel
Set: Murray Laufer
Costume Designer: Marie Day

Siegfried	Jean Cox
Brünnhilde	Ingrid Bjoner
Hagen	William Wildermann
Waltraute	Lili Chookasian
Gunther	Janos Tessenyi
Gutrune	Barbara Collier
First Norn	Lili Chookasian
Second Norn	Eleanor James
Third Norn	Barbara Collier
Woglinde	Jeannette Zarou
Wellgunde	Roxolana Roslak
Flosshilde	Eleanor James
Alberich	Severin Weingort

Héloise and Abélard　　　　**Charles Wilson/Eugene Benson**
September 8, 14, 26, 1973
Conductor: Victor Feldbrill
Director: Leon Major
Set: Murray Laufer
Costume Designer: Suzanne Mess

Héloise	Heather Thomson
Abélard	Allan Monk
Fulbert	Don McManus
Bernard of Clairvaux	Emile Belcourt

256

Madelon	Patricia Rideout	
Albéric	Phil Stark	
Lutolphe	Ronald Bermingham	
François	Garnet Brooks	
Eugène	Jacques Lareau	
Minstrel/Tavern Singer	Alan Crofoot	
Cardinal Conon	Donald Oddie	
Bishop of Chartres	Peter Barcza	
Priest/Bishop/Archbishop of Rheims		John Arab
Herald	James Anderson	
First Assassin	Bruce Kelly	
Second Assassin	John Dodington	
Amanuensis	Kathleen Ruddell	
Citizen	Richard Braun	
Citizen	Jill Pert	

Il barbiere di Siviglia   Gioacchino Rossini
In English
September 13, 15, 21, 24, October 9, 13, 1973
Conductor: Ernesto Barbini
Director: Constance Fisher
Set: William Lord
Costume Designer: William Lord

Fiorello	Roelof Oostwoud; Bruce Kelly; Henry Barney Ingram
Count Almaviva	John Walker
Figaro	Cornelis Opthof
Dr. Bartolo	Peter Milne
Rosina	Patricia Kern
Don Basilio	Claude Corbeil
Berta	Ann Cooper; Lynn Blaser
Sergeant	Phil Stark
Notary	Edward Matthiessen

The Merry Widow   Franz Lehár
In English
September 18, 22, 27, 29, Oct. 1, 3, 5, 13, 1973
Conductor: Victor Feldbrill
Director: Leon Major
Set: Murray Laufer
Costume Designer: Marie Day

St. Brioche	Alan Crofoot
Baron Zeta	Jan Rubes
Valencienne	Gwenlynn Little
Camille	Emile Belcourt
Cascada	Peter Barcza ·
Kromov	Edward Matthiessen
Olga	Lynn Blaser
Bogdanowitsch	Peter Milne
Sylvaine	Sonia Rohozynsky
Njegus	Allen Coates
Anna Glawari	Irene Salemka
Count Danilo	John Reardon
Lolo	Barbara Carter
Dodo	Kathleen Ruddell
Waiter	Herman Rombouts

Rigoletto   Giuseppe Verdi
September 19, 22, 28, October 2, 6, 8, 11, 1973
Conductor: Ernesto Barbini
Director: Peter Symcox
Set: Murray Laufer
Costume Designer: Marie Day

Rigoletto	Louis Quilico
Duke	Ruggero Bondino
Gilda	Maria Pellegrini
Maddalena	Judith Forst
Count Ceprano	John Dodington (Sep. 19, 28, Oct. 6, 11); Herman Rombouts (Sep. 22, Oct. 2, 8)
Marullo	Donald Oddie
Monterone	Gary Relyea
Sparafucile	Don McManus
Borsa	Roelof Oostwoud (Sep. 19, 28, Oct. 2, 8); Glyn Evans (Sep. 22, 28, Oct. 6, 11)
Countess Ceprano	Judith Lebane (Sep. 19,28, Oct. 6); Jill Pert (Sep. 22, Oct. 2, 8, 11)
Giovanna	Patricia Rideout (Sep. 19, 28, Oct. 6, 11); Nancy Greenwood (Sep. 22, Oct. 2, 8)
Page	Clare Bewley (Sep. 19, 28, Oct. 6, 11); Barbara Carter (Sep. 22, Oct. 2, 8)
Usher	Allen Coates (Sep. 19, 28, Oct. 6, 11); James Anderson (Sep. 22, Oct. 2, 8)

Fidelio   Ludwig van Beethoven
September 25, 29, October 4, 6, 10, 12, 1973
Conductor: Heinrich Bender
Director: Carlos Alexander
Set: Murray Laufer
Costume Designer: Marie Day

Jaquino	John Walker
Marzelline	Jeannette Zarou
Rocco	William Wildermann
Leonore	Helly Jedig
Don Pizarro	Avo Kittask
First Prisoner	Glyn Evans (Sep. 25, Oct. 4, 12); Roelof Oostwoud (Sep. 29, Oct. 6, 10)
Second Prisoner	Herman Rombouts
Florestan	Jean Cox
Don Fernando	Claude Corbeil
Officer	Jacques Lareau

1974

Bluebeard's Castle   Bela Bartok
In English
September 6, 14, 19, 25, 1974
Conductor: Thomas Blum
Director: John Leberg
Set: Murray Laufer
Costume Designer: Marie Day

Duke Bluebeard	Claude Corbeil

Judith	Lyn Vernon
Bard	Norman Welsh
Morning Wife	Anne Marie Albert
Noon Wife	Kristina Diobro
Evening Wife	Karin Mawson

L'heure espagnole **Maurice Ravel**
In English
September 6, 14, 19, 25, 1974
Conductor: Thomas Blum
Director: Constance Fisher
Set: Marie Day
Costume Designer: Marie Day

Concepción	Gwenlynn Little
Torquemeda	Alan Crofoot
Gonzalve	John Arab (Sep. 6, 19); Emile Belcourt (Sep. 14, 25)
Ramiro	Avo Kittask
Don Inigo Gomez	Peter Milne

Der fliegende Holländer **Richard Wagner**
September 7, 13, 18, 21, 26, October 1, 1974
Conductor: Heinrich Bender
Director: Carlos Alexander
Set: Murray Laufer
Costume Designer: Suzanne Mess

The Dutchman	Leif Roar
Daland	William Wildermann
Senta	Anna Green
Erik	Charles Hindsley
Mary	Patricia Rideout
Steersman	Phil Stark (Sep. 7, 13, Oct. 1); Roelof Oostwoud (Sep. 18, 21, 26)

Carmen **Georges Bizet**
September 11, 14, 20, 23, 28, October 3, 10, 1974
Conductor: Victor Feldbrill
Director: Charles Janssens
Set: Robert Prévost
Costume Designer: Suzanne Mess

Moralès	Donald Oddie (Sep. 11, 14, Oct. 3, 10); Bruce Kelly (Sep. 20, 23, 28)
Micaela	Jeannette Zarou
Don José	Ermanno Mauro
Zuniga	Claude Corbeil (Sep. 11, 23, 28, Oct. 10); Allen Coates (Sep. 14, 20, Oct. 3)
Carmen	Mignon Dunn
Frasquita	Barbara Collier (Sep. 11, 14, 20, 28, Oct. 3, 10); Roxolana Roslak (Sep. 23)
Mercédès	Carrol Anne Curry (Sep. 11, 20, 28, Oct. 10); Jill Pert (Sep. 14, 23, Oct. 3)
Escamillo	Allan Monk
Remendado	Alan Crofoot
Dancairo	Phil Stark

La Traviata **Giuseppe Verdi**
September 12, 17, 21, 30, October 5, 9, 11, 1974
Conductor: Bryan Balkwill
Director: Irving Guttman
Set: Robert Darling
Costume Designer: Suzanne Mess

Violetta	Maria Pellegrini
Alfredo	Ruggero Bondino
Germont	Cornelis Opthof
Flora	Sonia Rohozynsky (Sep. 12, 21, Oct. 9); Michèle Dowsett (Sep. 17, 30, Oct. 5, 11)
Annina	Clare Bewley (Sep. 12, 21, Oct. 5, 9); Veronica Kalfman (Sep. 27, 30, Oct. 11)
Gastone	Roelof Oostwoud (Sep. 12, 30, Oct. 11); Michele Strano (Sep. 17, 21, Oct. 5, 9)
Baron Douphol	David Varjabed (Sep. 12, 21, Oct. 9, 11); Donald Oddie (Sep. 17, 30, Oct. 5)
d'Obigny	James Anderson
Dr. Grenvil	Herman Rombouts
Giuseppe	Glyn Evans (Sep. 12, 30, Oct. 9, 11); Lary Benson (Sep. 17, 21, Oct. 5)

Boris Godunov **Modest Mussorgsky**
In English
September 24, 28, October 2, 4, 7, 10, 12, 1974
Conductor: Heinrich Bender
Director: Herman Geiger-Torel
Set: David Mitchell
Costume Designer: Suzanne Mess

Boris Godunov	Don Garrard
Shuisky	Emile Belcourt
Pimen	William Wildermann
Grigory	Luciano Rampaso
Marina	Lyn Vernon
Rangoni	Bernard Turgeon
Varlaam	Don McManus
Missail	Alan Crofoot (Sep. 24, Oct. 4, 7, 12); Edward Matthiessen (Sep. 28, Oct. 2, 10)
Hostess	Ivanka Myhal (Sep. 24, Oct. 2, 10, 12); Jane O'Brien (Sep. 28, Oct. 4, 7)
Krushchov	Jerold Norman
Feodor	Kathleen Ruddell (Sep. 24, Oct. 4, 7); Michèle Dowsett (Sep. 28, Oct. 2, 10, 12)
Xenia	Deborah Jeans (Sep. 24, Oct. 4, 7, 12); Janet Field (Sep. 28, Oct. 2, 10)
Nurse	Patricia Rideout
Simpleton	Henry Barney Ingram (Sep. 24, Oct. 2, 10, 12); Glyn Evans (Sep. 28, Oct. 4, 7)
Shchelkalov	Avo Kittask
Nikitish	James Anderson
Borderguard	Allen Coates
Lavitsky	Donald Oddie
Chernikovsky	Herman Rombouts
Mitiukha	David Varjabed
A Woman	Jane O'Brien (Sep. 24, Oct. 2, 12); Janet Stubbs (Sep. 28, Oct. 4, 7, 10)
A Man	Michele Strano (Sep. 24, Oct. 2, 10, 12);

258

Larry Benson (Sep. 28, Oct. 4, 7)

Faust   **Charles Gounod**
September 27, October 3, 5, 8, 12, 1974
Conductor: Ernesto Barbini
Director: John Leberg
Set: Les Lawrence
Costume Designer: Suzanne Mess

Faust	Jean Bonhomme
Méphistophélès	Jerome Hines
Valentin	Peter Barcza
Wagner	Guillermo Silva
Siébel	Ivanka Myhal (Sep. 27, Oct. 5, 8); Kathleen Ruddell (Oct. 3, 12)
Marguerite	Heather Thomson
Marthe	Sonia Rohozynsky (Sep. 27, Oct. 5, 12); Diane Loeb (Oct. 3, 8)

1975

I Pagliacci   **Ruggiero Leoncavallo**
September 5, 10, 13, 16, 20, 25, 1975
Conductor: Bryan Balkwill
Director: Leon Major
Set: Les Lawrence
Costume Designer: Andrea Grainger

Tonio	Louis Quilico
Canio	Luciano Rampaso
Villager	Bruce Kelly (Sep. 5, 16, 20); Jonas Vaskevicius (Sep. 10, 13, 25)
Villager	Paul Frey
Nedda	Carrol Anne Curry (Sep. 5, 10, 20); Deborah Jeans (Sep. 13, 16, 25)
Beppe	Henry Barney Ingram (Sep. 5, 13, 25); Glyn Evans (Sep. 10, 16, 20)
Silvio	Peter Barcza (Sep. 5, 10, 13, 20); David Varjabed (Sep. 16, 25)

Il Tabarro   **Giacomo Puccini**
September 5, 10, 13, 16, 20, 25, 1975
Conductor: Bryan Balkwill
Director: Constance Fisher
Set: Brian Jackson
Costume Designer: Brian Jackson

Michele	Louis Quilico
Giorgietta	Lucine Amara
Luigi	Luciano Rampaso
Tinca	John Arab (Sep. 5, 13, 16); Michele Strano (Sep. 10, 20, 25)
Talpa	Donald Oddie
Frugola	Rita De Carla
Song Seller	Glyn Evans (Sep. 5, 13, 25); Paul Trépanier (Sep. 10, 13, 25)

Young Lover	Deborah Jeans (Sep. 5, 10, 20); Kathleen Ruddell (Sep. 13, 16, 25)
Young Lover	Stephen Young

Manon Lescaut   **Giacomo Puccini**
September 6, 13, 17, 23, October 2, 6, 10, 1975
Conductor: Ernesto Barbini
Director: James de Blasis
Set: John Naccarato
Costume Designer: Suzanne Mess

Manon Lescaut	Heather Thomson
des Grieux	Ermanno Mauro
Lescaut	Alexander Gray
Geronte	Peter Milne (Sep. 6, 13, Oct. 2, 6); Janos Tessenyi (Sep. 17, 23, Oct. 10)
Edmondo	Larry Benson (Sep. 6, 17, Oct. 2, 10); John Keane (Sep. 13, 23, Oct. 6)
Innkeeper	Douglas McEachen (Sep. 6, 17, Oct. 2); Bruce Kelly (Sep. 13, 23, Oct. 6, 10)
Sergeant	Donald Oddie (Sep. 6, 17, 23, Oct. 2); Douglas McEeachen (Sep. 13, Oct. 6, 10)
Dance-Master	Paul Trépanier
Madrigal Singer	Kathleen Ruddell (Sep. 6, 17, 23); Janet Stubbs (Sep.13, Oct. 2, 6, 10)
Lamplighter	Alan Crofoot
Naval Commander	James Anderson
Hairdresser	Ron Hastings

Die Fledermaus   **Johann Strauss, Jr.**
In English
September 11, 19, 22, 27, 30, October 2, 8, 11, 1975
Conductor: Raffi Armenian
Director: Herman Geiger-Torel
Set: William Lord
Costume Designer: William Lord

Rosalinda	Lois McDonall
Eisenstein	Cornelis Opthof
Adele	Gwenlynn Little
Alfred	Alan Crofoot (Sep. 11, 22, 27, Oct. 8, 11); John Arab (Sep. 19, 30, Oct. 2)
Frank	Avo Kittask
Prince Orlofsky	Henry Barney Ingram
Dr. Falke	Emile Belcourt (Sep. 11, 19, Oct. 2, 8, 11); Gary Relyea (Sep. 22, 27, 30)
Frosch	Ron Hastings
Dr. Blind	Guillermo Silva-Marin (Sep. 11, 22, Oct. 2, 8); Larry Benson (Sep. 19, 27, 30, Oct. 11)
Fifi	Michele Dowsett (Sep. 11, 22, 30, Oct. 11); Janet Field (Sep. 19, 27, Oct. 2, 8)
Ivan	James Anderson (Sep. 11, 22, 30, Oct. 11); Jonas Vaskevicius (Sep. 19, 27, Oct. 2, 8)
Judge	Ron Hastings

Madama Butterfly   **Giacomo Puccini**
September 12, 18, 24, 29, October 4, 7, 11, 1975

Conductor: Ernesto Barbini
Director: Irving Guttman
Set: Robert Darling
Costume Designer: Suzanne Mess

Cio-Cio-San	Maria Pellegrini
Suzuki	Judith Forst
Pinkerton	Giuseppe Campora
Sharpless	Donald Rutherford (Sep. 12, 29, Oct. 7, 11); Peter Barcza (Sep. 18, 24, Oct. 4)
Goro	André Lortie
The Bonze	Janos Tessenyi
Yamadori	Thomas Park (Sep. 12, 29, Oct. 4, 7); José Hernandez (Sep. 18, 24, Oct 11)
Commissioner	David Varjabed (Sep. 12, 18, 29, Oct. 4); Guillermo Silva-Marin (Sep. 24, Oct. 7, 11)
Kate Pinkerton	Jill Pert (Sep. 12, 24, Oct. 4, 11); Linda Marcinkus (Sep. 18, 29, Oct. 7)
Dolore	Tera Goldblatt
Yakuside	Remo Marinucci
Mother	Louise Roy (Sep. 12, 24, Oct. 4, 7); Barbara Ianni (Sep. 18, 29, Oct. 11)
Cousin	Constance Adorno (Sep. 12, 24, Oct. 4, 7); Nancy Hermiston (Sep. 18, 29, Oct. 11)
Aunt	Judith Lebane (Sep. 12, 24, Oct. 4, 7); Rosemarie Landry (Sep. 18, 29, Oct. 11)

Salome   **Richard Strauss**
September 20, 26, October 1, 4, 1975
Conductor: Heinrich Bender
Director: Carlos Alexander
Set: Brian Jackson
Costume Designer: Suzanne Mess

Narraboth	Jerold Norman
Page	Janet Stubbs
First Soldier	James Anderson
Second Soldier	Donald Oddie
Cappadocian	Jonas Vaskevicius (Sep. 20, Oct. 1); Douglas McEachen (Sep. 26, Oct. 4)
Salome	Grace Bumbry
Slave	Jean MacPhail (Sep. 20, Oct. 1); Michèle Dowsett (Sep. 26, Oct. 4)
Jochanaan	Victor Braun
Herod	Phil Stark
Herodias	Lyn Vernon
First Jew	Thomas Park
Second Jew	John Keane
Third Jew	Henry Barney Ingram
Fourth Jew	David Astor
Fifth Jew	Guillermo Silva-Marin
First Nazarene	Janos Tessenyi
Second Nazarene	Michele Strano

Louis Riel   **Harry Somers/Mavor Moore**
September 25, 27, October 3, 9, 1975
Conductor: Victor Feldbrill

Director: Leon Major
Set: Murray Laufer
Costume Designer: Marie Day

William McDougall	Ronald Bermingham
British Soldier	Glyn Evans
Ambroise Lépine	André Lortie
Thomas Scott	Thomas Park
Joseph Delorme	Jonas Vaskevicius
Janvier Ritchot	John Nieboer
Elzéar Goulet	Lloyd Dean
André Nault	Phil Stark
Baptiste Lépine	Remo Marinucci
Elzéar Lagimodière	James Anderson
Louis Riel	Bernard Turgeon
Dr. Schultz	Peter Milne
Charles Mair	John Keane
O'Donaghue	John Arab
Bishop Taché	Jean-Pierre Hurteau
Sir John A. Macdonald	Donald Rutherford
Sir George Cartier	Paul Trépanier
Donald Smith	David Astor
Julie Riel	Patricia Rideout (Sep. 25, 27, Oct. 3); Diane Loeb (Oct. 9)
Sara Riel	Ann Cooper (Sep. 25, Oct. 3); Barbara Collier (Sep. 27, Oct. 9)
Colonel Wolseley	Avo Kittask
Hudson's Bay Scout	Stephen Young
Marguerite Riel	Roxolana Roslak
Gabriel Dumont	John Keane
James Isbister	Bruce Kelly
Poundmaker	Ronald Bermingham
General Middleton	David Astor
Father André	André Lortie
Wandering Spirit	Stan Kane
Clerk of the Court	James Anderson
Judge	Guillermo Silva-Marin
F. X. Lemieux	José Hernandez
B.B. Osler	John Nieboer
Dr. François Roy	Stephen Young
Prison Guard	Glyn Evans

1976

La grande duchesse de Gérolstein   **Jacques Offenbach**
In English and French
September 24, 27, 30, October 2, 5, 6, 16, 1976
Conductor: John O. Crosby
Director: Bliss Hebert
Set: Allen Charles Klein
Costume Designer: Suzanne Mess

Baron Grog	Jack Davison
Fritz	James Atherton (Sep. 24, 27, 30, Oct. 2, 5, 6); John Walker (Oct. 16)
Wanda	Barbara Shuttleworth
General Boum	Don McManus (Sep. 24, 27, 30, Oct. 2, 5, 6); Claude Corbeil (Oct. 16)

Baron Puck	Alan Crofoot
Nepomuc	Henry Barney Ingram
Prince Paul	Mark Pedrotti
Grand Duchess	Ann Howard
Iza	Michèle Dowsett
Olga	Nancy Hermiston
Amelie	Janet Field
Charlotte	Susan Gudgeon

Die Walküre   Richard Wagner
September 25, 29, October 8, 12, 1976
Conductor: Heinrich Bender
Director: Herman Geiger-Torel
Set: (Murray Laufer)
Costume Designer: Suzanne Mess

Siegmund	Richard Cassilly
Sieglinde	Alexandra Browning
Hunding	William Wildermann
Wotan	Leif Roar
Brünnhilde	Gunilla af Malmborg
Fricka	Lyn Vernon
Gerhilde	Barbara Collier
Waltraute	Janice Taylor
Schwertleite	Janet Stubbs
Ortlinde	Donna-Faye Carr
Helmwige	Belva Spiel
Siegrune	Jean MacPhail
Rossweisse	Florence Maltese
Grimgerde	Patricia Harton

La Bohème   Giacomo Puccini
September 28, 30, October 2, 7, 9, 11, 13, 15, 1976
Conductor: Ernesto Barbini
Director: James Lucas
Set: Marie Day
Costume Designer: Marie Day

Marcello	Cornelis Opthof (Sep. 28, 30, Oct. 2, 7, 11, 13); Peter Barcza (Oct. 9, 15)
Rodolfo	Ruggero Bondino
Colline	Giulio Kukurugya
Schaunard	Avo Kittask (Sep. 28, Oct. 2, 7, 13); James Anderson (Sep. 30, Oct. 9, 11, 15)
Benoit	Peter Milne (Sep. 28, Oct. 2, 9, 15); Guillermo Silva-Marin (Sep. 30, Oct. 7, 11, 13)
Mimi	Jeannette Zarou
Parpignol	Michele Strano (Sep. 28, Oct. 2, 7, 13); Antonio Zanet (Sep. 30, Oct. 9, 11, 15)
Musetta	Deborah Jeans (Sep. 28, 30, Oct. 2, 7); Barbara Shuttleworth (Oct. 9, 11, 13, 15)
Alcindoro	Phil Stark
Customs Officer	Joel Katz (Sep. 28, Oct. 2, 7, 13);Mark Pedrotti (Sep. 30, Oct. 9, 11, 15)
Customs Officer	Douglas McEachen (Sep. 28, Oct. 2, 7, 13); John Nieboer (Sep. 30, Oct. 9, 11, 15)

Tosca   Giacomo Puccini
October 1, 4, 9, 14, 16, 1976
Conductor: Bryan Balkwill
Director: Constance Fisher
Set: Lawrence Schäfer
Costume Designer: Suzanne Mess

Angelotti	William Wilderman
Sacristan	Don McManus
Cavaradossi	Ermanno Mauro
Tosca	Marisa Galvany
Scarpia	Leif Roar
Spoletta	Phil Stark
Sciarrone	James Anderson (Oct. 1, 4); Bruce Kelly (Oct. 9, 14, 16)
Jailer	James Shafer
Voice of Shepherd	Janet Stubbs (Oct. 1, 4, 16); Susan Gudgeon (Oct. 9, 14)

1977

Don Carlos   Giuseppe Verdi
September 14, 16, 18, 20, 22, 24, 1977
Conductor: Reynald Giovaninetti
Director: Lotfi Mansouri
Set: Wolfram Skalicki
Costume Designer: Suzanne Mess

Elizabeth de Valois	Clarice Carson
Thibault	Nancy Hermiston
Don Carlos	Ermanno Mauro
Le Comte de Lerme	Michele Strano
Un Moine	Ingemar Korjus
Rodriguez	Victor Braun
La Princesse	Tatiana Troyanos
Un Hérault	Glyn Evans
Philippe II	Paul Plishka
Voix dans le Ciel	Barbara Collier
Le Grand Inquisiteur	Don Garrard

Die Zauberflöte   Wolfgang Amadeus Mozart
September 28, 30, October 2, 4, 6, 8, 13, 1977
Conductor: Kenneth Montgomery
Director: Bliss Herbert
Set: Peter Rice
Costume Designer: Peter Rice

Pamina	Patricia Wells
Tamino	Leo Goeke
Papageno	Peter Barcza
Papagena	Colleen Letourneau
Queen of the Night	Deborah Cook
First Spirit	Nancy Hermiston
Second Spirit	Caralyn Tomlin
Third Spirit	Michèle Dowsett
First Lady	Claudette Leblanc
Second Lady	Carrol Anne Curry
Third Lady	Jean MacPhail

Sarastro	Robert Lloyd (Sep. 28, 30, Oct. 2, 4, 6, 8); Herbert Beattie (Oct. 13)
Monostatos	Phil Stark
Armed Man	Paul Frey
Armed Man	Avo Kittask
Priest	Janos Tessenyi
Priest	John Keane

La fille du régiment   **Gaetano Donizetti**
In English
October 12, 14, 16, 18, 20, 22, 28, 1977
Conductor: Boris Brott
Director: Bruce Donnell
Set: Beni Donnell
Costume Designer: Beni Donnell

Marie	Norma Burrowes (Oct. 12, 14, 16, 18, 20, 22); Colleen Letourneau (Oct. 28)
Marquise Berkenfield	Maureen Forrester
Hortensio	Michael Fletcher
Tonio	William Harness
Sulpice	Jules Bastin (Oct. 12, 14, 16, 18, 20); Avo Kittask (Oct. 22, 28)
Corporal	Gino Quilico
Dance Master	Donald Himes
Notary	Donald Himes
Duchess of Crakentorp	Anna Russell (Oct. 12, 18, 20, 22); Stuart Hamilton (Oct. 14, 16, 28)

Wozzeck   **Alban Berg**
October 21, 23, 25, 27, 29, 1977
Conductor: Raffi Armenian
Director: Lotfi Mansouri
Set: Murray Laufer
Costume Designer: Marie Day

Wozzeck	Allan Monk
Drum Major	William Neill
Andres	Martin Chambers
Captain	Phil Stark
Doctor	Ara Berberian
Fool	John Keane
Marie	Lyn Vernon
Margret	Janet Stubbs
Apprentice	Avo Kittask
Apprentice	James Anderson
Pianist	José Hernandez

1978 (Spring)

Le nozze di Figaro   **Wolfgang Amadeus Mozart**
In English
Royal Alexandra
April 3, 4, 5, (matinée and evening), 6, 7, 8 (matinée and evening), 10, 11, 1978

Conductor: Raffi Armeneian/Daniel Nazareth
Director: Graziella Sciutti
Set: Mary Kerr
Costume Designer: Mary Kerr

Figaro	William Dansby (Apr. 3, 5 (mat), 6, 8 (mat), 10); Ingemar Korjus (Apr. 4, 5 (eve), 7, 8 (eve), 11)
Susanna	Barbara Shuttleworth (Apr. 3, 5 (eve), 8 (eve)); Nancy Hermiston (Apr. 4, 6, 8 (mat), 10); Carrol Anne Curry (Apr. 5 (mat), 7, 11)
Count Almaviva	Raymond Hickman (Apr. 3, 5 (eve), 8 (mat), 10); Brent Ellis (Apr. 4, 6, 8 (eve), 11); Avo Kittask (Apr. 5 (mat), 7)
Countess Almaviva	Pamela Myers (Apr. 3, 5 (eve), 8 (eve), 10); Alexandra Browning (Apr. 4, 7); Riki Turofsky (Apr. 5 (mat), 6, 8 (mat), 10)
Cherubino	Janet Stubbs (Apr. 3, 5 (mat), 6, 8 (mat), 10); Kathleen Hegierski (Apr. 4, 5 (eve), 7, 8 (eve), 11)
Marcellina	Patricia Rideout (Apr. 3, 6 (mat), 6, 8 (mat & eve)); Darlene Hirst (Apr. 4, 5 (eve), 7, 10, 11)
Dr. Bartolo	Don McManus (Apr. 3, 5 (mat), 7, 8 (eve), 11); John Dodington (Apr. 4, 5 (eve), 7, 8 (mat), 10)
Don Basilio	John Keane (Apr. 3, 5 (mat), 6, 8 (mat), 10); Phil Stark (Apr. 4, 5 (eve), 7, 8 (eve), 11)
Don Curzio	Stephen Young (Apr. 3, 5 (mat), 6, 8 (mat), 10); Mark DuBois (Apr. 4, 5 (eve), 7, 8 (eve), 11)
Antonio	Joel Katz (Apr. 3, 5 (mat), 6, 8 (mat), 10); Christopher Cameron (Apr. 4, 5 (eve), 7, 8 (eve), 11)
Barbarina	Caralyn Tomlin (Apr. 3, 5 (mat), 6, 8 (mat), 10); Iris Fraser (Apr. 4, 5 (eve), 7, 8 (eve), 11)

La Traviata   **Giuseppe Verdi**
Royal Alexandra
April 12 (matinée and evening), 13, 14, 15 (matinée and evening), 17, 18, 19 (matinée and evening), 20, 1978
Conductor: Raffi Armenian/Daniel Nazareth/Timothy Vernon
Director: John Leberg
Set: Martin Johnson
Costume Designer: Suzanne Mess

Violetta	Riki Turofsky (Apr. 12 (mat), 14, 17, 19 (mat)); Maria Pellegrini (Apr. 12 (eve), 15 (eve), 19 (eve)); Pamela Myers (Apr. 13, 15 (mat), 18, 20)
Alfredo	Paul Frey (Apr. 12 (mat), 14, 18, 20); Rico Serbo (Apr. 12 (eve), 15 (eve), 17, 19); Martin Chambers (Apr. 13, 15 (mat), 19 (mat))
Germont	Gary Relyea (Apr. 12 (mat), 14, 18, 20); Brent Ellis (Apr. 12 (eve), 15 (eve), 17, 19);

	Bernard Turgeon (Apr. 13, 15 (mat), 19 (mat))
Flora	Janet Stubbs (Apr. 12 (mat), 13, 17, 19 (mat)); Darlene Hirst (Apr. 12 (eve), 14, 15 (eve), 18, 19); Slava Ziemelyte (Apr. 15 (mat))
Annina	Carrol Anne Curry (Apr. 12 (mat), 13, 15 (mat), 17, 19 (mat), 20); Nancy Hermiston (Apr. 12 (eve), 14, 15 (eve), 18, 19)
Gastone	Stephen Young (Apr. 12 (mat), 13, 15 (mat), 17, 19 (mat), 20); Mark DuBois (Apr. 12 (eve), 14, 15 (eve), 18, 19)
Baron Douphol	Allen Stewart-Coates (Apr. 12 (mat), 13, 15 (mat), 17, 19 (mat)); James Anderson (Apr. 12 (eve), 14, 15 (eve), 18, 19)
Marquis	Christopher Cameron (Apr. 12 (mat), 13, 15 (mat), 17, 19 (mat), 20); Don McManus (Apr. 12 (eve), 14, 15 (eve), 18, 19)
Dr. Grenvil	Ingemar Korjus (Apr. 12 (mat), 13, 15 (mat), 17, 19 (mat), 20); John Dodington (Apr. 12 (eve), 14, 15 (eve), 18, 19)
Giuseppe	James McLean
Commissiario	Joel Katz
Spanish Dancer	Terry Watson

Il barbiere di Siviglia   Gioacchino Rossini
Royal Alexandra
April 21, 22 (matinée and evening), 24, 25, 26 (matinée and evening) 27, 28, 29 (matinée and evening), 1978
Conductor: Raffi Armenian/Daniel Nazareth/Timothy Vernon
Director: Lotfi Mansouri
Set: Maurice Strike
Costume Designer: Maurice Strike

Fiorello	James Shafer (Apr. 21, 22 (eve), 25, 26 (eve), 28, 29 (eve)); James Anderson (Apr. 22 (mat), 24, 26 (mat), 27, 29)
Count Almaviva	George Livings (Apr. 21, 25, 27, 29 (mat)); Neil Rosenshein (Apr. 22 (mat), 26 (eve), 29 (eve)); Abram Morales (Apr. 22 (eve), 24, 26 (mat), 28);
Figaro	Brent Ellis (Apr. 21, 24, 26 (eve)); Raymond Hickman (Apr. 22 (mat), 25, 28, 29 (eve)); Lawrence Cooper (Apr. 22 (eve), 26 (mat), 27, 29)
Dr. Bartolo	Don McManus (Apr. 21, 22 (eve), 25, 26 (eve), 27, 29 (eve)); Avo Kittask (Apr. 22 (mat), 24, 26 (mat), 27, 29)
Rosina	Judith Forst (Apr. 21, 26 (eve), 29, (eve)); Janet Stubbs (Apr. 22 (mat), 24, 26 (mat), 28); Nancy Hermiston (Apr. 22 (eve), 25, 27, 29 (mat))
Don Basilio	John Dodington (Apr. 21, 22 (eve), 25, 27, 28, 29 (eve)); Ingemar Korjus (Apr. 22 (mat), 24, 26 (mat, eve), 29)
Berta	Darlene Hirst (Apr. 21, 22 (eve), 25, 26 (eve), 27, 29 (mat)); Carrol Anne Curry (Apr. 22 (mat), 24, 26 (mat), 28, 29)

Sergeant	Phil Stark
Notary	Joel Katz
Ambrogio	Briane Nasimok

1978 (Winter)

Joan of Arc   Pyotr Ilyich Tchaikovsky
September 13, 15, 17, 19, 21, 23, 1978
Conductor: Mario Bernardi
Director: Lotfi Mansouri
Set: Wolfram Skalicki
Costume Designer: Amrei Skalicki

Joan	Lyn Vernon (Sep. 13, 17, 21); Carol Wyatt (Sep. 15, 19, 23)
Charles VII	Pierre Duval
Agnes Sorel	Roxolana Roslak
Thibault	Claude Corbeil
Lionel	Brent Ellis
Dunois	Bernard Turgeon
Raymond	Stephen Young
Bertrand	Theodore Baerg
Cardinal	Leonid Skirko
Soldier	Joel Katz
Loret	John Dodington

Rigoletto   Giuseppe Verdi
September 27, 29, 30, October 1, 3, 5, 7, 1978
Conductor: Reynald Giovaninetti/Kenneth Montgomery
Director: Bliss Hebert
Set: Lawrence Schäfer
Costume Designer: Suzanne Mess

Rigoletto	Louis Quilico (Sep. 27, 29, Oct. 1, 3, 5, 7); Richard Fredricks (Sep. 30)
Duke of Mantua	Cesar-Antonio Suarez (Sep. 27, 29, Oct. 1, 3, 5, 7); Pierre Duval (Sep. 30)
Gilda	Mariana Niculescu (Sep. 27, 29, Oct. 1, 3, 5, 7); Faye Robinson (Sep. 30)
Maddalena	Janet Stubbs
Count Ceprano	Leonid Skirko
Marullo	Gino Quilico
Monterone	Theodore Baerg
Sparafucile	David Cornell
Borsa	Gerard Boyd
Countess Ceprano	Deborah Milsom
Giovanna	Patricia Rideout
A Page	Nancy Hermiston
Usher	James Anderson

Der Rosenkavalier   Richard Strauss
October 11, 13, 15, 17, 19, 21, 1978
Conductor: Kenneth Montgomery
Director: Lotfi Mansouri
Set: Robert O'Hearn
Costume Designer: Robert O'Hearn

Octavian	Judith Forst (Oct. 11, 15, 17, 21); Lyn Vernon (Oct. 13, 19)
Feldmarschallin	Heather Harper
Major Domo	Mark DuBois
Baron Ochs	Artur Korn
A Notary	Peter Milne
A Milliner	Deborah Milsom
Animal Trainer	Barry Stilwell
Valzacchi	Gerard Boyd
Annina	Janet Stubbs
A Singer	Pierre Duval
Leopold	Briane Nasimok
Herr Von Faninal	Alexander Gray
Sophie	Costanza Cuccaro
Marianne	Darlene Hirst
Major Domo to Faninal	Stephen Young
Innkeeper	Stephen Young
Police Commissioner	Leonid Skirko
Mahomet	Kwame Younge; Ruddy Hall

Don Giovanni   **Wolfgang Amadeus Mozart**
October 25, 27, 28, 29, 31, November 2, 4, 1978
Conductor: Raffi Armenian
Director: Lotfi Mansouri
Set: Lawrence Schäfer
Costume Designer: Suzanne Mess

Leporello	Stafford Dean (Oct. 25, 27, 29, 31, Nov. 2, 4); Peter Strummer (Oct. 28)
Donna Anna	Clarice Carson (Oct. 25, 27, 27, 29, 31, Nov. 4); Susan Godine (Oct. 28, Nov. 2)
Don Giovanni	Michael Devlin (Oct. 25, 27, 29, 31, Nov. 2, 4); Justino Diaz (Oct. 28)
The Commendatore	Robert Lloyd (Oct. 25, 27, 29, 31, Nov. 2, 4); David Cornell (Oct. 28)
Don Ottavio	Jon Garrison (Oct. 25, 27, 29, 31, Nov. 2, 4); John Aler (Oct. 28)
Donna Elvira	Johanna Meier (Oct. 25, 27, 29, Nov. 4); Alexandra Browning (Oct. 28, 31, Nov. 2)
Zerlina	Nancy Hermiston (Oct. 27, 29, 31, 4); Barbara Shuttleworth (Oct. 25, 28, Nov. 2)
Masetto	Robert Lloyd (Oct. 25, 27, 29, 31, Nov. 2, 4); Christopher Cameron (Oct. 28)

1979 (Spring)

Carmen   **Georges Bizet**
Royal Alexandra
April 23, 24, 25 (matinée and evening), 26, 27, 28 (matinée and evening), 30, May 1, 2 (matinée and evening), 3, 4, 5 (matinée and evening), 1979
Conductor: Kenneth Montgomery/Ruben Gurevich/Derek Bate
Director: Lotfi Mansouri
Set: Martin Johnson
Costume Designer: Suzanne Mess

Moralès	Mark Pedrotti (Apr. 23, 25 (mat), 26, 28 (mat), May 1, 2, 4, 5); Rod Campbell (Apr. 24, 25, 27, 28, 30, May 2)
Micaela	Roxolana Roslak (Apr. 23, 25 (mat), 26, 28 (mat), May 1, 2, 4, 5); Caralyn Tomlin (Apr. 24, 25, 27, 28, 30, May 2)
Don José	Frédéric de Marseille (Apr. 23, 25, 28, May 2, 4); Gene Bullard (Apr. 24, 26, 28 (mat), 30, May 2); John Sandor (Apr. 25 (mat), 27, May 1, 3, 5)
Zuniga	Maurice Brown (Apr. 23, 25, 27, 28, 30, May 2 (mat), 3, 5); John Dodington (Apr. 24, 25 (mat), 26, 28 (mat), May)
Carmen	Lyn Vernon (Apr. 23, 25, 28, 30, May 2, 4); Judith Forst (Apr. 24, 26, 28 (mat), May 2 (mat)); Janet Stubbs (Apr. 25 (mat), 27, May 1, 3, 5)
Frasquita	Katherine Terrell (Apr. 23, 25, 27, 28, 30, May 2 (mat), 3, 5); Iris Fraser (Apr. 24, 25 (mat), 26, 28 (mat), May)
Mercedes	Susan Gudgeon (Apr. 23, 25, 27, 28, 30, May 2 (mat), 3, 5); Darlene Hirst (Apr. 24, 25 (mat), 26, 28 (mat), May)
Escamillo	John Ostendorf (Apr. 23, 25, 28, 30, May 2, 4); Gino Quilico (Apr. 24, 26, 28 (mat), May 2 (mat)); Paul Aquino (Apr. 25 (mat), 27, May 1, 3, 5)
Remendado	Phil Stark (Apr. 23, 25 (mat), 26, 28 (mat), May 1, 2, 4, 5); Gerard Boyd (Apr. 24, 25, 27, 28, 30, May 2)
Dancairo	Stephen Young (Apr. 23, 25 (mat), 26, 28 (mat), May 1, 2, 4, 5); Barry Stilwell (Apr. 24, 25, 27, 28, 30, May 2)
Lillas Pastia	Yvon Paul Chartrand
Dancer	David Nixon
A Guide	Henri Loiselle

La Cenerentola   **Gioacchino Rossini**
In English
Royal Alexandra
May 7, 8, 9 (matinée and evening) 10, 11, 12 (matinée and evening), 14, 15, 16 (matinée and evening), 17, 18, 19 (matinée and evening), 1979
Conductor: Timothy Vernon/Derek Bate
Director: Jeannette Aster
Set: Maurice Strike
Costume Designer: Maurice Strike

Clorinda	Iris Fraser (May 7, 9 (mat), 10, 12 (mat), 15, 16, 18, 19); Caralyn Tomlin (May 8, 9, 11, 12, 14, 16 (mat), 17)
Tisbe	Darlene Hirst (May 7, 9 (mat), 10, 12 (mat), 15, 16, 18, 19); Susan Gudgeon (May 8, 9 11, 12, 14, 16 (mat), 17)
Cinderella	Judith Forst (May 7, 9, 11, 16, 19 (mat)); Janet Stubbs (May 8, 12, 14, 16 (mat), 18); Diane Loeb (May 9 (mat), 10, 12 (mat), 15)
Alidoro	Donnie Ray Albert (May 7, 9 (mat), 11,

264

	12, 15, 16, 17, 19 (mat)); John Dodington (May 8, 9, 10, 12 (mat)), 14, 16)
Don Magnifico	Raymond Hickman (May 7, 9, 11, 14, 16, 19 (mat)); Stephen Markuson (May 8, 10, 12, 16 (mat), 18); Christopher Cameron (May 9 (mat), 12 (mat), 15, 17)
Don Ramiro	Abram Morales (May 7, 9, 11, 16, 19 (mat)); Rico Serbo (May 8, 10, 12, 14, 16 (mat), 18); Mark DuBois (May 9 (mat), 12 (mat), 15, 17)
Dandini	Guillermo Silva-Marin (May 7, 9, 11, 14, 16 (mat), 18); Alexander Gray (May 8, 10, 12, 16, 19 (mat)); Samuel Byrd May 9 (mat), 12 (mat), 15, 17)

1979–1980

Simon Boccanegra   Giuseppe Verdi
September 19, 21, 23, 25, 27, 29, 1979
Conductor: Nicola Rescigno
Director: John Leberg/Lotfi Mansouri
Set: Wolfram Skalicki
Costume Designer: Amrei Skalicki

Paolo	Gino Quilico
Pietro	John Dodington
Simon Boccanegra	Louis Quilico
Jacopo Fiesco	Don Garrard
Amelia Boccanegra	Patricia Wells
Gabriele Adorno	Carlo Bini
Amelia's maidservant	Darlene Hirst
A Captain	Stephen Young

Tristan und Isolde   Richard Wagner
October 23, 26, 29, November 1, 4, 1979
Conductor: Kenneth Montgomery
Director: Lotfi Mansouri
Set: Annelies Corrodi
Costume Designer: Annelies Corrodi

Sailor	Michael Shust
Isolde	Johanna Meier
Brangäne	Maureen Forrester
Kurwenal	Peter Van Ginkel
Tristan	Spas Wenkoff
Melot	Theodore Baerg
King Marke	Don Garrard
A Shepherd	Stephen Young
A Steersman	Blair House

L'elisir d'amore   Gaetano Donizetti
December 5, 7, 9, 11, 13, 15, 1979
Conductor: Timothy Vernon
Director: Graziella Sciutti
Set: Robert Darling
Costume Designer: Robert Darling

Gianetta	Carrol Anne Curry
Nemorino	Beniamino Prior
Adina	Norma Burrowes
Belcore	Allan Monk
Dr. Dulcamara	Spiro Malas

Madama Butterfly   Giacomo Puccini
January 23, 25, 27, 29, 31, February 2, 1980
Conductor: Stefan Minde
Director: Sarah Ventura
Set: Robert Darling
Costume Designer: Robert Darling

Cio-Cio-San	Maria Pellegrini
Suzuki	Janet Stubbs
Pinkerton	Rico Serbo
Sharpless	Cornelis Opthof
Goro	Phil Stark
The Bonze	Janos Tessenyi
Prince Yamadori	Mark Pedrotti
Commissioner	Daniel Lichti
Kate Pinkerton	Eleanor James
Dolore	Alyson Court; Melissa MacDonald
Registrar	Michael Shust
Yakuside	Barry Stilwell
Mother	Louise Roy
Cousin	Colleen Letourneau-Galle
Aunt	Doreen Joachim

Werther   Jules Massenet
March 19, 21, 23, 25, 27, 29, 1980
Conductor: Jacques Delacôte
Director: Leon Major
Set: Steven Rubin
Costume Designer: Steven Rubin

The Bailiff	John Dodington
Johann	Robert Grenier
Schmidt	André Lortie
Sophie	Caralyn Tomlin
Werther	Benito Maresca
Charlotte	Judith Forst
Albert	Cary Archer Smith

Peter Grimes   Benjamin Britten
April 23, 25, 27, 29, May 1, 3, 1980
Conductor: Kenneth Montgomery
Director: Lotfi Mansouri
Set: Carl Toms
Costume Designer: Suzanne Mess

Hobson	Christopher Cameron
Swallow	John Dodington
Peter Grimes	William Neill
Ned Keene	Theodore Baerg
Reverend Horace Adams	John Keane
Bob Boles	Barry Stilwell
Auntie	Audrey Glass

Mrs. Sedley	Janet Stubbs
Ellen Orford	Heather Thomson
Captain Balstrode	Thomas Stewart
Niece	Caralyn Tomlin
Niece	Katherine Terrell
John	Brian Hyslop

1980-1981

Otello　　　　　　**Giuseppe Verdi**
September 10, 12, 14, 16, 18, 20, 1980
Conductor: Reynald Giovaninetti
Director: Lotfi Mansouri
Set: Wolfram Skalicki
Costume Designer: Richard Lorain

Montano	Greg Ryerson
Cassio	Michael Shust
Iago	Allan Monk
Roderigo	Stephen Young
Otello	James McCracken (Sep. 10, 14, 20); Richard Cassilly (Sep. 12, 16, 18)
Desdemona	Mariana Niculescu (Sep. 10, 14, 16); Ruth Falcon (Sep. 12, 18, 20)
Emilia	Janet Stubbs
A Herald	Theodore Baerg
Lodovico	Giulio Kukurugya

Lulu　　　　　　**Alban Berg**
October 15, 17, 19, 21, 23, 25, 1980
Conductor: Kenneth Montgomery
Director: Lotfi Mansouri
Set: Wolfram Skalicki
Costume Designer: Suzanne Mess

Lulu	Carole Farley (Oct. 15, 19, 23, 25); Claudia Cummings (Oct. 17, 21)
Countess Geschwitz	Evelyn Lear
A Dresser	Janet Stubbs
High School Boy/A Groom/Dr. Goll	Ferguson MacKenzie
A Painter	Gene Bullard
A Negro/Dr. Schön	Victor Braun
Jack/Alwa	William Pell
Schigolch	Jan Rubes
Animal Tamer	Theodore Baerg
Rodrigo/the Prince	Barry Stilwell
Manservant/Marquis/Theatre Manager	Greg Ryerson
Banker/Police Officer	Ken Baker
15 Year Old Girl	Cristen Gregory
Her Mother	Jean MacPhail
A Lady Artist	Eleanor James
Journalist	Mark Pedrotti
Clown	Shawna Farrell
Clown	Michael Shust
Colwn	Barry Stilwell

Die Entführung aus dem Serail　　　**Wolfgang Amadeus Mozart**
December 10, 12, 14, 16, 18, 20, 1980
Conductor: Mario Bernardi
Director: David Alden
Set: Toni Businger
Costume Designer: Malabar Ltd.

Belmonte	Jon Garrison
Osmin	Artur Korn
Pedrillo	Barry Stilwell
Selim	Tony Kramreither
Constanze	Costanza Cuccaro
Blonde	Caralyn Tomlin

The Merry Widow　　　　　　**Franz Lehár**
In English
January 21, 23, 24, 25, 27, 29, 30, 31, 1981
Conductor: Erich Kunzel
Director: Lotfi Mansouri
Set: Murray Laufer
Costume Designer: Suzanne Mess

St. Brioche	Michael Shust
Baron Zeta	Phil Stark
Valencienne	Barbara Shuttleworth (Jan. 21, 23, 25, 29, 31); Caralyn Tomlin (Jan. 24, 27, 30)
Camille	Neil Rosenshein (Jan. 21, 23, 25, 27, 29, 31); Mark DuBois (Jan. 24, 30)
Cascada	Theodore Baerg
Kromov	Gordon Masten
Olga	Lynn Blaser
Bogdanowitsch	Arnie Hardt
Sylvaine	Shawna Farrell
Njegus	Gerald Isaac
Anna Glawari	Elisabeth Söderström (Jan. 21, 23, 25, 27, 29, 31); Carole Farley (Jan. 24, 30)
Count Danilo	Alan Titus (Jan. 21, 23, 24, 27, 29, 30); Cornelis Opthof (Jan. 24, 31)
Maitre d'Hotel	Robert Godin
Zozo	Deborah Milsom
Pritschitsch	Barry Stilwell
Prasowia	Barbara Hamilton

Der fliegende Holländer　　　**Richard Wagner**
March 25, 27, 29, 31, April 2, 4, 1981
Conductor: Kenneth Montgomery
Director: Bodo Igesz
Set: Murray Laufer
Costume Designer: Suzanne Mess

Dutchman	Leif Roar
Daland	Don Garrard
Senta	Marita Napier
Erik	Alberto Remedios
Mary	Jean MacPhail
Steersman	Michael Shust

266

Norma **Vincenzo Bellini**
April 28, May 1, 4, 7, 10, 1981
Conductor: Richard Bonynge
Director: Lotfi Mansouri
Set: José Varona
Costume Designer: José Varona

Oroveso	Justino Diaz
Pollione	Francisco Ortiz
Flavio	Michael Shust
Norma	Joan Sutherland
Adalgisa	Tatiana Troyanos
Clotilde	Frances Ginzer
Norma's Child	Annabelle Chostek
Norma's Child	Paul Chostek

1981-1982

Un ballo in maschera **Giuseppe Verdi**
September 11, 14, 17, 20, 23, 26, 1981
Conductor: Cal Stewart Kellogg
Director: Lotfi Mansouri
Set: Wolfram Skalicki
Costume Designer: Suzanne Mess

Sam	Jeffrey Wells
Tom	John Dodington
Oscar	Caralyn Tomlin
Riccardo	Michail Svetlev
Renato	Louis Quilico
Judge	Roger Jones
Ulrica	Stella Silva
Silvano	Theodore Baerg
Servant	Ferguson MacKenzie
Amelia	Martina Arroyo

Les contes d'Hoffmann **Jacques Offenbach**
September 18, 21, 24, 27, 30, October 3, 1981
Conductor: Reynald Giovaninetti
Director: Lotfi Mansouri
Set: Gunther Schneider-Siemssen
Costume Designer: Gunther Schneider-Siemssen

Lindorf/Coppélius/Dappertutto/Dr. Miracle	Allan Monk
Andrès/Cochenille/Pittichinaccio/Franz	Martin Chambers
Luther	Vytautas Paulionis
Hermann	Viorel Dihel
Nathanael	Roger Jones
Hoffmann	Neil Shicoff
Nicklausse/The Muse	Janet Stubbs
Spalanzani	André Lortie
Giullietta/Stella	Evelyn Lear (Sep. 18, 24); Carol Gutknecht (Sep. 21, 27, 30, Oct. 3)
Antonia	Frances Ginzer (Sep. 18, 24); Carol Gutknecht (Sep. 21, 27, 30, Oct. 3)
Olympia	Claudia Cummings (Sep. 18, 24); Carol Gutknecht (Sep. 21, 27, 30, Oct. 3)

Schlémil/Crespel	Jeffrey Wells
Antonia's Mother	Eleanor James

Die Fledermaus **Johann Strauss, Jr.**
In English
January 15, 18, 21, 23, 24, 27, 29, 30, 1982
Conductor: Erich Kunzel/Derek Bate
Director: Peter Mark Schifter
Set: Robert O'Hearn
Costume Designer: Suzanne Mess

Rosalinda	Carol Gutknecht (Jan. 15, 21, 24, 30); Claudia Cummings (Jan. 18, 23, 27)
Eisenstein	Alan Titus (Jan. 15, 18, 21, 23, 27, 30); Theodore Baerg (Jan. 24, 29)
Adele	Caralyn Tomlin (Jan. 15, 21, 23, 27); Shawna Farrell (Jan. 18, 24, 29, 30)
Alfred	Ragnar Ulfung
Frank	Spiro Malas
Prince Orlofsky	Gerald Isaac
Dr. Falke	Mark Pedrotti (Jan. 15, 21, 23, 30); Guillermo Silva-Marin (Jan. 18, 24, 27, 29)
Frosch	Tom Kneebone
Dr. Blind	Phil Stark
Ivan	Arnie Hardt
Sally	Cristen Gregory

Lucia di Lammermoor **Gaetano Donizetti**
January 22, 25, 28, 31, February 3, 5, 6, 1982
Conductor: Paolo Peloso
Director: John Copley
Set: Henry Bardon
Costume Designer: Suzanne Mess

Normanno	Martin Chambers (Jan. 22, 28, 31, Feb. 6); Michael Shust (Jan. 25, Feb. 3, 5)
Lord Ashton	John Brocheler (Jan. 22, 25, 28, 31, Feb. 3, 6); Theodore Baerg (Feb. 5)
Raimondo	Pierre Charbonneau (Jan. 22, 25, 28, 31, Feb. 3, 6); John Seabury (Feb. 5)
Lucia	Gianna Rolandi (Jan. 22, 25, 28, 31, Feb. 3, 6); Caralyn Tomlin (Feb. 5)
Alisa	Eleanor James
Edgardo	Barry McCauley (Jan. 22, 25, 28, 31, Feb. 3, 6); James Schwisow (Feb. 5)
Lord Bucklaw	Roger Jones

Jenufa **Leos Janácek**
In English
April 8, 10, 14, 16, 18, 1982
Conductor: Mario Bernardi
Director: Lotfi Mansouri
Set: Maria Bjornson
Costume Designer: Maria Bjornson

Grandmother Buryja	Eleanor James

Laca Klemen	William Neill
Steva Buryja	William Pell
Kostelnicka Buryjovka	Elizabeth Connell
Jenufa	Patricia Wells
Starek	Theodore Baerg
Rychtar	Vytautas Paulionis
Rychtarka	Jean MacPhail
Karolka	Cristen Gregory
Pastuchnya	Anne Dlugokecki
Barena	Joanne Kolomyjec
Jano	Shawna Farrell
Aunt	Brenda Berge

La Traviata   **Giuseppe Verdi**
April 12, 15, 17, 21, 23, 24, 25, 1982
Conductor: Imre Pallo/Derek Bate
Director: Irving Guttman
Set: Pier Luigi Pizzi
Costume Designer: Pier Luigi Pizzi

Violetta	Mariana Niculescu (Apr. 12, 15, 17, 21, 23, 25); Roxolana Roslak (Apr. 24)
Alfredo	John Brecknock (Apr. 12, 15, 17, 21, 25); James Schwisow (Apr. 23, 24)
Germont	Cornelis Opthof (Apr. 12, 15, 17, 21, 23, 25); Viorel Dihel (Apr. 24)
Flora	Eleanor James (Apr. 12, 15, 17, 21, 23, 25); Brenda Berge (Apr. 24)
Annina	Cristen Gregory
Gastone	Roger Jones
Baron Douphol	Theodore Baerg
Marquis	Vytautas Paulionis
Dr. Grenvil	John Dodington
Giuseppe	Ferguson MacKenzie

1982-1983

Falstaff   **Giuseppe Verdi**
September 16, 21, 23, 26, 29, October 2, 1982
Conductor: Julius Rudel/Derek Bate
Director: John Copley
Set: Wolfram Skalicki
Costume Designer: Suzanne Mess

Sir John Falstaff	Louis Quilico
Dr. Caius	Martin Chambers
Bardolfo	Barry Stilwell
Pistola	John Dodington
Robin	Brennan Carson
Alice Ford	Roxolana Roslak
Nannetta	Caralyn Tomlin
Meg Page	Janet Stubbs
Mistress Quickly	Diane Curry
Ford	Allan Monk
Fenton	Mark DuBois

Die Zauberflöte   **Wolfgang Amadeus Mozart**
September 24, 27, 30, October 1, 3, 5, 7, 9, 1982
Conductor: Theo Alcantara/Derek Bate
Director: Frank Corsaro
Set: Maurice Sendak/Neil Peter Jampolis
Costume Designer: Maurice Sendak/Steven Feldman

Pamina	Costanza Cuccaro
Tamino	Anson Austin (Sep. 24, 27, 30, Oct. 3, 5, 9); Mark DuBois (Oct. 1, 7)
Papageno	Theodore Baerg (Sep. 24, 27, 30, Oct. 3, 5, 7, 9); Christopher Cameron (Oct. 1)
Papagena	Shawna Farrell (Sep. 24, 27, 30, Oct. 3); Shari Saunders (Oct. 5, 7, 9)
Queen of the Night	Claudia Cummings
First Spirit	Benjamin Carlson (Sep. 24, 27, 30, Oct. 3); Simon Blend (Oct. 1, 5, 7, 9)
Second Spirit	Justin Young (Sep. 24, 27, 30, Oct. 3); Justin Booth (Oct. 1, 5, 7, 9)
Third Spirit	David Yung (Sep. 24, 27, 30, Oct. 3); Lawrence Nichols (Oct. 1, 5, 7, 9)
First Lady	Claudette Leblanc (Sep. 24, 27, 30, Oct. 3, 5, 7, 9); Susan Austin (Oct. 1)
Second Lady	Irena Welhasch
Third Lady	Katharina Megli (Sep. 24, 27, 30, Oct. 3); Eleanor James (Oct. 1, 5, 7, 9)
Sarastro	Noel Mangin (Sep. 24, 27, 30, Oct. 3, 5, 7, 9); John Macurdy (Oct. 1)
Speaker	Viorel Dihel
Monostatos	Phil Stark
Armed Man	Ben Heppner
Armed Man	Gidon Saks
Priest	John Dodington
Priest	Roger Jones

La belle Hélène   **Jacques Offenbach**
In English
January 14, 18, 20, 22, 23, 26, 29, 1983
Conductor: Erich Kunzel
Director: Lotfi Mansouri
Set: Thierry Bosquet
Costume Designer: Thierry Bosquet

Calchas	Douglas Chamberlain
Philocomos	Gidon Saks
Euthycles	Barry Stilwell
Hélène	Shiela M. Smith (Jan. 14, 20, 23, 26); Elizabeth Knighton (Jan. 18, 22, 29)
Orestes	Gerald Isaac
Bacchis	Kristine Anderson
Parthaoenis	Irena Welhasch
Laeoena	Cristen Gregory
Paris	Alan Kays (Jan. 14, 20, 23, 26); Jerry Hadley (Jan. 18, 22, 29)
Ajax I	Martin Chambers
Ajax II	Theodore Baerg
Achilles	Ben Heppner
Menelaus	Claude Corbeil
Agamemnon	Jeffrey Wells

Elektra   **Richard Strauss**
January 21, 25, 27, 30, February 2, 5, 1983
Conductor: Gabor Ötvös
Director: Lotfi Mansouri
Set: Wolfram Skalicki
Costume Designer: Amrei Skalicki

First Maid	Martha Jane Howe
Second Maid	Lilian Kilianski
Third Maid	Eleanor James
Fourth Maid	Joanne Kolomyjec
Fifth Maid	Irena Welhasch
Overseer	Jean MacPhail
Elektra	Olivia Stapp
Chrysothemis	Viviane Thomas
Klytemnestra	Maureen Forrester
Confidante	Janet Smith
Trainbearer	Kristine Anderson
Young Servant	Ben Heppner
Old Servant	Christopher Cameron
Orestes	Tom Fox
Guardian	Jeffrey Wells
Aegisthus	Phil Stark

La fanciulla del West   **Giacomo Puccini**
April 8, 12, 14, 17, 20, 23, 1983
Conductor: Berislav Klobucar
Director: Lotfi Mansouri/John Leberg
Set: Robert O'Hearn
Costume Designer: Suzanne Mess

Harry	Roger Jones
Joe	Ben Heppner
Handsome	Rod Campbell
Nick	Martin Chambers
Happy	Paul Massel
Sid	Ross Thompson
Sonora	Theodore Baerg
Larkens	Avo Kittask
Trin	Phil Stark
Jake Wallace	Gidon Saks
Ashby	Jeffrey Wells
Minnie	Johanna Meier
A Pony Express Courier	Daniel Neff
José Castro	John Dodington
Dick Johnson (Ramerrez)	Giorgio Lamberti
Wowkle	Eleanor James
Billy Jackrabbit	Christopher Cameron
Sheriff Jack Rance	Cornelis Opthof

L'incoronazione di Poppea   **Claudio Monteverdi**
April 19, 22, 24, 26, 28, 30, 1983
Conductor: Kenneth Montgomey
Director: Lotfi Mansouri
Set: Ita Maximowna
Costume Designer: Ita Maximowna

Fortuna	Joanne Kolomyjec
Virtu	Diane Loeb
Amor	Jaimie Peters; David Yung
Ottone	Mark Pedrottti
Soldier	Ben Heppner
Soldier	Roger Jones
Poppea	Carmen Balthrop
Nero	Michael Myers
Arnalta	Alexander Oliver
Ottavia	Katherine Ciesinski
Nutrice	Patricia Kern
Drusilla	Irena Welhasch
Seneca	Kevin Langan
Valletto	Martin Chambers
Damigella	Shari Saunders
Liberto	Ross Thompson
Lucano	Barry Stilwell
Littore	Gidon Saks

1983-1984

Lohengrin   **Richard Wagner**
September 16, 20, 24, 28, October 2, 6, 1983
Conductor: Michel Tabachnik
Director: Nando Schellen
Set: Wilfried Werz
Costume Designer: Wilfried Werz

The King's Herald	Theodore Baerg (Sep. 16, Oct. 2, 6); Mark Pedrotti (Sep. 20, 24, 28);
Heinrich der Vogler	Donald Shanks
Friedrich von Telramund	Nicola Fabricci
Elsa von Brabant	Ellen Shade
Lohengrin	Siegfried Jerusalem (Sep. 16, 24, 28, Oct. 2); Warren Ellsworth (Sep. 20, Oct. 6)
Ortrud	Janis Martin
Noble of Brabant	Dennis Giesbrecht
Noble of Brabant	Ron Haney
Noble of Brabant	Edward Knuckles
Noble of Brabant	John Nieboer
Page	Lilian Kilianski
Page	Marjorie Sparks
Page	Deborah Stephens
Page	Susan Tsagkaris

Turandot   **Giacomo Puccini**
September 23, 27, 29, October 1, 5, 9, 1983
Conductor: Nicola Rescigno
Director: Lotfi Mansouri
Set: Allen Charles Klein
Costume Designer: Allen Charles Klein

A Mandarin	John Fanning
Liu	Maria Spacagna (Sep. 23, 29, Oct. 1, 9); Irena Welhasch (Sep. 27, Oct. 5)
Calaf	Ermanno Mauro (Sep. 23, 27, 29); Francisco Ortiz (Oct. 1, 5, 9)
Timur	Don Garrard
Prince of Persia	Ben Heppner
Ping	Theodore Baerg

Pang	Barry Stilwell
Pong	Guillermo Silva-Marin
Emperor	Phil Stark
Turandot	Martina Arroyo

The Merry Widow   **Franz Lehár**
In English
January 13, 15, 19, 21, 24, 25, 27, February 2, 4, 1983
Conductor: Erich Kunzel/Derek Bate
Director: John Leberg
Set: Murray Laufer
Costume Designer: Suzanne Mess

St. Brioche	Ross Thompson
Baron Zeta	Phil Stark
Valencienne	Caralyn Tomlin (Jan. 13, 19, 21, 24, Feb. 2); Irena Welhasch (Jan. 15, 25, 27, Feb. 4)
Camille	Mark DuBois (Jan. 13, 19, 21, 25, 27, Feb. 4); Martin Chambers (Jan. 15, 24, Feb. 2)
Cascada	Barry Stilwell
Kromov	Douglas Chamberlain
Olga	Tania Parrish
Bogdanowitsch	Arnie Hardt
Sylvaine	Shari Saunders
Njegus	Gerald Isaac
Anna Glawari	Sheri Greenawald (Jan. 13, 19, 25, 27, Feb. 4); Karen Huffstodt (Jan. 15, 21, 24, Feb. 2)
Count Danilo	John Reardon (Jan. 13, 19, 21, 25, 27, Feb. 2, 4); Theodore Baerg (Jan. 15, 24)
Maitre d'Hotel	Robert Godin
Zozo	Katharina Megli
Pritschitsch	Brian Pearcy
Prasowia	Barbara Hamilton

Carmen   **Georges Bizet**
January 20, 22, 26, 28, 31, February 1, 3, 5, 1984
Conductor: Michel Tabachnik/Derek Bate
Director: Lotfi Mansouri
Set: John Conklin
Costume Designer: Jane Greenwood

Moralès	John Fanning
Micaela	Jennifer Ringo (Jan. 20, 26, 28, Feb. 1); Caralyn Tomlin (Jan. 22, 31, Feb. 3, 5)
Don José	Harry Theyard (Jan. 20, 26, 28, Feb. 1); Barry McCauley (Jan. 22, 31, Feb. 3, 5)
Zuniga	John Dodington (Jan. 20, 26, 28, Feb. 1, 3, 5); Gidon Saks (Jan. 22, 31)
Carmen	Claire Powell (Jan. 20, 26, 28, Feb. 1, 5); Janet Stubbs (Jan. 22, 31, Feb. 3)
Frasquita	Joanne Kolomyjec (Jan. 20, 26, 28, Feb. 1); Cristen Gregory (Jan. 22, 31, Feb. 3, 5)
Mercédès	Katharina Megli (Jan. 20, 26, 28, Feb. 1); Odette Beaupré (Jan. 22, 31, Feb. 3, 5)
Escamillo	Michael Devlin
Remendado	Barry Stilwell (Jan. 20, 26, 28, Feb. 1); Ben Heppner (Jan. 22, 31, Feb. 3, 5)

Dancairo	Theodore Baerg (Jan. 20, 26, 28, Feb. 1); Ross Thompson (Jan. 22, 31, Feb. 3, 5)
A Guide	Robert Godin
Innkeeper	Dennis O'Connor

La Bohème   **Giacomo Puccini**
April 11, 13, 14, 15, 17, 18, 19, 20, 21, 1984
Conductor: Paolo Peloso
Director: John Copley
Set: Pier-Luigi Pizzi
Costume Designer: Pier-Luigi Pizzi

Marcello	J. Patrick Raftery (Apr. 11, 14, 17, 19); Theodore Baerg (Apr. 13, 15, 18, 20, 21)
Rodolfo	Tonio Di Paolo (Apr. 11, 14, 17, 19, 21); Franco Farina (Apr. 13, 15, 18, 20)
Colline	Eric Halfvarson (Apr. 11, 14, 17, 19, 20, 21); Gidon Saks (Apr. 13, 15, 18)
Schaunard	Samuel Byrd (Apr. 11, 14, 17, 19, 20, 21); John Fanning (Apr. 13, 15, 18)
Benoit	John MacMaster
Mimi	Kathryn Bouleyn (Apr. 11, 14, 17, 19, 21); Karen Hunt (Apr. 13, 15, 18, 20)
Parpignol	Peter Blanchet
Musetta	Katherine Terrell (Apr. 11, 14, 17, 19, 21); Irena Welhasch (Apr. 13, 15, 18, 20)
Alcindoro	Phil Stark
Customs House Sergeant	Maurice Brown

Anna Bolena   **Gaetano Donizetti**
May 22, 25, 28, 31, June 3, 1984
Conductor: Richard Bonynge
Director: Lotfi Mansouri
Set: John Pascoe
Costume Designer: Michael Stennett

Enrico	James Morris
Anna Bolena	Joan Sutherland
Giovanna Seymour	Judith Forst
Rochefort	Gidon Saks
Percy	Michael Myers
Smeton	Janet Stubbs
Hervey	Ben Heppner

La rappresentazione di Anima e di Corpo   **Emilio de' Cavalieri**
St. Michael's Cathedral
June 6, 8, 1984
Conductor: Kenneth Montgomery
Director: Peter Reichenbach

Tempo	John Fanning
Intelletto	Guillermo Silva-Marin
Anima	Irena Welhasch
Corpo	Mark Pedrotti
Consiglio	John Fanning
Piacere	Odette Beaupré
First Compagno	Peter Blanchet

Second Compagno	Theodore Baerg
Angelo Custode	Theodore Gentry
Vita Mondana	Martha Collins
Mondo	Christopher Cameron
Solo Anima Damnata	Maurice Brown
Solo Anima Beata	Shari Saunders

Death in Venice   **Benjamin Britten**
June 24, 26, 28, 30, 1984
Conductor: Richard Woitach
Director: Lotfi Mansouri
Set: Wolfram Skalicki
Costume Designer: Susan Benson

Gustav von Aschenbach	Kenneth Riegel
The Traveller	Allan Monk
Youth on Boat	Peter Blanchet
Youth on Boat	John Fanning
Youth on Boat	Dennis Giesbrecht
Youth on Boat	Ron Haney
Youth on Boat	John MacMaster
Youth on Boat	John Nieboer
Youth on Boat	Bruce Schaef
Youth on Boat	Guillermo Silva-Marin
Youth on Boat	Lenard Whiting
Elderly Fop	Allan Monk
Ship's Steward	Ross Thompson
Old Gondolier	Allan Monk
Lido Boatman	Theodore Baerg
Hotel Porter	Martin Chambers (June 24, 26, 28); Peter Blanchet (June 30)
Hotel Manager	Allan Monk
French Girl	Shari Saunders
French Mother	Odette Beaupré
American	Peter Blanchet
American	John MacMaster
German Mother	Anne McWatt
German Father	John Fanning
German Child	Alexandor Ritter
Danish Lady	Irena Welhasch
English Lady	Gaynor Jones
Russian Mother	Martha Collins
Russian Father	Christopher Cameron
Russian Child	Jennifer Dinelle
Russian Child	Michael Faigaux
Russian Child	Fleur Leslie
Russian Child	Tanya Moore
Russian Nanny	Anne Dlugokecki
Polish Father	Ron Haney
Hotel Waiter	Erik Oland
Polish Governess	Lilian Maher
Tadzio	Jeffrey Edwards
Tadzio's Sister	Heidi LeMoine
Tadzio's Sister	Kelly McDonald
Polish Mother	Olga Evreinoff
Waiter	Philip Barker
Waiter	Steven Domingo
Waiter	Brian Morey
Waiter	Glen Piper

Desk Clerk	Rob Sjoerds
Jaschiu	Alexander Sukonnik
Boy on Beach	Lloyd Adams
Boy on Beach	Robert Dungey
Boy on Beach	Darrell Komonko
Boy on Beach	Ron Ladd
Boy on Beach	David Malek
Boy on Beach	Gerard McIsaac
Boy on Beach	David Meinke
Boy on Beach	Ales Polacek
Boy on Beach	Gregory Pouchet
Cabana Boy	Gregory Pouchet
Cabana Boy	Ron Ladd
Cabana Boy	David Meinke
Photographer	John Nieboer
Guest on the Beach	Pat Drummond
Guest on the Beach	Barbara Scott
Guest on the Beach	Lynette Coleman
Strawberry Seller	Cristen Gregory
Guide	John Fanning
Lace Seller	Mary Jo Masterson
Glass Maker	Guillermo Silva-Marin
Newspaper Seller	Halyna Dytyniak
Beggar Woman	Lilian Kilianski
Flower Seller	Tania Parrish
Postcard Seller	John McMaster
Restaurant Waiter	Ross Thompson
Gondolier	Gordon Cowan
Gondolier	Dennis Giesbrecht
Gondolier	Ferguson MacKenzie
Venetian	Rosa Antony
Venetian	Renee Lynn Bouthot
Venetian	William Bowen
Venetian	Maurice Brown
Venetian	Erik Oland
Venetian	Bruce Schaef
Venetian	Susan Tsagkaris
Venetian	Lenard Whiting
Venetian	Heather Wilberforce
Voice of Apollo	Jeffrey Gall
Hotel Barber	Allan Monk
Priest	Maurice Brown
Leader of Strolling Players	Allan Monk
Strolling Player	Guillermo Silva-Marin
Strolling Player	Heather Wilberforce
Acrobat	Gerard McIsaac
Acrobat	Ales Polacek
Elder Player	Gael Rayment
English Clerk	Theodore Baerg
Voice of Dionysus	Allan Monk

1984-1985

Il Trovatore   **Giuseppe Verdi**
September 29, October 2, 5, 8, 11, 14, 17, 1984
Conductor: Cal Stewart Kellogg
Director: Lotfi Mansouri
Set: Wolfram Skalicki

Costume Designer: Gladstein and Co.

Ferrando	Jeffrey Wells (Sep. 29, Oct. 5, 11, 14); John Dodington (Oct. 2, 6, 17)
Inez	Odette Beaupré
Leonora	Margarita Castro-Alberty
Count di Luna	Allan Monk
Manrico	Maurizio Frusoni (Sep. 29, Oct. 2, 5, 8, 17); Ermanno Mauro (Oct. 11, 14)
Azucena	Livia Budai
A Gypsy	John Nieboer
Ruiz	Ben Heppner

Tosca　　　　　　**Giacomo Puccini**
October 13, 16, 18, 20, 22, 24, 26, 28, 1984
Conductor: Paolo Peloso
Director: Anne Ewers
Set: Lawrence Schäfer
Costume Designer: Suzanne Mess

Angelotti	John Dodington (Oct. 13, 18, 22, 26); Jeffrey Wells (Oct. 16, 20, 24, 28)
Sacristan	Christopher Cameron (Oct. 13, 18, 22, 26); Maurice Brown (Oct. 16, 20, 24, 28)
Cavardossi	Francisco Ortiz (Oct. 13, 26); Giorgio Lamberti (Oct. 16, 18, 20, 22, 24, 28)
Tosca	Martina Arroyo (Oct. 13, 18, 22, 26); Johanna Meier (Oct. 16, 20, 24, 28)
Scarpia	Cornelis Opthof
Spoletta	Barry Stilwell
Sciarrone	John Fanning
Shepherd Boy	Danny Auchincloss (Oct. 13, 16, 20, 28); Alexandra Tait (Oct. 18, 22, 26, 28)
Jailer	Maurice Brown (Oct. 13, 18, 22, 26); Christopher Cameron (Oct. 16, 20, 24, 28)

Candide　　　　　　**Leonard Bernstein**
January 19, 23, 25, 28, 31, February 2, 3, 5, 8, 9, 1985
Conductor: Erich Kunzel/Derek Bate
Director: Harold Prince
Set: Clarke Dunham
Costume Designer: Judith Dolan

Voltaire	Joseph McKee
Candide	David Eisler (Jan. 19, 25, Feb. 2, 5, 9); Mark DuBois (Jan. 23, 28, 31, Feb. 3, 8)
Huntsman	Maurice Brown
Paquette	Deborah Darr
Baroness	Martha Collins
Baron	Jack Harrold
Cunegonde	Marilyn Hill Smith (Jan. 19, 25, 31, Feb. 3, 8); Jennifer Ringo (Jan. 23, 28, Feb. 2, 5, 9)
Maximilian	Scott Reeve
Servant of Maximilian	Richard McMillan
Dr. Pangloss	Joseph McKee
Bulgarian Soldier	Maurice Brown
Bulgarian Soldier	Richard McMilan

Westphalian Soldier	Christopher Cameron
Westphalian Soldier	Ross Thompson
Don Issachar	Richard McMillan
Grand Inquisitor	Jack Harrold
Calliope Player	Martha Collins
Heresy Agent	Avery Saltzman
Inquisition Agent	Ross Thompson
Inquisition Agent	Maurice Brown
Judge	Richard McMillan
Old Lady	Arlene Meadows
Don	Maurice Brown
Don	Paul Dorsey
Don	Victor Edwards
Don	Marshall Pynkoski
Don	Avery Saltzman
Don	Ross Thompson
Businessman	Joseph McKee
Governor	Joseph McKee
Governor's Aide	Marshall Pynkoski
Slave Driver	Jack Harrold
Father Bernard	Richard McMillan
Sailor	Jim Brazier
Sailor	Paul Dorsey
Sailor	Victor Edwards
Pirate	Ross Thompson
Pink Sheep	Linda Bennett
Pink Sheep	Sandra Gavinchuk
Lion	Christopher Cameron
Pasha-Prefect	Jack Harrold
First Gambler	Richard McMillan
Second Gambler (Police Chief)	Joseph McKee
Sage	Joseph McKee

Faust　　　　　　**Charles Gounod**
January 26, 29, February 1, 4, 7, 10, 1985
Conductor: Reynald Giovaninetti
Director: Lotfi Mansouri
Set: Wolfram Skalicki
Costume Designer: Amrei Skalicki

Faust	Barry McCauley
Méphistophélès	Kevin Langan
Valentin	Theodore Baerg (Jan. 26, Feb. 1, 4, 10); Gaétan Laperrière (Jan. 29, Feb. 7)
Wagner	John Fanning
Siébel	Odette Beaupré
Marguerite	Elizabeth Knighton
Marthe	Jean MacPhail

Così fan tutte　　　　　　**Wolfgang Amadeus Mozart**
COCE, St. Lawrence Centre
February 21, 23, 25, 27, March 1, 3, 1985
Conductor: Derek Bate
Director: Lotfi Mansouri
Set: Beandesign
Costume Designer: Michael Stennett

Ferrando	Peter Blanchet
Guglielmo	Gaétan Laperrière (Feb. 21, 25, 27); John

	Fanning (Feb. 23, Mar. 1, 3)
Don Alfonso	Maurice Brown (Feb. 21, 23, Mar. 1, 3); Brian McIntosh (Feb. 25, 27)
Fiordiligi	Joanne Kolomyjec
Dorabella	Odette Beaupré
Despina	Susan Tsagkaris

Il barbiere di Siviglia   **Gioacchino Rossini**
April 10, 12, 13, 14, 16, 18, 19, 20, 1985
Conductor: Franco Mannino
Director: Bliss Hebert
Set: Robert Prévost
Costume Designer: Robert Prévost

Fiorello	John Fanning
Count Almaviva	Mark DuBois (Apr. 10, 13, 16, 19); Gary Bennett (Apr. 12, 14, 18, 20)
Figaro	Theodore Baerg (Apr. 10, 13, 16, 19); Stephen Dickson (Apr. 12, 14, 18, 20)
Dr. Bartolo	Maurice Brown (Apr. 10, 13, 16, 19); Christopher Cameron (Apr. 12, 14, 18, 20)
Rosina	Claire Powell (Apr. 10, 13, 16, 19); Janet Stubbs (Apr. 12, 14, 18, 20)
Basilio	William Wildermann (Apr. 10, 13, 16, 19); John Dodington (Apr. 12, 14, 18, 20)
Berta	Joanne Kolomyjec (Apr. 10, 13, 16, 19); Darlene Hirst (Apr. 12, 14, 18, 20)
Sergeant	Phil Stark
Ambrogio	Avery Saltzman

Die Meistersinger von Nürenberg   **Richard Wagner**
May 21, 24, 27, 30, June 2, 1985
Conductor: Gabor Ötvös
Director: Lotfi Mansouri
Set: Robert O'Hearn
Costume Designer: Robert O'Hearn

Eva	Mari Anne Häggander
Magdalene	Janet Stubbs
Walther von Stolzing	William Johns
David	James Atherton
Veit Pogner	Artur Korn
Sixtus Beckmesser	John Reardon
Kunz Vogelgesang	Ben Heppner
Konrad Nachtigall	John Fanning
Fritz Kothner	Gary Relyea
Hermann Ortel	Brian McIntosh
Balthasar Zorn	Guillermo Silva-Marin
Augustin Moser	Phil Stark
Ulrich Eisslinger	Barry Stilwell
Hans Foltz	Maurice Brown
Hans Schwarz	John Dodington
Hans Sachs	Siegfried Vogel
A Night Watchman	Gaétan Laperrière

The Rake's Progress   **Igor Stravinsky**
June 5, 7, 9, 11, 13, 15, 1985
Conductor: Michel Tabachnik
Director: John Leberg
Set: David Hockney
Costume Designer: David Hockney

Anne Trulove	Costanza Cuccaro
Tom Rakewell	John Stewart
Father Trulove	John Dodington
Nick Shadow	Allan Monk
Mother Goose	Martha Jane Howe
Baba the Turk	Sheila M. Smith
Sellem	Barry Stilwell
Keeper of the Asylum	Brian McIntosh

1985-1986

Hamlet   **Ambroise Thomas**
October 4, 7, 10, 13, 16, 19, 1985
Conductor: Richard Bonynge
Director: Lotfi Mansouri
Set: Wolfram Skalicki
Costume Designer: Desmond Digby/Michael Stennett

Claudius	Donald Shanks
Gertrude	Leslie Richards
Polonius	Maurice Brown
Hamlet	John Bröcheler
Ophélie	Joan Sutherland
Laërte	Mark DuBois
Horatio	Gaétan Laperrière
Marcellus	Martin Chambers
Ghost	Christopher Cameron
Player King	Daniel Hyatt
Player Queen	Brian Grist
Player Villain	Daryl Shuttleworth
First Gravedigger	Peter Blanchet
Second Gravedigger	Ingemar Korjus (Oct. 4, 16, 19); Gary Relyea (Oct. 7, 10, 13)

Madama Butterfly   **Giacomo Puccini**
October 9, 11, 15, 17, 20, 22, 24, 25, 26, 1985
Conductor: Michel Tabachnik
Director: Christopher Newton
Set: Toni Businger
Costume Designer: Toni Businger

Cio-Cio-San	Yoko Watanabe (Oct. 9, 15, 20, 24, 26); Maria Pellegrini (Oct. 11, 17, 22, 25)
Suzuki	Janet Stubbs (Oct. 9, 15, 20, 24, 26); Odette Beaupré (Oct. 11, 17, 22, 25)
Pinkerton	Franco Farina (Oct. 9, 15, 20, 24, 26); Gordon Greer (Oct. 11, 17, 22, 25)
Sharpless	Mark Pedrotti (Oct. 9, 15, 20, 24, 26); John Fanning (Oct. 11, 17, 22, 25)
Goro	Phil Stark
The Bonze	Gary Relyea (Oct. 9, 15, 20, 22, 26); Ingemar Korjus (Oct. 11, 17, 24, 25)

Prince Yamadori	Patrick Timney
Commissioner	Brian McIntosh
Kate Pinkerton	Kimberly Barber
Dolore	James Mills (Oct. 9, 15, 20, 24, 26); Andreane Beaupré (Oct. 11, 17, 22, 25)
Registrar	Dennis Giesbrecht
Yukasidé	John Avey
Mother	Lilian Kilianski
Cousin	Diane Lewarne
Aunt	Linda Bennett

The Mikado   W. S. Gilbert and Arthur S. Sullivan
January 17, 19, 21, 23, 25, 26, 28, 29, 31, 1986
Conductor: Alexander Faris
Director: Lotfi Mansouri
Set: Thierry Bosquet
Costume Designer: Thierry Bosquet

Mikado	Donald Adams
Nanki-Poo	Bruce Reed (Jan. 17, 21, 25, 26, 28); Mark DuBois (Jan. 19, 23, 29, 31)
Ko-Ko	James Billings (Jan. 17, 21, 25, 29, 31); Ragnar Ulfung (Jan. 19, 23, 26, 28)
Pooh-Bah	John Ayldon (Jan. 17, 21, 25, 26, 28); William Wildermann (Jan. 19, 23, 29, 31)
Pish-Tush	John Fanning
Yum-Yum	Marilyn Hill Smith (Jan. 17, 21, 25, 28); Claudette Peterson (Jan. 19, 23, 26, 29, 31)
Pitti-Sing	Kimberly Barber (Jan. 17, 21, 25, 28, 29, 31); Linda Bennett (Jan. 19, 23, 26)
Peep-Bo	Sharon Anne Miller
Katisha	Maureen Forrester (Jan. 17, 21, 25, 28); Anne Collins (Jan. 19, 23, 26, 29, 31)

Salome   Richard Strauss
January 24, 27, 30, February 1, 4, 6, 9, 1986
Conductor: Gabor Ötvös
Director: Lotfi Mansouri
Set: Wolfram Skalicki
Costume Designer: Amrei Skalicki

Narraboth	Peter Kazaras
Page	Odette Beaupré
First Soldier	John Ayldon
Second Soldier	Gaétan Laperrière
Cappadocian	Christopher Coyea
Salome	Kristine Ciesinski (Jan. 24, 30, Feb. 4, 9); Stephanie Sundine (Jan. 27, Feb. 1, 6)
Slave	Susan Tsagkaris
Jokanaan	Tom Fox
Herod Antipas	Ragnar Ulfung (Jan. 24, 30, Feb. 4, 9); Phil Stark (Jan. 27, Feb. 1, 6)
Herodias	Maureen Forrester
First Jew	Barry Stilwell
Second Jew	Peter Blanchet
Third Jew	John MacMaster
Fourth Jew	Richard Margison

Fifth Jew	Brian McIntosh
First Nazarene	Dennis Giesbrecht
Second Nazarene	Maurice Brown

The Beggar's Opera   John Gay
COCE Texaco Opera Theatre
February 26, 28, March 1, 2, 6, 7, 8, 9, 14, 15, 1986
Conductor: Stephen Lord
Director: William Farlow
Set: John Roslevich
Costume Designer: Opera Theatre of St. Louis & Malabar

The Beggar/Filch	Peter Blanchet
Jeremiah Peachum	Maurice Brown
Mrs. Peachum	Arlene Meadows
Polly Peachum	Susan Tsagkaris
Captain MacHeath	Gaétan Laperrière
Lucy Lockit	Odette Beaupré
Lockit	Brian McIntosh
Mrs. Diana Trapes	Arlene Meadows
Matt of the Mint	Patrick Timney
Ben Budge	Dennis Giesbrecht
Wat Dreary	David Fawcett
Crook-Finger'd Jack	John Avey
Harry Paddington	Christopher Coyea
Tom Tipple	Edward Knuckles
Potboy	Greg Tessaro
Potboy	Christopher Dunning
Supernumerary	Benedict Magnin
Jenny Diver	Linda Bennett
Mrs. Vixen	Lilian Kilianski
Dolly Trull	Anne McWatt
Molly Brazen	Kathy Domoney
Mrs. Slammekin	Mary Jo Masterson
Mrs. Coaxer	Halyna Dytyniak
Suky Tawdry	Tania Parrish

Aïda   Giuseppe Verdi
April 4, 7, 10, 13, 16, 19, 22, 25, 1986
Conductor: Paolo Peloso
Director: Nicolas Joël
Set: Pet Halmen
Costume Designer: Pet Halmen

Ramfis	Kevin Langan
Radames	Ernesto Veronelli
Amneris	Livia Budai (Apr. 4, 10, 13, 19, 22); Leslie Richards (Apr. 7, 16, 25)
Aïda	Leona Mitchell (Apr. 4, 7, 10, 13, 16, 19, 22); Viviane Thomas (Apr. 25)
King of Egypt	Christopher Cameron
Messenger	Michele Strano
Priestess	Joanne Kolomyjec (Apr. 4, 10, 13, 16, 19, 22); Susan Tsagkaris (Apr. 7, 19, 25)
Amonasro	Cornelis Opthof

Dialogues des Carmélites   Francis Poulenc
April 11, 15, 17, 20, 23, 26, 1986

Conductor: Jean Fournet
Director: Lotfi Mansouri
Set: Wolfram Skalicki
Costume Designer: Amrei Skalicki

Chevalier de la Force	Mark DuBois
Marquis de la Force	Gaétan Laperrière
Blanche de la Force	Irena Welhasch
Thierry	Patrick Timney
Mme. De Croissy	Maureen Forrester
Sister Constance	Harolyn Blackwell
Mother Marie	Janet Stubbs
M. Javelinot	Brian McIntosh
Mme. Lidoine	Carol Vaness
Father Confessor	Martin Chambers
Sister Mathilde	Kimberly Barber
Mother Jeanne	Odette Beaupré
First Commissary	Dennis Giesbrecht
Second Commissary	Christopher Coyea
Officer	Barry Stilwell
Jailer	John Fanning

La Traviata   Giuseppe Verdi
June 18, 20, 21, 22, 24, 25, 26, 27, 28, 1986
Conductor: Derek Bate
Director: John Leberg
Set: Pier Luigi Pizzi
Costume Designer: Pier Luigi Pizzi

Violetta	Nelly Miricioiu (June 18, 21, 25, 27); Maria Spacagna (June 20, 22, 24, 26, 28)
Alfredo	Patrick Power (June 18, 21, 25, 27); Tonio Di Paolo (June 20, 22, 24, 26, 28)
Germont	Allan Monk (June 18, 21, 25, 27, 28); Gaétan Laperrière (June 20, 22, 24, 26)
Flora	Kimberly Barber (June 18, 21, 24, 26, 28); Odette Beaupré (June 20, 22, 25, 27)
Annina	Susan Tsagkaris
Gaston	Peter Blanchet
Baron Douphol	John Fanning
Marquis	Christopher Cameron
Dr. Grenvil	Maurice Brown (June 18, 21, 22, 24, 25, 27, 28); Brian McIntosh (June 20, 26)
Giuseppe	Patrick Timney
Commissionario	Brian McIntosh (June 18, 21, 22, 24, 25, 27, 28); Maurice Brown (June 20, 26)
Flora's Servant	Rob Milne

1986-1987

Boris Godunov   Modest Mussorgsky
September 12, 17, 20, 23, 25, 28, October 1, 1986
Conductor: Berislav Klobucar
Director: Lotfi Mansouri
Set: Wolfram Skalicki
Costume Designer: David Collis

Boris Godunov	Gwynne Howell
Prince Shuisky	Alexander Oliver
Pimen	Kevin Langan
Grigory	Michael Myers
Marina Mnishek	Claire Powell
Rangoni	Gary Relyea
Varlaam	Donnie Ray Albert
Missail	Dennis Giesbrecht
Hostess	Arlene Meadows
The Boyar Khrushchov	Brian McIntosh
Feodor	Linda Bennett Maguire
Xenia	Sharon Anne Miller (Sep. 12, 25, 28); Susan Tsagkaris (Sep. 17, 20, 23, Oct. 1)
Xenia's Nurse	Lilian Kilianski
A Simpleton	Peter Blanchet
Andrei Shchelkalov	John Fanning
Nikitich	Brian Robertson
A Border Guard	Brian Robertson
Lavitsky	Patrick Timney
Chernikovsky	Christopher Coyea
Mitiukha	Brian McIntosh
A Boyar in Attendance	Gary Rideout

Macbeth   Giuseppe Verdi
September 19, 21, 24, 27, 30, October 2, 4, 1986
Conductor: Cal Stewart Kellogg
Director: Elijah Moshinsky
Set: Wolfram Skalicki
Costume Designer: Amrei Skalicki

Macbeth	Allan Monk
Banquo	Don Garrard
Lady Macbeth	Sylvia Sass
MacDuff	Walter MacNeil
Malcolm	Ben Heppner
Lady-in-Waiting	Lyudmila Pildysh
Murderer	Brian McIntosh
Doctor	Brian Robertson
First Apparition	John Nieboer
Second Apparition	Danny Auchincloss
Third Apparition	Craig Elliot
Herald	Benoit Boutet

Die Fledermaus   Johann Strauss, Jr.
In English
January 15, 18, 20, 23, 26, 28, 30, February 3, 7, 1987
Conductor: Derek Bate
Director: Lotfi Mansouri
Set: Robert O'Hearn
Costume Designer: Suzanne Mess

Rosalinda	Heather Thomson (Jan. 15, 20, 26, 30, Feb. 7); Katherine Terrell (Jan. 18, 23, 28, Feb. 3)
Eisenstein	André Jobin (Jan. 15, 20, 26, 30, Feb. 7); Theodore Baerg (Jan. 18, 23, 28, Feb. 3)
Adele	Cheryl Parrish (Jan. 15, 20, 26, 30, Feb. 7); Tracy Dahl (Jan. 18, 23, 28, Feb. 3)

Alfred	Bruce Reed (Jan. 15, 20, 26, 30, Feb. 7); Gregory Kundle (Jan. 18, 23, 28, Feb. 3)
Frank	John Del Carlo
Prince Orlofsky	Gerald Isaac
Dr. Falke	Mark Pedrotti (Jan. 15, 20, 26, 30, Feb. 7); John Fanning (Jan. 18, 23, 28, Feb. 3)
Frosch	Avery Saltzman
Dr. Blind	Phil Stark
Ivan	Arnie Hardt
Sally	Linda Bennett Maguire

Rigoletto   Giuseppe Verdi
January 24, 27, 29, 31, February 2, 4, 6, 8, 1987
Conductor: Richard Buckley
Director: John Leberg
Set: Lawrence Schäfer
Costume Designer: Claude Girard/E. K. Ayotte

Rigoletto	Allan Monk (Jan. 24, 29, Feb. 2, 6); John Rawnsley (Jan. 27, 31, Feb. 4, 8)
The Duke of Mantua	Tonio Di Paolo (Jan. 24, 27, Feb. 4, 8); Kristian Johannsson (Jan. 29, 31, Feb. 2, 6)
Gilda	Maria Spacagna (Jan. 24, 29, Feb. 2, 6); Costanza Cuccaro (Jan. 27, 31, Feb. 4, 8)
Maddalena	Janet Stubbs (Jan. 24, 29, Feb. 2, 6); Odette Beaupré (Jan. 27, 31, Feb. 4, 8)
Count Ceprano	Brian McIntosh
Marullo	Patrick Timney
Monterone	Theodore Baerg (Jan. 24, 29, Feb. 4, 8); John Fanning (Jan. 27, 31, Feb. 2, 6)
Sparafucile	Alfredo Zanazzo (Jan. 24, 29, 31, Feb. 2); Mark Doss (Jan. 27, Feb. 4, 6, 8)
Borsa	Dennis Giesbrecht
Countess Ceprano	Gabrielle Prata
Giovanna	Lilian Kilianski
Page	Susan Tsagkaris
Usher	John Avey

Idomeneo   Wolfgang Amadeus Mozart
March 28, April 2, 5, 8, 10, 14, 1987
Conductor: Leopold Hager
Director: Lotfi Mansouri
Set: Michael Levine
Costume Designer: Michael Levine

Ilia	Ruth Ann Swenson
Idamante	Delores Ziegler
Woman of Crete	Sharon Anne Miller
Woman of Crete	Gabrielle Prata
Trojan Soldier	Benoit Boutet (Mar. 28, Apr. 2, 5, 8, 10); Stephen McClare (Apr. 14)
Trojan Soldier	Brian McIntosh
Elettra	Carol Vaness
Arbace	Peter Kazaras
Idomeneo	Siegfried Jerusalem
High Priest of Neptune	Guillermo Silva-Marin
The Voice	Brian McIntosh

Adriana Lecouvreur   Francesco Cilea
April 3, 6, 9, 12, 15, 18, 1987
Conductor: Richard Bonynge
Director: John Copley
Set: C. M. Christini
Costume Designer: Michael Stennett

Mlle. Jouvenot	Irena Welhasch
Michonnet	Cornelis Opthof
Poisson	Dennis Giesbrecht
Mlle. Dangeville	Odette Beaupré
Quinault	Christopher Coyea
Abbé de Chazeuil	Martin Chambers
Prince de Bouillon	Gary Relyea
Adriana Lecouvreur	Joan Sutherland
Maurizio	Alberto Cupido
Princesse de Bouillon	Lorna Myers
Majordomo	Patrick Timney
Juno	Gloria Luoma
Athena	Amalia Schelhorn
Venus	Vanessa Harwood
Nymph	Denise Mitsche
Nymph	Kathleen Rea
Mercury	Bengt Jörgen
Cavalieri	Lloyd Adams
Cavelieri	Luc Amyôt
Cavelieri	Sean Boutilier
Paris	David Malek

Lucia di Lammermoor   Gaetano Donizetti
June 10, 11, 12, 13, 15, 17, 19, 20, 21, 1987
Conductor: Christian Badea
Director: Anne Ewers
Set: Henry Bardon
Costume Designer: Suzanne Mess

Normanno	Ben Heppner
Enrico	Gaétan Laperrière (June 10, 12, 15, 19, 21); Robert McFarland (June 11, 13, 17, 20)
Raimondo	Jeffrey Wells (June 10, 12, 15, 19, 21); Harry Dworchak (June 11, 13, 17, 20)
Lucia	Ruth Welting (June 10, 12, 15, 19, 21); Nelly Miricioiu (June 11, 13, 17, 20)
Alisa	Kimberly Barber
Edgardo	Richard Leech (June 10, 12, 15, 19, 21); Michael Myers (June 11, 13, 17, 20)
Arturo	Martin Chambers

Kismet   Robert Wright and George Forrest
Royal Alexandra
June 23, 24, 25 (matinée and evening), 26, 27, 28 (matinée and eveining), 1987
Conductor: Don Jones
Director: Theodore Pappas
Set: James Noone
Costume Designer: Michael Stennett

276

Iman	Michael Burgess
Muezzin	Wayne Berwick
Muezzin	Christopher Coyea
Muezzin	Dennis Giesbrecht
Muezzin	Barry Stilwell
First Beggar	Vince Metcalfe
Second Beggar	Ted Pearson
Third Beggar	Peter Barnes
Dervish	David Koch
Dervish	Jay Tramel
Omar	Don McManus
The Poet/Hajj	John Reardon
Marsinah	Beverly Lambert
Businessman	Barry Stilwell
Hassan Ben	Garry Gable
Jawan	Jack Duffy
Bangle Man	Dennis Giesbrecht
Silk Merchant	Wayne Berwick
Silk Merchant	Michael Burgess
Pearl Merchant	Barry Stilwell
Chief of Police	George Merner
Policeman	Greg Cross
The Wazir of Police	Avery Saltzman
Lalume	Judy Kaye
Princess of Ababu	Janie Brennan
Princess of Ababu	Rowena Modesto
Princess of Ababu	Laura Hartman
Slave Girl	Samantha Adamson
Slave Girl	Lorna Magarian
Slave Girl	Carol Schuberg
Slave Girl	Suzanne Van Johns
Slave to Lalume	Dale Azzard
Slave to Lalume	Joel Hawkins
Slave to Lalume	David Koch
Slave to Lalume	Jay Tramel
Lalume's Bodyguard	Alessandro Bandiera
Lalume's Bodyguard	Ernie Emmanuel
Ayah to Lalume	Christina James
Slave Merchant	Ron Rand
Informer	Timothy Cruickshank
Orange Merchant	Vince Metcalfe
Caliph	Michael Maguire
Widow Yussef's Servant	Ted Pearson
Prosecutor	Vince Metcalfe
Widow Yussef	Charlene Shipp
Manservant	Ron Rand
Zubbediya	Suzanne Van Johns
Ayah to Zubbediya	Arlene Meadows
Samaris	Carol Schuberg

1987-1988

La forza del destino   **Giuseppe Verdi**
September 17, 20, 22, 25, 28, 30, October 3, 1987
Conductor: Maurizio Arena
Director: John Copley
Set: Robin Don
Costume Designer: Susan Benson

Marquis	Joel Katz
Leonora	Stefka Evstatieva
Curra	Gabrielle Prata
Don Alvaro	Ernesto Veronelli (Sep. 17, 20, 22, 25); Yuri Marusin (Sep. 28, 30, Oct 3)
Alcalde	John Avey
Don Carlos	Allan Monk
Trabuco	Gary Rideout
Preziosilla	Judith Forst
Fra Melitone	Peter Strummer
Padre Guardiano	John Cheek
Surgeon	Robert Milne
Peddler	Gary Rideout

Tristan und Isolde   **Richard Wagner**
September 23, 26, 29, October 2, 5, 8, 11, 1987
Conductor: Berislav Klobucar
Director: Lotfi Mansouri
Set: Annelies Corrodi
Costume Designer: Annelies Corrodi

Sailor	Gary Rideout
Isolde	Sophia Larson
Brangäne	Katherine Ciesinski
Kurwenal	Victor Braun
Tristan	William Johns
Melot	Christopher Coyea
King Marke	Siegfried Vogel
A Shepherd	Benoit Boutet
A Steersman	Patrick Timney

Patria 1   **R. Murray Schafer**
Texaco Opera Theatre
November 21, 24, 25, 26, 27, 28, 1987
Conductor: Robert Aitken
Director: Christopher Newton
Set: Jerrard and Diana Smith
Costume Designer: Jerrard and Diana Smith

Sappho Silikens, Muhammed be Muslim		Alec Tebbutt
Syball Wong Schöps Fu	Brigitte Robinson	
Eddie Le Chasseur	Richard Waugh	
Afteb B. Noo, Rev. Rabbindranath Le Meul		Ian Prinsloo
Primavera Nicolson	Carole Pope	
Maurice Ayoub, Massimo Quigg		Paul Mulloy
Ovid Klein	George Dawson	
Mercedes Jardine	Patric Masurkevitch	
Glen Frever	Lance McDayter	
D.P.	Peter Millard	
Ariadne, the Party Girl	Martha Collins	
Ron Muck	Paul Larocque	
Voiceover	R. Murray Schafer	
Henry Judah Treece	Ross Driedger	
Sass Boomga	Richard Thorne	
Mimi Mippipopolous	Jo-Anne Kirwan Clark	
Nellie Frencheater	Gabrielle Jones	
Rodney Livermash Bashford, Charlie		Jim Jones
Runny Bumper, Sir Percival Schops		Grant Carmichael

H. Showell Stools, Amadeus Nagy Toth-Toth	Peter Hutt
Hieronymous Knicker, Hvar Mullin	Al Kozlik
Illich P. Vogler	Steven Cumyn
Ariadne, the six-year-old girl	Inga Braunstein
Sigismundo, Thaddeus J. McGuire	Kerry Dorey

The Merry Widow   Franz Lehár
In English
January 15, 16, 22, 25, 28, 30, 31, February 2, 3, 5, 1988
Conductor: Richard Bradshaw
Director: Theodore Pappas
Set: Murray Laufer
Costume Designer: David Collis

St. Brioche	Patrick Timney
Baron Zeta	Phil Stark
Valencienne	Linda Maguire (Jan. 15, 22, 28, 31, Feb. 3); Cristen Gregory (Jan. 16, 25, 30, Feb. 2, 5)
Camille	Mark DuBois (Jan. 15, 22, 28, 31, Feb. 3); Gregory Kunde (Jan. 16, 25, 30, Feb. 2, 5)
Cascada	Barry Stilwell
Kromov	Gordon Masten
Olga	Tania Parrish
Bogdanowitsch	Arnie Hardt
Sylvaine	Kathleen Brett
Njegus	Scott Robertson
Anna Glawari	Leigh Munro (Jan. 15, 22, 25, 31, Feb. 2); Katherine Terrell (Jan. 16, 28, 30, Feb. 3, 5)
Count Danilo	Richard Stilwell (Jan. 15, 22, 25, 31, Feb. 2); William Lewis (Jan. 16, 28, 30, Feb. 3, 5)
Maitre d'Hotel	Robert Godin
Zozo	Janet Stubbs (Jan. 15, 22, 28, 31, Feb. 3); Odette Beaupré (Jan. 16, 25, 30, Feb. 2, 5)
Praskowia	Marilyn Boyle

Lady Macbeth of Mtsensk   Dmitri Shostakovich
January 23, 26, 29, February 1, 4, 7, 1988
Conductor: Richard Buckley
Director: Lotfi Mansouri
Set: Thomas J. Munn
Costume Designer: Thomas J. Munn

Katerina Lvovna Ismailova	Mary Jane Johnson
Boris Timofeyevich Ismailov	Cornelis Opthof
Zinovy Borisovich Ismailov	Ben Heppner
Millhand	Steven Horst
Sergey	Michael Myers (Jan. 23, 26, 29, Feb. 1, 4, 7); William Lewis (Feb. 7)
Aksinya	Mary Anne Barcellona
Coachman	Ronald Rand
Village Drunk	Dennis Giesbrecht
Porter	Robert Milne
Steward	Patrick Timney
Foreman	Stephen Young
Foreman	Stephen McClare
Foreman	Steven Horst
Priest	Christopher Cameron
Chief of Police	Joel Katz
Policeman	John Avey
Teacher	Benoit Boutet
Drunken Guest	Ronald Rand
Sentry	Brian McIntosh
Sonyetka	Gabrielle Prata
Old Convict	Robert Milne
Female Convict	Adrianne Pieczonka

The Turn of the Screw   Benjamin Britten
Texaco Opera Theatre
February 24, 26, 28, March 2, 4, 5, 1988
Conductor: Martin Isepp
Director: Lotfi Mansouri/Tom Diamond
Set: Vladimir Vukovic
Costume Designer: Carol Holland

Prologue	Gary Rideout (Feb. 24, 26, Mar. 2, 5); Dennis Giesbrecht (Feb. 28, Mar. 4)
Governess	Christiane Riel (Feb. 24, 28, Mar. 4); Kathleen Brett (Feb. 26, Mar. 2, 5)
Mrs. Grose	Marcia Swanston (Feb. 24, 28, Mar. 4); Lilian Kilianski (Feb. 26, Mar. 2, 5)
Flora	Valerie Gonzalez
Miles	Thomas Reynolds(Feb. 24, 28, Mar. 4); Jesse Clark (Feb. 26, Mar. 2, 5)
Peter Quint	Benoit Boutet (Feb. 24, 28, Mar. 4); Dennis Giesbrecht (Feb. 26, Mar. 2, 5)
Miss Jessel	Linda Maguire (Feb. 24, 28, Mar. 4); Gabrielle Prata (Feb. 26, Mar. 2, 5)

Don Giovanni   Wolfgang Amadeus Mozart
April 2, 6, 8, 12, 15, 17, 18, 21, 23, 1988
Conductor: Peter Maag
Director: Lotfi Mansouri/Graziella Sciutti
Set: Lawrence Schäfer
Costume Designer: Suzanne Mess

Leporello	Louis Quilico (Apr. 2, 8, 12, 15, 17, 21, 23); Peter Strummer (Apr. 6, 18)
Donna Anna	Carol Vaness (Apr. 2, 8, 12, 15, 17, 21, 23); Marilyn Mims (Apr. 6, 18)
Don Giovanni	Gino Quilico (Apr. 2, 8, 12, 15, 17, 21, 23); Jeffrey Wells (Apr. 6, 18)
The Commendatore	Stephen Dupont (Apr. 2, 6, 18, 21, 23); Jeffrey Wells (Apr. 8, 12, 15, 17)
Don Ottavio	Randall Outland (Apr. 2, 8, 17, 21, 23); Benoit Boutet (Apr. 6, 12, 15, 18)
Donna Elvira	Rachel Yakar (Apr. 2, 8, 12, 15, 17, 21, 23); Joanne Kolomyjec (Apr. 6, 18)
Zerlina	Donna Brown (Apr. 2, 8, 17, 21, 23); Linda Maguire (Apr. 6, 12, 15, 18)
Masetto	Stephen Dupont (Apr. 2, 6, 18, 21, 23); John Avey (Apr. 8, 12, 15, 17)

Ariadne auf Naxos   Richard Strauss
April 9, 11, 14, 16, 19, 22, 24, 1988
Conductor: Christian Badea
Director: Lotfi Mansouri
Set: Wolfram Skalicki
Costume Designer: Amrei Skalicki

The Music Master	Cornelis Opthof
Majordomo	Jan Rubes
Lackey	Joel Katz
Officer	Benoit Boutet
Composer	Judith Forst
Tenor/Bacchus	William Johns
Wigmaker	Patrick Timney
Zerbinetta	Tracy Dahl (Apr. 9, 14, 19, 22); Constance Hauman (Apr. 11, 16, 24)
Prima Donna/Ariadne	Elizabeth Connell
Dancing Master	Peter Blanchet
Arlecchino	Theodore Baerg
Brighella	Dennis Giesbrecht
Truffaldino	Christopher Cameron
Scaramuccio	Guillermo Silva-Marin
Naiad	Mary Anne Barcellona
Dryade	Gabrielle Prata
Echo	Kathleen Brett

Les contes d'Hoffmann Jacques Offenbach
June 15, 17, 18, 19, 21, 23, 24, 25, 1988
Conductor: Jean Fournet
Director: Lotfi Mansouri
Set: Gunther Schneider-Siemssen
Costume Designer: Gunther Schneider-Siemssen

Lindorf/Coppélius/Dappertutto/Dr. Miracle	Allan Monk (June 15, 18, 21, 24); Tom Fox (June 17, 19, 23, 25)
Andrès/Cochenille/Pittichinaccio/Franz	Peter Blanchet
Luther	Robert Milne
Hermann	Patrick Timney
Nathanael	Christopher Coyea
Hoffmann	Jerry Hadley (June 15, 18, 21, 24); Robert Grayson (June 17, 19, 23, 25)
Nicklausse/The Muse	Janet Stubbs (June 15, 18, 21, 24); Kimberly Barber (June 17, 19, 23, 25)
Spalanzani	Benoit Boutet
Guillietta/Stella	Odette Beaupré (June 15, 18, 21, 24); Eirian Davies (June 17, 19, 23, 25)
Antonia	Christiane Riel (June 15, 18, 21, 24); Eirian Davies (June 17, 19, 23, 25)
Olympia	Constance Hauman (June 15, 18, 21, 24); Eirian Davies (June 17, 19, 23, 25)
Schlémil/Crespel	Joel Katz
Antonia's Mother	Gabrielle Prata

1988-1989

Don Carlos   Giuseppe Verdi
October 1, 7, 11, 13, 16, 19, 1988
Conductor: Cal Stewart Kellogg
Director: Lotfi Mansouri
Set: Wolfram Skalicki
Costume Designer: Suzanne Mess

Elizabeth de Valois	Leona Mitchell
Thibault	Kathleen Brett
Don Carlos	Stefano Algieri
Le Comte de Lerme	Gary Rideout
Un Moine	Gary Relyea
Rodriguez	Gaétan Laperrière
La Princesse	Nina Terentieva (Oct. 1, 13, 16); Claire Powell (Oct. 7, 11, 19)
Un Hérault	Steven Horst
Philippe II	Kevin Langan
Voix dans le Ciel	Chrisitiane Riel
Le Grand Inquisiteur	Don Garrard
The Countess of Aremberg	Christiane Riel
Flemish Deputy	John Avey
Flemish Deputy	Christopher Cameron
Flemish Deputy	Robert Milne
Flemish Deputy	John Nieboer
Flemish Deputy	Patrick Timney

The Queen of Spades   Pyotr Ilyich Tchaikovsky
October 8, 12, 14, 17, 20, 23, 1988
Conductor: Richard Bonynge
Director: Hans Nieuwenhuis
Set: Robert O'Hearn
Costume Designer: Robert O'Hearn

Tchekalinsky	Gary Rideout
Sourin	Robert Milne
Herman	Yuri Marusin
Count Tomsky	Allan Monk
Prince Yeletsky	Gary Relyea
The Countess	Maureen Forrester
Lisa	Mari Anne Häggander
Pauline	Claire Powell
Governess	Marcia Swanston
Mascha	Mary Anne Barcellona
Master of Ceremonies	Christopher Coyea
Chloe	Mari Anne Häggander
Daphnis	Claire Powell
Plutus	Allan Monk
Tchaplitsky	Keith Boldt
Narumov	Christopher Cameron
Dancer	Andrej Baczynskyj

Tosca   Giacomo Puccini
January 14, 15, 19, 20, 23, 24, 28, February 1, 3, 1989
Conductor: Richard Bradshaw
Director: Frank Corsaro
Set: Lawrence Schäfer
Costume Designer: Suzanne Mess

Angelotti	Philip Skinner
Sacristan	Peter Strummer (Jan. 14, 19, 20, 24, 28,

Feb. 1, 3); Christopher Cameron (Jan. 15, 23)

Cavaradossi	Vyacheslav Polozov (Jan. 14, 19, Feb. 1, 3); Vladimir Popov (Jan. 15, 24, 28)
Tosca	Stefka Evstatieva (Jan. 14, 19, 24, Feb. 1, 3); Elizabeth Holleque (Jan. 15, 20, 23, 28)
Scarpia	Tom Fox (Jan. 14, 19, 20, 24, 28); Cornelis Opthof (Jan. 15, 23, Feb. 1, 3)
Spoletta	Guillermo Silva-Marin
Sciarrone	John Avey
Jailer	Robert Milne

La Bohème   **Giacomo Puccini**
June 15, 16, 17, 18, 20, 21, 22, 23, 24, 1989
Conductor: Bruno Rigacci
Director: Christopher Mattaliano
Set: Wolfram Skalicki
Costume Designer: Amrei Skalicki

Marcello	Gaétan Laperrière (June 15, 17, 20, 22, 24); Theodore Baerg (June 16, 18, 21, 23)
Rodolfo	Neil Wilson (June 15, 17, 20, 22, 24); John Fowler (June 16, 18, 21, 23)
Colline	Kenneth Cox (June 15, 17, 20, 22, 24); David Pittsinger (June 16, 18, 21, 23)
Schaunard	John Avey (June 15, 17, 20, 22, 24); Patrick Timney (June 16, 18, 21, 23)
Benoit	André Lortie
Mimi	Hei-Kyung Hong (June 15, 17, 20, 22, 24); Ruth Golden (June 16, 18, 21, 23)
Parpignol	Gary Rideout
Musetta	Katherine Terrell (June 15, 17, 20, 22, 24); Linda Maguire (June 16, 18, 21, 23)
Alcindoro	Phil Stark
Sergeant	Steven Horst

The Makropulos Case   **Leos Janácek**
January 21, 25, 27, 30, February 2, 5, 1989
Conductor: Berislav Klobucar
Director: Lotfi Mansouri
Set: Leni Bauer-Ecsy
Costume Designer: Michael Stennett

Vitek	Richard Margison
Albert Gregor	Graham Clark
Kristina	Kathleen Brett
Dr. Kolenaty	Robert Orth
Emilia Marty	Stephanie Sundine
Jaroslav Prus	Cornelis Opthof
Charwoman	Marcia Swanston
Stagehand	Steven Horst
Janek	Benoit Boutet
Count Hauk-Sendorf	Gary Rideout
Chambermaid	Gabrielle Prata

Il ritorno d'Ulisse in patria   **Claudio Monteverdi**
Texaco Opera Theatre

February 25, 27, March 1, 3, 5, 1989
Conductor: William Hicks
Director: Hans Nieuwenhuis/Roman Hurko
Set: Hans Nieuwenhuis
Costume Designer: Carol Holland

Anfinomo	Rebecca Hass
Pisandro	Keith Boldt
Antinoo	Robert Milne
Telemaco	Doug MacNaughton
Iro	Christopher Coyea
Eumete	Steven Horst
Minerva	Mary Anne Barcellona
Ulisse	Patrick Timney
Eurimaco	Gary Rideout
Melanto	Kathleen Brett
Penelope	Gabrielle Prata
Amore	Valerie Gonzalez
La Fortuna	Kathleen Brett
Il Tempo	Robert Milne
L'Umana Fragilita	Rebecca Hass

Andrea Chénier   **Umberto Giordano**
April 5, 8, 13, 16, 18, 21, 1989
Conductor: Julius Rudel
Director: Lotfi Mansouri
Set: Wolfram Skalicki
Costume Designer: Amrei Skalicki

Majordomo	Steven Horst
Carlo Gérard	Allan Monk
Maddalena di Coigny	Aprile Millo
Contessa di Coigny	Lois McDonall
Bersi	Jean Stilwell
Pietro Fléville	Doug MacNaughton
Andrea Chénier	Ermanno Mauro
The Abbé	Gary Rideout
Dancer	Vanessa Harwood
Dancer	Sean Boutilier
Mathieu	Joel Katz
L'Incredibile	Peter Blanchet
Roucher	John Fanning
Madelon	Judith Farris
Dumas	John Avey
Fouquier-Tinville	Christopher Coyea
Schmidt	Robert Milne

Die Zauberflöte   **Wolfgang Amadeus Mozart**
April 7, 10, 11, 14, 15, 19, 20, 22, 23, 1989
Conductor: Reinhard Peters
Director: Lotfi Mansouri
Set: Thierry Bosquet
Costume Designer: Thierry Bosquet

Pamina	Ruth Ann Swenson (Apr. 7, 11, 15, 20, 23); Donna Brown (Apr. 10, 14, 19, 22)
Tamino	Laurence Dale (Apr. 7, 11, 15, 20, 23); Bruce Reed (Apr. 10, 14, 19, 22)

Papageno	Theodore Baerg (Apr. 7, 11, 15, 20, 23); Stephen Dickson (Apr. 10, 14, 19, 22)
Papagena	Kathleen Brett (Apr. 7, 11, 15, 20, 23); Valerie Gonzalez (Apr. 10, 14, 19, 22)
Queen of the Night	Sally Wolf (Apr. 7, 11, 15, 20, 23); Rachel Rosales (Apr. 10, 14, 19, 22)
First Spirit	Bronwen Low (Apr. 7, 11, 15, 20, 23); Jesse Clark (Apr. 10, 14, 19, 22)
Second Spirit	Curtis Eisenberg (Apr. 7, 14, 19, 22); Charles Dekerckhove (Apr. 10, 15, 20, 23); Gilly Kirkland (Apr. 11)
Third Spirit	Gabriel Radford (Apr. 7, 11, 15, 20, 23); Charles Erlichman (Apr. 10, 14, 19, 22)
First Lady	Christiane Riel
Second Lady	Kimberly Barber
Third Lady	Rebecca Russell
Sarastro	Kevin Langan (Apr. 7, 11, 15, 20, 23); Ken Cox (Apr. 10, 14, 19, 22)
The Speaker	Mark Doss
Monostatos	John Duykers
First Armoured-Man	Gary Rideout
Second Armoured-Man	Robert Milne
First Priest	Dennis Giesbrecht
Second Priest	Joel Katz

1989-1990

Un ballo in maschera   Giuseppe Verdi
September 22, 27, October 2, 5, 8, 11, 14, 1989
Conductor: John Fiore
Director: Keith Warner
Set: Wolfram Skalicki
Costume Designer: Suzanne Mess

Count Ribbing	Frank Curtis
Count Horn	Robert Milne
Oscar	Harolyn Blackwell
Gustavus III	Taro Ichihara
Count Anckarström	Lajos Miller
Judge	Keith Boldt
Madame Arvidson	Nuala Willis
Christian	Steven Hosrt
Servant	Craig Ashton
Amelia	Leona Mitchell

Il barbiere di Siviglia   Gioacchino Rossini
September 29, 30, October 3, 4, 7, 10, 12, 13, 15, 1989
Conductor: Bruno Rigacci
Director: Anthony Besch
Set: Alfred Siercke
Costume Designer: John Stoddart

Fiorello	John Avey
Count Almaviva	Raúl Giménez (Sep. 29, Oct. 3, 7, 12, 15); Richard Croft (Sep. 30, Oct. 4, 10, 13)
Figaro	Theodore Baerg (Sep. 29, Oct. 3, 7, 12, 15); Robert Orth (Sep. 30, Oct. 4, 10, 13)
Dr. Bartolo	Peter Strummer (Sep. 29, Oct. 3, 7, 12, 15); Jan Opalach (Sep. 30, Oct. 4, 10, 13)
Rosina	Patricia Schuman (Sep. 29, Oct. 3, 7, 12, 15); Linda Maguire (Sep. 30, Oct. 4, 10, 13)
Don Basilio	Jeffrey Wells (Sep. 29, Oct. 3, 7, 12, 15); James Patterson (Sep. 30, Oct. 4, 10, 13)
Berta	Marcia Swanston
Sergeant	Phil Stark
Notary	John Ash
Ambrogio	Gordon Masten

Carmen   Georges Bizet
January 18, 19, 26, 29, 30, February 3, 4, 7, 9, 10, 1990
Conductor: Graeme Jenkins
Director: Aidan Lang
Set: John Bury
Costume Designer: John Bury

Moralès	Patrick Timney (Jan. 18, 26, 30, Feb. 4, 9); Steven Horst (Jan. 19, 29, Feb. 3, 7, 10)
Micaela	Cynthia Haymon (Jan. 18, 26, 30, Feb. 4, 9); Christiane Riel (Jan. 19, 29, Feb. 3, 7, 10)
Don José	Barry McCauley (Jan. 18, 26, 30, Feb. 4, 9); Jacque Trussel (Jan. 19, 29, Feb. 3, 7, 10)
Zuniga	John Dodington
Carmen	Cynthia Clarey (Jan. 18, 26, 30, Feb. 4, 9); Claire Powell (Jan. 19, 29, Feb. 3, 7, 10)
Frasquita	Kathleen Brett (Jan. 18, 26, 30, Feb. 4, 9); Shari Saunders (Jan. 19, 29, Feb. 3, 7, 10)
Mercédès	Gabrielle Prata (Jan. 18, 26, 30, Feb. 4, 9); Odette Beaupré (Jan. 19, 29, Feb. 3, 7, 10)
Escamillo	Tom Fox (Jan. 18, 26, 30, Feb. 4, 9); Robert McFarland (Jan. 19, 29, Feb. 3, 7, 10)
Remendado	Gary Rideout (Jan. 18, 26, 30, Feb. 4, 9); Keith Boldt (Jan. 19, 29, Feb. 3, 7, 10)
Dancairo	Christopher Coyea (Jan. 18, 26, 30, Feb. 4, 9); Erik Oland (Jan. 19, 29, Feb. 3, 7, 10)
Lillas Pastia	Dennis O'Connor
A Guide	Robert Godin

Wozzeck   Alban Berg
January 27, 31, February 2, 6, 8, 11, 1990
Conductor: David Atherton
Director: Lotfi Mansouri
Set: Michael Levine
Costume Designer: Michael Levine

Wozzeck	Allan Monk
Drum Major	William Pell
Andres	Benoit Boutet
Captain	Stuart Kale
Doctor	Siegfried Vogel
Fool	Peter Blanchet

Marie	Judith Forst
Margret	Gabrielle Prata
First Workman	John Avey
Second Workman	Christopher Coyea
Marie's Child	Ryan Hili; Jennifer Bertram

Otello   **Giuseppe Verdi**
April 7, 11, 16, 19, 22, 24, 27, 1990
Conductor: Maurizio Arena
Director: Lotfi Mansouri
Set: Wolfram Skalicki
Costume Designer: Ray Diffen

Montano	Robert Milne
Cassio	Robert Brubaker
Iago	Allan Monk
Roderigo	Gary Rideout
Otello	Ermanno Mauro
Desdemona	Stefka Evstatieva
Emilia	Odette Beaupré
A Herald	Steven Horst
Lodovico	James Patterson

La rondine   **Giacomo Puccini**
April 14, 17, 18, 20, 23, 26, 28, 29, 1990
Conductor: Graeme Jenkins
Director: Lotfi Mansouri
Set: Ralph Funicello
Costume Designer: Sam Kirkpatrick

Yvette	Kathleen Brett
Bianca	Gabrielle Prata
Suzy	Odette Beaupré
Prunier	James Hoback
Magda	Sheri Greenawald (Apr. 14, 28, 30, 23, 26, 29); Elizabeth Knighton Printy (Apr. 17, 28)
Lisette	Cheryl Parrish
Crébillon	Brian McInstosh
Gobin	Keith Boldt
Périchaud	Doug MacNaughton
Rambaldo	Cornelis Opthof
Ruggero	Vinson Cole (Apr. 14, 28, 30, 23, 26, 29); Robert Brubaker (Apr. 17, 28)
Georgette	Wendy Nielsen
Gabriella	Catherine Janus
Lolette	Joanne Hounsell
Adolfo	Keith Boldt
Rabonier	Steven Horst
A Steward	John Nieboer

Der Rosenkavalier   **Richard Strauss**
June 20, 22, 24, 26, 28, 30, 1990
Conductor: Julius Rudel
Director: Stephen Lawless
Set: Elizabeth Dalton
Costume Designer: Elizabeth Dalton

Octavian	Delores Ziegler
Feldmarschallin	Josephine Barstow
Major Domo	Guillermo Silva-Marin
Baron Ochs	Artur Korn
A Notary	Christopher Coyea
A Milliner	Valerie Gonzales
Animal Trainer	Blaine Hendsbee
Valzacchi	Peter Blanchet
Annina	Jean Stilwell
Noble Orphan	Norine Burgess
Noble Orphan	Sandra Gavinchuk
Noble Orphan	Joanne Hounsell
A Singer	Richard Margison
Leopold	William Grenzberg
Herr Von Faninal	Peter Strummer
Sophie	Cheryl Parrish
Marianne	Christiane Riel
Major Domo	Keith Boldt
Innkeeper	Guillermo Silva-Marin
Police Commissioner	Desmond Byrne
Mahomet	Devi Dahl; Naomi Dawkines
Servant	William Bowen
Servant	Russell Braun
Servant	Brian Gow
Servant	Bruce Schaef
Waiter	Russell Braun
Waiter	André Clouthier
Waiter	John Nieboer
Waiter	Bruce Schaef
A Hairdresser	Kelly McCallum
A Scholar	Paul Oros
A Noble Widow	Barbara Scott
Boots	John Avey

1990-1991

Madama Butterfly   **Giacomo Puccini**
September 20, 21, 28, October 1, 3, 6, 11, 13, 14, 1990
Conductor: Maurizio Arena
Director: Brian Macdonald
Set: Susan Benson
Costume Designer: Susan Benson

Cio-Cio-San	Yoko Watanabe (Sep. 20, 28, Oct. 3, 6, 11, 14); Nikki Li Hartliep (Sep. 21, Oct. 1, 13)
Suzuki	Sandra Graham (Sep. 20, 28, Oct. 3, 11, 14); Gabrielle Prata (Sep. 21, Oct. 1, 6, 13)
Pinkerton	Marcello Giordani (Sep. 20, 28, Oct. 3, 6, 11, 14); Allan Glassman (Sep. 21, Oct. 1, 13)
Sharpless	Cornelis Opthof (Sep. 20, 28, Oct. 3, 11, 14); Mark Pedrotti (Sep. 21, Oct. 1, 6, 13)
Goro	Damon Evans
The Bonze	Robert Milne
Prince Yamadori	Patrick Timney
Commisioner	Phil Stark
Kate Pinkerton	Wendy Nielsen
The Offical Registrar	Gordon MacLeod
Yakuside	Russell Braun

282

Mother	Gaynor Jones
Cousin	Catherine Janus
Aunt	Lilian Kilianski

Eugene Onegin   **Pyotr Ilyich Tchaikovsky**
September 29, October 2, 4, 7, 10, 12, 1990
Conductor: Richard Bradshaw
Director: John Copley
Set: Robin Don
Costume Designer: Michael Stennett

Tatyana	Carol Vaness
Olga	Louise Winter
Madame Larina	Gabrielle Lavigne
Filipyevna	Enid Hartle
Lensky	John Graham-Hall
Eugene Onegin	Sergei Leiferkus
A Captain	Patrick Timney
Triquet	Craig Ashton
Zaretsky	Cornelis Opthof
Guillot	Phil Stark
Prince Gremin	Gwynne Howell

Die Fledermaus   **Johann Strauss, Jr.**
In English
January 19, 23, 26, 29, February 1, 4, 7, 8, 10, 1991
Conductor: Richard Bradshaw
Director: Anthony Besch
Set: Zack Brown
Costume Designer: Zack Brown

Rosalinda	Gwynne Geyer
Eisenstein	John Janssen
Adele	Constance Hauman
Alfred	Tonio Di Paolo
Frank	Spiro Malas
Prince Orlofsky	Delia Wallis
Dr. Falke	Allan Monk
Frosch	Richard McMillan
Dr. Blind	Dennis Petersen
Ivan	John Kriter
Ida	Joanne Hounsell

Guacamayo's Old Song and Dance   **John Oliver**
Imperial Oil Opera Theatre
February 26, 28, March 2, 1991 (Toronto), March 8, 10 (Banff)
Conductor: Richard Bradshaw
Director: François Racine
Set: Laara Cassells
Costume Designer: Laara Cassells

Guacamayo	Gary Rideout
Ixbalanque	Norine Burgess
Hunahpu	Valerie Gonzalez
Ixmucane	Wendy Nielsen
Ixpyacoc	Robert Milne

I Pagliacci   **Ruggiero Leoncavallo**
April 6, 11, 14, 17, 19, 22, 25, 1991
Conductor: Julius Rudel
Director: Ken Cazan
Set: Jean-Pierre Ponnelle
Costume Designer: Jean-Pierre Ponnelle

Tonio	John Rawnsley
Canio	Ermanno Mauro
First Villager	Matthew Thomas
Second Villager	John Kriter
Nedda	Gwynne Geyer
Beppe	Guillermo Silva-Marin
Silvio	Gaétan Laperrière

Suor Angelica   **Giacomo Puccini**
April 6, 11, 14, 17, 19, 22, 25, 1991
Conductor: Julius Rudel
Director: Ken Cazan
Set: Robert Perdziola
Costume Designer: Robert Perdziola

Suor Angelica	Nikki Li Hartliep
The Monitor	Marcia Swanston
First Lay Sister	Wendy Nielsen
Second Lay Sister	Gaynor Jones
Mistress of the Novices	Norine Burgess
Suor Osmina	Catherine Janus
Suor Genovieffa	Irena Welhasch Baerg
A Novice	Valerie Gonzalez
Suor Dolcina	Avalee Beckman
First Alms Sister	Monica Whicher
Second Alms Sister	Tania Parrish
The Abbess	Jean MacPhail
The Princess	Yevgenia Gorohovskaya
A Child	Jennifer Bertram

Lulu   **Alban Berg**
April 13, 15, 18, 21, 24, 26, 1991
Conductor: Lothar Zagrosek
Director: Nicholas Muni
Set: Derek McLane
Costume Designer: Suzanne Mess

Lulu	Rebecca Caine
Countetss Geschwitz	Emily Golden
Wardrobe Technician	Rebecca Hass
The Groom	Rebecca Hass
The Schoolboy	Rebecca Hass
Dr. Goll	John Nieboer
The Painter	Michael Myers
The African	Michael Myers
Dr. Schön	Victor Braun
Jack the Ripper	Victor Braun
Alwa	Barry McCauley
Schigolch	Donald Adams
An Usher	Theodore Baerg
The Prince	Gary Rideout

The House Servant	Gary Rideout
The Marquis	Gary Rideout
The Theatre Director	Brian McIntosh
The Banker	Brian McIntosh
Fifteen-Year-Old Girl	Valerie Gonzalez
The Girl's Mother	Marcia Swanston
The Female Artist	Norine Burgess
The Journalist	Doug MacNaughton
The Valet	Gordon MacLeod
The Acrobat	Theodore Baerg
Police Commissioner	John Kriter
Professor	John Nieboer

Così fan tutte   Wolfgang Amadeus Mozart
Elgin Theatre
June 1, 4, 6, 8, 10, 13, 16, 20, 22, 1991
Conductor: Yakov Kreizberg
Director: Nikolaus Lehnoff
Set: Jorge Jara
Costume Designer: Jorge Jara

Fiordiligi	Joanne Kolomyjec
Dorabella	Louise Winter
Despina	Mimi Lerner
Ferrando	Richard Croft
Guglielmo	Anthony Michaels-Moore
Don Alfonso	Federico Davia

La clemenza di Tito   Wolfgang Amadeus Mozart
Elgin Theatre
June 5, 7, 9, 11, 15, 18, 21, 1991
Conductor: Leopold Hager/Bruno Ferrandis
Director: Stephen Wadsworth
Set: Thomas Lynch
Costume Designer: Dunya Ramicova

Sextus	Susan Quittmeyer
Vitellia	Margaret Marshall
Annius	Jean Stilwell
Titus	Richard Margison
Publius	Robert Milne
Servilia	Donna Brown

Le nozze di Figaro   Wolfgang Amadeus Mozart
Elgin Theatre
June 14, 17, 19, 23, 25, 27, 29, 1991
Conductor: Jane Glover
Director: Stephen Lawless
Set: Toni Businger
Costume Designer: Toni Businger

Figaro	Jan Opalach
Susanna	Harolyn Blackwell
Count Almaviva	Gaétan Laperrière
Countess Almaviva	Rita Cullis
Cherubino	Norine Burgess
Marcellina	Gabrielle Lavigne

Dr. Bartolo	James Patterson
Don Basilio	Jonathan Green
Don Curzio	Peter Blanchet
Antonio	Desmond Byrne
Barbarina	Valerie Gonzalez
First Peasant Girl	Kathy Domoney
Second Peasant Girl	Anne McWatt

Elektra   Richard Strauss
January 25, 28, 31, February 3, 6, 9, 1991
Conductor: Richard Armstrong
Director: Lotfi Mansouri
Set: Wolfram Skalicki
Costume Designer: Amrei Skalicki

Serving Woman	Cristiane Young
Serving Woman	Norine Burgess
Serving Woman	Marcia Swanston
Serving Woman	Wendy Nielsen
Serving Woman	Irena Welhasch Baerg
Overseer	Gaynor Jones
Elektra	Johanna Meier
Chrysothemis	Stephanie Sundine
Klytemnestra	Anny Schlemm
Confidante	Tania Parrish
Trainbearer	Valerie Gonzalez
Young Servant	Craig Ashton
Old Servant	Gordon MacLeod
Orestes	Tom Fox
Tutor of Orestes	Robert Milne
Aegisthus	William Neill

1991-1992

La Traviata   Giuseppe Verdi
September 20, 25, 28, 30, October 3, 5, 8, 10, 13, 1991
Conductor: Richard Bradshaw
Director: Brian Macdonald
Set: John Ferguson
Costume Designer: John Pennoyer

Violetta	Nancy Gustafson
Alfredo	Jorge Lopez-Yanez
Germont	Luis Girón May
Flora	Norine Burgess
Annina	Marcia Swanston
Gaston	Jay Hunter Morris
Baron Douphol	Cornelis Opthof
Marquis	Richard Woods
Dr. Grenvil	Brian McIntosh
Giuseppe	John Kriter
Messenger	John Nieboer
Flora's Servant	Matthew Thomas

Fidelio   Ludwig van Beethoven
September 26, 29, October 1, 4, 7, 9, 12, 1991

284

Conductor: Mario Bernardi
Director: Richard Monette
Set: Laara Cassells
Costume Designer: Laara Cassells

Jaquino	Benoit Boutet
Marzelline	Dawn Kotoski
Rocco	Claude Corbeil
Leonore	Helena Does
Don Pizarro	Allan Monk
First Prisoner	André Clouthier (Sep. 26, 29, Oct. 1, 4, 7, 9); Stephen McClare (Oct. 12)
Second Prisoner	Christopher Cameron
Florestan	Mark Baker
Don Fernando	Phillip Ens

Albert Herring   **Benjamin Britten**
Elgin Theatre
October 26, 28, 30, November 1, 2, 5, 6, 8, 10, 13, 15, 17, 1991
Conductor: David Lloyd-Jones
Director: Martin Duncan
Set: Phillip Silver
Costume Designer: Ann Curtis

Florence Pike	Marcia Swanston
Lady Billows	Heather Thomson
Miss Wordsworth	Nancy Hermiston
Mr. Gedge	John Avey
Mr. Upfold	Guillermo Silva-Marin
Superintendent Budd	James Patterson
Emmie	Valerie Gonzalez
Cis	Donna Bennett
Harry	Patrick Torcat (Oct. 26, 30, Nov. 2, 6, 10, 15); Matthew Elek (Oct. 28, Nov. 1, 5, 8, 13, 17)
Sid	Gerald Finley
Albert Herring	Charles Workman (Oct. 26, 30, Nov. 2, 5, 8, 10, 13, 15, 17); Craig Ashton (Oct. 28, Nov. 1, 6)
Nancy	Gabrielle Prata (Oct. 26, 28, 30, Nov. 1, 2, 5, 8, 10, 13, 15); Helen Yu (Nov. 6)
Mrs. Herring	Patricia Kern

La Bohème   **Giacomo Puccini**
January 16, 21, 24, 26, 29, 31, February 3, 6, 8, 1992
Conductor: Myer Fredman
Director: Dieter Kaegi
Set: Wolfram Skalicki
Costume Designer: Amrei Skalicki

Marcello	Theodore Baerg
Rodolfo	Keith Olsen (Jan. 16, 21, 24, 29); J. Hunter Morris (Jan. 26, 29); Richard Margison (Jan. 31, Feb. 3, 6, 8)
Colline	Robert Milne
Schaunard	Desmond Byrne
Benoit	André Lortie
Mimi	Yoko Watanabe
Parpignol	John Kriter
Musetta	Gianna Rolandi (Jan. 16, 24, 26, 28, 31, Feb. 3, 6, 8); Catherine Janus (Jan. 21)
Alcindoro	André Lortie
Sergeant	John Nieboer

Roméo et Juliette   **Charles Gounod**
January 22, 25, 28, 30, February 1, 4, 7, 9, 1992
Conductor: Jacques Delacôte
Director: Bernard Uzan
Set: Claude Girard
Costume Designer: Claude Girard

Tybalt	Jay Hunter Morris
Pâris	Russell Braun
Capulet	Cornelis Opthof
Juliette	Hei-Kyung Hong
Mercutio	Gaétan Laperrière
Benvolio	Craig Ashton
Roméo	Marcello Giordani
Gertrude	Gabrielle Lavigne
Grégorio	Steven Horst
Frère Laurent	James Patterson
Stéphano	Joanne Hounsell
The Duke of Verona	Robert Milne

Falstaff   **Giuseppe Verdi**
April 9, 11, 14, 16, 18, 22, 24, 26, 1992
Conductor: Richard Bradshaw
Director: Jonathan Eaton
Set: Wolfram Skalicki
Costume Designer: Suzanne Mess

Sir John Falstaff	Timothy Noble
Dr. Cajus	Peter Blanchet
Bardolfo	Guillermo Silva-Marin
Pistola	James Patterson
Alice Ford	Nancy Gustafson
Nannetta	Tracy Dahl
Meg Page	Jean Stilwell
Mistress Quickly	Shiela Nadler
Ford	Gaétan Laperrière
Fenton	Mark DuBois

Mario and the Magician Harry Somers/Rod Anderson
Elgin Theatre
May 19, 20, 21, 23, 26, 28, 1992
Conductor: Richard Bradshaw
Director: Robert Carsen
Set: Michael Levine
Costume Designer: Michael Levine

Stefan	Theodore Baerg
Martha	Marcia Swanston
Franzl	Matthew Elek
Klara	Laura Bertram
Mario	Benoit Boutet

The Hotel Porter	Stephen McClare
The Head Waiter	Gordon MacLeod
The Hotel Manager	Russell Braun
The Hotel Doctor	Matthew Thomas
Silvestra	Monica Whicher
Principe/Old Fisherman	William Bowen
Principessa/Old Fisherwoman	Wendy Nielsen
The English Governess	Adreana Braun
Man in the Bowler Hat/Young Fisherman	Blaine Hendsbee
A Roman Gentleman	John Avey
A Florentine Colonel	Cornelis Opthof
Maso	Sanford Riley
Lisetta	Bronwen Low
Maso and Lisetta's Mother	Gaynor Jones
Maso and Lisetta's Father	John Nieboer
Tonio	Elliot Bryant
Tonio's Father	Craig Ashton
Fuggiero	Patrick Torcat
Fuggiero's Mother	Kathleen Brett
Lady from the Bus	Anne McWatt
Elderly Man from the Bus	Gordon Cowan
Young Wife from the Bus	Avalee Beckman
Young Husband from the Bus	Robert Dirstein
The Pedlar	John Kriter
A Taxi Driver	André Clouthier
Signora Angiolieri	Heather Thomson
Signor Angiolieri	Martin Spencer
The Neopolitan Tourist	Lenard Whiting
The Neopolitan Tourist's Wife	Kathryn Domoney
The Municipio Officer/The Crier	James Patterson
Cavaliere Cipolla	David Rampy

Il barbiere di Siviglia   Gioacchino Rossini
June 18, 19, 20, 22, 23, 24, 26, 27, 28, 1992
Conductor: Richard Buckley/Samuel Wong
Director: Anthony Besch
Set: John Stoddart
Costume Designer: John Stoddart

Fiorello	John Avey
Count Almaviva	Richard Croft (June 18, 20, 23, 26, 28); Michael Schade (June 19, 22, 24, 27)
Figaro	Theodore Baerg (June 18, 20, 23, 26, 28); Russell Braun (June 19, 22, 24, 27)
Dr. Bartolo	François Loup (June 18, 20, 23, 26, 28); Peter Strummer (June 19, 22, 24, 27)
Rosina	Susanne Mentzer (June 18, 20, 23, 26, 28); Ning Liang (June 19, 22, 24, 27)
Don Basilio	Claude Corbeil
Berta	Marcia Swanston
Sergeant	John Kriter
Notary	John Ash
Ambrogio	Gordon Masten

1992-1993

Rigoletto   Giuseppe Verdi
September 19, 22, 25, 27, 30, October 2, 5, 8, 10, 1992
Conductor: Richard Bradshaw

Director: Nicholas Muni
Set: George Tsypin
Costume Designer: Martin Pakledinaz

Rigoletto	Brent Ellis
The Duke of Mantua	Jorge Lopez-Yanez
Gilda	Young Ok Shin
Maddalena	Jean Stilwell
Count Ceprano	Robert Milne
Marullo	Russell Braun
Monterone	Desmond Byrne
Sparafucile	Mark S. Doss
Borsa	Jay Hunter Morris
Countess Ceprano	Pamela MacDonald
Giovanna	Anne McWatt
Page	Jackalyn Pipher

Werther   Jules Massenet
September 26, 29, October 1, 4, 7, 9, 1992
Conductor: Mario Bernardi
Director: Ken Cazan
Set: Neil Peter Jampolis
Costume Designer: Martin Pakledinaz

The Bailiff	James Patterson
Fritz	Isaac Seo
Max	Ian Vickers
Hans	Paul Miklasevics
Karl	Thomas Watkins
Gretel	Allison Scott
Clara	Desiree Jones
Johann	Cornelis Opthof
Schmidt	Christopher Coyea
Sophie	Tracy Dahl
Werther	Neil Wilson
Charlotte	Delores Ziegler
Brühlmann	Matthew Thomas
Kätchen	Jackalyn Pipher
Albert	Luis Girón May

Don Giovanni   Wolfgang Amadeus Mozart
Elgin Theatre
November 4, 6, 10, 12, 14, 17, 19, 21, 25, 27, 29, December 2, 4, 6, 1992
Conductor: Yakov Kreizberg/Richard Bradshaw
Director: Nikolaus Lehnhoff
Set: Jorge Jara
Costume Designer: Jorge Jara

Leporello	Herbert Perry
Donna Anna	Dominique Labelle
Don Giovanni	Richard Cowan
The Commendatore	Robert Milne
Don Ottavio	Charles Workman
Donna Elvira	Joanne Kolomyjec
Zerlina	Alison Hagley
Masetto	Desmond Byrne

286

Così fan tutte   **Wolfgang Amadeus Mozart**
Elgin Theatre
November 11, 13, 15, 18, 20, 22, 24, 26, 28, December 1, 3, 5, 1992
Conductor: Richard Bradshaw/Bruno Ferrandis
Director: Nikolaus Lehnhoff
Set: Jorge Jara
Costume Designer: Jorge Jara

Fiordiligi	Wendy Nielsen
Dorabella	Charlotte Hellekant
Despina	Rebecca Caine (Nov. 11, 13, 15, 18, 20, 22, 24, 28, Dec. 1, 3); Pamela MacDonald (Nov. 26)
Ferrando	Richard Croft
Guglielmo	Russell Braun
Don Alfonso	Rudolf Mazzola

Hänsel und Gretel   **Engelbert Humperdinck**
January 15, 21, 24, 27, 30, February 2, 5, 1993
Conductor: Steuart Bedford
Director: Ross A. Perry
Set: Beni Montresor
Costume Designer: Beni Montresor

Gretel	Abbie Furmansky
Hänsel	Kimberly Barber
Gertrude	Heather Thomson
Peter	Allan Monk
The Sandman	Monica Whicher
The Dew Man	Valerie Gonzalez
The Witch	Steven Cole

Bluebeard's Castle   **Bela Bartok**
January 22, 26, 28, 31, February 3, 6, 1993
Conductor: Richard Bradshaw
Director: Robert Lepage
Set: Michael Levine
Costume Designer: Michael Levine

Duke Bluebeard	Victor Braun
Judith	Jane Gilbert

Erwartung   **Arnold Schoenberg**
January 22, 26, 28, 31, February 3, 6, 1993
Conductor: Richard Bradshaw
Director: Robert Lepage
Set: Michael Levine
Costume Designer: Michael Levine

The Woman	Rebecca Blankenship

Tosca   **Giacomo Puccini**
April 2, 7, 10, 13, 15, 18, 21, 24, 1993
Conductor: Richard Armstrong
Director: Frank Corsaro
Set: Lawrence Schäfer

Costume Designer: Suzanne Mess

Cesare Angelotti	Alexander Savtchenko
A Sacristan	Peter Strummer
Mario Cavaradossi	Fabio Armiliato
Floria Tosca	Barbara Daniels
Baron Scarpia	Timothy Noble
Spoletta	John Kriter
Sciarrone	John Avey
Shepherd Boy	Curtis Eisenberg (Apr. 2, 10, 15, 18); Andrew Moore (Apr. 7, 13, 21, 24)
Jailer	Bruce Schaef

The Bartered Bride   **Bedrich Smetana**
April 8, 14, 17, 20, 23, 25, 1993
Conductor: Hermann Michael
Director: Christine Mielitz
Set: Reinhard Heinrich
Costume Designer: Reinhard Heinrich

Marenka	Gwynne Geyer
Jeník	Jay Hunter Morris
Kecal	Spiro Malas (Apr. 8, 17, 20, 23, 25); Ludék Vele (Apr. 14)
Vasek	Benoit Boutet
Krusina	Allan Monk
Ludmilla	Gaynor Jones
The Indian	Randall Jakobsh
Esmeralda	Valerie Gonzalez
Háta	Marcia Swanston
Micha	Alexander Savtchenko
Ringmaster	John Kriter

1993-1994

Carmen   **Georges Bizet**
September 24, 25, 26, 28, 29, 30, October 1, 2, 3, 6, 7, 8, 9, 1993
Conductor: Richard Bradshaw/David Lloyd-Jones
Director: François Racine
Set: John Bury
Costume Designer: John Bury

Moralès	Russell Braun
Micaela	Rebecca Caine (Sep. 24, 26, 29, Oct. 1, 3, 7, 9); Christiane Riel (Sep. 25, 28, 30, Oct. 2, 6, 8)
Don José	Jacque Trussel (Sep. 24, 26, 29, Oct. 1, 3, 7, 9); Fabio Armiliato (Sep. 25, 28, 30, Oct. 2, 6, 8)
Zuniga	James Patterson
Carmen	Katherine Ciesinski (Sep. 24, 26, 29, Oct. 1, 3, 7, 9); Jean Stilwell (Sep. 25, 28, 30, Oct. 2, 6, 8)
Frasquita	Sally Dibblee
Mercédès	Pamela MacDonald
Escamillo	Richard Cowan (Sep. 24, 26, 29, Oct. 1, 3, 7, 9); Charles Austin (Sep. 25, 28, 30,

Oct. 2, 6, 8)

El Remendado	Guillermo Silva-Marin
El Dancairo	Brian Nickel
Lillas Pastia	Robert Godin

Le nozze di Figaro   **Wolfgang Amadeus Mozart**
Elgin Theatre
November 4, 6, 11, 13, 16, 19, 21, 24, 26, 28, 1993
Conductor: Richard Bradshaw
Director: Robin Phillips
Set: Morris Ertman
Costume Designer: Ann Curtis

Figaro	Gerald Finley
Susanna	Alison Hagley
Count Almaviva	Dwayne Croft
Countess Almaviva	Wendy Nielsen
Cherubino	Charlotte Hellekant
Marcellina	Marcia Swanston
Dr. Bartolo	Peter Strummer
Don Basilio	John Kriter
Don Curzio	John Kriter
Antonio	Cornelis Opthof
Barbarina	Jackalyn Pipher
Bridesmaid	Lilian Kilianski

Die Zauberflöte   **Wolfgang Amadeus Mozart**
Elgin Theatre
November 12, 14, 18, 20, 23, 25, 27, December 1, 3, 5, 1993
Conductor: Bruno Ferrandis
Director: Martha Clarke
Set: Robert Israel
Costume Designer: Robert Israel

Pamina	Rebecca Caine
Tamino	Michael Schade (Nov. 12, 14, 18, 20, 23, 25, 27); Tracey Welborn (Dec. 1, 3, 5)
Papageno	Russell Braun
Papagena	Valerie Gonzalez
Queen of the Night	Felicia Filip
First Spirit	Carlos Pascual-Leone
Second Spirit	Adam Tunnicliffe
Third Spirit	Thomas Watkins
First Lady	Monica Whicher
Second Lady	Norine Burgess
Third Lady	Tania Parrish
Sarastro	Reinhard Hagen
The Speaker	Peter Becker
Monostatos	César Oulloa
First Armoured-Man	Clifton Forbis
Second Armoured-Man	Randall Jakobsh
Priest	John Kriter
Deus ex machina	Gus Solomons Jr.

Nosferatu   **Randolph Peters/Marilyn Gronsdale Powell**
du Maurier Theatre Centre

December 8, 10, 12, 1993
Conductor: Richard Bradshaw
Director: Marilyn Gronsdal Powell
Set: Peter Horne
Costume Designer: Peter Horne

Camilla and Mina	Sally Dibblee
Nosferatu	Barry Busse
The Mayor	Brian Nickel
The Sequin Lady	Helen Yu
The Nurse	Pamela MacDonald
Josef	Allison Scott
Josef's Mother	Gaynor Jones
Josef's Father	Robert Dirstein
The Banker	Kenneth Baker
The Policeman	Randall Jakobsh
Nzbana	Marcia Swanston
Tomas	John Avey

Katya Kabanová   **Leos Janácek**
Elgin Theatre
January 15, 20, 23, 26, 29, February 1, 4, 1994
Conductor: Richard Bradshaw
Director: Robert Carsen
Set: Patrick Kinmonth
Costume Designer: Patrick Kinmonth

Vanya Kudryas	Benoit Boutet
Glasha	Sonya Gosse
Dikoy	Cornelis Opthof
Boris Grigoryevic	Clifton Forbis
Feklusha	Lilian Kilianski
Kabanicha	Felicity Palmer
Tichon Kabanov	Miroslav Kopp
Katya Kabanová	Stephanie Sundine
Varvara	Jane Gilbert
Kuligin	Matthew Thomas
A Woman	Jayne Smiley
A Bystander	Stephen Young

Le Comte Ory   **Gioacchino Rossini**
January 28, 30, February 2, 5, 8, 10, 12, 1994
Conductor: John Fisher
Director: Keith Warner/Pierre Péloquin
Set: John Conklin
Costume Designer: John Conklin

Comte Ory	Paul Austin Kelly (Jan. 28, 30, Feb. 2, 5); Charles Workman (Feb. 8, 10, 12)
Raimbaud	Gaétan Laperrière
Alice	Joanne Hounsell
Ragonde	Marcia Swanston
Tutor	Donato Di Stefano
Isolier	Kimberly Barber
Adèle	Susan Patterson
First Nun	Benjamin Butterfield
Second Nun	Bruce Schaef
Lady-in-Waiting	Anne McWatt

288

Madama Butterfly   **Giacomo Puccini**
April 2, 8, 10, 13, 15, 17, 19, 21, 23, 1994
Conductor: Samuel Wong
Director: Brian Macdonald
Set: Susan Benson
Costume Designer: Susan Benson

Cio-Cio-San	Barbara Daniels (Apr. 2, 8, 10, 13, 17, 19, 23); Christiane Riel (Apr. 15, 21)
Suzuki	Gabrielle Prata
Pinkerton	Arthur Davies
Sharpless	Mark Pedrotti
Goro	John Kriter
The Bonze	James Patterson
Prince Yamadori	Patrick Timney
Commissioner	Brian Nickel
Kate Pinkerton	Tania Parrish
Dolore	Corey Ireland; Théa Pel
Yakuside	Marcus Wilson
Mother	Gaynor Jones
Cousin	Margaret Ann
Aunt	Catherine Duff

La Traviata   **Giuseppe Verdi**
April 9, 12, 14, 16, 20, 22, 24, 1994
Conductor: Jan Latham-Koenig
Director: François Racine
Set: John Ferguson
Costume Designer: John Pennoyer

Violetta	Gwynne Geyer
Alfredo	Stephen Mark Brown
Germont	Sigmund Cowan
Flora	Tania Parrish
Annina	Anita Krause
Gaston	Jay Hunter Morris
Baron Douphol	Patrick Timney
Marquis	Christopher Cameron
Dr. Grenvil	James Patterson
Giuseppe	Stephen Young
Messenger	John Nieboer
Flora's Servant	Bruce Schaef

1994–1995

La Bohème   **Giacomo Puccini**
September 22, 23, 24, 25, 27, 28, 29, 30, October 1, 2, 1994
Conductor: Richard Bradshaw
Director: Michael Albano
Set: Wolfram Skalicki
Costume Designer: Amrei Skalicki

Marcello	Gaétan Laperrière (Sep. 22, 24, 27, 29, Oct. 1); John Hancock (Sep. 23, 25, 28, 30, Oct. 2);
Rodolfo	Vicente Ombuena (Sep. 22, 24, 27, 29, Oct. 1); Miroslav Dvorsky (Sep. 23, 25, 28, 30, Oct. 2)

Colline	Robert Milne
Schaunard	Nathan Berg
Benoit	Cornelis Opthof
Mimi	Helena Kaupova (Sep. 22, 24, 27, 29, Oct. 1); Adrianne Pieczonka (Sep. 23, 25, 28, 30, Oct. 2)
Parpignol	John Kriter
Musetta	Katherine Terrell (Sep. 22, 24, 27, 29, Oct. 1); Sally Dibblee (Sep. 23, 25, 28, 30, Oct. 2)
Alcindoro	Cornelis Opthof
Sergeant	Bruce Schaef

Don Pasquale   **Gaetano Donizetti**
Elgin Theatre
November 4, 6, 8, 10, 12, 15, 17, 19, 23, 25, 27, 1994
Conductor: Bramwell Tovey/Dwight Bennett
Director: David Gately
Set: Tony Fanning
Costume Designer: Helen E. Rodgers

Don Pasquale	François Loup
Dr. Malatesta	Theodore Baerg
Ernesto	Tracey Welborn
Norina	Lisa Saffer
Notary	John Kriter

Il rè pastore   **Wolfgang Amadeus Mozart**
Elgin Theatre
November 5, 9, 11, 13, 16, 18, 22, 24, 26, 1994
Conductor: Daniel Beckwith
Director: Mark Lamos
Set: John Conklin
Costume Designer: John Conklin

Aminta	Brenda Harris
Elisa	Monica Whicher
Agenore	Gordon Gietz
Alessandro	Mark DuBois
Tamiri	Laura Tucker

Bluebeard's Castle   **Bela Bartok**
January 11, 13, 14, 17, 19, 20, 22, 1995
Conductor: Richard Bradshaw
Director: Robert Lepage
Set: Michael Levine
Costume Designer: Michael Levine

Duke Bluebeard	Victor Braun
Judith	Jane Gilbert

Erwartung   **Arnold Schoenberg**
January 11, 13, 14, 17, 19, 20, 22, 1995
Conductor: Richard Bradshaw
Director: Robert Lepage
Set: Michael Levine

Costume Designer: Michael Levine

The Woman	Rebecca Blankenship

Lucia di Lammermoor Gaetano Donizetti
April 8, 11, 15, 20, 22, 26, 28, 30, 1995
Conductor: Richard Buckley
Director: Frank Matthus
Set: Henry Bardon
Costume Designer: Peter J. Hall

Normanno	Clifton Forbis
Lord Enrico Ashton	Sigmund Cowan
Raimondo	Gary Relyea
Lucia	Young-Ok Shin
Alisa	Anita Krause
Edgardo	Michael Rees Davis
Lord Arturo Bucklaw	John Uhlenhopp

Eugene Onegin Pyotr Ilyich Tchaikovsky
April 19, 21, 23, 25, 27, 29, 1995
Conductor: Richard Bradshaw
Director: John Copley
Set: Robin Don
Costume Designer: Michael Stennett

Tatyana	Gwynne Geyer (Apr. 19); Sonya Gosse (Apr. 19, 21); Ljuba Kazarnovskaya (Apr. 23, 25, 27, 29)
Olga	Jane Gilbert
Madame Larina	Marcia Swanston
Filipyevna	Gwenneth Bean
Lensky	Clifton Forbis
Eugene Onegin	Vassily Gerello
A Captain	Igor Emelianov
Triquet	Benjamin Butterfield
Zaretsky	Cornelis Opthof
Guillot	Stephen Young
Prince Gremin	Robert Milne

1995-1996

Ariadne auf Naxos Richard Strauss
September 30, October 3, 6, 12, 15, 18, 1995
Conductor: Richard Bradshaw
Director: Tom Diamond
Set: Wolfram Skalicki
Costume Designer: Amrei Skalicki/Julia Tribe

The Music Master	Cornelis Opthof
Major Domo	David William
Lackey	Bruce Schaef
Officer	Dan Chamandy
Composer	Kristine Jepson
Tenor/Bacchus	David Rampy
Wigmaker	Patrick Timney

Zerbinetta	Tracy Dahl
Prima Donna/Ariadne	Isabelle Vernet
Dancing Master	John Kriter
Arlecchino	Russell Braun
Brighella	Alberto Sanchez
Truffaldino	David Watson
Scaramuccio	Ya Lin Zhang
Naiad	Nathalie Paulin
Dryade	Norine Burgess
Echo	Rayanne Dupuis

Jenufa Leos Janácek
October 7, 11, 13, 17, 19, 22, 1995
Conductor: Richard Bradshaw
Director: Nicholas Muni
Set: Derek McLane
Costume Designer: Martin Paklidinaz

Grandmother Buryja	Marcia Swanston
Laca Klemen	Quade Winter
Steva Buryja	Miroslav Dvorsky
Kostelnicka	Judith Forst
Jenufa	Gwynne Geyer
Karolka	Rayanne Dupuis
Pastuchnya	Anne McWatt
Barena	Sonya Gosse
Jano	Nathalie Paulin
Tetka	Karen Olinyk
Foreman	John Avey
Mayor	Cornelis Opthof
Mayor's Wife	Anita Krause

Red Emma Gary Kulesha/Carol Bolt
COCE du Maurier Theatre Centre
November 28, 29, December 1, 2, 3, 1995
Conductor: Gary Wedow
Director: David William
Set: Teresa Przybylski
Costume Designer: Teresa Przybylski

Emma	Anita Krause (Nov. 28, Dec. 1, 3); Sonya Gosse (Nov. 29, Dec. 2)
Helen	Nathalie Paulin (Nov. 28, Dec. 1, 3); Rayanne Dupuis (Nov. 29, Dec. 2)
Fedya	Dan Chamandy
Sasha	Igor Emelianov
Johann Most	Matthew Lord
Kreiderman	Marcos Pujol
Parks	Bruce Schaef
Henry Clay Frick	Robert Milne

Der fliegende Holländer Richard Wagner
January 26, 28, 31, February 2, 6, 8, 10, 1996
Conductor: Richard Bradshaw
Director: Christopher Alden
Set: Allen Moyer
Costume Designer: Allen Moyer

The Dutchman	Richard Paul Fink
Daland	Gidon Saks
Senta	Eva-Marie Bundschuh
Erik	Patrick Raftery
Mary	Martha Jane Howe
Steersman	Gordon Gietz

Gianni Schicchi **Giacomo Puccini**
January 27, 30, February 1, 3, 7, 9, 11, 1996
Conductor: Richard Buckley
Director: Michael Albano
Set: Claude Girard
Costume Designer: Robert Prévost

Zita	Mimi Lerner
Simone	Cornelis Opthof
Rinuccio	Ya Lin Zhang
Marco	Igor Emelianov
La Ciesca	Anita Krause
Gherardo	John Kriter
Nella	Sonya Gosse
Betto	John Avey
Gherardino	Gregory Tranah (Jan. 27, Feb. 3, 9, 11); Paul Shopiro (Jan. 30, Feb. 1, 7)
Gianni Schicchi	Renato Capecchi
Lauretta	Sally Dibblee
Spinelloccio	Marcos Pujol
Guccio	Kenneth Baker
Pinellino	Bruce Schaef
Amantio di Nicolao	Christopher Cameron

I Pagliacci **Ruggiero Leoncavallo**
January 27, 30, February 1, 3, 7, 9, 11, 1996
Conductor: Richard Buckley
Director: Ken Cazan
Set: Claude Girard
Costume Designer: Mérédith Caron

Tonio	Sigmund Cowan
Canio	Ben Heppner
Nedda	Helena Kaupová
Beppe	Benjamin Butterfield
Silvio	John Hancock

Rigoletto **Giuseppe Verdi**
April 10, 13, 18, 20, 23, 26, 28, 1996
Conductor: Mark Ermler
Director: Frank Matthus
Set: George Tsypin
Costume Designer: Martin Pakledinaz

Rigoletto	Sigmund Cowan
The Duke of Mantua	Miroslav Dvorsky
Gilda	Laurence Janot
Maddalena	Jean Stilwell
Count Ceprano	Robert Milne
Marullo	Doug MacNaughton

Monterone	Igor Emelianov
Sparafucile	Alexander Anisimov
Borsa	Dan Chamandy
Countess Ceprano	Rayanne Dupuis
Giovanna	Sonya Gosse
Page	Nathalie Paulin
Usher	Marcos Pujol

La Cenerentola **Gioacchino Rossini**
April 11, 14, 16, 19, 21, 24, 27, 1996
Conductor: Randall Behr
Director: Albert Takazauckas
Set: Jean-Pierre Ponnelle
Costume Designer: Jean-Pierre Ponnelle

Clorinda	Sally Dibblee
Tisbe	Anita Krause
Cinderella	Anna Caterina Antonacci
Alidoro	Umberto Chiummo
Don Magnifico	Enzo Dara
Don Ramiro	Jorge Lopez-Yanez
Dandini	Brent Ellis

1996-1997

Salome **Richard Strauss**
September 27, October 1, 6, 10, 16, 19, 1996
Conductor: Richard Bradshaw
Director: Atom Egoyan
Set: Derek McLane
Costume Designer: Catherine Zuber

Narraboth	Jon Villars
A Page	Norine Burgess
First Soldier	Igor Emelianov
Second Soldier	Thomas Goerz
A Cappadocian	Bruce Schaef
Salome	Ljuba Kazarnovskaya
A Slave	Allyson McHardy
Jokanaan	Simon Estes
Herod	David Rampy
Herodias	Jane Gilbert
First Jew	Matthew Lord
Second Jew	Stephen McClare
Third Jew	John Kriter
Fourth Jew	Robert Martin Reid
Fifth Jew	Robert Milne
First Nazarene	Brian McIntosh
Second Nazarene	James Westman
Dancer	Carolyn Woods

Elektra **Richard Strauss**
October 2, 5, 8, 11, 17, 20, 1996
Conductor: John Crosby
Director: James Robinson
Set: Derek McLane
Costume Designer: Anita Stewart

First Maid	Gwenneth Bean
Second Maid	Sonya Gosse
Third Maid	Norine Burgess
Fourth Maid	Rayanne Dupuis
Fifth Maid	Sally Dibblee
Overseer	Gaynor Jones
Elektra	Susan Marie Pierson
Chrysothemis	Makvala Kasrashvili
Klytemnestra	Susan Shafer
Confidante	Karen Ydenberg
Trainbearer	Allyson McHardy
Young Servant	Matthew Lord
Old Servant	Robert Milne
Orestes	Claudio Otelli
Tutor	Brian McIntosh
Aegisthus	Quade Winter

La Calisto   Francesco Cavalli
COCE du Maurier Theatre Centre
November 29, 30, December 1, 1996
Conductor: Gary Wedow
Director: Tom Diamond
Set: Lori Hickling
Costume Designer: Lori Hickling

Natura	Allyson McHardy
Eternità	Karen Ydenberg
Giove	Robert Martin Reid
Mercurio	Dan Chamandy
Calisto	Nathalie Paulin
Diana	Karen Ydenberg
Endimione	James Westman
Linfea	Rayanne Dupuis
Satirino	Dan Chamandy
Pane	Robert Martin Reid
Giunone	Allyson McHardy

Béatrice et Bénédict   Hector Berlioz
January 21, 24, 29, February 1, 6, 9, 1997
Conductor: Richard Bradshaw
Director: Robin Phillips
Set: Morris Ertman
Costume Designer: Christina Poddubiuk

The Elder Béatrice	Fiona Reid
The Elder Bénédict	Barrie Ingham
Léonato	William Webster
Héro	Nancy Allen Lundy
Béatrice	Jane Gilbert
A Messenger	Andrew Jackson
Don Pedro	Gidon Saks
Claudio	John Hancock
Bénédict	Gordon Gietz
Somarone	François Loup
Ursule	Anita Krause
First Servant	Glen Gaston
Second Servant	Timothy French
A Scrivener	John Kriter

Soldier	Eric Coates
Soldier	David Hogan
Soldier	Kent Staines

Dialogues des Carmélites   Francis Poulenc
January 25, 28, 30, February 2, 5, 7, 1997
Conductor: Kenneth Montgomery
Director: Diana Leblanc
Set: Wolfram Skalicki
Costume Designer: Amrei Skalicki

Chevalier de la Force	Benoit Boutet
Marquis de la Force	John Fanning
Blanche de la Force	Anne-Sophie Schmidt
Thierry	Kenneth Baker
Mme. De Croissy	Rita Gorr
Sister Constance	Élizabeth Vidal
Mother Marie	Nadine Denize
M. Javelinot	Bruce Schaef
Mme. Lidoine	Lauren Flanigan
Father Confessor	Mark DuBois
Sister Mathilde	Sonya Gosse
Mother Jeanne	Buffy Baggott
First Commissary	Dan Chamandy
Second Commissary	Marcos Pujol
Officer	James Westman
Jailer	Doug MacNaughton

Manon Lescaut   Giacomo Puccini
April 8, 11, 16, 19, 24, 27, 1997
Conductor: Maurizio Arena
Director: Bruce Donnell
Set: Allen Charles Klein
Costume Designer: Suzanne Mess

Manon Lescaut	Elizabeth Byrne
des Grieux	Badry Maisuradze
Lescaut	Gaétan Laperrière
Geronte	Cornelis Opthof
Edmondo	Dan Chamandy
Innkeeper	Christopher Cameron
Sergeant of the Royal Archers	Niculae Raiciu
Dance-Master	John Kriter
Madrigal Singer	Anita Krause
Lamplighter	Stephen McClare
Naval Commander	Bruce Schaef
A Wig-Maker	Marcus Wilson
Sergeant	James Westman

Luisa Miller   Giuseppe Verdi
April 12, 15, 17, 20, 23, 25, 1997
Conductor: Richard Bradshaw
Director: Paula Suozzi
Set: George Tsypin
Costume Designer: Suzanne Mess

Laura	Rayanne Dupuis

Miller	Evgenij Dmitriev
Luisa Miller	Marina Mescheriakova
Rodolfo	Luca Lombardo
Wurm	Gidon Saks
Count Walter	Gregory Reinhart
Federica	Hélène Perraguin
A Peasant	James Westman

1997-1998

Oedipus Rex with Symphony of Psalms   Igor Stravinsky
September 27, October 3, 7, 9, 15, 19, 1997
Conductor: Richard Bradshaw
Director: François Girard
Set: Michael Levine
Costume Designer: Michael Levine

The Speaker	Colm Feore
Oedipus	Michael Schade
Creon	Victor Braun
Tiresias	Vladimír Kubovcik
Jocasta	Judith Forst
A Messenger	James Westman
A Shepherd	Yves Saelens

Turandot   Giacomo Puccini
October 2, 5, 8, 11, 14, 17, 1997
Conductor: Marco Armiliato
Director: James Robinson
Set: Anita Stewart
Costume Designer: Anna Oliver

A Mandarin	John Avey
Liu	Svetelina Vassileva
Calaf	Jon Villars
Timur	Hao Jiang Tian
Prince of Persia	Robert Martin Reid
Ping	Theodore Baerg
Pang	Dan Chamandy
Pong	Yves Saelens
The Emperor of China	Gerard Boyd
Princess Turandot	Galina Kalinina

The Emperor of Atlantis   Viktor Ullmann/Peter Kien
In English
Imperial Oil Opera Theatre
November 23, 25, 27, 29, 30, 1997
Conductor: Richard Bradshaw/Bruno Ferrandis
Director: John Neville
Set: Teresa Przybylski
Costume Designer: Teresa Przybylski

The Loudspeaker	John Avey
Harlequin	Dan Chamandy
Death	Thomas Goerz
The Drummer-Girl	Allyson McHardy

Emperor Overall	James Westman
A Soldier	Robert Martin Reid
A Girl	Karen Ydenberg

Hänsel und Gretel   Engelbert Humperdinck
January 23, 25, 28, February 1, 3, 5, 7, 1998
Conductor: Randall Behr
Director: Frank Corsaro
Set: Maurice Sendak
Costume Designer: Maurice Sendak

Gretel	Clare Gormley
Hänsel	Kristine Jepson
Gertrude	Alexandra Hughes
Peter	John Fanning
The Sandman	Isabel Bayrakdarian
The Dew Man	Karen Ydenberg
The Witch	Gary Rideout

The Cunning Little Vixen   Leos Janácek
January 27, 29, 31, February 4, 6, 8, 1998
Conductor: Richard Bradshaw
Director: Frank Corsaro
Set: Neil Peter Jampolis/Maurice Sendak
Costume Designer: Steven Feldman/Maurice Sendak

Bartos	Richard Paul Fink
A Cricket	Jordana Talsky
A Grasshoper	Tamara Rusque
A Mosquito	Giancarlo Pecchia
A Frog	Nikki Hutchinson
The Vixen as a Baby	Hallie Reynolds
Mrs. Bartos	Marcia Swanston
The Vixen	Rebecca Caine
The Dog/an Owl	Allyson McHardy
Frantík	Alex Cushman
Pepík	Eitan Rosenberg
A Cock/Terynka	Rayanne Dupuis
A Hen	Kathryn Domoney
A Badger	Thomas Goerz
Ant	Sarah Chiddy
Ant	Meredith Winning
Spider	Jennifer Dalton
Spider	Natalie Dyck
Beetle	Rhiannon Jones
Beetle	Laura Winton
The Priest	John Avey
The Schoolmaster	Benjamin Butterfield
Pásek	John Kriter
The Fox	Beth Clayton
A Jay	Ingrid Martin
A Woodpecker	Karen Olinyk
Harasta	John Fanning
Little Fox	Sarah Angus
Little Fox	Rebecca Brenner
Little Fox	Kari Carpenter
Little Fox	Robin Dann
Little Fox	Hallie Reynolds

Little Fox	Mia Shulman
Mrs. Pásek	Gaynor Jones

Fidelio **Ludwig van Beethoven**
April 8, 11, 16, 21, 24, 26, 1998
Conductor: Richard Bradshaw
Director: Richard Monette
Set: Laara Cassells
Costume Designer: Laara Cassells

Jaquino	Benoit Boutet
Marzelline	Elzbieta Szmytka
Rocco	Raymond Aceto
Leonore	Sophia Larson
Don Pizarro	Kevin Short
First Prisoner	John MacMaster
Second Prisoner	Chrisopher Cameron
Florestan	Clifton Forbis
Don Fernando	Jay Baylon

Madama Butterfly **Giacomo Puccini**
April 9, 14, 17, 19, 22, 25, 1998
Conductor: Maurizio Barbacini
Director: Brian Macdonald
Set: Susan Benson
Costume Designer: Susan Benson

Cio-Cio-San	Marina Mescheriakova
Suzuki	Anita Krause
Pinkerton	Badry Maisuradze
Sharpless	Cornelis Opthof (Apr. 9, 17, 22, 25); James Westman (Apr. 14, 19)
Goro	Jonathon Green
The Bonze	Raymond Aceto
Prince Yamadori	Doug MacNaughton
Commisioner	Robert Martin Reid
Kate Pinkerton	Karen Ydenberg
Dolore	Carleigh Beverly (Apr. 9, 17, 22, 25); Laurie Fletcher (Apr. 14, 19)
The Official Registrar	John Kriter
Yakuside	Kenneth Baker
Mother	Gaynor Jones
Cousin	Marian Sjölander
Aunt	Anne McWatt

1998-1999

Norma **Vincenzo Bellini**
September 24, 27, 30, October 3, 6, 9, 1998
Conductor: Stephen Lord
Director: James Robinson
Set: Allen Moyer
Costume Designer: Anna Oliver

Oroveso	Alexander Anisimov
Pollione	Jean-Pierre Furlan
Flavio	Michael Colvin

Norma	Marina Mescheriakova
Adalgisa	Ruxandra Donose
Clotilde	Krisztina Szabó

Tosca **Giacomo Puccini**
September 25, 29, October 1, 4, 7, 10, 1998
Conductor: Richard Bradshaw
Director: David William
Set: Ulisse Santicchi
Costume Designer: Ulisse Santicchi

Cesare Angelotti	Alain Coulombe (Sep. 25, Oct. 1, 4, 10); Bruce Schaef (Sep. 29, Oct. 7)
A Sacristan	Eric Garrett
Mario Cavaradossi	César Hernández
Floria Tosca	Sylvie Valayre
Baron Scarpia	Jean Philippe Lafont (Sep. 25, 29, Oct. 1, 4); Franck Ferrari (Oct. 7, 10)
Spoletta	John Kriter
Sciarrone	Andrew Tees
Shepherd Boy	Andrew Harper; Peter Neelands; Alexander Cushman
Jailer	Bruce Schaef (Sep. 25, Oct. 1, 4, 10); Alain Coulombe (Sep. 29, Oct. 7)

Giasone **Francesco Cavalli**
COCE du Maurier Theatre Centre
December 11, 12, 13, 1998
Conductor: Gary Wedow
Director: Tom Diamond
Set: Dany Lyne
Costume Designer: Dany Lyne

Apollo/Aegeus	Michael Colvin
Cupid/Alinda	Barbara Hannigan
Hercules/Oreste	Andrew Tees
Besso	Alain Coulombe
Giasone	Liesel Fedkenheuer
Medea	Krisztina Szabó
Isifile	Tamara Hummel
Demo/Delfa	John Kriter

Il barbiere di Siviglia **Gioacchino Rossini**
January 21, 24, 27, 29, February 2, 6, 1999
Conductor: Richard Bradshaw
Director: Albert Takazauckas
Set: John Stoddart
Costume Designer: John Stoddart

Fiorello	Andrew Tees
Count Almaviva	Michael Colvin (Jan. 21, 24, Feb. 2, 6); Alain Gabriel (Jan. 27, 29)
Figaro	Russell Braun
Dr. Bartolo	Donato Di Stefano
Rosina	Isabel Bayrakdarian (Jan. 21, 24, Feb. 2); Mika Shigematsu (Jan. 27, 29, Feb. 6)
Don Basilio	Umberto Chiummo

294

Berta	Allyson McHardy
Officer	Bruce Schaef
Ambrogio	John Kriter

Xerxes **George Friederich Handel**
January 26, 28, 30, February 3, 5, 7, 1999
Conductor: Noel Davies
Director: Stephen Wadsworth
Set: Thomas Lynch
Costume Designer: Martin Pakledinaz

Xerxes	Kimberly Barber
Arsamene	David Daniels
Elviro	Doug MacNaughton
Romilda	Kathleen Brett
Atalanta	Susannah Waters
Amastre	Phyllis Pancella
Ariodate	Jan Opalach

Il Trovatore **Giuseppe Verdi**
April 6, 9, 14, 18, 22, 24, 1999
Conductor: Richard Buckley
Director: Nicholas Muni
Set: John Conklin
Costume Designer: John Conklin

Ferrando	Mark Doss
Inez	Liesel Fedkenheuer
Leonora	Eva Urbanová
Count Di Luna	Evgenij Dmitriev
Manrico	Richard Margison
Azucena	Irina Mishura
Ruiz	David Pomeroy

The Golden Ass **Randolph Peters/Robertson Davies**
April 13, 15, 17, 21, 23, 25 1999
Conductor: Richard Bradshaw
Director: Colin Graham
Set: Susan Benson
Costume Designer: Susan Benson

Festus	Theodore Baerg
Scholar	Michael Colvin
Merchant	Thomas Goerz
Philospher	Doug MacNaughton
The Boy	Decker LaDouceur
Lucius	Kevin Anderson
Fotis	Rebecca Caine
Milo	Raymond Aceto
Pamphilea	Judith Forst
Antiope	Judith Forst
Charis	Tamara Hummel
Seedy Bandit	Alain Coloumbe
Leader of the Bandits	Raymond Aceto
Psyche	Raymond Gibson
Psyche's Sister	Barbara Glazar
Psyche's Sister	Laurence Racine

Venus	Kathleen Renaud
Cupid	Daniel Touchette
Persephone	Nicholas Gede-Lange
Jupiter	Reuben Wright
Stage Manager of the Ballet	David Meinke
Bandit/Citizen	Margaret Evans
Bandit/Citizen	Alex Fleuriau Chateau
Bandit/Citizen	Sonya Gosse
Bandit/Citizen	Gaynor Jones
Bandit/Citizen	John Kriter
Bandit/Citizen	Stephen McClare
Bandit/Citizen	David Pomeroy
Bandit/Citizen	Krisztina Szabó

1999-2000

La Traviata **Giuseppe Verdi**
September 23, 26, 29, October 2, 5, 8, 1999
Conductor: Richard Bradshaw
Director: Dmitry Bertman
Set: Igor Nezhny
Costume Designer: Tatiana Tulubieva

Violetta	Zvetelina Vassileva
Alfredo	Vladimir Grishko
Flora	Krisztina Szabó
Germont	Gaétan Laperrière
Marquis	Andrew Tees
Baron Douphol	Cornelis Opthof
Gastone	Michael Colvin
Annina	Liesel Fedkenhuer
Dr. Grenvil	Alain Coulombe
Giuseppe	John Kriter
Flora's Servant	Alex Fleuriau Chateau
A Messenger	Bruce Schaef

L'elisir d'amore **Gaetano Donizetti**
September 24, 28, 30, October 3, 6, 9, 1999
Conductor: Maurizio Barbacini/Richard Bradshaw
Director: Paolo Montarsolo
Set: Naoji Kawaguchi
Costume Designer: Malabar Ltd.

Giannetta	Tamara Hummel
Nemorino	Michael Schade
Adina	Henriette Bonde-Hansen
Dr. Dulcamara	John Del Carlo
Belcore	Louis Otey

The Rape of Lucretia **Benjamin Britten**
du Maurier Theatre Centre
November 23, 25, 26, 28, 1999
Conductor: Richard Bradshaw, Judith Yan
Director: Diana Leblanc
Set: Astrid Janson
Costume Designer: Astrid Janson

Male Chorus	Michael Colvin
Female Chorus	Cheryl Hickman
Collatinus	Alain Coulombe
Junius	Gregory J. Dahl
Tarquinius	Andrew Tees
Lucretia	Liesel Fedkenheuer (Nov. 23, 26); Krisztina Szabó (Nov. 25, 28)
Bianca	Krisztina Szabó (Nov. 23, 26); Liesel Fedkenheuer (Nov. 25, 28)
Lucia	Tamara Hummel

Der fliegende Holländer   Richard Wagner
January 20, 23, 26, 29, February 1, 4, 2000
Conductor: Richard Bradshaw
Director: Christopher Alden
Set: Allen Moyer
Costume Designer: Allen Moyer

The Dutchman	Gidon Saks (Jan. 20, 23, 26, 29); Richard Paul Fink (Feb. 1, 4)
Daland	Raymond Aceto
Senta	Frances Ginzer (Jan. 20, 26, 29, Feb. 4); Susan Marie Pierson (Jan. 23, Feb.1)
Mary	Susan Schafer
Steersman	Gordon Gietz
Erik	David Rendall

Don Giovanni   Wolfgang Amadeus Mozart
January 21, 25, 27, 30, February 2, 5, 2000
Conductor: Nicholas Cleobury
Director: James Conway
Set: Jorge Jara
Costume Designer: Jorge Jara

Leporello	Gilles Cachemaille
Donna Anna	Monica Colonna
Don Giovanni	Davide Damiani
The Commendatore	Theodore Coresi
Don Ottavio	Michael Colvin
Donna Elvira	Alwyn Mellor
Zerlina	Isabel Bayrakdarian (Jan. 21, 25, 27, 30); Krisztina Szabó (Feb. 2, 5)
Masetto	Alain Coulombe

La Bohème   Giacomo Puccini
April 6, 8, 11, 14, 16, 19, 22, 2000
Conductor: Richard Bradshaw/Bruno Ferrandis
Director: Albert Takazauckas
Set: Wolfram Skalicki
Costume Designer: Amrei Skalicki

Marcello	Evgenij Dmitriev
Rodolfo	Joseph Calleja
Colline	Alain Coulombe
Schaunard	Alfredo Daza
Benoit	Cornelis Opthof
Mimi	Eszter Sümegi

Parpignol	John Kriter
Musetta	Rosalind Sutherland
Alcindoro	Cornelis Opthof
Sergeant	Bruce Schaef

Pelléas et Mélisande   Claude Debussy
April 7, 9, 12, 15, 18, 20, 2000
Conductor: Richard Bradshaw
Director: Nicholas Muni
Set: Dany Lyne
Costume Designer: Dany Lyne

Goland	Monte Pederson
Mélisande	Elzbieta Szmytka
Geneviève	Susan Shafer
Arkel	Dimitri Kavrakos
Pelléas	Jean-François Lapointe
Yniold	Elizabeth Skillings
The Doctor	Alain Coulombe

Appendix III

296

COC Tours

1958

Il barbiere di Siviglia   Gioacchino Rossini
In English
November 12–December 9, 1958 (19 performances)
Ontario, Eastern Canada
Conductor: George Brough
Director: Herman Geiger-Torel
Set Designer: Brian Jackson
Costume Designer: Suzanne Mess

Fiorello	Andrew MacMillan; Ernest Adams
Villager	Victor Braun
Villager	Alan Crofoot
Count Almaviva	John Arab; Kelvin Service
Figaro	Alexander Gray; Murray Kenig
Dr. Bartolo	Ernest Adams; Andrew MacMillan
Rosina	Patricia Snell; Sheila Piercey
Don Basilio	Jan Rubes
Berta	Patricia Rideout
Sergeant	Alan Crofoot; John Arab
Policeman	Ernest Adams; Alan Crofoot
Notary	Ernest Adams

1959

Il barbiere di Siviglia   Gioacchino Rossini
In English
November 2–December 5, 1959 (22 performances)
Conductor: George Brough
Director: Herman Geiger-Torel
Set Designer: Brian Jackson
Costume Designer: Suzanne Mess

Fiorello	Andrew MacMillan; Ernest Adams
Two Villagers	Victor Braun; Alan Crofoot
Count Almaviva	John Arab; Kelvin Service
Figaro	Alexander Gray; Murray Kenig
Rosina	Patricia Snell; Sheila Piercey
Policeman	Ernest Adams; Alan Crofoot
Don Basilio	Jan Rubes
Berta	Patricia Rideout
Sergeant	Alan Crofoot; John Arab
Dr. Bartolo	Ernest Adams; Andrew MacMillan
Notary	Ernest Adams

1960

Die lustigen Weiber von Windsor   Otto Nicolai
In English
January 31–March 14, 1960 (23 performances)
Ontario, Eastern Canada
Conductor: Mario Bernardi
Director: Herman Geiger-Torel
Set Designer: William Lord
Costume Designer: Suzanne Mess

Alice Ford	Patricia Snell; Barbara Strathdee
Meg Page	Elsie Sawchuk; Darlene Hirst
Mr. Page	Victor Braun; Donald Young
Mr. Slender	Robert Briggs; Danny Tait
Mr. Ford	Alexander Gray; Ernest Adams
Fenton	John Arab; Roger Doucet
Dr. Cajus	Cornelis Opthof; James Whicher
Falstaff	Andrew MacMillan; Jan Rubes
Ann Page	Sheila Piercey; Marnie Patrick

Die lustigen Weiber von Windsor   Otto Nicolai
In English
November 1–December 22, 1960 (40 Performances)
Conductor: Mario Bernardi
Director: Herman Geiger-Torel
Set Designer: William Lord
Costume Designer: Suzanne Mess

Alice Ford	Barbara Strathdee; Dodi Protero
Meg Page	Darlene Hirst; Elsie Sawchuk
Mr. Page	Victor Braun; Donald Young
Mr. Slender	Phil Stark; Danny Tait
Mr. Ford	Alexander Gray; Ernest Adams
Fenton	Robert Briggs; John Arab
Dr. Cajus	Cornelis Opthof
Falstaff	Andrew MacMillan; Jan Rubes
Ann Page	Sheila Piercey

1961

Orphée aux enfers   Jacques Offenbach
In English
January 23–March 14, 1961 (30 performances)
Eastern Canada
Conductor: George Brough/Leo Mueller
Director: Herman Geiger-Torel
Set Designer: William Lord/Brian Jackson
Costume Designer: Suzanne Mess

Public Opinion	Joanne Ivey
Eurydice	Dodi Protero; Barbara Strathdee
Orpheus	Danny Tait; Phil Stark
Pluto	Jan Rubes; Victor Braun
Chloe	Joyce Hill
Cupid	Daphne Drake
Venus	Sheila Piercey
Jupiter	Andrew MacMillan; Ernest Adams
Juno	Elsie Sawchuk
Diana	Arlene Meadows
Mercury	Cornelis Opthof
Hebe	Franki Pannell
Minerva	Kathryn Newman
Mars	Donald Young
Morpheus	Robert Briggs
Bacchus	Alan Crofoot

Orphée aux enfers **Jacques Offenbach**
In English
October 23–December 20, 1961 (44 performances)
Western Canada
Conductor: George Brough
Director: Herman Geiger-Torel/Mavor Moore
Set Designer: William Lord/Brian Jackson
Costume Designer: Suzanne Mess

Public Opinion	Joanne Ivey
Eurydice	Dodi Prtoero; Barbara Strathdee
Orpheus	Phil Stark; Danny Tait
Pluto	Victor Braun; Jan Rubes
Chloe	Joyce Hill
Cupid	Kathryn Newman
Venus	Sheila Piercey
Jupiter	Ernest Adams; Peter Mews
Juno	Elsie Sawchuk
Diana	Arlene Meadows
Mercury	Robert Briggs
Hebe	Dianne Gibson
Morpheus	Tito Dean
Bacchus	Alan Crofoot

1962

La Bohème **Giacomo Puccini**
In English
February 2–April 14, 1962 (41 performances)
Ontario, Eastern Canada, United States
Conductor: James Craig/Leo Mueller
Director: Herman Geiger-Torel
Set Designer: Joanne Ivey
Costume Designer: Suzanne Mess

Vendors/Officers	Kathryn Newman; Eraine Schwing; Joseph Macko; Wallace Williamson
Marcello	Victor Braun; Alexander Gray
Rodolfo	John Arab; Robert Briggs; Thomas Clerke
Colline	Peter van Ginkel; Jan Rubes; Andrew

	MacMillan
Schaunard	Ernest Adams; Cornelis Opthof
Benoit	Tito Dean
Mimi	Gwenlynn Little; Barbara Strathdee; Sheila Piercey
Musetta	Constance Fisher; Sheila Piercey; Franki Pannell
Alcindoro	Phil Stark

La Bohème **Giacomo Puccini**
In English
October 29–December 21, 1962 (40 performances)
Conductor: James Craig
Director: Herman Geiger-Torel
Set Designer: Joanne Ivey
Costume Designer: Suzanne Mess

Vendors/Officers	Kathryn Newman; Eraine Schwing; Joseph Macko; Wallace Williamson
Marcello	Victor Braun; Alexander Gray
Rodolfo	John Arab; Robert Briggs; Thomas Clerke
Colline	Peter van Ginkel; Jan Rubes; Andrew MacMillan
Schaunard	Ernest Adams; Cornelis Opthof
Benoit	Tito Dean
Mimi	Gwenlynn Little; Barbara Strathdee; Sheila Piercey
Musetta	Constance Fisher; Sheila Piercey; Franki Pannell
Alcindoro	Phil Stark

1963

Così fan tutte **Wolfgang Amadeus Mozart**
In English
January 28–April 6, 1963
Ontario, Eastern Canada
Conductor: George Brough
Director: Herman Geiger-Torel
Set Designer: Les Lawrence
Costume Designer: Suzanne Mess

Ferrando	Phil Stark; John Arab
Guglielmo	Alexander Gray; Cornelis Opthof
Don Alfonso	Peter van Ginkel; Jan Rubes
Fiordiligi	Arlene Meadows; Constance Fisher
Dorabella	Elsie Sawchuk; Cecilia Ward
Despina	Kathryn Newman; Dodi Protero
Servants	Ron Hastings; Joseph Rutten

Così fan tutte **Wolfgang Amadeus Mozart**
In English
October 14–December 20, 1963
Western Canada
Conductor: George Brough

Director: Herman Geiger-Torel
Set Designer: Les Lawrence
Costume Designer: Suzanne Mess

Ferrando	Phil Stark; John Arab
Guglielmo	Alexander Gray; Cornelis Opthof
Don Alfonso	Peter van Ginkel; Jan Rubes
Fiordiligi	Arlene Meadows; Heather Thomson; Constance Fisher
Dorabella	Elsie Sawchuk; Cecilia Ward
Despina	Kathryn Newman; Dodi Protero
Servants	Ron Hastings; Joseph Rutten

1964

Die Fledermaus **Johann Strauss, Jr.**
In English
January 24–April 19, 1964
Eastern Canada
Conductor: James Craig/Leo Mueller
Director: Herman Geiger-Torel
Set Designer: William Lord
Costume Designer: Eve Mautner/William Lord

Alfred	Alan Crofoot; John Arab
Adele	Dodi Protero; Sheila Piercey
Rosalinda	Arlene Meadows; Heather Thomson; Constance Fisher
Eisenstein	Cornelis Opthof; Thomas Clerke
Dr. Blind	Joseph Macko; Tito Dean
Dr. Falke	Alexander Gray; Peter van Ginkel
Frank	William Copeland; Robert Briggs
Prince Orlofsky	Phil Stark; Jan Rubes
Ivan	Joseph Macko
Frosch	Joseph Rutten; Ron Hastings
Orlofsky's Guests	Maria Pellegrini; Roberta Ging; Tito Dean; Wallace Williamson

1965

Die Fledermaus **Johann Strauss, Jr.**
In English
January 11–April 3, 1965 (54 performances)
Conductor: James Craig
Director: Herman Geiger-Torel
Set Designer: William Lord
Costume Designer: Eve Mautner/William Lord

Alfred	John Arab; Phil Stark
Adele	Dodi Protero; Sheila Piercey; Kathryn Newman
Rosalinda	Arlene Meadows; Constance Fisher
Eisenstein	Raymond Chiarella; Wallace Williamson
Dr. Blind	Tito Dean
Dr. Falke	Alexander Gray; Peter van Ginkel
Frank	William Copeland

Prince Orlofsky	Phil Stark; Jan Rubes
Ivan	Ronald Nipper
Frosch	Ron Hastings
Orlofsky's Guests	Anne Harrington; Elsie Sawchuk; Tito Dean; John Clancy

1966

Carmen **Georges Bizet**
In English and French
January 17–April 30 1966 (76 performances)
Eastern Canada
Conductor: George Brough
Director: Herman Geiger-Torel
Set Designer: William Lord
Costume Designer: Warren Hartman

Micaela	Sheila Piercey; Jeannette Zarou
Don José	Guy Lavoie; Jean Louis Pellerin;
Zuniga	Oskar Raulfs
Carmen	Marija Kova; June Genovese; Geneviève Perrault
Frasquita	Constance Fisher; Kathryn Newman
Mercédès	Geneviève Perrault; Elsie Sawchuk
Escamillo	Roland Richard; Donald Young
Remendado	Thomas Park; Wallace Williamson

1967

Don Pasquale **Gaetano Donizetti**
In English
January 15–May 13, 1967 (82 performances)
Western Canada
Conductor: James Craig
Director: Herman Geiger-Torel
Set Designer: William Lord
Costume Designer: Warren Hartman

Servants	Ronald Nipper; Warren Hartman
A Notary	Phil Stark
Norina	Sheila Piercey; Eleanor Calbes
Ernesto	Ernest Atkinson; Leonard Bilodeau
Dr. Malatesta	Alexander Gray; Richard Braun
Don Pasquale	Jan Rubes; Eugene Green

1968

Don Pasquale **Gaetano Donizetti**
In English
January 14–March 2, 1968 (33 performances)
Eastern Canada
Conductor: John Fenwick
Director: Herman Geiger-Torel
Set Designer: William Lord

Costume Designer: Warren Hartman

Servants	Elsie Sawchuk; Donald Young
A Notary	Phil Stark
Norina	Sheila Piercey; Eleanor Calbes
Ernesto	John Arab; Ernest Atkinson
Dr. Malatesta	Alexander Gray; Cornelis Opthof
Don Pasquale	Maurice Brown; Jan Rubes

Il barbiere di Siviglia   Gioacchino Rossini
In English
October 21–December 20 (43 performances)
Western Canada
Conductor: John Fenwick
Director: Herman Geiger-Torel
Set Designer: William Lord
Costume Designer: Warren Hartman

Fiorello	Richard Braun
Villager	Giuseppe Macina
Count Almaviva	John Arab; Jerold Siena
Figaro	Alexander Gray; Cornelis Opthof
Dr. Bartolo	Oskar Raulfs; Eugene Green
Rosina	Sheila Piercey; Dodi Protero
Don Basilio	Jan Rubes; Maurice Brown
Berta	Kathryn Newman; Elsie Sawchuk
Sergeant	Phil Stark
Policeman	Giuseppe Macina; Richard Braun
Notary	Giuseppe Macina

1969–1970

Il barbiere di Siviglia   Gioacchino Rossini
In English
October 27–December 12, 1969 and January 5–February 21, 1970
(81 performances)
Eastern Canada
Conductor: John Fenwick/Raffi Armenian
Director: Herman Geiger-Torel
Set Designer: William Lord
Costume Designer: Warren Hartman

Count Almaviva	John Arab; Bernard Fitch
Figaro	Cornelis Opthof; William Covington; Donald Rutherford
Dr. Bartolo	Stephen Henrikson; Peter Milne
Rosina	Sheila Piercey; Dodi Protero
Don Basilio	Jan Rubes; Richard Mundt
Berta	Kathryn Newman; Elsie Sawchuk
Sergeant	Phil Stark
Policeman	Ralph Oostwoud
Notary	Ralph Oostwoud

1970–1971

Orphée aux enfers   Jacques Offenbach
In English
November 2–December 19, 1970 and January 4–April 5, 1971 (117 performances)
Western Canada
Conductor: John Fenwick/Errol Gay
Director: Herman Geiger-Torel
Set Designer: Elsie Sawchuk
Costume Designer: Elsie Sawchuk

Public Opinion	Elizabeth Mawson
Eurydice	Sheila Piercey; Dodi Protero
Orpheus	Phil Stark
Pluto	Cornelis Opthof
Cupid	Lynda Boothby
Venus	Loro Farell
Jupiter	Peter Milne; Don McManus
Juno	Elsie Sawchuk
Diana	Anne Linden
Mercury	Richard Braun
Hebe	Susan Gay
Bacchus	Alan Crofoot
Mars	Gerard Boyd

1971–1972

Orphée aux enfers   Jacques Offenbach
In English
November 10–December 12, 1971 and January 3–March 23, 1972
(90 performances)
Eastern Canada
Conductor: John Fenwick/Errol Gray
Director: Herman Geiger-Torel
Set Designer: Elsie Sawchuk
Costume Designer: Elsie Sawchuk

Eurydice	June Cooper; Dodi Protero
Orpheus	Phil Stark
Pluto	Jan Rubes
Cupid	Lynda Boothby
Venus	Susan Gay
Jupiter	Avo Kittask; Peter Milne
Juno	Elsie Sawchuk
Diana	Annemarie Clark
Mercury	Herman Rombouts
Hebe	Kathleen Ruddell
Bacchus	John Arab; Alan Crofoot; David Meek
Mars	David Meek

1972–1973

Così fan tutte   Wolfgang Amadeus Mozart
November 5–December 16, 1972 and January 8–March 24, 1973 (91 performances)

Western Canada
Conductor: John Fenwick/Errol Gay
Director: Herman Geiger-Torel
Set Designer: Georg Schlögl
Costume Designer: Andrea Grainger

Ferrando	John Arab; Garnet Brooks
Guglielmo	Donald Oddie; Peter Barcza
Don Alfonso	Jan Rubes; Peter Milne
Fiordiligi	Helly Jedig; Barbara Collier
Dorabella	Nancy Greenwood; Kathleen Ruddell
Despina	Dodi Protero; Ann Cooper; Sandra Darling; Carol Wilcox; Gwenlynn Little
Servants	Phil Stark; Steven Thomas

1973–1974

Così fan tutte   **Wolfgang Amadeus Mozart**
November 4–December 15, 1973 and January 7–March 21, 1974 (91 performances)
Eastern Canada
Conductor: John Fenwick/Errol Gay
Director: Herman Geiger-Torel
Set Designer: Georg Schlögl
Costume Designer: Andrea Grainger

Ferrando	John Arab; Garnet Brooks
Guglielmo	Peter Barcza; Ronald Bermingham
Don Alfonso	Jan Rubes; Peter Milne
Fiordiligi	Barbara Collier; Jeannette Dagger
Dorabella	Kathleen Ruddell; Carrol Anne Curry
Despina	Ann Cooper; Gwenlynn Little
Servants	Phil Stark; Briane Nasimok

1974–1975

La Bohème   **Giacomo Puccini**
In English
October 28–December 1, 1974 (29 performances)
Western Canada
Conductor: Errol Gay/Melvin Margolis
Director: Jan Rubes
Set Designer: William Lord
Costume Designer: Andrea Grainger

Marcello	Peter Barcza; Avo Kittask
Rodolfo	John Arab; Glyn Evans
Colline	Ronald Bermingham
Schaunard	James Anderson
Mimi	Barbara Collier; Ann Cooper
Musetta	Carrol Anne Curry; Deborah Jeans
Alcindoro	Phil Stark
Parpignol	Henry Barney Ingram
Headwaiter	Briane Nasimok

1975–1976

La Bohème   **Giacomo Puccini**
In English
November 6–30, 1975 (18 performances)
Eastern Canada
Conductor: Errol Gay/William Shookhoff
Director: Jan Rubes
Set Designer: William Lord
Costume Designer: Andrea Grainger

Marcello	Guillermo Siva-Marin; Peter Barcza
Rodolfo	John Arab; Glyn Evans
Colline	Giulio Kukurugya
Schaunard	James Anderson
Benoit	Peter Milne
Mimi	Barbara Collier; Ann Cooper
Musetta	Lynn Blaser; Deborah Jeans
Alcindoro	Bruce Kelly
Parpignol	Henry Barney Ingram

La Bohème   **Giacomo Puccini**
In English
January 7–March 7, 1976 (50 performances)
United States
Conductor: Errol Gay/William Shookhoff
Director: Jan Rubes
Set Designer: William Lord
Costume Designer: Andrea Grainger

Marcello	Guillermo Silva-Marin; Peter Barcza; Avo Kittask
Rodolfo	John Arab; Glyn Evans
Colline	Giulio Kukurugya; Ronald Bermingham
Schaunard	James Anderson
Benoit	Peter Milne
Mimi	Barbara Collier; Ann Cooper; Lynn Blaser; Deborah Jeans
Musetta	Carrol Anne Curry; Deborah Jeans; Lynn Blaser
Alcindoro	Phil Stark; Henry Barney Ingram
Parpignol	Henry Barney Ingram; Michele Strano
Headwaiter	Michele Strano

La Bohème   **Giacomo Puccini**
In English
March 26–April 24, 1976 (16 performances)
Ontario
Conductor: Errol Gay/William Shookhoff
Director: Jan Rubes
Set Designer: William Lord
Costume Designer: Andrea Grainger

Marcello	Peter Barcza; Avo Kittask
Rodolfo	John Arab; Glyn Evans
Colline	Ronald Bermingham
Schaunard	James Anderson
Benoit	Peter Milne

Mimi	Barbara Collier; Ann Cooper; Lynn Blaser; Deborah Jeans
Musetta	Deborah Jeans; Lynn Blaser
Alcindoro	Phil Stark; Bruce Kelly
Monsieur Parpignol	Michele Strano
Headwaiter	Michele Strano

La Traviata **Giuseppe Verdi**
March 26–April 24, 1976 (8 performances)
Conductor: Errol Gay/William Shookhoff
Director: John Leberg
Set Designer: Murray Laufer
Costume Designer: Andrea Grainger

Violetta	Ann Cooper; Heather Thomson
Flora	Deborah Jeans
Doctor Grenvil	Peter Milne
d'Obigny	James Anderson
Douphol	Ronald Bermingham
Gastone	John Arab; Michele Strano
Alfredo	Glyn Evans; Perry Price
Annina	Diane Loeb
Germont	Peter Barcza
Waiter/Friend of Flora	Phil Stark
Friend of Violetta	Lynn Blaser

1976–1977

La Traviata **Giuseppe Verdi**
November 1–December 5, 1976 (29 performances)
Western Canada
Conductor: Raffi Armenian/Timothy Vernon
Director: John Leberg
Set Designer: Murray Laufer
Costume Designer: Andrea Grainger

Violetta	Lorna Castaneda; Barbara Carter
Flora	Susan Gudgeon
Doctor Grenvil	James Anderson; Monte Jaffe
d'Obigny	Peter Milne
Douphol	Henri Louiselle
Gastone	Michele Strano
Alfredo	Glyn Evans; Paul Frey
Annina	Nancy Hermiston
Germont	Peter Barcza; Jonas Vaskevicius; Avo Kittask; Lawrence Cooper
Waiter/Friend of Flora	Phil Stark; John Nieboer
Friend of Violetta	Darlene Hirst

La Traviata **Giuseppe Verdi**
United States
Conductor: Timothy Vernon/Dwight Bennett
Director: John Leberg
Set Designer: Murray Laufer
Costume Designer: Andrea Grainger

Violetta	Lorna Castaneda; Barbara Carter
Flora	Darlene Hirst
Doctor Grenvil	Monte Jaffe
d'Obigny	Peter Milne
Douphol	John Nieboer
Gastone	Michele Strano
Alfredo	Glyn Evans; Paul Frey
Annina	Nancy Hermiston
Germont	Guillermo Silva-Marin; Avo Kittask; Lawrence Cooper
Waiter/Friend of Flora	Douglas McEachen
Friend of Violetta	Lois Marsh

La Bohème **Giacomo Puccini**
In English
January 6–March 11 1977 (36 performances)
United States
Conductor: Timothy Vernon/Dwight Bennett
Director: John Leberg
Set Designer: William Lord
Costume Designer: William Lord

Marcello	Avo Kittask; Lawrence Cooper; Guillermo Silva-Marin
Rodolfo	Glyn Evans; Paul Frey
Colline	Monte Jaffe
Schaunard	Douglas McEachen
Benoit	Peter Milne
Mimi	Lorna Castaneda; Lois Marsh
Musetta	Nancy Hermiston; Barbara Carter
Alcindoro	Peter Milne
Parpignol	Michele Strano

La Traviata **Giuseppe Verdi**
March 6–April 23, 1977 (7 performances)
Ontario
Conductor: Timothy Vernon/Dwight Bennett
Director: John Leberg
Set Designer: Murray Laufer
Costume Designer: Andrea Gainger

Violetta	Lorna Castaneda
Flora	Susan Gudgeon
Doctor Grenvil	Janos Tessenyi; John Dodington
d'Obigny	Peter Milne
Douphol	John Nieboer
Gastone	Michele Strano
Alfredo	Glyn Evans
Annina	Nancy Hermiston
Germont	Avo Kittask; Peter Barcza
Waiter/Friend of Flora	Phil Stark
Friend of Violetta	Darlene Hirst

Il barbiere di Siviglia **Gioacchino Rossini**
In English
March 6–April 23, 1977 (13 Performances)
Ontario

Conductor: Timothy Vernon
Director: Lotfi Mansouri
Set Designer: Maurice Strike
Costume Designer: Andrea Grainger

Fiorello	John Nieboer
Count Almaviva	Glyn Evans; Henry Barney Ingram
Figaro	William Pell; Peter Barcza
Dr. Bartolo	Avo Kittask; Peter Milne
Rosina	Lorna Castaneda; Nancy Hermiston; Janet Stubbs
Don Basilio	Janos Tessenyi; John Dodington
Berta	Susan Gudgeon; Darlene Hirst
Notary	John Nieboer
Ambrogio	Phil Stark

1977–1978

La Traviata **Giuseppe Verdi**
November 7–December 3, 1977, January 15–March 12, 1978
Eastern Canada, United States
Conductor: Timothy Vernon/Jose Hernandez
Director: John Leberg
Set Designer: Murray Laufer
Costume Designer: Andrea Grainger

Violetta	Riki Turofsky; Barbara Collier
Flora	Janet Stubbs; Kathleen Hegierski; Darlene Hirst
Doctor Grenvil	Janos Tessenyi; John Dodington
Marquis	Don McManus; Peter Milne
Baron Douphol	John Nieboer; James Shafer
Gastone	Modesta Crisci; Michele Strano
Alfredo	Michele Strano; Abram Morales
Annina	Nancy Hermiston; Kathleen Hegierski; Iris Fraser
Germont	Forrest Lorey; Peter Barcza; Ronald Corrado; Guillermo Silva Marin
Waiter/Friend of Flora	James Shafer
Friend of Violetta	Darlene Hirst; Iris Fraser

Il barbiere di Siviglia **Gioacchino Rossini**
In English
November 7, 1977–March 12, 1978 (67 performances)
Ontario, Eastern Canada, United States
Conductor: Timothy Vernon/Jose Hernandez
Director: Lotfi Mansouri
Set Designer: Maurice Strike
Costume Designer: Maurice Strike

Fiorello	John Nieboer; James Shafer
Count Almaviva	Abram Morales; Modesto Crisci
Figaro	Peter Barcza; Forret Lorey
Dr. Bartolo	Peter Milne; Don McManus
Rosina	Janet Stubbs; Nancy Hermiston
Don Basilio	John Dodington; Janos Tessenyi
Berta	Barbara Collier; Darlene Hirst

Sergeant	James Shafer; John Nieboer
Soldier/Notary	John Nieboer; James Shafer
Ambrogio	Michele Strano

1978–1979

Le nozze di Figaro **Wolfgang Amadeus Mozart**
In English
January 13–March 15, 1979
Ontario, United States
Conductor: Peter McCoppin/Timothy Vernon
Director: John Leberg
Set Designer: Mary Kerr
Costume Designer: Mary Kerr

Figaro	Maruice Brown; Ingemar Korjus
Susanna	Eleanor Calbes; Caralyn Tomlin
Dr. Bartolo	John Dodington; Peter Milne
Marcellina	Darlene Hirst; Dorothy Jean Lloyd
Cherubino	Susan Gudgeon; Kathleen Murison
Count Almaviva	Raymond Hickman; Gino Quilico
Don Basilio	Phil Stark; Gerard Boyd
Countess Almaviva	Darlene Hirst; Rosemarie Landry; Roxolana Roslak
Antonio	Herman Rombouts
Don Curzio	Steven Young
Barbarina	Iris Fraser

1979–1980

Le nozze di Figaro **Wolfgang Amadeus Mozart**
In English
November/December 1979 (22 performances)
Eastern Canada
Conductor: Derek Bate/Harvey Sachs
Director: John Leberg
Set Designer: Mary Kerr
Costume Designer: Mary Kerr

Figaro	Jean-Clement Bergeron; John Ostendorf
Susanna	Claudia Cummings; Iris Fraser
Dr. Bartolo	Peter Milne; John Dodington
Marcellina	Patricia Rideout; Rosa Antony
Cherubino	Deborah Milsom; Eleanor James
Count Almaviva	Theodore Baerg; Allan Glassman
Don Basilio	Gerard Boyd; Phil Stark
Countess Almaviva	Roxolana Roslak; Sally Wolf
Antonio	Herman Rombouts
Don Curzio	Stephen Young
Barbarina	Sandra Gavinchuk

La Cenerentola **Gioacchino Rossini**
In English
January and February 1980
Ontario

Conductor: Dwight Bennett/Derek Bate
Director: Jeanette Asher
Set Designer: Maurice Strike
Costume Designer: Maurice Strike

Clorinda	Katherine Terrell; Janet Field
Tisbe	Rosa Antony; JoAnn Thompson
Cinderella	Deborah Milsom; Diane Loeb
Alidoro	Maurice Brown; John Dodington
Don Magnifico	Stephen Markuson; Peter Milne
Don Ramiro	David Eisler; Mark Dubois
Dandini	Sam Byrd; Theodore Baerg

The Magic Mozart   **Mavor Moore**
February 1980
Conductor: Derek Bate

Soprano	Katherine Terrell
Mezzo	Deborah Milsom
Tenor	Mark DuBois
Baritone	Theodore Baerg

1980–1981

Hello ...Boheme (La Bohème)   **Giacomo Puccini**
In English
Fall 1980
Ontario
Conductor: Stuart Hamilton
Director: John Leberg
Set Designer: Tayie Abdel-Rehem

Rodolfo	Michael Shust; Roger Ohlsen
Mimi	Roxolana Roslak
Marcello	Theodore Baerg; Mark Pedrotti
Musetta	Shawna Farrell; Eleanor James
Alcindoro	Mark Pedrotti; Theodore Baerg
Waiter	Roger Ohlsen; Michael Shust

Hänsel und Gretel   **Engelbert Humperdink**
In English
March 1981
Northern Ontario
Conductor: Derek Bate
Director: Stuart Hamilton
Set Designer: Ann Ewers
Costume Designer: Elsie Sawchuck

The Witch	Henry Barney Ingram; Barry Stilwell
Hansel	Eleanor James; Deborah Milsom
Gretel	Shawna Farrell

1981–1982

Little Red Riding Hood   **Seymour Barab**
Fall 1981
Ontario
Conductor: Derek Bate/Leslie Uyeda
Director: Lotfi Mansouri
Set Designer: Elsie Sawchuck
Costume Designer: Elsie Sawchuck

The Wolf	Theodore Baerg; Vytautas Paulionis
The Woodsman	Theodore Baerg; Vytautas Paulionis
Little Red Riding	Shawna Farrell; Cristen Gregory
Mother	Brenda Berge; Eleanor James
Grandmother	Brenda Berge; Eleanor James

Il barbiere di Siviglia   **Gioacchino Rossini**
In English
November 1981
Sourthen Ontario
Conductor: Derek Bate/Leslie Uyeda
Director: Jeanette Asher
Set Designer: Anne Ewers
Costume Designer: Patricia Bentley and Carol Perdu

Figaro	Theodore Baerg; Guillermo Silva-Marin
Count Almaviva	Barry Stilwell
Don Basilio	Vytautas Paulionis
Dr. Bartolo	Christopher Cameron
Rosina	Eleanor James; Shawna Farrell
Berta	Cristen Gregory; Brenda Berge
Sergeant	Roger Jones

1982–1983

Die Fledermaus   **Johann Strauss, Jr.**
In English
March 2–13, 1983
Northern Ontario
Conductor: Leslie Uyeda
Director: Christopher Newton
Set Designer: George Schlögl

Alfred	Ben Heppner; Barry Stilwell
Adele	Shari Saunders; Janet Smith
Rosalinda	Irena Welhasch
Eisenstein	Theodore Baerg; Ross Thompson
Dr. Falke	Avo Kittask
Frank	Christopher Cameron
Princess Orlovska	Lilian Kilianski; Katharina Megli
Frosch	Ben Heppner; Barry Stilwell

1983–1984

The Merry Widow   **Franz Lehár**
In English
November 23–29, 1983 (4 performances)
Southern Ontario
Conductor: Derek Bate
Director: John Leberg
Set Designer: George Schlögl
Costume Designer: Suzanne Mess

Sylviane	Odette Beaupré
Olga	Tania Parrish
Vicomte Cascada	Henry Barney Ingram
Raoul de St. Brioche	John Fanning
Valencienne	Cristen Gregory; Shari Saunders
Camille de Rosillon	Peter Blanchet; Ben Heppner
Baron Mirko Zeta	Gidon Saks
Anna Glawari	Joanne Kolomyjec; Irena Welhasch
Danilo	Theodore Baerg; Ross Thompson

1984–1985

La Bohème   **Giacomo Puccini**
In English
October 29–December 8, 1984
Sourthern Ontario
Conductor: Derek Bate
Director: Michael Albano

Waiter	Larry Tayler
Rodolfo	Ben Heppner; Guillermo Silva-Marin
Marcello	John Fanning; Gaétan Laperrière
Colline	Brian McIntosh
Schaunard	Erik Oland
Mimi	Joanne Kolomyjec; Susan Tsagkaris
Musetta	Cristen Gregory; Tania Parrish
Benoit/Alcindoro	Peter Blanchet

1985–1986

La Traviata   **Giuseppe Verdi**
In Italian and English
November 4–November 28, 1985
Ontario
Conductor: Brian Jackson
Director: Hans Nieuwenhuis
Set Designer: Cameron Porteous
Costume Designer: E.K. Ayotte

Violetta	Joanne Kolomyjec; Lyudmila Pildysh
Flora	Kimberly Barber
Dr. Grenvil	Brian McIntosh
D'Obigny	Christopher Coyea
Douphol	Patrick Timney
Gastone	Peter Blanchet; Dennis Giesbrecht

Alfredo	Guillermo Silva-Marin; Dennis Giesbrecht
Annina	Susan Tsagkaris; Sharon Anne Miller
Germont	John Fanning; Gaétan Laperrière

1986–1987

La Cenerentola   **Gioacchino Rossini**
In English
November 14–December 6 (11 performances), 1986
Ontario
Conductor: Derek Bate
Director: Sarah Ventura
Set Designer: Barbara Matis
Costume Designer: Maurice Strike

Clorinda	Sharon Anne Miller; Susan Tsagkaris
Tisbe	Gabrielle Prata; Kimberly Barber
Cinderella	Kimberly Barber; Linda Bennett Maguire
Alidoro	Brian McIntosh; Joel Katz
Don Magnifico	Maurice Brown; Brian McIntosh
Don Ramiro	Dennis Giesbrecht; Benoit Boutet
Dandini	Patrick Timney; Christopher Coyea

1987–1988

Les contes d'Hoffmann Jacques Offenbach
In English
October 14–November 14, 1987 (23 performances)
Eastern Canada
Conductor: Derek Bate
Director: Hans Nieuwenhuis
Set Designer: Astrid Janson
Costume Designer: Gunther Schneider-Siemssen

The Muse/Nicklausse	Tania Parrish; Gabrielle Prata
Luther	Joel Katz; Robert Milne
Lindorf	John Avey; Christopher Coyea; Joel Katz
Andrès	Peter Blanchet; Lenard Whiting
Nathanael	Stephen McClare
Hermann	Robert Milne; Patrick Timey
Hoffmann	Benoit Boutet; Dennis Giesbrecht
Spalanzani	Peter Blanchet; Lenard Whiting
Cochenille	Christopher Coyea; Patrick Timney
Coppélius	John Avey; Christopher Coyea; Joel Katz
Olympia	Mary Anne Barcellona; Kathleen Brett; Christiane Riel
Antonia	Mary Anne Barcellona; Kathleen Brett; Christiane Riel
Crespel	Joel Katz; Robert Milne
Frantz	Peter Blanchet; Lenard Whiting
Doctor Miracle	John Avey; Christopher Coyea; Joel Katz
Antonia's Mother	Tania Parrish; Marcia Swanston
Giulietta	Mary Anne Barcellona; Kathleen Brett; Christiane Riel
Pittichinaccio	Peter Blanchet; Lenard Whiting
Schlémil	Joel Katz; Patrick Timney
Dapertutto	John Avey; Christopher Coyea; Joel Katz
Stella	Mary Anne Barcellona; Kathleen Brett; Christiane Riel

1988–1989

Les contes d'Hoffmann Jacques Offenbach
In English
November 10–December 3, 1988 (15 performances)
Western Canada
Conductor: Derek Bate
Director: Hans Nieuwenhuis
Set Designer: Astrid Jansen
Costume Designer: Gunther Schneider-Siemssen

The Muse/Nicklausse	Rebecca Hass; Tania Parrish
Luther	John Avey; Robert Milne
Lindorf	John Avey; Christopher Coyea; John Fanning
Andrès	Peter Blanchet; Keith Boldt
Nathanael	Craig Ashton; Keith Boldt
Hermann	Robert Milne; Patrick Timey
Hoffmann	Dennis Giesbrecht; Gary Rideout
Spalanzani	Peter Blanchet; Keith Boldt
Cochenille	Christopher Coyea; Patrick Timney
Coppélius	John Avey; Christopher Coyea; John Fanning
Olympia	Mary Anne Barcellona; Kathleen Brett; Christiane Riel
Antonia	Mary Anne Barcellona; Kathleen Brett; Christiane Riel
Crespel	John Avey; Robert Milne
Frantz	Peter Blanchet; Keith Boldt
Doctor Miracle	John Avey; Christopher Coyea; John Fanning
Antonia's Mother	Tania Parrish; Marcia Swanston
Giulietta	Mary Anne Barcellona; Kathleen Brett; Christiane Riel
Pittichinaccio	Peter Blanchet; Keith Boldt
Schlémil	John Fanning; Patrick Timney
Dapertutto	John Avey; Christopher Coyea; John Fanning
Stella	Mary Anne Barcellona; Kathleen Brett; Christiane Riel

1989–1990

Le nozze di Figaro   Wolfgang Amadeus Mozart
In English
October 26–November 25, 1989 (21 performances)
Eastern Canada
Conductor: Georg Tintner
Director: Duncan McIntosh
Set Designer: Chrisina Poddubiuk
Costume Designer:

Figaro	Steven Horst; John Avey
Susanna	Kathleen Brett; Valerie Gonzalez; Joanne Hounsell
Dr. Bartolo	Robert Milne
Marcellina	Marcia Swanston
Cherubino	Rebecca Hass; Norine Burgess
Count Almaviva	Doug MacNaughton; Patrick Timney
Don Basilio	Henry Barney Ingram
Countess Almaviva	Wendy Nielsen; Christiane Riel
Antonio	Tom Oliver
Don Curzio	Blaine Hendsbee
Barbarina	Joanne Hounsell; Valerie Gonzalez

1990–1991

L'incoronazione di Poppea   Claudio Monteverdi
In English
October 27–November 18, 1990 (11 performances)
Southern Ontario
Conductor: Daniel Beckwith
Director: Stephen Wadsworth
Set Designer: Michael Goodwin
Costume Designer: Michael Goodwin

Fortune	Irena Welhasch Baerg
Virtue	Wendy Nielsen
Amor	Valerie Gonzalez
Ottone	Gabrielle Prata; Patrick Timney
First Soldier	Blaine Hendsbee
Second Soldier	Christopher Coyea
Nero	André Clouthier; Rebecca Hass
Poppea	Irena Welhasch Baerg
Arnalta	Marcia Swanston
Ottavia	Wendy Nielsen
Seneca	Robert Milne
Pallade	Valerie Gonzalez
Drusilla	Joanne Hounsell
Liberto	Tom Oliver
Followers of Seneca	Christopher Coyea; Blaine Hendsbee; Gordon MacLeod; Tom Oliver
Lucano	Christopher Coyea
A Lictor	Gordon MacLeod
Coronation Voices	Christopher Coyea; Blaine Hendsbee; Gordon MacLeod; Tom Oliver

Appendix IV

Toronto Mainstage Productions in Other Cities

1954
Hamilton: *The Consul* (March 8)
                   Rigoletto (March 9)
Kitchener: *La Bohème* (March 10)
London: *The Consul* (March 12)
                   Rigoletto (March 13)

1955
Kitchener: *Die Fledermaus* (March 14)
                   La Traviata (March 15)
Hamilton: *La Traviata* (March 16)

1956
Kitchener: *Carmen* (March 12)
Hamilton: *Madama Butterfly* (March 13)
Ottawa: *Madama Butterfly* (March 15)

1957
Hamilton: *Tosca* (March 13)
London: *Die Fledermaus* (November 22)
                   The Merry Widow (November 23)
Ottawa: *Die Fledermaus* (December 2)
                   The Merry Widow (December 3)
Montreal: *Die Fledermaus* (December 4)

1967
Montreal: *Les contes d'Hoffmann* (October 18, 20, 22)
                   Louis Riel (October 19, 21)

1969
Ottawa: *Rigoletto* (October 15, 17)
                   Die Fledermaus (October 16, 18)

1970
Ottawa: *Carmen* (October 21, 23)
                   Don Giovanni (October 22, 24)

1971
Ottawa: *Lucia di Lammermoor* (October 20, 22)
                   The Merry Widow (October 21, 23)

1972
Ottawa: *Eugene Onegin* (October 18, 20)
                   Tosca (October 19, 21)

1973
Ottawa: *Héloise et Abélard* (October 17, 19)
                   Fidelio (October 18, 20)

1974
Ottawa: *Faust* (October 17, 19)
                   Der fliegende Holländer (October 16, 18)

1975
Ottawa: *Louis Riel* (October 17)
                   Die Fledermaus (October 14, 16, 18)
Washington, DC, USA: *Louis Riel* (October 23)

1976
Ottawa: *La Bohème* (October 20, 22)
                   La Grande Duchesse de Gérolstein (October 21, 23)

1993
Brooklyn, NY, USA: *Bluebeard's Castle/Erwartung* (February 10, 12, 13)
Edinburgh, Scotland: *Bluebeard's Castle/Erwartung* (August 28, 29)

1994
Melbourne, Australia: *Bluebeard's Castle/Erwartung* (October 13, 15, 16)

1995
Hong Kong: *Bluebeard's Castle/Erwartung* (February 27, 29, March 1)

Appendix V

Concert Performances of Operas in Toronto

Dido and Aeneas (Purcell) - St. Lawrence Centre, February 26, 1981

Capriccio (R. Strauss) - Roy Thomson Hall, September 15, 1982

Apollo et Hyacinthus (Mozart) - Imperial Oil Opera Theatre, April 28, 1991

L'isola disabitata (Haydn) - St. Lawrence Centre, December 12, 1992

Iolanta (Tchaikovsky) - George Weston Recital Hall, October 16, 1998

Giovanna d'Arco (Verdi) - George Weston Recital Hall, March 18, 2000